Deferring the Self

STUDIES IN SOCIAL SCIENCES, PHILOSOPHY AND HISTORY OF IDEAS

Edited by Andrzej Rychard

VOLUME 2

PETER LANG
EDITION

Szymon Wróbel

Deferring the Self

PETER LANG
EDITION

Bibliographic Information published by the Deutsche Nationalbibliothek
The Deutsche Nationalbibliothek lists this publication in the Deutsche Nationalbibliografie; detailed bibliographic data is available in the internet at http://dnb.d-nb.de.

This publication was financially supported by the Faculty of "Artes Liberales" of the University of Warsaw and the Institute of Philosophy and Sociology of the Polish Academy of Sciences.

Reviewers: Prof. Dr. hab. Mirosław Loba (Professor of French and Italian Literature and Director of the Institute of Romance Philology at Adam Mickiewicz University in Poznań, Poland) andProf. Dr. hab. Krzysztof Ziarek (Professor of English Literature and Director of Graduate Studies, Department of ComparativeLiterature, University at Buffalo)

Proofreading: Jakub Bielak, Bartłomiej Reszuta, Artur Skweres

Library of Congress Cataloging-in-Publication Data

Wróbel, Szymon.
Deferring the self / Szymon Wróbel. -- First edition
pages cm. -- (Studies in social sciences, philosophy and history of ideas ; v. 2)
ISBN 978-3-631-64161-3
1. Psychoanalysis--Social aspects. 2. Psychoanalysis and art. 3. Political science. I. Title.
BF175.W76 2013
150.19'5--dc23

2013028636

ISSN 2196-0151
ISBN 978-3-631-64161-3 (Print)
E-ISBN 978-3-653-03223-9 (E-Book)
DOI 10.3726/978-3-653-03223-9

Peter Lang Edition is an Imprint of Peter Lang GmbH.
Peter Lang – Frankfurt am Main · Bern · Bruxelles · New York · Oxford · Warszawa · Wien

This book is part of the Peter Lang Edition list and was peer reviewed prior to publication.

www.peterlang.com

Contents

Introduction: Practicing the Humanities

[...] if one considers accident as unworthy of determining our fate, it is only a relapse to the pious aspect of life, the overcoming of which Leonardo himself prepared when he put down in writing that the sun does not move. We are naturally grieved over the fact that a just God and a kindly providence do not guard us better against such influences in our most defenseless age. We thereby gladly forget that as a matter of fact everything in our life is accident from our very origin through the meeting of spermatozoa and ovum, accident, which nevertheless participates in the lawfulness and fatalities of nature, and lacks only the connection to our wishes and illusions. The division of life's determinants into the "fatalities" of our constitution and the "accidents" of our childhood may still be indefinite in individual cases, but taken altogether one can no longer entertain any doubt about the importance of precisely our first years of childhood. We all still show too little respect for nature, which in Leonardo's deep words recalling Hamlet's speech "is full of infinite reasons which never appeared in experience".

Sigmund Freud[1]

The author is the principle of thrift in the proliferation of meaning. [...] The author is therefore the ideological figure by which one marks the manner in which we fear the proliferation of meaning.

Michel Foucault[2]

A rhetorical critic can regard a defense as a concealed trope. A psychoanalytical interpreter can regard a trope as a concealed defense. An antithetical critic will learn to use both in turn, relying upon the substitution of analogues as being one with the poetic process itself.

Harold Bloom[3]

---

1 Sigmund Freud (1910), *Leonardo da Vinci. A Psychosexual Study of an Infantile Reminiscence*, trans. A. Brill, [in:] *The Standard Edition of the Complete Psychological Works of Sigmund Freud*, Volume XI, ed. James Strachey, (London: Hogarth Press, 1957), p. 324.

2 Michel Foucault (1984), *What Is an Author?*, trans. P. Rabinow, [in:] Paul Rabinow, ed. *The Foucault Reader* (New York: Pantheon Books, 1984), p. 230.

3 Harold Bloom, *A Map of Misreading* (New York: Oxford University Press, 1975), pp. 88-89.

1. The politics of reading

The present book does not result from a single cognitive effort. It is a result of many years of studies on psychoanalysis, politics, and art. For the last ten years, supported mainly by my home universities I have been able to freely conduct research in the direction I chose and be fully responsible for those choices. The topics appearing in this book – populism, the limits of the political, identity, melancholy, the peculiarity of psychoanalytical interpretation, authority and its limitations, the connection between theater and politics, the relation between the human and the animal world – have long motivated my reflections. The partial results of my research have been submitted to public scrutiny in specialist scientific journals. I thought, nonetheless, that it was time to gather all those fragmented thoughts to shape them in a more uniform structure and look into them in their entirety. This intent of gathering the texts in one place is not simply conducive to something which may be regarded as a simple summary of my efforts, their gathering and locking in one space; therefore, it is not just to find a pretext to glance at the results of my work from a certain perspective, which is enabled by the passage of time and the unity of space and action, with which the instrument of a book endows the author. I believe the issue here is more than that.

This is a book about reading. It is a book about the practice of reading. I am writing about the practice of reading as a form of spiritual exercise as if I was writing about the ethical techniques and practices, as though I treated the latter as therapeutic techniques and practices. This is the case, in fact: I treat ethics as a domain of practical reasoning and not in the Kantian sense, but rather as a domain of spiritual exercises which are to bring one to reflection on life's principles, rules of conduct, exercises activating within us the most insecure and constantly endangered virtue of justice – enabling us to make the most informed decisions. Reading is always endangered by injustice and there is no greater temptation for the reader than the temptation of being unjust. Perception of ethics in the manner of spiritual exercises, recognizing an ethical exercise in reading is not my original idea; I am pursuing the path charted, *inter alia*, by the writings of Pierre Hadot,[4] a late work of Michel Foucault written before his death,[5] but also some works by Alexander Nehamas.[6]

4 Pierre Hadot, *Philosophy as a Way of Life*, trans. M. Chase (Oxford: Blackwell's, 1995).

5 Michel Foucault (1984) *The Uses of Pleasure*, and *Care of the Self*, trans. R. Hurley, [in:] Michel Foucault, *History of Sexuality*, 3 Volumes (New York: Vintage Books, 1988-90).

6 Alexander Nehamas, *The Art. Of Living. Socratic Reflections from Plato to Foucault* (Berkeley/Los Angeles/London, 1998).

Ethics, in the sense which has interested Hadot, Foucalt, Nehemas and me, is a set of procedures with which people not only establish the rules of conduct, but also try to change themselves, transform their individual, mortal existence and make their own life a work complying with the requirements of style. The great ethicists of reading were always accompanied by the belief that only in reading, in confrontation with the texts of others, it is possible for us to attain our identity. If we intend to associate morality with the concern for oneself, then by morality we should understand not just a set of principles and rules of conduct, which are presented to individuals and groups by various obligation-imposing institutions, but rather as the actual behavior of individuals towards the imposed rules. Morality would then define the way in which individuals oppose or submit to forbiddance or obligation. Moral acts would be that kind of practice thanks to which the human would not only reproduce the constraint of society but would also create a certain lifestyle, characteristic of an ethical subject. In this sense the practice of reading would be a political act, drawing the outline of intellectual closeness and remoteness, boundaries of agreement and its lack, activating the forces of attraction and repulsion, creating affinity maps. In this sense, for the action to be worthy of being designated as ethical, it should not be equaled to acting according to rules, laws, or values. Any moral action assumes a certain attitude to the code to which it makes reference, but it also connotes the relationship of the individual to oneself.

Roland Barthes said that "there is no Literature without an Ethic of language", but the same Barthes in the very same text, while discussing the emergence and end of literature, began his story with the purest form or writing, which is the product of fighting and power.[7] Barthes does not formulate a clear ethics of writing, he does formulate, however, a clear suggestion that political writing is preceded by novel and poetical writing. What is more, he formulates a diagnosis according to which there appears the possibility of new humanism, in which "widespread mistrust towards language in the entire modern literature would be supplanted by the writer's reconciliation with the words of ordinary people". Is it possible that literature, born from the words of power and blood, has dissipated and become life itself, abolishing all authority through the creation of a linguistic project of Noah's Ark, keeping countless hallmarks of countless dialects afloat? And does this practice of writing/reading create a community which is no longer shameful, a community of people cultivating and practicing the politics of affects which are at the same time concepts? Does in such practice of reading/writing a community emerge in which the speech of the

7 Roland Barthes, *Writing Degree Zero*, trans. A. Lavers, C. Smith (New York: Hill and Wang, 1968), p. 14.

reader blends with the language of the writer to such a degree that they begin to serve as each other's inside and outside, its justification and possible forms of coexistence? It is an open matter.

In this book I engage in polemical discourse. In this sense, I follow the tracks identified and laid by Michel Foucault. According to the basic insight of Foucault (and also his argumentation, to some extent), polemics is rather an obstacle in the search for the truth. Very schematically, it seems to him that we can recognize the presence in polemics of three models. First, there is the religious model according to which polemics sets itself the task of determining the intangible point of dogma, the fundamental and necessary principle that the adversary has neglected, ignored, or transgressed; and it denounces this negligence as a moral failing. Second, there is the juridical model according to which polemics allows for no possibility of an equal discussion; rather, it examines a case; it is not dealing with an interlocutor, it constitutes processing a suspect; it collects the proofs of his guilt, designates the infraction he has committed, and pronounces the verdict and sentence to him. The third one is the political model according to which polemics defines alliances, recruits partisans, unites interests or opinions, represents a party; it establishes the other as an enemy, an upholder of opposed interests, against which one must fight until the moment this enemy is defeated and either surrenders or disappears. For Foucault, the reactivation of these political, juridical, or religious practices in polemics is nothing more than theatre.

> In this comedy, one mimics war, battles, annihilations, or unconditional surrenders, putting forward as much of one's killer instinct as possible. But it is really dangerous to make anyone believe that he can gain access to the truth by such paths, and thus to validate, even if in a merely symbolic form, the real political practices that could be warranted by it.[8]

Similarly to Foucault, instead of polemics, I prefer discussions. In the serious play of questions and answers, in the work of reciprocal elucidation, the rights of each person are in some sense immanent in the discussion. They depend only on the dialogue situation. The person asking the questions is merely exercising the right that has been given him: to remain unconvinced, to perceive a contradiction, to require more information, to emphasize different postulates, to point out faulty reasoning, etc. As for a person answering the questions, he too exercises a right that does not go beyond the discussion itself; by the logic of his own discourse he is tied to what he has said earlier, and by the acceptance of dialogue he is tied to the questioning of the other. Questions and answers depend

---

8 Michel Foucault, *Polemics, Politics, and Problemzations: An Interview,* [in:] Paul Rabinow, ed. *The Foucault Reader* (New York: Pantheon Books, 1984), pp. 382-383.

on the game – a game that is at once pleasant and difficult – in which each of the two partners takes pains to use only the rights given to him by the other and by the accepted form of dialogue.

I would like to believe that this book remains such an open discussion, more than just religious, political, or juristic polemics.

2. The question of method

With regards to a book such as this, one must ask about the principles governing its integrity. Does it even form a coherent whole? Does friendship, even agonistic, even imbued with hostile elements, even ambivalent friendship, can become a force which unifies the text, or rather its plurality? Perhaps the best description of the method of thinking presented here is something which Walter Benjamin called "literary montage", in which the potency of juxtaposing elements alien to each other is no less significant than the conceptual continuity of the argument. To a certain degree I find close the idea of raising great constructions from the tiniest, clear and clean cut building elements as well as the conviction that one needs even during the analysis of singular, small elements notice the shape of the whole historic process. Capture the construction of history itself, through the structure of the commentary.[9] There is something in this book, however, which exceeds the limits of literary montage. Perhaps the only mark of unity of such a multitude of stories about difficult friendships developed and documented here is the category of style.

The author is left to believe that this style is strong enough for the formal unity of the text to enable the author to transcend the multitude of scattered friendships in which he entangles himself. It is not the method, not the purity of heart, not goodwill, not individual experience, not even the desire for power, not even valiance – *virtù* – the set of political skills enabling one to control one's fortune, in Niccolò Machiavelli's sense, but the power of writing itself seeking literature and an impossible friendship. The inability to conclusively explain a text is not only the equivalent of the inability of conclusive identification, it is a triumph of the rule of differentiation, division, multiplication, exposing the fundamental multiplicity of speech. Not friendship but friendships in the plural are the subject of this book.

9 Walter Benjamin, *The Arcades Project*, trans. H. Eiland and K. McLaughlin, ed. R. Tiedemann (New York: Belknap Press, 2002), p. 506.

3. Styles of practicing the humanities

A book is a form of practicing the humanities. But the humanities how understood? I shall skip the organizational – one could say "disciplinary" – issues, that is, those related to the division of the university departments. I shall also skip the organizational constraints of the idea of interdisciplinarity, and, instead, I shall focus on generating potential styles, or rather, potential orders of thinking about interdisciplinarity. Reflecting on the question of how the idea of interdisciplinarity can work in the humanities, I reached the conclusion that there are three variants, or rather styles, of practicing interdisciplinarity in the humanities. The key thing is not to define or list these options, but rather to realize what conditions need to be met to enable interdisciplinarity in each of the three approaches.

In the first approach, the humanities develop a dialogue with science – science narrowly understood as natural science. The assumption is that the humanities would not only develop simultaneously with science, but that they would reflect the explanatory procedures developed by researchers. The condition of this kind of interdisciplinarity is the preliminary assumption that science, and only science, is the form of organization of intellectual life worth the investment of energy, a form that is qualitatively different from wishful thinking, religious thinking, magical thinking, or other forms of thinking conceived of as infantile. This is the direction contemporary cognitive science is now following. It is assumed that cognitive science is essentially an interdisciplinary meeting ground for the languages of psychology, computer science, or neuroscience; interdisciplinarity is therefore achieved thanks to ontological naturalism, or at least naturalism. This means rejecting the specific and unique explanations of the humanities; instead, such uniqueness now stands for eccentricity, and on these grounds it is abolished or terminated. The basic belief is that science, at least at the explanatory or methodological level, is one. What we hear today about the so-called third culture, that is a new synthesis of the humanities and natural sciences, follows this direction. I am deeply convinced that it is a manifestation of demagoguery, as this variant seems threatened by a form of reductionism (qualifying or not – that is debatable). We could be convinced of this after reading the works of Steven Pinker, Daniel Dennett and other evolutionary psychologists, who are trying to reduce all the so-called "higher forms" of cognitive and emotional functioning to adaptation strategies, or differently understood evolutionary games, which can be described with the help of categories from the natural sciences. In this scenario, studying expands our knowledge of the mechanisms governing the brain, or, more broadly, the central nervous system, as it allows us to understand our relationship with the natural world. However, we must remember that the "synthesis" of the humanities and natural science means the absorption of the humanities by natural science, and not the other way round.

Fortunately, this is not the only approach to the humanities we have. In the second variant, the humanities follow the model and share the paradigmatic point of departure of literature and literary criticism. This is the approach of Harold Bloom and Richard Rorty. Their demand, as formulated by Rorty, is that the humanities become poetical and romantic, and thus liberate our culture. Literature is a "paradoxical" institution which, to paraphrase Derrida, seems aware of the idiomatic human experience and dramas in which we are involved. Literature is the most humanizing factor. In this sense, reading Thomas Mann and Marcel Proust is a much more interesting intellectual endeavor for scholars than reading Burrhus Skinner or Steven Pinker. A key point of departure in this scenario is an attempt to show what Sigmund Freud called "instincts and their vicissitudes". Man is a biological structure and a collection of impulses, but these drives operate in the world, in the environment, and all have their own stories which constitute the essence of our very existence. A humanist is someone who gives an account – be it anthropological, sociological, historical or psychological – of these individual, unique and fateful instincts in the human environment. Humanist narratives attempt to show the complexity of human existence suspended between genesis and structure, strength and meaning, norm and disease – these and other mysterious connections which to a humanist are, or rather should be, the most important in a discourse concerning humans.

Finally, the third option, which I call a sociopolitical project, understands the humanities as a political project or social theory. This is founded on the belief that man is by nature a political being, or that man is a being that shapes his collective life for good and for bad, and this cannot be avoided. The contemporary Frankfurt School, critical social theory and contemporary political theories are examples of such practice calibrating the humanities. This is not solely limited to the idea of interdisciplinarity, as it is not limited solely to the impact of social concepts on philosophical concepts, but the key thing is to develop a transdisciplinary language, to build such a social theory that not only unites social order with the order of philosophy, but inhibits the assumption that the social order in which we operate is ultimate and unique. The overt intention of such thinking is denaturalization of our thinking about society. Although we might see our environs as a finite fossilized effect of evolution, which is in congruity with the eternal law of nature, it is in fact only a casual moment in the life of a culture that already knows it is mortal.

In my opinion, none of these options is fully optimal. They are not optimal because they are limited solely to juxtaposing scientific and nonscientific disciplines. If we think of interdisciplinarity in terms of disciplines colliding with one another, I find the whole idea trivial and uninteresting. The real idea of interdisciplinarity is basically transdisciplinarity and it means abandoning the disciplinary nature of science. What I would expect from a person engaged in such thinking is to forget that they are a representative of any given scientific discipline and to remind them that the only obligation is to address ensuing problems, which are always entangled in various languages. I would claim that any genuine scientific enterprise in the humanities of the 20th century was the result of forgetting about university disciplines and implementing the transdisciplinarity of research problems.

As far as the Polish humanities are concerned, the question is how to cope with these three variants of interdisciplinary practice. Another thing is how the humanities are prepared for taking on the fourth model, which from my perspective is optimal, that is abandoning the disciplinary nature of science and perceiving the field of investigation as a smooth surface to be covered with virtually all possible concepts and to be approached with all possible research tools. Unfortunately, as a representative of the Polish humanities I have no reason to feel at ease. The hardest thing to achieve is being original within the limits of the first approach. It is an especially demanding field in terms of "instrumentation" of research. It is difficult for us Poles to reach "the limits of human thought". The question is, how well are we prepared for dealing with the second and third approach? In my opinion, after a period of more or less reflexive mimicry, after the reception of events that took place worldwide in the humanities (this phase lasted for over ten years), it is time for Polish science to enter the phase of "maturity", as Kant put it, that is, the phase of intellectual independence. How far are we able to engage in the world debate? What can we add to the discussion of interdisciplinarity based on our particular local experience? Unfortunately, I have no reliable answer here.

4. The practices of dislocation

What, then, is my own position? Does it set the parameters of my own speech, my own voice, my own writing? What kind of exercise do I propose to my readers in this book? Is there a hidden political, theoretical, or esthetic strategy behind my thinking process? Do I make use of some tactics allowing me to effectively practice the humanities in areas which at first glance seem so different: psychoanalysis, politics, and art? What hermeneutic tactics or strategy of reading texts am I suggesting? Do I at all recommend any form (practice) of presence in the world? Does it have ethical implications, or is it just a form of aestheticizing oneself? Do we even have the right to talk about politics here, or are we dealing in this book with a subject that is avoiding politics, that is being in the world, with people or against them?

Surely I cannot agree with the traditional postulate about some kind of natural division into the objectivity of the scholar and the subjectivity of the writer, as if one was endowed with "freedom" and the other with a "calling" and as if both could open the real borders of their situation. To the contrary: I want to fully experience the contradictions of my time in which satire, and even sarcasm can be the condition of truth. Moreover, I believe that literature, criticism, or art become a subversive factor not when they do terrify, move or even stigmatize, but when they give us too much to think about. Yet, what does it mean "to fully experience the contradictions of my time"? And when does literature, criticism, or art "give us too much to think about"?

As a matter of fact, I recommend in this book something which I call the practice of dislocation or rather the practices of dislocation, with the desire to underline the plurality of practices and the plurality of dislocations. A practice may be psychoanalytical (sensitive to biographical truth), political (sensitive to the collective events), and, finally, artistic (aimed at the configuration of affects). Dislocation can occur in the epistemological field (disrupting the order of knowledge), aesthetical field (disrupting the order of sensitivity), as well as ethical one (causing moral anxiety). I claim that only a constant translocation, a constant movement of deterritorialization and dislocation can save us from death and intellectual inertia. The humanities are a discipline which is constantly exposed to the risk of inflation, the risk of the death of the meanings of its main terms, or even whole lexicons which it uses. Trauma, narration, body, gesture, discourse, amalgamation, figure, position, paradigm – here is the set of concepts which emerged one day and like an imperious despot started to regulate the traffic of our speech. We cannot stop in our constant escape from the linguistic collapse, the clinical death of the leading terminology which once seemed invigorating and energizing, and which has today degenerated into a mere semantic vampire.

Hence, politics and practice of dislocation is not reduced to the practice of the idea of interdisciplinarity or transdisciplinarity – it is not reduced to the juxtaposition of social and philosophical terms or to mixing the literary terms with those borrowed from the natural sciences. It is more the notion of developing a new, live language, of building such a theoretical practice that would not only link together the social order with the philosophical order, but would prevent the acceptance of the given linguistic order, in which we function, as definitive and singular. An explicit intention of such thinking is the denaturalization of our "natural" perception of the world and language. What in our surroundings would seem a finite, evolutionary fossil inscribed in the eternal laws of nature is but a passing moment in the life of a certain culture, which already realizes its mortality. A person practicing politics of dislocation undertakes the risk of creating a living language, denaturalizing that which is dead in the human and in culture. Such practice calls us to a life intensified, to living up to the demands of a multiplied humanity, multiplied and supplemented through constant association with other species.

The practice of dislocation then is the cultivation in oneself the movement of the chess knight, who executes movements in space and shifts in time. The subject of displacement is never settled, never at home, he is also always out of touch, always somewhere else. His resistance is the resistance against time, space, and the well-defined disciplines which surround him. The practice of dislocation is a constant deterritorialization of one's thinking, experiencing, and action. Only by practicing the politics of dislocation do we fully experience the contradictions of our time.

5. Psychoanalysis, politics and art

Jacques-Alain Miller, wondering about Jacques Lacan's famous statement that the "unconscious is politics", says that "for Lacan psychoanalysis is the opposite of politics".[10] We have tolerable knowledge about politics, and no reliable knowledge about the unconscious, therefore the unconscious is the category which needs defining, and politics is the defining category. The Freudian unconscious is not autonomic and hidden and does not remain in its unreality just for itself, it is rather the unconscious structurally coordinated with the discourse of the Other, it is therefore something for the Other, something which needs an audience and a spectacle. The unconscious then is a relation or something which occurs as a part of relations. A joke without an audience does not exist. If that were true, psychoanalysis would in a way be prisoner and hostage to politics. When Miller adds that no psychoanalysis exists where no one can be ironic and question ideals, then he actually says that psychoanalysis cannot be reconciled with the totalitarian regime, and, as a result, liberalism is the political condition for psychoanalysis. Moreover, when he adds that "psychoanalysis is undoubtedly not revolutionary", but it is "subversive" and claims that despite this subversion of psychoanalysis "psychoanalysts have a spontaneously conservative attitude", then in principle it subordinates

10 Jaques-Alain Miller, *Lacan et la politique.* Entretien avec Jaques-Alain Miller propos recueillis par Jean-Pierre Clero et Lynda Lotte, [in:] "Cités. Philosophie, Politique, Histoire", T 16, 2003.

psychoanalysis to a kind of politics of moderation. On the other hand, when we recall the famous episode in Lacan's life when, during his stay at the Psychoanalytical Congress in Marienbad, he attended the Olympic Games in Munich, was introduced to Goebbels, and stated that "clasping his hand I felt that he has been analyzed", then we seem to realize that psychoanalysis towers over politics, because it analyzes without being analyzed.

Miller admits he "believes that politics of desire exists – even if only because politics plays with identifications, and there is no such identification which is not based on a desire. And in this sense psychoanalysis is not politics but a kind of ethics – acting in reverse".[11] Yet the same Miller notes that politics does not exist without identification, and politics itself heads towards seizing, seducing the subject and in a way identifying it. Nonetheless, psychoanalysis works against the final identification, returning the subjects their initial emptiness, the element of lack of identification, exposing their primal phantasm. Would this mean then that psychoanalysis is, nonetheless, subversive and even revolutionary?

In this book I assemble three words: psychoanalysis, politics, and art. I assemble them on purpose, because all these three "institutions" – psychoanalysis, politics, and art – are a kind of practice and do not exist in the absence of the practical element. Psychoanalysis, in a nutshell, is to me a form of practicing truth, personal truth, truth which needs to be one's own, truth which is not a result of anonymous, scholarly discourse but is the result of a real clash with one's own experience. Politics, on the other hand, is the practice of being with others, it is the cultivation of antagonistic relations with others, it is the fight for liberation from hitherto unknown forms of coexistence. Finally, art is above all the practice aiming at giving one's life the mark of something unique, it is the very practice of life.

Psychoanalysis is most of all the practice of speaking. The analysand is telling his analyst about his suffering, his symptom. This symptom is articulated in the unconscious matter, constructed from things which were said to the subject that hurt him or her and things with respect to which it is impossible to tell whether they make the subject hurt. The power of speech and the effect of truth which it enables, which is called interpretation, constitute the very power of the unconscious. Interpretation manifests itself both on the part of the analysand and on the part of the analyst. However, neither has the same attitude towards this unconscious because one of them has gone through the experience, and the other has not. The psychoanalytic session is a place where the most long-lasting identifications in which the subject was entangled can relax.

---

11 Jaques-Alain Miller, *Lacan et la politique*.

Politics is above all else a practice of coexistence. By "the political" I understand an aspect of antagonism, which I consider constructive for human relations of societies, and by "politics" – the set of practices and institutions the purpose of which is to organize human existence in conditions of conflict stemming from the political. This order always results from ordering practices, which occur in conflict-afflicted areas within the framework of a given configuration of power relations. If I say that the political is a constitutive feature of human life, in other words, that the human ceases to be a human when he removes the dimension of the political from his life, this statements signifies that a human loses humanity by abandoning that which is political.

The theatricality of contemporary politics has been stressed many times. It has been also frequently stressed that theater is a political art form *par excellence*. Yet the idea of politics does not lead to creating a political space which in itself would be a work of art, that is a collective performance. Politics understood as a space of appearances, as a perceptual spectacle, as a place of emergent esthetics of the world is not consistent with the vision of politics of storytelling. The issue is not the aestheticizing of politics, just as it is not politicizing esthetics. The aestheticizing of politics was led to extremes by Nazism and Albert Speer's architecture. The politicization of esthetics, on the other hand, ended with socialist realism. A total work of art is not the fulfillment of the idea of politics – it does not reveal the nonpolitical nature of contemporary politics, but rather its demise. Not only politics', but also art's demise. This demise takes place every day on our television screens.

Art is above all the practice of life. Art can be regarded as a form of practicing the art of survival. Here is a simple example. I assert that in the contemporary world no one portrayed better the problem of infinity and logical paradoxes connected with it, no one rendered better the Kantian thought of geometry and mathematics as forms of human worldview/ *Weltanschaung* than Roman Opałka. Roman Opałka, who had lived for 40 years in France and died on 6 August 2011, was a painter of numeral paintings. Their subject is time and numbers. He covered canvasses of identical sizes with consecutive numbers. He named his work *Opałka 1965/1-?*. This question mark enquires about the artist's date of death. Now it is known. The question mark has now been replaced by the infinity symbol. During his work, Opałka read the painted numbers aloud and recorded his voice, he also photographed his face. In Atlas Sztuki in Lodz, where a gallery devoted to his works is situated, a perfect figure was built – an octagon. Seven paintings hang on seven walls, while the eighth wall remains open to infinity. The background of the paintings is increasingly pale and white, the numbers more and more blurred. The octagon has white walls, a white floor and a white ceiling, the voice of the painter is projected from hidden loudspeakers, counting. Seven people can enter the exhibition at one time, so that nothing disrupts the reception: one viewer – one painting. When I confront Opałka I begin to understand that human life constitutes the measuring of one's unique vector of being towards death and that this death gives human life a dimension of uniqueness. Death is a gift, death is the greatest generosity, only death makes us human. We have reasons to talk about and demand not only the right to live but the right to die.

Let us therefore forget about philosophy as a battle for the final form of truth and forget about art as a battle for the final form of beauty and instead try to use the diagnostic power of art, the power to recognize and document acts of violence, which we inflict on ourselves and nature every day, let us instead use the therapeutic power of psychoanalysis, which can restore our courage to stop the politically correct and psychologically deadly art of silence.

6. The clinic of politics

Let us return once more to the question concerning the relation between psychoanalysis and politics. I assume that the most substantial psychoanalytical experience is the clinical experience, experience deriving from relations with the patient. Surely, we know today already that psychoanalysis is not a science of the unconsciousness, it is also not generalized hermeneutics of culture, finally, it is not psychotherapy, a kind of "treatment" of mental disorders. What is it then? My rather risky reply to this question is: perhaps today psychoanalysis is above all a clinic of politics. Politics today is nothing but a collective spectacle demonstrating collective traumas and individual abilities of seducing the masses. The moment psychoanalysis transformed into politics, politics became a kind of collective psychoanalysis.

In *The Birth of the Clinic* Foucault demonstrates the hermeneutic status of the doctor's profession.[12] The doctor in his trade is forever fated to interpretation. When a patient consults him with a cough as the main symptom, and the doctor cannot use a stethoscope or x-ray his chest, or examine the sputum of the patient, he will have great difficulties pronouncing if the reason for the cough is pneumonia, asthma, or perhaps tuberculosis. In the clinical method the goal is not the examination, but deciphering. What does that mean? It means that the experience is interpreted immediately, and interpreted from a certain angle. The clinical interpretation is an interpretation which integrates

12 Michel Foucault (1963), *The Birth of the Clinic: An Archaeology of Medical Perception*, trans. A. M. Sheridan Smith, London: Routledge 1997.

knowledge and experience into one diagnosing-deciphering whole. Psychoanalysis is nothing but such a generalized clinical experience. The clinical interpretation thus constructed and modeled is moved by psychoanalysis from the "sick man's body" to other objects: cultural, linguistic, or social – monuments, literary works, dream fantasies, slips of the tongue, images, fantasies, and finally the mechanisms of power. Psychiatrization of politics (bringing it to the level of the clinic) achieved by contemporary psychoanalysis is neither an exception nor aberration or anomaly, it is simply a consequence of the dominant role of the clinical interpretation.

Yet, after such a juxtaposition of psychoanalysis and politics one methodological question arises: how does the clinical practice of psychoanalysis negotiate its dictionary with the language of politics, which is the language concerning the relations of power, its legitimization, forms of rule, kinds of political system, democracy, state and its constitution, tyranny, elections, single-member or multi-seat constituencies? How do these two dictionaries – a dictionary of the clinic composed of concepts such as psychosis, neurosis, slip of the tongue, forgetting, defense mechanisms, etc., and the dictionary of politics constituted by notions such as domination, oligarchy, social reproduction, violence, party, etc., meet in something which I here call the clinic of politics? To be more concrete: what does the case of the rat man, analyzed by Freud, bring into our knowledge about the social contract? Or the other way around: what does the knowledge of the social contract tell us about the symptoms of the rat man? What does the case of Schreber, frequently commented by psychiatry, transfer into our knowledge about panoptic structures of power? Or the other way around: what do the panoptic structures of power tell us on the subject of Schreber's symptom? What does the case of Dora bring into our knowledge about the masses and the process of identification? Or the other way around: what do the hypnotized masses tell us about Dora? What is here the explanatory category, and what is the explained category? And if we negate this classification, then why and in the name of what do we negate it? Does the political sphere explain the clinical or the clinical the political?

All these are very legitimate questions. The problem is that the traditional, positivist methodological classification within this system of thought is no longer functioning. There is no explanatory side and no explained side, there are no categories which are interpreting or interpreted, there is no subject of cognition, which is beyond the political reality, and there is no politics which would not have epistemological consequences. Psychoanalysis transformed from the couch hidden in Freud's domicile into a collective media spectacle. Politics, on the other hand, transformed from the electoral and party fight for power into a series of dramas, struggles, negotiations, stratagems, and tactics used in parliament, at home, at university and in the supermarket. At the same time, when psychoanalysis becomes public, politics is carried into the intimate sphere of our homes.

7. Deferring (*nachträglich*) the Self

This is a book about reading and a book about deferring (nachträglich) the Self. This is a book about rehearsing friendship in reading and nurturing enmity towards the Self in writing. As a matter of fact the only form of friendship feasible to me is an agonistic friendship intermediated by reading. Make no mistake, I befriend nobody, I only exercise friendship. I am constantly deferring the Self by multiplying the presence of others in textual proximity. These exercises make up for the inability to make friends and allow me to pair with or position against the others, to walk hand in hand with some of them and to step aside from myself. Moreover, the work of reading is to coerce a disposition to speak to others and about others - which most probably implies that my constitution is that of hostility and indifference, and that brotherhood is something for which I need to persevere. In other words this is a spiritual practice, a little like that of the Stoics. To be a philosopher is – the way I have come to perceive it – to master both the internal and the external discourse, i.e. to first evoke and then master anxiety. What makes my politics of reading so different from spiritual exercises of the Stoics is that I can no longer discriminate between the inside and the outside, anxiety and tranquillity, friendship and hostility. Thus, evoking internal anxiety, coming to hostility, and pursuing external conflict is neither a form of speaking to myself nor addressing the other in me, but a third kind encounter with the alien which is neither a friend nor enemy. While reading I arouse anxiety in the work of thinking initiated by someone else in my own thinking, but I also arouse anxiety in someone else's text. In fact, reading incites anxiety in my relations with the world and incites war against myself, or more precisely, an irreconcilable agonism between me and myself.

Marcel Proust, in his essay *On Reading* says – "There are perhaps no days of our childhood we lived so fully as those we believe we left without having lived them, those we spent with a favourite book."[13] Certainly, days spent with a book are days spent with oneself – not with the other. Days with a book justify our absence in the world and so Marcel Proust sought in reading a justification for his absence in the world. To Proust, reading should never be confused with a

13 Marcel Proust, *On Reading*, trans. Jean Autret and William Burford (New York, 1971).

conversation for even provided the interlocutors were the wisest of men; it is not wisdom that matters but the way we communicate. Reading, unlike having a conversation – while both are ways to communicate with the thoughts of another, does not impede our loneliness and sovereignty; in its course we may enjoy the power of our intellect reserved to solitude and lost in a conversation.

Reading – according to Proust – is on the threshold of the life of the mind; it brings it out rather than substitutes it. The latter constitutes a pathological case akin to a spiritual depression where reading becomes a sort of curative discipline reintroducing a lazy mind in perpetuity into the life of the mind and where books play a role analogous to that of psychotherapists with certain neurasthenics. The above, I think, is a correct diagnosis of my case – that of spiritual depression. However, contrary to Proust and in line with some of the intuitions of Sigmund Freud I would claim that passivity, or spiritual laziness, is inherent to our spiritual activity, hence our perpetual demand for the measures to reintroduce mind to the spiritual life.

Proust, notwithstanding his premonition of the desire of being dependent, deluded himself into believing that just as our passion for books grows along the intellect, the associated risks lose momentum. Proust, who himself excelled in being dependant, believed that autonomous mind can subject reading to spiritual activity. Doubtlessly, some readings can be recuperative. These readings, however, are often unfair. Proust believed in the logic of sovereignty and injustice. Despite feeling endangered and in poor health he entrusted his will to be one day independent and to regain health. Although, as he claimed, it is only in reading and in contact with other minds that the mind adopts certain manners, gains a kind of intellectual "advantage" and ascribes to the nobility in order to transmit tradition, we still expect much more from the writer than from the reader who at best excels in spiritual depression. Surely, had we lived in Proust's times we could at least have entertained guests to veil our low disposition. In our times, however, under constant threat of pandemics and blessed with the Internet we rather browse and chat, reading comes least and last. And when it finally does, under the guise of health we let in the most infected visitors. Epidemics are what can't be escaped, allowing the deferment of the Self and justifying our permanent absence in the world.

Friendship – being concerned with the others – is a most casual thing, and this is exactly the form of friendship nurtured in reading. However, as it concerns the dead and the absent, sincerity and selflessness – the values young Proust believed in – are never pledged. The problem with my policy of friendship and the practice of reading affected by my activity (disease) is that not only they concern the living but that these living are all around me. This is a peculiar and dissocial form of friendship where it often appears that I care more of the works than their authors. We remain largely indifferent to our bodies and our deeds and we are much preoccupied with our recorded thoughts. We thus constitute a dissocial, if not openly hostile, a community of friends. If – as Marcel Proust suggests – all of us, the living, are in fact the dead who have not yet taken up their role, then our etiquette sporting respect, gratitude or devotion, so often entwined with lies and deceit, is indeed idle and burdensome.

However, we do not even pretend friendship. In the case of reading friendship is never restored to the original state of purity. Reading is at best an invitation to open hostility. Along reading books, we not so much lose our gentility as we gain sobriety. Entertaining such friends is a way of relieving real and everyday hostility. Unhealthy arousal induced by hostility tends to disappear in the course of reading, where friendship is dynamic and fighting. Reading days are days of fighting. Reading days are days of war. Reading days are days justifying our absence in the world by disease – spiritual depression, and the imperative to reintroduce the mind into spiritual life. Reading days are days of deferring the Self. Beyond respect and pure friendship, pure reading is bathed in silence clearer than words. As much as we speak to the others, we are silent to ourselves. Silence, unlike speaking, bears no trace of our ill disposition. Its purity is almost like that of the air – clear after the battle.

8. Practice

I therefore claim that what links psychoanalysis, politics and art is practice: the practice of life. But what do I consider as the practice of life, which is the art of courageous, unique dying, nontrivial death? Gilles Deleuze in a famous conversation with Michele Foucault talks as follows about this new relation between practice and theory:

> Possibly we're in the process of experiencing a new relationship between theory and practice. At one time, practice was considered an application of theory, a consequence; at other times, it had an opposite sense and it was thought to inspire theory, to be indispensable for the creation of future theoretical forms. In any event, their relationship was understood in terms of a process of totalisation. For us, however, the question is seen in a different light. The relationships between theory and practice are far more partial and fragmentary. On one side, a theory is always local and related to a limited field, and it is applied in another sphere, more or less distant from it. The relationship which holds in the application of a theory is never one of resemblance. Moreover, from the moment a theory moves into its proper domain, it begins to encounter obstacles, walls, and blockages which require its relay by another type of discourse (it is through this other discourse that it eventually passes to a different domain). Practice is a set of relays from one theoretical point to

> another, and theory is a relay from one practice to another. No theory can develop without eventually encountering a wall, and practice is necessary for piercing this wall.[14]

The art of living might in fact be a name, on the one hand, for the rupturing quality of art: its power to break our habitual ways of being and acting in the world (our reactive selves); and on the other, for a concomitant second moment: the production of something new. We might say then that what is at stake with aesthetics is what Deleuze would call a genuine encounter. For Deleuze such an encounter is always with an object of sense that in itself involves the short-circuiting of sorts of our cognitive and conceptual capacities. We might add to this, following some of my comments above, that such an object of encounter might also operate to rupture certain circuits of reception and consumption and other habits of "spectatorship" (those that reinforce a certain "knowledge" of art, or even a given subjectivity) whilst opening us up to other perhaps more unfamiliar but more productive economies.

Affect names the intensive quality of life. The risings and fallings, the movement from one state of being to another, the becomings. For Deleuze-Spinoza, ethics would be the organization of one's life so as to increase specially joyful affects, those that increase our capacity to act in the world. This ethics will then involve certain kinds of encounter, for example when we come across an object with which we positively resonate, or when two or more individuals come together that essentially "agree" (albeit this agreement might operate below that of apparent complicity in a register of becoming, as it were). This is to move the register from one of rupture to one of conjunction. In Spinoza's terms it is to form a "common notion" that refers to an essence shared by two or more modes. It is in this sense that the concept of "disinterest" I introduced above might be seen to involve the mobilization of a "common notion" in that it moves the dynamics of an encounter away from purely subjective coordinates towards those of the longitudes and latitudes that determine the limits of wider assemblages.

The art of living, though a practical art, is practiced in writing. The question whether its practitioners applied it successfully to themselves is secondary and in most cases impossible to answer. We want a philosophy that consists of views in harmony with the actions, with the mode of life of those who hold them. But the main question still is not whether, as a matter of historical fact, someone else succeeded in living that way but whether one can construct such a life oneself.

14 Gilles Deleuze, *Intellectuals and power: A conversation between Michel Foucault and Gilles Deleuze*, [in:] Michel Foucault, *Language, counter-memory, practice: selected essays and interviews*, ed D Bouchard (Cornell University Press, Ithaca 1977), pp. 205-217.

That can be done in two ways. One can either try to apply someone else's conception to one's own life, and to that extent live well, perhaps, but derivatively; or one can formulate one's own art of living. But it is difficult to imagine that one can formulate one's own art of living without writing about it because it is difficult to imagine that the complex views that such an art requires can be expressed in any other way. Further, unless one writes about it, one's art will not be able to constitute a model for others in the longer run. And the moment one writes about the art of living, the question for others again becomes not whether its originator succeeded in practicing it but whether they can in turn practice it on their own. Socrates himself wrote nothing. But had not Plato created an art of living in his name – and in writing – there would be nothing for us to think about, no art and no model to accept, reject, manipulate, or even pass by indifferently. The same is true of Montaigne, Nietzsche, and Foucault. The purpose of philosophy as the art of living is, of course, living. But the life it requires is a life in great part devoted to writing. The monument one leaves behind is in the end the permanent work, not the transient life.

Those who practice philosophy as the art of living construct their personalities through the investigation, the criticism, and the production of philosophical views – views, that is, that belong to the repertoire of philosophy as we have come to understand it. The connection is historical: even though the philosophers of the art of living often introduce new questions, their inspiration always comes from the tradition that we already accept as the tradition of philosophy. More importantly, the philosophers of the art of living make the articulation of a mode of life their central topic: it is by reflecting on the problems of constructing a philosophical life that they construct the life their work constitutes. The body of work that reflects on the philosophical life is the very content of the life it composes. The project of establishing a philosophical life is largely self-referential. Philosophical lives differ from others, to the extent that they do, because they proceed from a concern with issues that have traditionally been considered philosophical and because those issues provide the material out of which they are fashioned.

In this book I draw heavily on the ideas I have already presented in the following publications:

- *In Praise For Monstrosities. The Case of Niccolo Machiavelli*, "Polish Sociological Review", 4, 180, 2012, pp. 455-475.
- *Friedrich Nietzsche's Three Hypotheses about the Origins of the Tragic Chorus*, [in:] Dorota Semenowicz, Katarzyna Tórz (ed.), *Malta Festival Poznań Forum 2011: The Boundaries of Exclusion. Between Aesthetics and Ethics*, Poznań: Fundacja Malta, 2012, pp. 58-68.

- *Mourning Populism. The Case of Poland*, “Polish Sociological Review”, 4, 171, pp. 437-457.
- *Three Styles of Practicing Interdisciplinarity in the Humanities*, [in:] Barbara Bokus (ed.), *The Humanities Today and the Idea of Interdisciplinary Studies*, Warsaw: Matrix, 2011, pp. 291-294.
- *Either Thinking or Art*, [in:] Bożena Czubak (ed.), *Quotations Marks.* Warsaw: Profile Foundations, 2010, pp. 237-254.
- *Between Kinship and Alienation. Three Fantastic Tales About Man in Nature*, [in:] Katarzyna Marciniak (ed.), *Birthday Beasts' Book. Cultural Studies in Honour of Jerzy Axer*, Warsaw: Wilczyska Press, 2011, pp. 471-488.
- *Foucault reads Freud: The dialogue with unreason and Enlightenment*, “Polish Sociological Review”, 3, 171, 2010, pp. 271-289.
- *A Metaphysician in the Land of Cyborgs. On Robert Piłat's Book* On the Nature of Concepts, “Polish Journal of Philosophy”, II/2, 2008, pp. 127-139.
- *Beyond Identity. Beyond Europe,* [in:] Małgorzata Kowalska (ed.), *The New Europe. Uncertain Identity and Borders* Białystok: Wydawnictwo Uniwersytetu w Białymstoku, 2007, pp. 123-141.

All the above mentioned texts have undergone, for the purpose of this book, a thorough overhaul. During the successive stages of work on the English version of the book I was helped with the translations by Bartłomiej Rcszuta, Jakub Bielak and Artur Skweres. I would like to thank all these gentlemen for their help during the consecutive stages of work on the book. I also thank Professors Krzysztof Ziarek and Mirosław Loba for an insightful reading of the book that allowed me to improve it considerably.

PART ONE:
PSYCHOANALYSIS

I. Consent and Resistance to Psychoanalysis

Widerstand.-Es.: resistencia.-Fr.: résistance.-I.: resistenza.-P.: resistência. In psycho-analytic treatment the name 'resistance' is given to everything in the words and actions of the analysand that obstructs his gaining access to his unconscious. By extension, Freud spoke of resistance to psycho-analysis when referring to a hostile attitude towards his discoveries in so far as they exposed unconscious desires and inflicted a 'psychological blow' upon man.

Jean Laplanche, Jean-Bertrand Pontalis[1]

Why this interest in psychoanalysis, an interest justified neither by the competence of an analyst nor by the experience of having been analyzed?

Paul Ricoeur[2]

Although The Interpretation of Dreams was published over a century ago, the integration of psychoanalysis into the broad matrix of modern social and cultural history has barely begun.

Eli Zaretsky[3]

1. The renaissance of psychoanalysis in question

In his booklet, which is a sort of introduction to the psychoanalysis of Jacques Lacan, Slavoj Žižek says explicitly that "it is only today that the time of psychoanalysis has arrived" as "Freud's key insights finally become visible in their true dimension".[4] The true dimension of psychoanalysis, if I correctly understand the logic behind it, is now being elucidated by visual, political and literary culture. Erica Jong's pronouncements on German toilets, Dick Cheney's stand on torture, Hans Christian Andersen's narrative *The Emperor's New Clothes*, Tom Cruise and Nicole Kidman's final dialogue in Stanley Kubrick's *Eyes Wide Shut*, the deadly creature in Ridley Scott's *Alien*, a few scenes in one of the major Hollywood film classics *Casablanca* by Michael Curtiz, and of course *Bobek* by Fyodor Dostoyevsky, as well as Shakespeare's plays such as

1 Jean Laplanche, Jean-Bertrand Pontalis, *The Language of Psychoanalysis*, trans. D. Nicholson-Smith, with an introd. by Daniel Lagache (London: Hogarth Press, 1973), p. 394.

2 Paul Ricoeur (1965), *Freud and Philosophy. An Essay on Interpretation*, trans. D. Savage (New Haven and London: Yale University, 1970), p. 3.

3 Eli Zaretsky, *Secrets of the Soul: A Social and Cultural History of Psychoanalysis* (New York: Knopf, 2004), p. 114.

4 Slavoj Žižek, *How to Read Lacan* (London: Granta Books, 2006), p. 15.

Richard II, are the most sublime illustrations of the complex concepts of Freud and Lacan. It is thanks to these and other works that truth can no longer be obscured and instead it becomes public.

It is not my intention to dispute Žižek's diagnosis, nor even to reproach it with mannerist eclecticism, but to frame this type of diagnosis as a symptom of what psychoanalysis is today. I think we are all subject to this symptom, which means that our apparent fascination with psychoanalysis and the resistance to psychoanalysis orbit the same phenomenon. The position of psychoanalysis in contemporary culture is thus paradoxical: the weakening of its position in the clinic parallels its increasing impact on the humanities, social sciences and global culture. Žižek asks the important question – Is psychoanalysis today really outdated? – and he answers: it seems that it is, on three interconnected levels: (1) that of scientific knowledge, where the cognitivist-neurobiologist model of the human mind appears to supersede the Freudian model; (2) that of psychiatric clinic, where psychoanalytic treatment is rapidly losing ground against pills and behavioral therapy; (3) that of the social context, where the image of a society and of social norms, which represses the individual's sexual drives, no longer appears valid with regard to today's predominant hedonistic permissiveness. Nonetheless, in contrast to the diagnosis and acclamations of how psychoanalysis is dead, Žižek's aim is to demonstrate that "it is only today that the time of psychoanalysis has arrived".[5]

It is an open issue how to diagnose the reasons for this state of affairs. It seems to me that the omnipresence of psychoanalysis and its presumed paradoxicality does not result from questioning the authority of science and the collapse of the Enlightenment, and neither is it a consequence of its weakened position in the dimension of the clinic. Simply put, I see this as a result of ostentatious claims of psychoanalysis to general ontology seen as descriptive language of the foundations of the social world.

It is then rather pointless to discuss the renaissance of psychoanalysis or the death of psychoanalysis. Yet, what is worth examining in detail are the expansionist intentions concealed in the work of Freud and Lacan. If Žižek is correct and indeed it is the time of psychoanalysis, it is not because certain conditions have been satisfied to allow its renaissance – such as the collapse of science in a narrow (positivist) sense, but the sheer fact that we have departed from seeing psychoanalysis as a regional psychology, a form of psychiatric therapy, the clinic, and even the art of reading of both written and spoken texts (hermeneutics), and that we have come to see it as a general ontology which says something about the emergence of the foundations of the social world.

---

5 *Ibid.*, p. 15.

Hence, terms such as: "relationship with the object", *Besetzung* ("investment"), "pleasure principle", *das Es*, *das Über-Ich*, "desire", "attachment", "death drive", *Genuss* (*jouissance*, "enjoyment"), and the four terms which are used in reference to the concept of a drive: "impetus" (*Drang*), "aim" (*Ziel*), "source" (*Quelle*) and "object" (*Objekt*), are not expressions that would belong to some regional psychological dictionary (in humanities) that psychologists often restrict them to, but instead they constitute elements of strictly philosophical lexicon, that is, they are of ontological nature. This is the only explanation I can think of considering the widespread contemporary interest in psychoanalysis – that of political scientists, culture analysts and philologists, and the use of psychoanalysis for the study of political, cultural and textual world. I think that in particular studies focused on the phenomenon of the political seek to explain the birth of power, and the resulting consistency and sustainability of all collective life. In consequence, they become the ontology of the political and social world in general.

I think, moreover, that these radical claims of psychoanalysis can be discouraging and provoking resistance to the works of Freud and Lacan, while at the same time they can be fascinating and therefore attractive. Resistance to psychoanalysis is not so much resistance to the child's sexuality, lack of falsification of the allegations posed by psychoanalysis, or its antiscience, but it is a resistance to its claim (or various claims) that its dictionary is the exclusive lexicon allowing explanations to virtually all phenomena. This is what many find too disturbing in psychoanalysis, too irritating, or even frightening, and it also makes it a method many find implausible. For this last reason Žižek, cited at the outset of this paper, is often taken for a humbug by the vast majority sporting standardized type of knowledge. It is not the case though, since his method of psychoanalysis is so ostentatious and nondeceptive that it is almost legitimate (as ambiguous as this may sound). He is an individual enchanted with the ontological and inexhaustible potential of the works by Freud.

Another researcher following this ontological trail is Joana Copjec. Copjec is fully aware that the psychoanalytic categories are not regional, and that they belong to the general ontology. For her, the theory developed by Freud poses classical ontological questions such as: What is an object?, What is the externality?, What is the interiority?, What is representation?, Where do the categories to classify objects come from?, What is language?, What is Real?, ans so on and so forth. In this connection, Copjec writes:

> This term, "object of lack", cannot be understood outside the Timaean/*la-mellian* myth from which it derives. The partial object or object of lack is the one that emerges *out of the lack*, the void, opened by the loss of the original Plenum or *das Ding*. In place of the mythical satisfaction derived from being at one with the maternal Thing, the subject now experiences satisfaction in this partial object [...].

> The elevation of the external object of the drive – let us stay with the example of the milk – to the status of the breast (that is, to the status of the object capable of satisfying something more than the mouth or stomach) does not depend on its cultural or social value in relation to other objects. Its surplus "breast value", let us say, depends solely on the drive's election of it as an object of satisfaction.[6]

In the same vein today, Ernesto Laclau writes explicitly that the moment of social mythical fullness that we are looking for in the historical social experiments, with communism at the helm, is a futile search for the restoration of unity of mother and child, which in political terms means the establishment of totally reconciled society. We may find this assertion irritating, sensing that psychoanalytic terms are not privileged to extend so far, that is, they only allow for a genealogical explanation of stability and irremovability of some phantasms, but that they cannot equal political concepts. Thus critiques of psychoanalysis accuse Laclau of not being able to understand that one thing is to provide explanation of our ideas and sources of mental fixation, and another is to provide ideological justifications for political projects which may be born of these fixations, but are not exhaustively explained by them alone. Laclau responds to these objections referring back to Freud:

> The main ontological consequence of the Freudian discovery of the unconscious is that the category of representation does not simply reproduce, at a secondary level, a fullness preceding it which could be grasped in a direct way but, on the contrary, representation is the absolutely primary level in the constitution of objectivity.[7]

Is not my intention to attempt to resolve the arguments of both sides here, my intention is solely to voice one plain thesis: our attitude towards the ideas, such as those of Joan Copjec and Ernesto Laclau, depends entirely on whether we are willing to treat psychoanalysis as a first ontology or not, and in this sense such conditioning is symptomological. It in fact betrays our most basic preferences. Those who first found first ontology in phenomenology, Hegellianism, cognitivism or Aristotelianism will systematically oppose claims – for them entirely idiosyncratic – equalling, for example, the search for a transparent social order with the search for the mythical fullness of the prenatal period. This resistance may prove just and reasonable, because what we ought to call for now are arguments to convince us that the work of Freud and Lacan indeed provides such an attractive ontology.

In other words, we should ask ourselves whether the lexicon of standard psychoanalytic concepts, and in the first resort the list of defense mechanisms,

---

6 Joan Copjec, *Imagine There's No Woman: Ethics and Sublimation* (Cambridge: MIT Press, 2002), p. 60.

7 Ernesto Laclau, *On Populist Reason* (London: Verso, 2005), p. 115.

allows us to do more than engage in mechanical spinning of prayer wheels? Is it credible at all? Were we not put into a coma watching the main concepts of psychoanalysis penetrate one by one the universal culture (thus being vulgarized) so that we lost the sense of credibility of the project itself and this dictionary? Or, to put it yet another way, is it not reasonable today to try make inventory of this lexicon of universal ontology and refresh this dictionary, and maybe even (at least partially) abandon some of its entries?

Here we return to Slavoj Žižek, who at the beginning of the introduction to Lacan puts forward three conscious questions addressing psychoanalysis: (1) In what sense can the Freudian model compete today with the cognitive-neurobiological model of human mind/brain? And (2) In what sense can the Freudian model compete today with the pharmaco-behavioral model of the clinic? (3) In what sense the Freudian notion of a society trapped in a "repressive hypothesis" and the shackles of Victorian society can be an adequate set of tools to describe hedonistic permissiveness dominating in the world of second modernity? It is interesting that Žižek only enumerates those doubts, but never returns to provide answers. Well, he does answer them otherwise.

2. Psychoanalysis as an anthropology

Perhaps in contemporary culture the discourse of psychoanalysis has acquired a rather monopolistic position in representing human fate. It may have been due to the remarkable rise of interest in political history and memory, while at the same time all universal anthropological projects suffered from intensified processes of delegitimization. But perhaps it happened only because other discourses in the humanities got secluded due to specialized jargon and have become an incomprehensible and anonymous type of academic discourse, which common researchers found to be out of their reach and were thus unable to identify with. Perhaps psychoanalysis has given us the most persuasive vocabulary to describe the dynamics of human behaviour, and language to understand the intense invasion of the human realm of various types of mechanical monstrosities, human look-alikes operating somewhere in no man's zone on the border of human and nonhuman. If that were the case we would have reached the explanation why psychoanalysis became the monopolist on the market of the humanities as far as description of what is human is concerned, and even – this time – a monopolist in describing what is prehuman, what is only to become human.

If, however, psychoanalysis is the kind of discourse, which gets us accustomed with the ambiguity of the term "man", and is the kind of vernacular allowing us to get accustomed with the world inhabited by look-alikes of what aspires to be "man's existence", then this incredible capacity of psychoanalysis implies nothing more than ambivalence of the psychoanalytic discourse, which conceals equal amount of condemnation and support for human aspirations, thereby demonstrating how much of a machine is in man and how much of man is in the machine. Through psychoanalysis I have discovered – let this confession be finally heard – how much of the mechanical monstrosity resides in myself, but also, how much humanity resides in each mechanical monstrosity that mankind tries to distance itself from.

Finally, is it not because of this ambiguity that psychoanalytical discourse is trapped between the reconstitution of subjectivity and its violent disintegration?! Does it not give us inspiration for both the far-reaching antihumanism driving man to the grave, and neo-humanist discourse calling for the renewal of humanity? Is it not because of all the ambiguity that there is today that we feel all urged to take shots at Freud and we feel all somehow related to Freud? Do we not use and abuse Freud to accomplish our own aims? Maybe to continue this analytical work we will have to start forgetting the word "psychoanalysis".

3. Unreason and Enlightenment

Freud's Enlightenment is rather suspicious: this is because at the same time it is murky, dark, sensual, and analytical. Freud's imagination is inhabited by both "murky" middle class writers and "dark" denouncers thinking of truth as a "moving army of metaphors". According to Freud, only sublimation makes possible thoughts free from their erotic past, and transforms the drive without killing it. In a sense, thought is never truly free from its erotic past and always carries the stigma of wishful thinking. On the other hand, as we read in *Die Zukunft einer Illusion*, thought is slow, or better said, when it comes to imposing discipline it is always late, persistently, and relentlessly. We find the following in *The Future of an Illusion:*

> We may insist as often as we like that man's intellect is powerless in comparison with his instinctual life, and we may be right in this. Nevertheless, there is something peculiar about this weakness. The voice of the intellect is a soft one, but it does not rest till it has gained a hearing. Finally, after a countless succession of rebuffs, it succeeds.[8]

8 Sigmund Freud (1927), *The Future of an Illusion*, trans. J. Strachey, [in:] *The Standard Edition of the Complete Psychological Works of Sigmund Freud,* Volume 21 (London: Hogarth Press (1968), p. 150.

On the one hand, the shaping of death drive as a prototype of all drives makes Freud a late cousin of Marquis de Sade. Was it not Freud who noted that death stands at the very beginning of life, which may defend itself against death only with the economy of death, postponing it, repeating it, and resonating death? On the other hand, Freud's work on narcissism and psychology of human assemblage makes him akin to Hobbes, dark middle class writer. It is in Freud's writings on culture, especially in *Civilization and Its Discontents*, that we find the suggestion that "[t]he liberty of the individual is no gift of civilization. It was greatest before there was any civilization, though then, it is true, it had for the most part no value, since the individual was scarcely in a position to defend it".[9] The studies on sublimation and children's eroticism in turn make Freud a distant relative of Schiller and Kierkegaard, sharing the legacy of anthropology of "man the player". It seems that Freud finds connection between representation and libido in early symbolic games of a child, the one in which a child – just after his/her mother left, starts playing a game of coming and leaving with a spool and a string. Freud decodes and deciphers the *Vor und Da* game and later finds it to be the prototype of effective release of a trauma. And finally there is Freud's early imagining of unconsciousness as optical apparatus, a typewriter or a copying machine, which he has never gone beyond, and which relates him to the linkage of rationality, determinism, and even positivism. Freud, with his most scientific projects, appears to be the prisoner of the methodology of natural sciences which he cannot transcend – unlike Galileo described by Edmund Husserl in *Die Krisis der europäischen Wissenschaften und die transzentale Phänomenologie*. Once again the short quotation from *Die Zukunft einer Illusion*: "[n]o, our science is no illusion. But an illusion it would be to suppose that what science cannot give us we can get elsewhere".[10]

Beyond eighteenth century psychology and, very broadly, beyond the psychologistic modernity of the nineteenth century, beyond the positivist institution of psychology, does it not seem as if Freud were joining back up with a certain classical age or at least with whatever in this age does not determine madness as a psychical illness but as unreason, that is, as something that has to do with reason? In the classical age, if such a thing exists (a hypothesis of Foucault that I take here, in this context, as not debatable), unreason is no doubt reduced to silence; one does not speak with it. One interrupts or forbids dialogue, and this suspension or interdiction would have received from the

9 Sigmund Freud (1930), *Civilization and Its Discontents*, trans. J. Strachey, [in:] *The Standard Edition of the Complete Psychological Works of Sigmund Freud,* Volume 21 (London: Hogarth Press, 1968), p. 42.

10 Sigmund Freud, *The Future of an Illusion*, p. 123.

Cartesian *cogito* the violent form of a sentence. For Freud too madness would be unreason (and in this sense, at least, there would be a neo-Cartesian logic at work in psychoanalysis). But this time one should resume speaking with it: one would reestablish a dialogue with unreason and lift the Cartesian interdiction.

What else, if not these ambiguities, trap psychoanalytical discourse in between restitution of subjectivity and its rapid disintegration? Does it not provide inspiration to both antihumanistic extremists who focus their attention on the human grave as well as neo-humanists who are calling for restoration of humanity? The ambiguities also seem to allow many to speak on Freud and feel justified in their comments. So maybe we use and abuse Freud for our own reasons? Maybe even as refined an analyst as Foucault fell victim to this ambiguity in the later stages of his work?

It is probably not such a good idea to follow Jürgen Habermas and to reproach Freud with his incorrect and flawed self-understanding: his ontological naturalism explicitly incoherent with his ostentatious methodological antinaturalism.[11] It is not a good idea to follow Paul Ricoeur, and justify Freud claiming that psychoanalysis has yet to work out a mixed language combining dictionaries of dynamics, energy and even hydraulics of the impulses with the vocabulary of the exegesis.[12] Those mixed concepts do not prove there are mistakes in the conceptual system of psychoanalysis, but quite the opposite, they correctly identify space where discourse appears, the tangle of power and meaning, impulse and discourse, energetics and semantics. Similarly, it is a bad idea to call Freud for support or fierce critique of the Enlightenment. It is a bad idea altogether to point to evidence in his own work to support this or that thesis. The thing about Freud is above all to honour his work in its complexity, it is about refusal of "blackmail of the Enlightenment" – in Foucault's own words: one has to be "for" or "against" the Enlightenment.[13] I suppose that in that way and only in that way we really do justice to Freud.

4. *Kultur* or fantasies about nature

The fluctuation in Freud's writings between medical investigation and a theory of culture bears witness to the scope of the Freudian project. True, the major texts on culture are to be found in the last part of Freud's work. However, psychoanalysis should not be regarded as a form of individual psychology,

11 Jürgen Habermas, *Erkenntnis und Interesse*, (Frankfurt am Main: Suhrkamp, 1968), p. 214.

12 Paul Ricoeur, *Freud and Philosophy: An Essay on Interpretation*.

13 Michel Foucault, *What is Enlightenment?*, trans. C. Porter. [in:] P. Rabinow (ed.), *The Foucault Reader* (New York: Pantheon Books, 1984), p. 48.

tardily transposed into a sociology of culture. A summary glance at the Freudian bibliography shows that the first texts on art, morality, and religion follow upon *The Interpretation of Dreams* and are then developed alongside the great doctrinal texts that constitute the *Papers on Metapsychology* (1913-17), *Beyond the Pleasure Principle* (1920), and *The Ego and the Id* (1923). In fact, to grasp how the theory of culture is related to the theory of dreams and the neuroses, it is necessary to go back to *The Interpretation of Dreams* of 1900, for it is here that the connection with mythology and literature was first established. Ever since 1900 the *Traumdeutung* had proposed that dreams are the dreamer's private mythology and myths the waking dreams of peoples, that Sophocles' *Oedipus* and Shakespeare's *Hamlet* are to be interpreted in the same way as dreams.

Whatever the outcome of this difficulty, the entrance of psychoanalysis into the general contemporary discussion about language is not due solely to its interpretation of culture. By making dreams not only the first object of his investigation but a model of all the disguised, substitutive, and active expressions of human wishing or desire, Freud invites us to look to dreams themselves for the various relations between desire and language. First, it is not the dream as dreamed that can be interpreted, but rather the text of the dream account; analysis attempts to substitute for this text another text that could be called the primitive speech of desire. Thus, analysis moves from one meaning to another meaning; it is not desires as such that are placed at the center of the analysis, but rather their language. Later we will discuss how this semantics of desire relates to the dynamics expressed in the notions of discharge, repression, cathexis, and so on. But it is important to stress from the start that this dynamics – or energetics, or even hydraulics – is articulated only in semantics: the "vicissitudes of the instincts", to use one of Freud's expressions, can be attained only in the vicissitudes of meaning. Therein lies the deep reason for all the analogies between dreams and wit, dreams and myth, dreams and works of art, dreams and religious illusion, etc. All these psychical productions belong to the area of meaning and come under a unified question: How do desires achieve speech? How do desires make speech fail, and why do they themselves fail to speak? This new approach to the whole of human speech, to the meaning of human desire, is what entitles psychoanalysis to its place in the general debate on language.

The German word *Kultur*, which Freud used in the German title of his book *Das Unbehagen in der Kultur* [*Civilization and Its Discontents*] should not be translated into English as "civilization". Perhaps the proper translation should be: *The Uneasiness in Culture*. For Freud, *Kultur*/civilization consists of (1) the institution governing our relationship with nature (science and technology), (2) institutions governing relationships among human persons and groups (state and law order), and finally, (3) strictly "cultural" institutions such as religion and art. With such a broad sense of the concept, *Kultur*/civilization has both repressive functions and at the same time a comforting and consoling function. Civilization, although its purpose would seem to be amelioration of human misery and suffering, is actually partially responsible for that suffering. This explains our subliminal hostility toward civilization.

What is the purpose of civilization? (1) It protects humans from nature, provides a line of defense. (2) It adjusts and regulates the mutual relations among human beings. (3) Aside from these more pragmatic, utilitarian aspects, civilization also promotes things that seems useless: for example, beauty (art), order, rules of cleanliness, etc. In short, civilization also produces luxuries. One of the major dangers of interpretation of Freud is the temptation to overestimate Freud's distinction nature/culture, and as a result – the famous and many-times-interpreted myth/story about the Founding Murder, the Killing of the Pre-Father, which has become the threshold of the birth of civilization. But Freud never treated this hypothesis as realistic and never refers to this hypothesis as to historical or anthropological fact. This hypothesis was for him merely a Phantasm, an insight about the so-called primary stage of humanity, which is essentially unavailable to us. As a result, nature appears in Freud only as a culture, only processed by the culture, as some Image, Representation. Similarly, in the social contract theory from Hobbes to Rawls, which tries to depict the transition of man from a state of nature to a state of civil society, this transition is not treated as an empirical hypothesis, but as a kind of thought experiment, that is, purely hypothetically. Is Freud a slave of Enlightenment thinking, and remains a philosopher of the Enlightenment? The answer is: yes and no. Yes, because he pretends that he was speaking in the name of science against the illusions that have to die in the future, such as religion. No, because Freud claims that the purpose of life is simply the programme of the pleasure principle and he explores various styles of human adaptation used to secure happiness from the world while also trying to avoid or limit suffering. The illusion, therefore, must be constantly maintained, even if it adopts other names. This illusion will continue as long as life will continue.

Freud's application of the topographic-economic point of view to works of art serves more than one design. It was a diversion for the clinician, who was also a great traveler, collector, and avid bibliophile, a great reader of classical literature – from Sophocles to Shakespeare to Goethe to contemporary poetry – and a student of ethnography and the history of religions. For the apologist of his own doctrine – especially during the period of isolation that preceded the first world war – it was a defense and an illustration of psychoanalysis open to the general, nonscientific public. It was even more a proof and test of truth for the theoretician of the metapsychology. And last, it was a milestone in the direction of the great philosophical design that Freud never lost sight of and which was both masked and manifested by the theory of the psychoneuroses.

Let us consider the economic interpretation of culture in *Civilization and Its Discontents*. Cultural development, like the growth of the individual from infancy to adulthood, is the fruit of Eros and Ananke, of love and work; we must even say it is the fruit of love more than of work, for the necessity of uniting in work in order to exploit nature is but a small thing compared with the libidinal tie which unites individuals in a single social body. It seems then, that the same Eros inspires the striving for individual happiness and wishes to unite men in ever wider groups. But the paradox soon appears: as the organized struggle against nature, culture gives man the power that was once conferred on the gods; but this resemblance to the gods leaves man unsatisfied: civilization and its discontents. And so the question arises: Why does man fail to be happy? Why is man as a cultural being dissatisfied? The analysis here reaches its turning point. Confronting man is an absurd commandment: to love one's neighbor as oneself; an impossible demand: to love one's enemies; a dangerous order: to turn the other cheek. These precepts squander love, put a premium on being bad, and lead to ruin anyone imprudent enough to obey them.

The instinct that thus disturbs man's relations with man and requires society to rise as the implacable dispenser of justice is, of course, the death instinct, identified here with the primordial hostility of man toward man. With the death instinct there appears what Freud henceforward calls an anticultural instinct. From now on social ties cannot be regarded as a mere extension of the individual libido, as in *Group Psychology and the Analysis of the Ego*. Thus the reinterpretation of the sense of guilt at the end of *Civilization and Its Discontents* is seen to be the climax in the series of figures of the death instinct. By mortifying the individual, culture places death at the service of love and reverses the initial relationship between life and death.

5. The future of psychoanalysis

Perhaps – and this is my last strong thesis – there are reasons to view psychoanalysis as a tool developed by culture to allow recreation of our family affairs, that is, to enable the establishment of one's own history, and as a result one's own freedom. Perhaps there are reasons to view psychoanalysis as a tool raised by culture to allow everyone to achieve greater freedom to sculpt one's own past and make use of one's own body and will for the sake of yet greater self-realization. This would however mean that psychoanalysis is a tool for building one's own identity, a sense of integrity with one's past. But does this self-realization mean reference to a tool allowing us to accept the suppressed, forgotten or unconscious truth about oneself, or, rather, is it recognition of the explanatory potential of this tool as a means to narrate the dimension of truth in human existence, that is, to explain how – to use the jargon of Michel Foucault – we become part of truth regimes, which begin to dominate over us. This brings us to the core issue – the stake of psychoanalytic discourse. I therefore ask: What is at stake in psychoanalytic discourse?

Psychoanalysis was, from the very beginning, drifting between two poles: the temptation to integrate with standardized psychiatric-clinical discourse and as a result to become part of clinical psychology, and the temptation of separatism, uniqueness, the special type of dialect, which would, as a result, condemn it to the fate of cursed science, suspicious, ambiguous, singular, and eventually alienated. The first temptation ends with the exaltation of the depressive position as the only acceptable position for a mature man. The second seeks to encourage cultivation of one's own idiosyncrasies and becoming a free subject, that is, an entity capable of creating itself, an entity which located in itself a disposition to confront the most primitive element of human existence. For Freud, autonomy means above all freedom in searching for what one wishes to do with one's life. This oscillation between the discourse of freedom, which is an open invitation to become a creator of one's own biography, and the discourse of reconciliation, which enables wise (meaning: depressive) life in the world, is constantly present in psychoanalysis. It also results – I should think – in an ambiguous response of the commentators of the works of Freud to psychoanalysis.

This oscillation of the psychoanalytic discourse and of the related views between the worshipping glorification and absolute condemnation makes me believe today that there is no such thing as "psychoanalysis", just as there is no such thing as "Freud", and *a fortiori* "Lacan". Eli Zaretsky writes in this vein that "[i]n truth, there had always been two Freuds: a conservative institutionalized pragmatist and a utopian revolutionary".[14] Personally, I think there were more than two. There are some threads in Freud's metapsychology that assert a conservative stance. Indeed, Freud speaks, above all, on the inability to distance onself from the past and the need to constantly be alert to the past perfect tense. The abandoned past tense shall one day return as a masked monstrosity. However, Freud can also be seen as a radical ideologue who is constantly exhorting the yet unfinished and unfulfilled project of

14 Eli Zaretsky, *Secrets of the Soul: A Social and Cultural History of Psychoanalysis*, p. 115.

Enlightenment. Indeed, Freud mentions a second chance, which is our only chance for freedom, a second chance, which, if used creatively, would allow us to become someone other than we had been, or, if our determination and skills are deficient, would at least allow us to act for the rest of our days in a neurotic armour, that is, to repeat mechanically our own ontogenetic past: the past actions, but also thoughts and feelings. Finally, Freud can be seen as a cool rationalist, who with the help of analytical instruments scrutinizes geysers and eruptions of volcanic deposits without sinking into the abyss of thoughts and without a desire to enter the deepest circle of hell. Is this not what captivates us in the first reading of *Die Traumdeutung* (1899), this anatomical attitude, this stand enabling him to surgically cut into ever smaller pieces Irma's dreams, which explain almost at the molecular level the visible structure of dreams!?

All of these incarnations of Freud which are true and untrue about him are true and untrue about psychoanalysis. Freud, as one of the few 20th century writers presents us with a suggestion that thinking can be passion: a passion which does not subordinate nor oppress other passions and talents, but brings in some order and overcomes them. We have so much got used to the opposition of reason and passion, spirit and life, that a newfound idea of passionate thinking still catches us unaware and disturbs us greatly, only after we have regained our balance. We have so much got used to these oppositions that the sole idea of intellectual erotica (or erotic intelligence) leaves us astounded. Living and thinking, as presented by Freud, have not much to do with the Buddhist self-renunciation, nor is it Georges Bataille's movement of transgression – it is more about controlled erotic life hoping for something unconsciously sought for: truth and gratification. Sometimes, there's no difference between. This said, we have perhaps argument supporting Foucault's diagnosis which is this time not in contradiction with Freud's basic insight: we are part of a society with sex and we see no other gratification than that which life under the spell of the pleasure principle may ever bring.

II. Foucault reads Freud: the Dialogue with Unreason and Enlightenment

One day we must do justice to Freud, he did not make speak a madness that had genuinely been a language for centuries [...] he dried it out; he forced its words back to their source, all the way back to that blank region of auto-implication where nothing is said.

Michel Foucault[1]

Foucault speaks little of Freud in this book [Histoire de la folie à l'âge classique].

Jacques Derrida[2]

1. Presence of the name

Michel Foucault made substantial efforts to divert our attention from the sources of his inspiration which rested in Freud and were underpinning his lines of thinking. Instead, we were encouraged to investigate Nietzsche's influence. For reasons that remain unknown, Foucault preferred to be remembered as a Nietzscheanist rather than Freudist. However, Freud's name is always present in Foucault's writings and, as for the volume, it outbids Nietzsche by a generous

1 Michel Foucault (1961), *Madness and Civilization: A History of Insanity in the Age of Reason*, trans. R. Howard (New York: Random House, 1965), p. 411. Foucault wrote in the book *in extenso*: "[t]his is why we must do justice to Freud. Between Freud's *Five Case Histories* and Janet's scrupulous investigations of *Psychological Healing*, there is more than the density of a discovery; there is the sovereign violence of a return. Janet enumerated the elements of a division, drew up his inventory, annexed here and there, perhaps conquered. Freud went back to madness at the level of its language, reconstituted one of the essential elements of an experience reduced to silence by positivism; he did not make a major addition to the list of psychological treatments for madness; he restored, in medical thought, the possibility of a dialogue with unreason". Foucault comes back also to the sentence in the *Preface* to *Madness and civilization*: "[o]ne day we must do justice to Freud, he did not make *speak* a madness that had genuinely been a language for centuries [...] he dried it out; he forced its words back to their source, all the way back to that blank region of auto-implication where nothing is said". Michel Foucault, *Madness, the Absence of Work (d'œuvre),* [in:] A. I. Davidson (ed.), *Foucault and his Interlocutors*, (London and Chicago: Chicago University Press 1997), p. 102.

2 Jacques Derrida, *"To Do Justice to Freud": The History of Madness in the Age of Psychoanalysis*, trans. A. Pascale Brault, M. Naas. "Critical Inquiry", 1994.

marigin. Freud's name and the word "psychoanalysis" is constantly inflected in yet new ways, new contexts and in shifting histories. Similarly, Foucault is constantly shifting his position in relation to psychoanalysis, changing in his evaluations and granting it more or less importance.

Right here, I need to confess that it is not my intention to investigate this changeable nature of Foucault's approach to psychoanalysis – a rather futile endeavour considering Foucault's commitment to philosophy of discontinuation and intermittence. I would rather investigate these swings and sways separately, and see them as symptoms of our own uncertainty concerning the evaluation of Freud's work, knowing that the structure of his work – is no help either. I believe that this examination is significant, as it allows us to relate Foucault's ever changing diagnosis of psychoanalysis and his ever changing bid for the importance of psychoanalytic discourse. In our culture, we have so far been unable to decide what the true value of psychoanalysis is and to define the rolc it has played.

Foucault's approach to psychoanalysis is ambivalent. Foucault hesitates whether to praise or to condemn it. While in the *Histoire de la folie à l'âge classique* the psychoanalitic theory of subject is employed to secretly break up the dialogue between insanity and unreason, the dialogue essential for the rational consciousness of the West, already in *Les Mots et les choses* (translated into English as *The Order of Things*), Foucault makes of it a critical science, which releases desire from the bonds of human subjectivity. There is one passage in *Les Mots et les choses* which says: "all this knowledge, within which Western culture had given itself in one century a certain image of man, pivots on the work of Freud".[3] The author of *Jenseits des Lustprinzips* more than anyone else brings knowledge of man this close to the model of linguistics and philology, and is the first one to undertake a breakneck task of bridging the gap between the positive and the negative, the normal and the pathologic, understandable and the inexpressible, the meaning and the meaningless. An excerpt from *Les Mots et les choses*:

> Psychoanalysis and ethnology occupy a privileged position in our knowledge – not because they have established the foundations of their positivity better than any other human science, and at last accomplished the old attempt to be truly scientific; but rather because, on the confines of all the branches of knowledge investigating man, they form an undoubted and inexhaustible treasure-hoard of experiences and concepts, and above all a perpetual principle of dissatisfaction, of calling into question, of criticism and contestation of what may seem, in other respects, to be established. Now, there is a reason for this that concerns the object they respectively

---

3 Michel Foucault (1966), *The Order of Things. An Archaeology of the Human Sciences*, (London: Vintage, 1992).

> give to one another, but concerns even more the position they occupy and function they perform within the general space of the *episteme*.[4]

In 1966, Foucault saw in psychoanalysis a critical science, directly addressing the issue of unconsciousness, that is directing our attention to a place by definition inaccessible to any other theoretical cognition, where we see three elements cross: silent repetition of Death, naked openness of Desire, and language – the expression of Law. From the standpoint of a certain epistemological trihedron (life, work, and language, or biology, economy, and philology), the human sciences are seen to be at once inclusive and exclusive. As for this inclusive exclusion, Freud's work, to which Foucault unwaveringly assigns a model that is more philological than biological, occupies the place of the hinge. Foucault in fact speaks about the place and workings of a "pivot": all this knowledge, within which Western culture had given itself in one century a certain image of man, pivots on the work of Freud.

At the time of writing, Foucault was particularly interested in the analytics of finitude and started describing human figure by mixing in the discourses on work, language and life. In his own words, psychoanalysis is a discipline with a potential for revealing the combination of the above discourses, also in its negative aspect, by uncovering death where previously only life was seen, exposing desires in place of desired work results, and declaring the mighty existence of words where others saw the orderly work of grammar.

It was here in *Les Mots et les choses*, where psychoanalysis earned the label of antiscience, side by side with ethnology. Foucault returns to this concept in his famous lectures at the College de France in 1976, published in a larger work: *Il faut défendre la société*. In these lectures Foucault compares psychoanalysis to Marxism, claiming that both types of discourse are rather suspicious forms of knowledge. Foucault turns our attention to the fact that the scientific knowledge of both Marxism and psychoanalysis were often questioned. So, is psychoanalysis a science at all?

Maybe we should reverse our traditional way of reasoning, and before we ask: to what extent Marxism or psychoanalysis resemble scientific practice – that is the rules by which we establish knowledge and the ways we investigate truth, and even before we ask about the scientific nature of psychoanalysis, we should perhaps analyse the sole ambition to possess knowledge, which is implied in all claims to science. Foucault says:

> The question or questions that have to be asked are: What types of knowledge are you trying to disqualify when you say you are a science? What speaking subject, what discursive subject, what subject of experience and knowledge are you trying to

4 *Ibid.*, p. 432.

> minorize when you begin to say "I speak this discourse, I am speaking a scientific discourse, and I am a scientist".[5]

Foucault's point of view allows a certain critique of psychoanalysis and Marxism, namely it reveals their pretence to science, and their attempts to reach the level of scientific approval (no matter how it is defined). These efforts, made under the influence of the academic world in order to provide these forms of knowledge the framing of positive science, only reveal the will to adjust to the disciplinary regimes of knowledge and, also, that the extensive discourses have internalized some kind of a reflected, mirrored self (also imposed on the self).

Let me put forward a daring thesis, that big names in human sciences of the 20th century – Freud, Lévi-Strauss, Chomsky, Foucault, but also Piaget, have become great names because all transgressed the limits of their native discipline – psychiatry, anthropology, linguistics, history, and psychology – and entered the territory of philosophy, the land of total discourse. It docs not mean, however, that the discourses of psychoanalysis, structural anthropology, generative grammar or genetic epistemology were nonscientific in nature; what it means is that they were extensive enough to generate a dictionary for description of reality, which was no longer subjected to the traditional methods of verification and refutability.

All of the thinkers concerned, before they pioneered antisciences, had first subjected thcir cognitive efforts to discipline, and had first imposed new scientific methods in their primary disciplines. Reaching high level of cognitive intensity allowed for the exteriorisation (and extrapolation) of their discoveries, and sending them out into new research areas. In this way, they were designing their discourse as a philosophical undertaking. To say that all those triumphs of the humanities in the 20th century are nonscientific is to admit that all those accomplishments are in a sense philosophical. I am pleased to agree with this finding. But on one condition, namely that by "philosophical" character I understand one intending to proceed beyond verifiable (falsifiable) empirical knowledge.

It makes damage to Freud to name him a psychologist or a therapist; as we do in fact know, his field was philosophical anthropology or critical hermeneutics of culture. Similarly, it makes damage to Lévi-Strauss, to classify him as a structural anthropologist and to limit his achievements to working out a few complicated systems of kinship. All the more so given how far reaching the observations included in his major work, *La Pensée sauvage*, were. Chomsky's influence on cognitive psychology was great, and so was the influence of

---

5 Michel Foucault, *Society Must Be Defended. Lectures at the Collège de France, 1975-76*, trans. D. Macey (London: Macmillan, 2003), p. 23.

Foucault on history, or Piaget's on development psychology. Still, we know too well that Chomsky's psycholinguistic project, Foucault's archaeology (genealogy), and Piaget's genetic epistemology all surpass fragmented research projects and their aspirations reach out higher. The novelty of their work was so intense and unexpected that at least at the beginning their projects were classified as antiscience and counterscience, which destabilised the system of established and institutional knowledge. At some point this counterscience receives academic recognition and is gradually assimilated into the system of academic knowledge. There are however some costs involved.

The tendency to make all systems of knowledge a positive science and to tame counterdiscourses relate to a withdrawal and elimination of those assertions which fall short of academic formula. Is it not the case with academic psychology, which makes Freud the central figure and yet conceals the most fundamental and revolutionary idea included in the concept of the death drive? Is this not the case with cultural anthropology, which allows Lévi-Strauss to spin tales on the logics of myths, but silences his thesis that "the final aim of human sciences is not to constitute a man, but to dismember him and find answer to the riddle he is"?[6] What about Foucault, who diagnosed death of a man and yet is predominantly perceived as a historian pondering on unwanted and repressed microhistories? Finally there is Piaget, whose ideas on accommodation and assimilation are widely shared in psychology classes, but whose ambitious project of saving unity of human cognition (genetic epistemology) is widely unknown. It seems that the surplus meaning, the added value hidden in the work of the above authors is crucial when it comes to assessing their greatness, but paradoxically, it is also distant to the disciplines which owe them a lot.

2. Freud in Foucault's work: critical presence

So there we have Freud as the founder of the antiscience calling itself "psychoanalysis". However, Freud's name is present in Foucault's work in yet another form. This presence, let's make it clear, is more critical towards the author of *Totem and Taboo*. This negative presence relates mainly to two extensive narrations by Foucault – one relating to insanity and second to sexuality. In both Freud plays a key role, in a sense bringing to an end these discourses initiated by the Enlightenment. In *Histoire de la folie à l'âge classique*, insanity is deposed. Madness has changed into thoughtlessness, with its most primary and most obvious

---

6 Claude Lévi-Strauss (1962), *The Savage Mind*, trans. G. Weidenfeld, Nicolson Ltd. (Oxford: Oxford University Press, 1996), p. 370.

manifestation – stupidity. We no longer explore madness to find the excess meaning which is on its own the most wonderful source of authentic discourse, the source of double language which exists only in speech, capable of communicating itself only through a language system, the matrix of all languages. Instead, in madness today we hear mumbling and unwarranted excess, which – precisely speaking – says nothing. Madmen in the age of reason are incapable of generating grammatical speech, they are unable to work productively, and they are incapable of establishing a lasting family. The exclusion of the figure of madman from the network of social relations and medicalization of madness have opened the world to a monologue type of the civilisation of reason, where systematic rationalisation and normalisation set the new order of things.

In the final message of history of insanity Foucault suggested that psychology is possible either as a form of critique of modern man, and then it becomes psychiatry or its version – clinical psychology, or as a self-critique, turning itself into a methodology (science about science), but it no longer being psychology (science about man). According to Foucault, psychology using "language of alienation":

> Always and as of its nature is at the crossroads: It is either to follow a deepened negation of man up to the final point where love and death are almost inseparable, like day and night, in the eternal rush of passing seasons, to finish at the point of philosophical craziness, or it is to start once again and again to match subject and the object, the internal and the external, experience and cognition. It was necessary for psychology – as it appeared – to follow that second path, but that choice is now denied.[7]

Freud's role in this exclusion and medicalisation is important, he is closing what Descartes started when he distanced himself from the threat of insanity.

Foucault's accusation focuses on Freud's exploitation of the role of a doctor, on the "exaggeration of doctor's wonderful thaumaturgical nature", granting a doctor "the status of almost a god", making of a doctor the "exclusive subject" and the "absolute Vision", making him "a judge, who punishes and rewards without the need to issue judgements", and "a mirror, in which madness turns to itself in a slow motion, and turns away from itself".[8]

Freud's listening to patients bridges speech and madness, the clue of the treatment is *talking cure*, even though he himself goes silent and "does not hear, cannot hear the voice of unreason, and he cannot read the signs of nonsense".[9] He may be treating some forms of madness, but the sovereign work of unreason

7 Michel Foucault, *Madness and Civilization: A History of Insanity in the Age of Reason*, trans. R. Howard. (New York: Random House, 1965), p. 376.

8 *Ibid.*, pp. 458-459.

9 *Ibid.*

is inaccessible to him. Here, psychoanalysis is not seen as a critical science, contra-science, but an element of an emerging disciplinary system, which will later – with the help of soft methods – control and pacify life and language of the Enlightened man.

This accusatory tone will once again return in the first volume of the *Histoire de la sexualité*, where Foucault shall undertake analysis of "confession" – beginning from the rite known from the church and finishing at the doctor's couch. Only this time Freud's work will be placed in the context of the construction of sexual apparatus and the new biopolitical construction of power typical for the world, where life and intensification of life becomes more valuable than a good and short life. With a special sentiment, Foucault attributes the so-called repressive hypothesis to Freud. According to this hypothesis, as to the principle power performs repressive functions, suppressing human drives and forcing them to impose on themselves serious limitations.[10] From this perspective, we see that power is not masked, its work is not secret; in fact the opposite is true, as power is masquerading in the costume of excessive and almighty Superego (*das Über-Ich* in Freud's terminology) which is the source of authority and law, brought into the individual's focus by the figure of Father, and in the social context by the figure of the State.

According to repressive hypothesis: (1) The relation between power and sex is always negative; power uses rejection, exclusion, refusal, suppression, and rarely needs to mask itself either way. (2) Power is a legal factor in sex. Sex is subdued by the regime of legality and illegality, prohibition and consent. (3) There is only one provision law applies to sex – it is prohibition and censorship, aiming at the rejection of pleasure: sex is supposed to denounce pleasure, and therefore denounce itself. (4) The influence of power on sex is similarly seen at all levels: at state and family level, from the princes to fathers, from priests to teachers. In all these places there is the same mechanics of power.

Foucault contrasts the so called *Reich hypothesis* – where the mechanism of power is repression, with *Nietzsche's hypothesis* – where the foundation of power is in the warring nature of the powers. Still, Foucault shares the assumption that both hypotheses are not necessarily contradictory. "Quite credibly – says Foucault – they even seem to merge: what is repression if not a political result of war, a little like oppression for classical theory of political rights, which was an abuse of sovereignty in the system of law".[11] Then, Reich

10 Herbert Marcuse, *Eros and Civilization. A Philosophical Inquiry into Freud*, trans. A. Blunden (Boston: Beacon Press, 1966).

11 Michel Foucault, *Society Must Be Defended. Lectures at the Collège de France, 1975-76.*

hypothesis does not annul Nietzsche's, and, as a consequence, these two ways of reasoning are not in a state of war.

There are fragments of *Histoire de la sexualité: la volonté de savoir* which suggest it is not a novelty for Foucault that the history of western societies in the last couple of centuries does not reveal the repressive games of power. For example, Foucault says: "in fact, it is not a novelty that sex is not repressed. It has been confirmed long ago by psychoanalysts". Without hesitation, however, Foucault accuses psychoanalysts of contributing to the discoursification of sex on the West and exploitation of repressive hypothesis. In *Histoire de la folie à l'âge classique* Foucault suggests that "psychoanalysis, according to Freud's own definition, is all about lifting prohibitions".[12] Psychoanalysts knew very well, that the unconscious is to some extent constituted by power relations, and that to free unconscious language is to lift the logic of consciousness. Foucault swiftly goes from this "psychoanalytical discovery" straight to his repression thesis. He does not seem to be worried about the fact that what he says is probably what Freud and Reich had said long ago, knowing that his reference is the social body, not an individual.

All Foucault's assertions relating to Freud may seem controversial to someone who knows the effort Freud had made to distinguish gender and sexuality. What relates to gender aims at procreation, says Freud. And what is sexual aims at pleasure. It is only thanks to this single differentiation that Freud grants himself the privilege of opening the discourse of children's sexuality. All Foucault's insinuations concerning Freud may seem largely controversial to those who are aware of Freud's intense decoding of power (relations) and complex relations between *Superego* and *Id*, the pleasure principle and all our efforts that are at first glance beyond this principle.

It seems though that Foucault uses the term "psychoanalysis" instrumentally and subjects interpretation of his work to his own conceptual construct. In this construction western culture suffers from a kind of hyper-developed sexuality discourse, theory of sexuality, that is the science of sexuality (*scientia sexualis*). On the other hand, the abundance of articles on sexuality finds its negative reflection in some kind of inhibition of the individual sexuality of every one of us. This inhibition became the core issue of Freud's analysis, who began his work with a description of symptoms of hysteria, where one of the basic symptoms of disorder is forgetting of one's self and one's desires, which is all about sexuality. For Foucault, individual's inability to perceive one's desires and

12 Michel Foucault, *Madness, the Absence of Work (d'œuvre),* [in:] A. I. Davidson (ed.), *Foucault and his Interlocutors*, (London and Chicago: Chicago University Press 1997), p. 97-104.

the general hyper-knowledge of sexuality in society are not contradictory trends: theoretical hyper-production in relation to sexuality in western societies was the effect of shunning sexuality, which has been made at the individual level, in the subject itself. And so, it opens a question: Why for centuries we Europeans were yearning for more truth about sex rather than increase of pleasure?[13] This is what makes Freud so important. Freud colligated our will to knowledge with desire and acknowledged that it is the truth about oneself and the truth about one's sexuality which is the fundamental obsession of man in the West.

In the two final paragraphs of *Histoire de la sexualité: la volonté de savoir* Foucault ridicules our human need of freedom and our past reception of Freud's work:

> People will be amused at the reproach of pansexualism that was once aimed at Freud and psychoanalysis. But the ones who will appear to have been blind will perhaps be not so much those who formulated the objection as those who discounted it out of hand, as if it merely expressed the fears of an outmoded prudishness. For the first, after all, were only taken unawares by a process which had begun long before and by which, unbeknown to them, they were already surrounded on all sides; what they had attributed solely to the genius of Freud had already gone through a long stage of preparation; they had gotten their dates wrong as to the establishment, in our society, of a general deployment of sexuality. But the others were mistaken concerning the nature of the process; they believed that Freud had at last, through a sudden reversal, restored to sex the rightful share which it had been denied for so long; they had not seen how the good genius of Freud had placed it at one of the critical points marked out for it since the eighteenth century by the strategies of knowledge and power, how wonderfully effective he was – worthy of the greatest spiritual fathers and directors of the classical period – in giving a new impetus to the secular injunction to study sex and transform it into discourse.[14]

In these final pages of the first volume of *The History of Sexuality,* the accusation of pansexualism, which was often levelled against psychoanalysis, naturally comes up. Those most blind in this regard, says Foucault, were not those who denounced pansexualism out of prudishness. Their only error was to have attributed solely to the bad genius [*mauvais genie*] of Freud what had already gone through a long stage of preparation. The opposite error, the symmetrical lure, corresponds to a more serious mystification. It is the illusion that could be called emancipator, the aberration of the Enlightenment, the misguided notion on the part of those who believed that Freud, the good genius of Freud, had finally freed sex from its repression by power. The good genius of Freud would thus be

13 Michel Foucault (1976), *The History of Sexuality Vol. 1: The Will to Knowledge*, translated by R. Hurley (London: Penguin, 1998), pp. 158-159.

14 Michel Foucault, *The History of Sexuality Vol. 1: The Will to Knowledge*, p. 139.

worse than the bad one. It would have consisted in getting itself well placed, in spotting the best place in an old strategy of knowledge and power.

Freud is thus torn between the good and the bad spirit of Freud, even though Freud himself does only as much as is expected according to the common perception of the sexuality issue: he assigns any sex other than heterosexual to psychiatry, children's sexuality to pedagogics, marital sex to socialisation and female sex to hysteria. Our civilisation Freud equips with sex, and links knowledge of one's sexuality with the knowledge of one's identity. The truth about us lays in the truth about our sex.

Let me return to my main concern, that is, who exactly is Freud and what exactly is his work? Is this work part of antiscience, which by methods of analysis and critique allows us to directly confront unconsciousness and to awaken it from anthropological snooze? Maybe it is rather a kind of work directly related to, and even akin to modern apparatus of power, driving madness into the realm of normalization discourse in psychiatry, and sexuality into the biopolitical machinery invented upon a discovery power once made; that it no longer relates to people but a population. What about Freud in Foucault's work? Is he what Napoleon was to Hegel? A real life fulfillment of theoretical postulates? Or what Isaac Newton to Kant? A generalisation of certain local knowledge elevated to the level of the absolute knowledge?

In a short article *Nietzsche, Freud, Marx* Foucault claims that the authors of *Der Wille zur Macht, Das Kapital,* and *Die Traumdeutung* all construct new hermeneutics. What we find there is that Marx, Freud, and Nietzsche profoundly modified the space of distribution in which signs can be signs. Moreover, they create a new figure of an interpreter, whose direction is opposite to the direction of the interpretation itself.

> For if the interpreter must go to the bottom himself, like an excavator, the movement of interpretation is, on the contrary, that of a projection [*surplomb*], of a more and more elevated projection, which always leaves depth above it to be displayed in more and more visible fashion; and depth is now restored as an absolutely superficial secret.[16]

Are we supposed to believe this declaration pointing to yet another Freud, Freud – the interpreter, who had to turn into the "underground man", and like miners and gnomes do, dive into the "goldmine of meanings" in order to save the interpretation?

---

15 Michel Foucault, *Nietzsche, Freud, Marx*, trans. Alan D. Schrift, [in:] Gayle L. Ormiston and Alan D. Schrift, ed., *Transforming the Hermeneutic Context From Nietzsche to Nancy* (Albany: State University of New York Press, Albany, 1990), pp. 55-67.

16 *Ibid.*, pp. 55-67.

3. Who reads what?

It is not my intention to reprimand Foucault and reproach him for unjust reading of Freud, not much letter-bound as to what had really been said, and for using Freud's name for his own intellectual reasons. It is not my intention to reprimand Foucault – Jacques Derrida did it so much better in the paper *"To Do Justice to Freud": The History of Madness in the Age of Psychoanalysis*. Here, he suggested that despite his claim that "we must do justice to Freud", Foucault must have still felt temptation to do injustice to Freud, and to be a little unfair to him. Foucault regularly attempts to objectify psychoanalysis and to reduce it to that of which he speaks rather than to that out of which he speaks.[17] The title Derrida has proposed for the reflections about the history of madness in the age of psychoanalysis clearly indicates his intentions. It is no longer a question of the age described by a *History of Madness*. It is no longer a question of an epoch

17 Jacques Derrida, *"To Do Justice to Freud": The History of Madness in the Age of Psychoanalysis*, pp. 227-266. Derrida relates to *Histoire de la folie a l'âge Classique* on two ocaasions. First, in a polemic article *Cogito and the History of Madness* (Jacques Derrida, *Cogito and the History of Madness*, [in:] *Writing and Difference*, trans. Alan Bass, (London & New York: Routledge, 1978)). Here, the controversy between Foucault and Derrida relates to Descartes, and his role in the exclusion of madness from the space of reason. In another article, *"To Do Justice to Freud"* – originally designed as a speech commemorating the 20th anniversary of publication of *The History of Madness* – Derrida argues with Foucault about Freud, and whether Freud managed to rebuild communication with reason previously excluded by Descartes. What is noteworthy is that the "joust" between Derrida and Foucault related to the names and their role in destabilizing historical time. Derrida reading and questioning Foucault's book gives rise to the question: What makes the history of madness possible? Such a question should have led him toward the situation of psychiatry and psychoanalysis rather than toward a questioning of a reading of Descartes. But if Derrida substituted Descartes for Freud, it was perhaps not only because of the significant and strategic place that Foucault confers upon the Cartesian moment in the interpretation of the Great Confinement and of the Classical Age, at least implicitly, but because of the role that the reference to a certain Descartes played in the thought of the time, in the early sixties, as close as possible to psychoanalysis, in the very element, in truth, of a certain Lacanian theory of psychoanalysis. This theory developed around the question of the subject and the subject of science. Whether it was a question of anticipated certainty and logical time or of the role of the *cogito* and of the deceitful God in *La science et la verite*, Lacan returned time and again to a certain unsurpassability of Descartes. In 1945, Lacan associated Descartes with Freud in his *Propos sur la causalité psychique* and concluded by saying that "neither Socrates, nor Descartes, nor Marx, nor Freud, can be surpassed insofar as they led their research with this passion for unveiling whose object is the truth". Jacques Lacan, *Propos sur la causalité psychique* (1946) [in:] Jacques Lacan, *Écrits*, Paris: Seuil 1966, p. 193.

or period, such as the classical age, that would, inasmuch as it is its very object, stand before that history of madness as Foucault writes it. It is a question today of the age to which the book itself belongs, the age in which it takes place, the age that provides its situation; it is a question of the age that is describing rather than the age that is described. In the title, "the history of madness" must be within quotation marks since the title designates the age of book, the *History of Madness* – as a book – in the age of psychoanalysis and not the history of madness, of madness itself, in the age of psychoanalysis. Foucault regularly attempts to objectify psychoanalysis and to reduce it to that of which he speaks rather than to that out of which he speaks. What is especially interesting for Derrida is the time and historical conditions in which the book is rooted, those that it takes as its point of departure, and not so much the time or historical conditions that it recounts and tries in a certain sense to objectify.

Derrida asks: Would Foucault's project have been possible without psychoanalysis, with which it is contemporary and of which it speaks little and in such an equivocal or ambivalent manner in the book? Does the project owe psychoanalysis anything? Would the debt, if it had been contracted, be essential? Or would it, on the contrary, define the very thing from which the project had to detach itself, in a critical fashion, in order to take shape? In a word, what is the situation of psychoanalysis at the moment of, and with respect to, Foucault's book? And how does this book situate its project with respect not only to psychoanalysis in general, but to a particular psychoanalysis, at a particular phase of its history, in one or another of its figures?

Indeed, Foucault does and does not want to situate Freud in a historical place that is stable, identifiable, and open to a univocal understanding. Sometimes Foucault wants to credit Freud, sometimes discredit him, unless he is doing both indiscernibly and at the same time. The Freudian place in the work of Foucault is not only the techno-historical apparatus, the artefact called hinge. Foucault does and does not want to situate Freud in a historical place that is stabilizable, identifiable, and open to a univocal understanding. The interpretation or topography of the Freudian moment with which he presents us is always uncertain, divided, mobile, some would say ambiguous, other ambivalent, confused, or contradictory.

Freud is going to be doubly situated, twice implicated in the chiasmus – the subject of Foucault' and Derrida's interest. On the one hand, Freud was immediately associated with Nietzsche, as a person who is able to reopen the dialogue with unreason that was interrupted in the West. On the other hand, in a more indirect way, to recall the necessity of taking into account a certain evil genius of Freud, namely, the presence of the demonic, the devil, the limping devil, and so on in *Beyond the Pleasure Principle,* where psychoanalysis finds its greatest speculative power but also the place of greatest resistance to psychoanalysis (death drive, repetition compulsion, and so on and forth!).

Freud is reintegrated into the modernity out of which *The History of Madness* is written and from which he had been banished at regular intervals. It is by taking account of death as "the concrete a priori of medical experience" that the "beginning of that fundamental relation that binds modern man to his originary finitude" comes about.[18] This modern man is also a "Freudian man":

> the experience of individuality in modern culture is bound up with that of death: from Hölderlin's *Empedocles* to Nietzsche's *Zarathustra*, and on to Freudian man, an obstinate relation to death prescribes to the universal its singular face, and lends to each individual the power of being heard forever.[19]

Originary finitude is a finitude that no longer arises out of the infinity of a divine presence. It now unfolds "in the void left by the absence of the gods".[20] What we have here, than, is, in the name of death, so to speak, a reinscription of Freudian man into a "modern" grouping or whole from which he was sometimes excluded.

Freud himself will in fact take on the ambiguous figure of a doorman or doorkeeper. Derrida says:

> Freud as the doorman of the today, the holder of the keys, of those that open as well as those that close the door, that is, the *huis*: onto the today [*l'aujourd'hui*] or onto madness. He [*lui*], Freud, is the double figure of the door or doorkeeper. He stands guard and ushers in. Alternatively or simultaneously, he closes one epoch and opens another. And as we will see, this double possibility is not alien to an institution, to what is called the analytic situation as a scene behind closed doors [*huis clos*]. That is why – and this would be the paradox of the serial law – Freud does and does not belong to different series in which Foucault inscribes him.[21]

Perhaps this is the reason why in the same book Freud is sometimes associated with and sometimes opposed to the great witnesses of madness and excess, such as Nietzsche, Artaud, Van Gogh, Nerval and Hölderlin, and sometimes he is associated with and sometimes he is opposed to the great doctors and psychiatrists like Pinel, Tuke, Janet, Brunschvicg. But suggesting injustice in Foucault's reading of Freud, we must still remember that the 20th century got us used to unjust readings so much that today we expect nothing else. We have

18 Michel Foucault (1963), *The Birth of the Clinic: An Archaeology of Medical Perception*, trans. A. M. Sheridan Smith (London: Routledge, 1997), 198-199.

19 Michel Foucault, *Madness, the Absence of Work (d'œuvre)*, p. 199.

20 *Ibid.*, p. 200.

21 Jacques Derrida, *"To Do Justice to Freud": The History of Madness in the Age of Psychoanalysis*, p. 234.

already seen unjust reading of Plato by Nietzsche, unjust reading of Nietzsche by Heidegger, and of Heidegger by Derrida. However, what Foucault does with Freud is truly unique and exceptional. Is this, what Foucault does with Freud, called reading at all? Did Foucault actually read Freud?

Anyway, the resemblance of the two is striking. Both are fascinated with the entanglement of life and death, excess life and all-pervading death. In Freud, the controlling instance is directed at investigating the driving forces of *das Es*, in Foucault the disciplines and inspections are related to birth and death, but he goes beyond the individual level and refers to population. Both had a feeling that the will to live is only a reading (translation) of the death drive. I think it is not a coincidence that both felt archaeologists at heart, that both put their cognitive activity to excavation work and to bringing to daylight mouldering monuments of the past. Those, at first sight, meaningless traces (scars), influence our actions, our speaking and living. Both shared dctective passion – obsessively searching for and archiving traces where no one would spot them. It sometimes feels that whereas Freud provides a method for investigating the internal workings of the psyche, Foucault seeks to show how the method itself is an ancient technique of self-fashioning which has over the centuries shaped the mind externally. Our conception of the psyche, Foucault

---

22 Patrick H. Hutton, *Foucault, Freud, and The Technologies of the Self,* [in:] *Technologies of the Self,* ed. Luther Martin, Huck Gutman, Patrick H. Hutton, (Massachusetts: University of Massachusetts Press, 1988), p. 121. The similarities between Foucault and Freud should not blur the obvious differences between the two. All boil down to what follows. (1) Psychoanalysis was the method that Freud invented to oblige the unconscious psyche to open its secret history, to reveal to the conscious psyche those unrequited desires or unresolved conflicts that unconsciously paralyze its actions. For Foucault our human nature is not a hidden reality to be discovered through self-analysis but the aggregate of the forms we have chosen to provide public definitions of who we are, so there is no such thing as human nature. (2) Freud believes that the knowledge of the self enhances one's power to cope more realistically with present problems. Knowledge drawn from the unconscious restores lost dimensions of *ego's* identity. Foucault rather believes that it is not knowledge of our sexuality (and the past) that gives us power over ourselves (as Freud taught), but our will to establish power over sexuality that incites our search for self-knowledge. (3) Foucault inverts Freud's proposition about the relationship between knowledge and power. Whereas Freud sought to explain how knowledge gives us power over the self, Foucault seeks to demonstrate how power shapes our knowledge of the self. (4) Freud is concerned with origins. He insists on the determining power of experience as a precedent for future behaviour. But if human nature for Freud is shaped by the recollection of past experiences, it is for Foucault constructed through humankind's activity as a maker of forms. We are beings that create form which ironically imprisons our creativity. (5) Freud would counter the psyche is a discrete reality workings of which we can

contends, has been sculpted by the techniques that we have devised to probe its secrets, to oblige it to give up hidden knowledge that will reveal to us the truth about who we are. Psychoanalysis is from a historical perspective a late addition to that enterprise, born of a long but erratic lineage of techniques for the care of the self.

The symmetry of interests and methods of research and the totalizing discourse is so evident that it may provoke a question: Which of the two thinkers created stronger and more spacious conceptual and interpretative apparatus? At first sight it seems it is Foucault who interprets the work of Freud, putting him in the context of emerging power games and to some extent exposing the cultural role of psychoanalysis in the civilisation of reason and of the Enlightenment, which lost touch with unreason and equally well with sovereign, patriarchal power structures. It seems though that the instrumental use of Freud's work, the pinnacle of which is *Histoire de la sexualité* by Foucault, is not the last word in this game of dependence and control. We could apply psychoanalysis to *Histoire de la sexualité* and see it as a vain search for a place where the Master's discourse was replaced by a plenitude of anonymous academic discourses which are shaped as truth, and where cognitive subject is lacking. *Histoire de la sexualité* for Jacques-Alain Miller does justice to psychoanalysis suggesting that Foucault got caught in the phantasmal loop in his search for the exact moment when the order of western sexuality was established. Foucault deepens his search and leaves modernity behind, then finds this moment when the ancient ethics of self-concern disintegrates into Christian confession ethics. If we look closer at the last two volumes of *Histoire de la sexualité: L'usage des plaisirs,* and *Le souci de soi,* which are devoted to pre-Christian ethics, we will see that they differ from the previous interference with the power, knowledge and sexuality complex – instead of micropractices they provide a kind of history of ideas, which in itself is enough to deepen our worry whether Foucault's Greece and Rome are not, by any chance, pure phantasms. If we followed that trace and employed psychoanalysis to look through the work of Foucault, we could possibly interpret it as a quest for father function in the world seemingly deprived of it.

objectively understand. Our conception of the psyche may be limited by the images we employ to describe it. But the inadequacy of our theory does not diminish the reality of the object it seeks to define. Foucault, to the contrary, argues that the self is not an objective reality to be described by our theories but a concept that is actually constituted by them.

4. There once was a star on which clever animals invented knowledge

In some remote corner of the universe, there once was a star on which clever animals invented knowledge. That was the most arrogant and the most untruthful moment in 'world history'.

Friedrich Nietzsche[23]

In the West the traditional approach to the study of thought has consisted in focusing only on positive phenomena. During the past few years, however, Freud, Lévi-Strauss, and Foucault have explored a method that makes it possible to reveal the negative structure in any society or culture. For Foucault it was a matter not of knowing what is affirmed and valorised in a society or a system of thought but of studying what is rejected and excluded. According to Foucault the most important feature of our societies is a binary system: a distinction that is black and white so that things are thought of as only one or the other. "Power is essentially – wrote Foucault in *The History of Sexuality* – what dictates its law to sex. Which means first of all that sex is placed by power in a binary system: licit and illicit, permitted and forbidden".

The whole work of Foucault is a search for the Others. The means by which society establishes itself as a binary system are "dividing practices". The normal subject through this process is divided from Others (Madmen, Ills, Offenders, Transgressors, Women, etc.). Foucault declares programmatically that he wants to write the history of the boundaries, by which our culture reprobates something that lies outside it. He classifies insanity among those borderline experiences in which Western Logos sees itself, with extreme ambivalence, faced with something heterogeneous. Boundary-transgressing experiences include contact with and even immersion in the Oriental world (Schopenhauer), rediscovery of the tragic element and the archaic in general (Nietzsche), penetration of the dream sphere (Freud) and the archaic prohibitions (Bataille), and even the exoticism nourished by anthropological reports.

Foucault omits Romanticism from this list, aside from the mention of Hölderlin. Schelling and the Romantic philosophy of nature had earlier conceived of madness as the other of reason, but of course within a perspective of reconciliation alien to Foucault. To the extent that the bond of communication between the madman (or even the criminal) and the rationally constituted context of the public life is severed, both parts suffer a deformation. Madness and evil negate normality by endangering it in two ways – as what disrupts

23 Friedrich Nietzsche (1873), *On Truth and Lying in an Extra-Moral Sense*, trans. S. L. Gilman, [in:] *Friedrich Nietzsche on Rhetoric and Language*, (Oxford: Oxford University Press), p. 246.

normality and puts it in question, but also as something that evades normality by withdrawing from it.

The immature Nietzsche recognizes that in Apollo, the Greeks divinised individuation, the observance of the limits of the individual. But Apollonian beauty and moderation only hid the Titanic and barbaric underground that erupted in the ecstatic tone of Dionysian festival. Already in the *Birth of Tragedy* art opens access to the Dionysian only at the cost of ecstasy – at the cost of a painful de-differentiation, a de-delimitation of the individual, a merging with amorphous nature. Standing behind the art is will to illusion. Will to power is at the same time will to illusion, will to simplification, to masks, to the superficial; arts count as man's genuine activity, because life itself is based on illusion, deception, optics, the necessity of perspective and error. Hence, for Nietzsche Illusion is the first name of the Other.

For Freud the childhood and youth of men were endowed with an ambiguous power: to tell of the birth of truth; but also to put to the test the tardy truth of men, to rectify it, to bring it closer to its nudity. The child became the immediate master of the adult insofar as true education was identified with the very genesis of truth. In every child things tirelessly repeat their youth, the world resumes contact with its native form. For these reasons for Freud the Child is the first name of the Other.

In his later work Foucault replaces the model of domination based on repression (developed in the tradition of Enlightenment by Marx and Freud) by a plurality of power strategies. These power strategies intersect one another and succeed one another; they are distinguished according to the type of their discourse formation and the degree of their intensity; but they cannot be judged under the aspect of their validity, as was the case with consciously working through conflicts in contrast to unconsciously doing so. In this place we find the reasons of Foucault's objections against the Freudian model of the repression of drives, and emancipation through heightened awareness. On the other hand the idea of the "unconsciousness", as we understand it in a proper way, was very close to Foucault. In this convention unconsciousness is a state that mediates between *me* and *another*. By fathoming its date we do not extend ourselves towards ourselves. Rather, we find a level which without taking us outside ourselves enables our contact with forms of activity that are common to *us* as well the *others*, forms which are a prerequisite for all mental life of all people and of all time. In the *Foreword* to the English edition of *The Order of Things* Foucault wrote explicitly:

> What I would like to do, however, is to reveal a positive unconscious of knowledge: a level that eludes the consciousness of the scientist and yet is part of scientific

> discourse, instead of disputing its validity and seeking to diminish its scientific nature.[24]

Foucault as the historian of science tries to restore what eluded that consciousness: the influences that affected it, the implicit philosophies that were subjacent to it, the unformulated thematics, the unseen obstacles – that is the unconscious of science. This unconscious is always the negative side of science – that which resists it, deflects it, or disturbs it.

Foucault, along with Bataille and Nietzsche, renounces this figure of thought from Idealism, which is supposed to grasp a dialectic inherent in reason itself. Foucault has learned from Nietzsche that reason develops its structure only by way of the exclusion of heterogeneous elements and only by way of monadic centering within itself. There was no reason before monological reason. This reason appears here as just that fiction by which the Occident makes itself known in its specialness and with which it assumes such a chimerical universality, and whose claim to global dominance it at the same time both hides and pursues.

Western Man – in Foucault's work – could constitute himself in his own eyes as an object of science only in the opening created by his own elimination: from the experience of Unreason (*Madness and Civilisation*) psychology was born; from the integration of Death and Illness (*The Birth of the Clinic*) into medical thought a medicine is born that is given as a science of individual; from the experience of Woman (*The History of Sexuality*) is born a modern concept of subject; and from the experience of Crime (*Discipline and Punish*) was born modern law order that is given as a science of what is legal.

Foucault explicitly defines his thinking as questioning what is taken to be universal and necessary:

> It is one of my targets to show people that a lot of things that are a part of their landscape – that people think are universal – are the result of some very precise historical changes. All my analyses are against the idea of universal necessities in human existence.[25]

In another place Foucault explicitly maintains that we have to get rid of the idea of an analytical or necessary link between ethics and other social or economic or political structures.

> For centuries we have been convinced that between our ethics, our personal ethics, our everyday life, and the great political and social and economic structures, there

24 Michel Foucault (1966), *The Order of Things. An Archaeology of the Human Sciences* (London 1974), p. xi.

25 Michel Foucault, *Truth, Power, Self*, trans. John Johnston [in:] *Foucault Live*, ed. Lotringer Sylvere, (New York: Semiotext(e), 1989), p. 11.

> were analytical relations, and that we couldn't change anything, for instance, in our sex life or our family life, without ruining our economy, our democracy, and so on.[26]

This statement is of course in clear contrast with the former statement that the field of mind must be coextensive with the field of social process. Richard Rorty points out that in his analyses Michel Foucault does not appeal to any "we" whose consensus, values, or traditions constitute the framework for thought and define the conditions in which it can be validated.[27] Foucault's answer to this objection of Rorty is that it is not actually suitable to place oneself within a "we" in order to assert the principles one recognizes and the values one accepts. The "we" must not be previous to the question; it can only be the result – and the necessarily temporary result – of the question as it is posed in the new terms in which one formulates it. For example, at the time when Foucault wrote the history of madness, there was not a preexisting and receptive "we" to which he would only have had to refer in order to write his book, and of which this book would have been the spontaneous expression. Laing, Cooper, Basaglia (the champion thinkers of the so-called anti-psychiatry movement) and Foucault had no community, nor any relationship. But the problem posed itself to those who had read these thinkers, gave rise to emergence the possibility of establishing a "we" on the basis of the work that had been done, a "we" that would also be likely to form a community of action.[28]

Instead of an exclusive concept of reason, which is instrumental and repressive, we need an inclusive concept of reason that incorporated even the other of reason in its totality. The point is – there is no comprehensive reason. One should have learned from Freud or even from Nietzsche that reason does not exist apart from its other and that – functionally considered – it becomes necessary in virtue of this other. The other of reason is nature, the human body, fantasy, desire, the feelings – or better: all this insofar as reason has not been able to appropriate it. Thus, it is directly the vital forces of split-off and repressed subjective nature, it is the sorts of phenomena rediscovered by Romanticism – dreams, fantasies, madness, orgiastic excitement, ecstasy – it is the aesthetic, body-centered experiences of a decentered subjectivity that function as the placeholders for the other of reason. Early Romanticism still wanted to establish art, in the form of a new mythology, as a public institution in

---

26 Michel Foucault, *On the Genealogy of Ethics: An Overview of Work in Progress,* [in:] *The Foucault Reader,* Ed. Rabinow Paul (New York 1984), p. 355.

27 Richard Rorty, *Moral Identity and Private Autonomy: The Case of Foucault,* [in:] Richard Rorty, *Essays on Heidegger and Others. Philosophical Papers,* Volume 2 (Cambridge 1991), p. 195.

28 Michel Foucault, *Polemics, Politics, and Problemizations: An Interview,* [in:] *The Foucault Reader,* Ed. Paul Rabinow (New York 1984), p. 385.

the midst of social life; it wanted to elevate the excitement radiating from it into an equivalent for the unifying power of religion. Nietzsche was the first to transfer this potential for excitement into the beyond of modern society and of history overall. The modern origin of aesthetic experience heightened in an avant-garde fashion remains concealed.

In Nietzsche and Foucault, subjective nature as the placeholder for the other of reason is brought into scientific discourse as the individual or collective unconscious in the concepts of Freud or Jung, of Lacan or Lévi-Strauss. Whether in the form of archaeology or of genealogy, Nietzsche and Foucault want to initiate a special discourse that claims to operate outside the horizon of reason without being utterly irrational. Reason is supposed to be criticisable in its historical forms from the perspective of the other that has been excluded from it; this requires, then, an ultimate act of self-reflection that surpasses itself.

The other they seek, which is heterogeneous to reason and still related to it as its heterogeneous factor, results from a radical finitizing of the absolute for which subjectivity had falsely substituted itself. Foucault chooses the dimension of spatial centering in the experience of one's own body and conceives the Other of reason as the anonymous source of the empowerment of interactions tied to the body.

5. Freedom and psychoanalysis

As Julia Kristeva (1999) accurately remarked in the paper *Psychoanalysis and Freedom*: "freedom is not a psychoanalytic concept".[29] If we are to believe the Index to the *Standard Edition*, Freud employs the word very rarely – in *The Uncanny* (*Das Unheimliche*) (1919), and especially in *Civilization and Its Discontents* (*Das Unbehagen in der Kultur*) (1929) – to convey the sense of an instinctual urge shackled by the necessity for humans to live in communities. This libidinal urge proves to be profoundly ambivalent, always more or less taken up, or dominated, by the death instinct which civilization refuses to accept. In resuming and deepening the propositions in *Totem and Taboo* (*Totem und Tabu: Einige Übereinstimmungen im Seelenleben der Wilden und der Neurotiker*) (1913) on the founding myth of the murder of the father, Freud specifies the two conditions inherent in being human, which limit the absolute freedom Freud attributes to the individual, namely, the realization of his desires. On the one hand, there is the need to share satisfactions with the other members

29 Julia Kristeva, *Psychoanalysis and Freedom*, trans. C. Levin, [in:] "Canadian Journal of Psychoanalysis", Vol. 7, 1: 1 1999.

of the community on whom the individual depends, given his physical weakness and the inadequacy of his technological mastery of nature. On the other hand, there is the consciousness itself (or conscience), which is constituted at the origin, precisely through a limitation on the freedom of the drives imposed by repression and censorship, or, in other words, "civilization". Through censorship, conscience transforms the reined-in desire into remorse and guilt, but also into self-destruction, in which aggression takes the ego as its target in masochism or melancholia.

Moral consciousness and its organ, the *super-ego*, thus impose, from the beginnings of primitive man, a renunciation of freedom drive, which Freud partly regrets but must eventually accept as a necessary compromise in the name of survival. Freud seems to begin with a naturalistic conception of pleasure: with the man of pleasure who wants to satisfy his drives naturally. This concept is situated not far from a Greek idea of freedom as "I can", as opposed to "I want", which implies an objective state in the body, without a constraint emanating from a master or a physical force. For the Greeks, freedom *(éleutheria)* is essentially freedom of movement (Freud says *Drang*). However, this freedom comes face to face with the fable of the "murder of the father", implying another conception of freedom which is consecutive to a commandment. The tyranny of the assimilated/introjected father becomes moral consciousness, the conscience or *super-ego*, which forbids: you should not sleep with your mother, and you should not kill your father. This biblical resurgence in Freudian thought, which structures the psychoanalytic conception of the psychic apparatus, is the starting point for what Jacques Lacan,[30] reader of *Civilization and Its Discontents*, calls an ethic "beyond the notion of a command, beyond what offers itself with a sense of obligation". This means that desire is not subordinated to a commandment exterior to it. To state this more positively, moral obligation is rooted in desire itself; it is the energy of desire that engenders its own censorship.

The human subject who recognizes himself there recognizes himself first as a subject of human plurality: concretely, the plurality of his family but also that of his analyst and of other analysands. Thus, with the help of the analyst, the helplessness of the end of my analysis, that is, that I expect nothing from anyone is first felt as a shared fate, something in common with the suffering of others. But this community is not really a community, for no institution will officially embrace this shared experience, this perception of the plurality of the "discarded". Moreover, to the extent that my analysis is terminated but not

---

30 Jacques Lacan, *The Ethics of Psychoanalysis: Seminar Book 7, 1959-1960,* trans. D. Porter, ed. Jacques-Alain Miller, (New York: Norton 1992).

finished, the suspension of the transferential bond in which a portion of my life drive and my desires is left unelaborated and unsublimated incites me to turn my aggression against every unity, identity, norm, and value: in short, to make myself the subject of a perpetual rebellion, an incessant questioning, a perpetual analysand.

Ultimately, for this reason exactly – the liberation of my desire through its elaboration or sublimation – I am in a state of perpetual rebirth at the end of my analysis. Donald Winnicott says something new and incontrovertible on this subject. He seems to hold that birth already presupposes an autonomy of bio-psychological life, making it possible for the infant to withdraw from environmental impingement and to avoid the traumatic violence of labour and delivery. This nuclear independence would be the precondition, in a way, of the later "internal world", which Winnicott[31] considers the most precious and mysterious freedom inherent in being human. Indeed, human being is here meant in the sense of being, as opposed to doing or acting. Winnicott rediscovers this freedom equally in the capacity to be alone and in the isolation of the secret ballot in the democratic voting booth. Better still, he finds it in the process of analytic treatment, in the undoing of the false self constructed as a defence against external impingement, and the recovery of that native interiority that, however, must always be recreated, and thus alone makes us free. Freedom thus becomes synonymous with an interiority to be recreated in relation to an external world to be internalised. This is not freedom in the sense of resisting the two tyrants of instinctual desire and external reality, as Freud thinks; but rather freedom as the interiorization of the outside, if and only if this outside (to begin with the mother) allows for play, and lets itself be played with.

In sum, at the end of an analysis terminated but still unfinished, we are able to refine ourselves, and we rediscover ourselves, because we have unveiled the freedom-unto-death of our desires, not only as mortality, but as "natality" – to use Hannah Arendt's[32] term in *The Life of the Mind*. This brings us to yet another perspective on freedom in psychoanalysis: far from the unrestraint of the one who will not give ground relative to her desire, freedom in psychoanalysis implies two kinds of issue that have already been encountered in philosophy. But psychoanalysis broaches each of them in a new way: the issue of *choice* and the issue of *beginning*.

---

31 Donald Woods Winnicott, *The Child, the Family, and the Outside World.* (London: Penguin Books, 1964).

32 Hannah Arendt, *The Life of the Mind: Volume II: Willing*, edited by Mary McCarthy (New York: Brace Harcourt, 1978), pp. 108-109.

In history of philosophy there have been elaborated two models of freedom: freedom as adaptation, and freedom as revelation. The first of these (freedom as adaptation) was announced by Immanuel Kant, along with the French Revolution, in the *Critique of Pure Reason* (*Kritik der reinen Vernunft*) (1781) and *Critique of Practical Reason* (*Kritik der praktischen Vernunft*) (1789). Echoing the *initium* of Augustine, Kant defines freedom for the first time not negatively as the transgression of a limit or a constraint, but positively as a *self-beginning* (*Selbstanfang*) understood as the capacity of each to undertake an action, to initiate an act from within. This is a magnificent idea of freedom, but we can already see the possible deviations contained within it: we are free to undertake moral obligations within the terms of a preestablished logical order, the moral logic of a good, the economic logic of free enterprise, and globalization.

The second model of freedom was linked by Martin Heidegger, in his reading of Kant, to pre-Socratic thought prior to the establishment of logical categories and values. This other freedom has to do with the revelation of self in the presence of the other through speech. Here I am not concerned with making a point about the Christian connotations of pre-Socratic philosophy, or details about the deconstruction of metaphysics implied in Heidegger's debate with Kant; and even less with the problem of political disengagement that Hannah Arendt tries to solve in her proposed philosophy of "judgement". I would say only that if this freedom as revelation, as opposed to freedom as adaptation, has more than a speculative existence, it would be in the transference-countertransference experience that it is actualized. Associating freely in the transference, the subject confronts both the unspeakability of the instinctual drives, his/her desires, and their traumas, and also the injunction that is imposed by the very fact of language (the capacity to symbolize) as well as the place of the analyst. The subject constitutes his/herself within his/herself for the other, and in this sense he/she reveals him/herself: in the strong sense of the word, he/she becomes free.

Analytic discourse is a constant process of questioning. Questioning, or putting into question (which has nothing to do with posing questions or answering them) is the method *par excellence* of expression in psychoanalysis. Its eternal return puts us in the timelessness of the temporal frame of the session, which actualizes, through analytic speech, the timelessness of the unconscious. It challenges identities and values, but it also provisionally restructures the subject in a new rebirth, as enabled by his transferential bond.

However, if this bond is itself undone by terminating the treatment, it does not mean that the patient is restructured once and for all by his/her analyst or a particular school of analysis. Rather, it means that he/she has achieved a psychic flexibility capable of traversing the repression barrier, of remobilizing drives, and thus of promoting creative adventure in his/her subsequent experiences of life as a subject. An aptitude for the renewal of relational bonds, links, and connections is thus established in the optimal conclusion of treatment. Of course, we all know how often we remain far from achieving this optimal result. Nevertheless, the implicit significance of it is obvious, insofar as it is true that the analyzed subject is an irreconcilable subject, a subject necessarily in revolt. To say that the analyzed individual discovers his/her irreconcilable conflictuality, the dramatic split that constitutes him/her and detaches him/her from any will toward control, power, or even unity, means that this freedom of which we have been speaking distances psychoanalysis from the moralistic or beatifying kind of humanism.

III. The Concept of the Death Drive. Reading Slavoj Žižek's *Opera's Second Death*

The truth is the whole. The whole, however, is merely the essential nature reaching its completeness through the process of its own development. Of the Absolute it must be said that it is essentially a result, that only at the end is it what it is in very truth; and just in that consists its nature, which is to be actual, subject, or self-becoming, self-development.

Georg Wilhelm Friedrich Hegel[1]

In what way is the instinctive connected with the compulsion to repetition? At this point the idea is forced upon us that we have stumbled on the trace of a general and hitherto not clearly recognized – or at least not expressly emphasized – characteristic of instinct, perhaps of all organic life. According to this, an instinct would be a tendency innate in living organic matter impelling it towards the reinstatement of an earlier condition, one which it had to abandon under the influence of external disturbing forces – a kind of organic elasticity, or, to put it another way, the manifestation of inertia in organic life.

Sigmund Freud[2]

This death of the higher organisms is, it is true, a natural one, a death from inner causes, but it does not depend on an inherent quality of the living substance, is not to be conceived as an absolute necessity based on the nature of life. Death is rather a purposive contrivance, a phenomenon of adaptation to the external conditions of life, because after the differentiation of the corporeal cells into soma and germ-plasm the indefinite prolongation of the life of the individual would have become a quite inexpedient luxury.

Sigmund Freud[3]

1. Plan

My plan will not aspire to be a serious interpretation of Slavoj Žižek's book on Wagner, or even a comment on it, it does not aspire also to provide an interesting and strong interpretation of the very complex work of Richard

---

1 Georg Wilhelm Friedrich Hegel (1807), *Phenomenology of Spirit*, trans. A. V. Miller (London: Oxford University Press, 1970 [1807]), p. 26.

2 Sigmund Freud (1920), *Beyond the Pleasure Principle*, [in:] *The Standard Edition of the Complete Psychological Works of Sigmund Freud.* Volume XVIII. (London: Hogarth Press, 1920-1922).

3 *Ibid.*

Wagner.[4] The only intention which guided me is rather more modest, that is: surround the book with some remarks that may help us to understand the main intention of Žižek and the plan of action of this ambiguous impact of Wagner's operas and psychoanalytical diagnosis. Creating the atmosphere and the intellectual environment around Žižek's book, I would therefore answer a few basic and important questions: firstly, why did Žižek turn attention toward the operas of Wagner at all? Secondly, what did Žižek find in these operas? Is there in the contents of the operas something unexpected and unsettling, especially for Žižek himself? Thirdly, what is the prototype of Wagnerian hero, and how does Žižek describe him/her? What kind of characteristics, what kind of set of features does Žižek attribute to him/her? Could the prototype of Wagnerian hero be in the same sense a man and a woman?[5] Fourthly, how does Žižek define and conceive the fundamental psychoanalytic concept of the death drive, and why does he insist on the strong claim that Wagner's heroes remain in the service of this concept? And finally, thus methodically prepared, I proceed to what is perhaps the most important question for us: Why do the dead return at all? What unfinished business do they still have with us or do we still have with them? The contemporary audiovisual culture floods us with a massive assault of films in which the vampire is a crucial figure. Is this return of vampirism in today's world, just as the whole work of Wagner, the herald of something important about contemporary relationships between the living and the dead, and is not the herald a sensible suggestion that we could not completely bury our dead? Do the dead not return precisely because the real work of mourning did not occur and because we could not weep for the dead, and in this say farewell to them?

Let me start with one more methodological reflection. Often it is said that the process of interpretation, especially with regards to such a complex work as the operas of Wagner, is exposed to a double danger. Interpretation can be either reductionist, that is, it may reduce a work of art to something it is not, for example, the embodiment of the drive, a certain policy or a set of philosophical beliefs, or – on the other hand – the process of interpretation can be tautological, saying that the work of art is simply what it is. Žižek, from the very beginning of the book exposes a reductionist interpretation of the plea; however, the awareness of this threat does not prevent him from falling victim to it. At least in a simple manner. In an important passage of his book he refers to Marx's famous passage recalling the *Introduction* to *Grundrisse*. In the fragment Marx

4 Slavoj Žižek, *I do not Order my Dreams,* [in:] Mladen Dolar, Slavoj Žižek, *Opera's Second Death* (New York: Routledge, 2002).

5 See also: Luce Irigaray, *The Eternal Irony of the Community*, in: *Speculum of the Other Woman*, trans. Gillian Gill, Ithaca: (Cornell University Press, 1985); Judith Butler, *Antigone's Claim*, (New York: Columbia University Press, 2000).

mentions how easy it is to explain Homer's poetry from the point of view of its unique historical context – it is much more difficult to explain its universal appeal, that is why it continues to give us artistic pleasure long after its historical context disappeared. If we reduce a great work of art to its historical context, we miss its universal dimension: in the case of Freud and above all Wagner, it is easy to describe his roots in the atmosphere of the epoch – it is much more difficult to demonstrate how this very specific situation enabled Wagner and Freud to formulate universal, theoretical insights. One of the tasks that I will just put myself to is find a permanent element, the common discovery of Wagner and Freud, which says something important about the relationship between life and death.

2. Wagner und haunted subjects

When asked about the reasons for his interest in Wagner, Žižek formulates a straight answer: Wagner's operas mark a unique achievement, a turning point which enables us to interpret properly retroactively the ambiguities and divides between the previous composers. Žižek recalls Jorge Louis Borges's famous statement uttered in the context of Kafka that some writers have the power to create their own precursors – this is the logic of retroactive restructuring of the past through the intervention of a new point: a truly creative act not only restructures the field of future possibilities, it restructures the past, resignifying the past contingent traces as pointing towards the present. Žižek put this claim in a naive and direct way: Tristan and Parsifal simply and effectively are the two single greatest, absolute, works of art in the history of humankind.

Of course, we can agree with the assertion that the past is still subject to constant reinterpretation by the present. Nevertheless the question remains: What kind of force of impact is present in Wagner's and Freud's work? What are these two stories equipped with that gives them such power not only at present, but also in the past? Above all, we must ask about the most basic issue: What links overall psychoanalysis with Wagner's opera? Žižek answers in a direct manner. The very historical connection between opera and psychoanalysis is provoking: the moment of the birth of psychoanalysis (the beginning of the 20th century) is also generally perceived as the moment of opera's death – as if, after psychoanalysis, opera, at least in its traditional form, were no longer possible. Moreover, Žižek adds that from its very beginning opera was dead, a still-born child of the musical art. One of the standard complaints about the opera today is that it is no longer a fully autonomous art – it always has to rely in a parasitic way on other arts – on pure music or on theater. If I interpret correctly the so openly expressed intention, it mostly seems to suggest that the primary object of Wagner's fascination and of psychoanalytic enterprise is simply death. Death is the very concept that combines opera, especially Wagner's opera, with psychoanalysis. To put it bluntly, Wagner's operas are about unfulfilled, more or less explicit desires of death. Psychoanalysis is about the hidden motive, the characteristics of all human activity, the motive which Freud called the "death drive".

Since we already understood the main intent, methodology, and the reason for Žižek's interest, let us consider the main thesis. The thesis is also open and suggests that Wagner's hero is doomed to an existence marked by being a living corpse doomed to eternal suffering. And it is this endless suffering that does not allow this hero to simply die. Žižek is constantly looking for the best candidate for a Wagnerian hero. Tannhaeuser is too common, simply split between pure spiritual love (for Elizabeth) and the excess of earthly erotic enjoyment (provided by Venus); Lohengrin is, on the contrary, too celestial, a divine creature longing to live like a common mortal with a faithful woman who would trust him absolutely. Neither of the two is in the position of a proper Wagnerian hero, condemned to the undead existence of eternal suffering. Hence Žižek offers us to read Wagner's *Tristan* as the zero-level work, as the perfect, ultimate formulation of a certain philosophical vision, and then to read the later works of Wagner himself as well as of other composers as the variations on this theme.[6] Žižek suggests at the end of Act III that Tristan is already a living dead, dwelling between the two deaths, no longer at home in reality, pulled back into the daily life from the blissful domain of the night and longing to return there.[7]

3. Death drive

This brings us to the most difficult problem: What assures us in the belief that what Žižek finds in the operas of Wagner and in his heroes is just what Freud and Lacan called the death drive? Is the urge which haunts the Wagnerian hero the equivalent of what Freud called the death drive (*Todestrieb*)? As is known, it took Freud twenty years, from *Traumdeutung* (1900; *The Interpretation of Dreams*) to *Jenseits des Lustprinzips* (1920; *Beyond the Pleasure Principle*), to formulate the concepts of the death drive and repetition compulsion. It also took Lacan basically fifteen years, from the second seminar (1954-1955) to the seventeenth (1969-1970), to formulate systematically "the path toward death" as

6 Richard Wagner (1874), *The Ring of the Nibelung*, (New York: Norton, 1977).

7 Theodor W. Adorno, *In Search of Wagner*, trans. Rodney Livingstone, (Verso Books, London 2009).

"that which is called enjoyment". It is no accident that to name this function Lacan selected the Hegelian master's enjoyment (*Genuß*), as opposed to the slave's pleasure and desire (*Lust and Begierde*). But, beyond the sexual and the exploitative connotations introduced through the French translation of the term (*jouissance*), Lacan revised thoroughly the Hegelian concept by reading Hegel via Marx, in an original configuration, in which the two are juxtaposed as divergent philosophical systems.

Hegel's limit is anthropological because he remains trapped within the intersubjective or "reciprocal alienation" between a master and a slave who always crave to be in one another's position. The originality of what Freud contributes in relation to Hegel lies in the fact that he got out of the limits of this dialectic, because Freud is not a humanist, and therefore, he was able to make the discovery that man is not entirely in man. Freud began to think of the body as a machine and as energy, and the meaning of this energy is the manifestation of a certain beyond of the Hegelian interhuman reference, which is in all strictness the symbolic beyond, the "network of signifiers", insofar as the latter is an "automaton" programmed to perform the single operation of "repetition". While Hegel's dialectic remains constrained within the imaginary relationship structuring intersubjectivity, Freud is concerned with the machine beyond it, which eventually leads him to the elaboration of the beyond of the pleasure principle and of the death drive, with its "need for repetition". But the question is: What needs to be repeated or reproduced?

My very naive answer to this question is: what calls on us to repeat is the Other. The true Other may be only someone outside of the reality of the living. Hence the necessity of the living dead, hence the need for a vampire and Wagnerian hero. For, on the one hand, the Other constantly tells me to do things, and on the other, it has no will that could justify the suggested course of action. I have to repeat the discourse until it emerges, as an effect of this repetition. For *Wiederholen* (repeating) is related to *Erinnerung* (remembering), and it is for this reason that repetition is a "function" that reveals the relation between the thought and the reality, the impossible and necessary will of the Other. Freud begins *Beyond the Pleasure Principle* by confidently reasserting the centrality of the pleasure principle in psychoanalytic theory: "[i]n the theory of psychoanalysis we have no hesitation in assuming that the course taken by mental events is automatically regulated by the pleasure principle".[8] But as the book progresses, Freud accumulates evidence that something other than the pleasure principle is at work in the unconscious. In particular, in some patients a "compulsion to repeat" overrides the pleasure principle, since what is repeated is

8 Sigmund Freud, *Beyond the Pleasure Principle*.

not associated with past or present pleasure. So Freud speculates that there may be death drives, independent of and antagonistic to the life drives. The life drives seek to prolong life, to create and to maintain ever-greater bonds; the death drives tend towards the destruction of the organism in which they are lodged, of the bonds it creates, of other organisms, and of the external world more generally. Freud concedes that his theory of the death drives is "speculation, often far-fetched speculation, which the reader will consider or dismiss according to his individual predilection"; he develops the idea "out of curiosity to see where it will lead".[9]

But in the same paper *Beyond the Pleasure Principle*, on the verge of launching into his speculations on the death drives, Freud observes that the compulsion to repeat can be observed in the lives of "normal people". Alluding to Nietzsche, Freud calls this tendency in life the "perpetual recurrence of the same thing"; and because the compulsion to repeat cannot be explained purely in terms of the pleasure principle, it leads Freud "beyond the pleasure principle" to the death drives. It is significant here that the compulsion to repeat is manifested in brief narratives, comprising the pared-down life histories of Freud's acquaintances. Identical or near-identical stories are compulsively re-enacted. The psychoanalytic resonance of serialized films can be initially suggested by the fact that, in them, the compulsion to repeat effectively becomes a fundamental principle of narrative construction.

In the years following the war, Freud's thought took a turn: in his wartime essays, Freud refers for the first time to a "death wish" residing in the unconscious. Rather than a desire for our own demise, this death wish is a hostility towards others. Our unconscious is, Freud insists, just as inaccessible to the idea of our own death, just as murderously inclined towards strangers, as was the primeval man; elsewhere he writes that our unconscious has as little use now as it ever had for the idea of its own mortality. So the death wish does not, at this stage, throw into doubt the primacy of the pleasure principle which Freud discerned as the motive force behind all mental functioning. After the war Freud would revise his views on this subject, at first in hypothetical mode in *Beyond the Pleasure Principle* (1920), and then with increasing certainty in *The Ego and the Id* (1923) and subsequent texts. Freud begins *Beyond the Pleasure Principle* by confidently reasserting the centrality of the pleasure principle in psychoanalytic theory: In the theory of psychoanalysis we have no hesitation in assuming that the course taken by mental events is automatically regulated by the pleasure principle.

---

9 *Ibid.*

But as the book progresses Freud accumulates evidence that something other than the pleasure principle is at work in the unconscious. In particular, in some patients a "compulsion to repeat" overrides the pleasure principle, since what is repeated is not associated with past or present pleasure. So Freud speculates that there may be death drives, independent of and antagonistic to the life drives. The life drives seek to prolong life, to create and to maintain ever-greater bonds; the death drives tend towards the destruction of the organism in which they are lodged, of the bonds it creates, of other organisms, and of the external world more generally. In Freud's work the death drives began as a hypothesis, as a possible way of explaining a gap left unfilled by his established conceptual framework. They rapidly became intellectually compelling, as Freud conceded in *Civilization and its Discontents*: "[t]o begin with it was only tentatively that I put forward the ideas that I have developed here, but in the course of time they have gained such a hold upon me that I can no longer think in any other way".[10] So the death drives begin as an explanatory fiction which accounts for an otherwise unexplained tendency to destroy, and they then acquire an irresistible power of seduction over the theorizing psychic apparatus. They destroy and repel, but also become indispensable.

What then is the ontological and epistemological status of the death drive? First of all, it should be stressed that what we call a "principle" or "law" is, in the first place, that which governs a particular field; it is in this sense that we speak of an empirical principle or law such as the pleasure principle. But there is another and quite distinct question, namely, in virtue of what is a field governed by a principle, there must be a second-order principle which accounts for the necessary compliance of the field with the empirical principle. It is this second-order principle that we call transcendental. I maintain this "transcendental" principle is the death drive. Freud is concerned not with the exceptions to this principle but with its foundations. However, the crucial and undecided point lies in the assertion that the death drive is "something not homogeneous with" the pleasure principle – does this statement entail that the death drive is to be ostracized from the empirical field, just as freedom is from Kant's civil society? Some answers to this question would be the suggestion that in terms of set theory it is both heterogeneous and homogeneous, since it is both an exception to and a member of its field.

When, after these theoretical considerations, we return to Wagner, the question is whether such an approach to the problem brings us a slightly better understanding of Wagner and his heroes troubled by desire for death and the

---

10 Sigmund Freud (1930), *Civilization and its Discontents*, [in:] *The Standard Edition of the Complete Psychological Works of Sigmund Freud.* Volume 21 (London: Hogarth Press, 1930/1968).

impossibility of satisfying this desire? Moreover, does Wagner possess any insight on the solution to the dilemma formulated by Freud? Does Wagner's opera offer us some premonition of solutions to the struggle between the pleasure principle and the death drive? Žižek's answer is most emphatically yes. Wagner's solution to Freud's antagonism between *Eros* and *Thanatos* is thus the identity of the two poles: love itself culminates in death, its true object is death, and the longing for the beloved is the longing for death. It is precisely the reference to Wagner which enables us to see how the Freudian death drive has nothing whatsoever to do with the craving for self-annihilation, for the return to the inorganic absence of any life-tension. Death drive does not reside in Wagnerian heroes' longing for death, to find peace in it; on the contrary, it is the very opposite of dying – a name for the undead eternal life itself, for the horrible fate of being caught in the endless repetitive cycle of wandering around in guilt and pain. The final passing-away of the Wagnerian hero (the death of the Dutchman, Wotan, Tristan, Amfortas) is therefore the moment of their liberation from the clutches of the death drive.

The paradox of Freud/Wagner is that the name "death drive" is the name for its very opposite, for an uncanny excess of life, for an undead urge which persist beyond the (biological) cycle of life and death. The ultimate lesson of psychoanalysis and Wagner's operas is the same: human life is never just life: humans are not simply alive, they are possessed by the strange drive to enjoy life in excess, passionately attached to a surplus which sticks out and derails the ordinary run of things. Such a striving to experience life at its excessive fullest is what Wagner's operas are about. This excess inscribes itself into the human body in the guise of a wound which makes the subject undead, depriving him of the capacity to die, apart from Tristan's and Amfortas's wound: when this wound is healed, the hero can die in peace. It should not, therefore, be a surprise to us that already Žižek noticed that Wagner's opera *Tristan and Isolde* is about the failure in love, characteristic for the whole of our Western culture. The myth of Tristan and Isolde was the first to give full expression to the axiom of courtly love: love is an act of radical transgression which suspends all socio-symbolic links and, as such, has to culminate in the ecstatic self-obliteration of death.

4. The death drive as the mask of the symbolic order

Lacan's view of the death drive is a case in point. He mentions, only to dismiss them, those who equate Freud's principle of constancy with the actual death of the organism. For Lacan, this equation confuses the pleasure principle with what we think Freud designated under the name of the death drive. Lacan says "what we think" because when Freud speaks of the death drive, he is, thank God, designating something less absurd, less antibiological, antiscientific. Lacan, in short, refuses to take Freud's word for it – for Freud does very clearly equate constancy with organic death. Instead, "thank God", Lacan's Freud is obliged to think the great thought of the death drive because the detour called human experience, human interchanges, or intersubjectivity is what truly interests him. For Lacan, we know, all analytic experience is an experience of signification. And thus, to the extent that the human being goes beyond the real which is biologically natural to it, he or she must struggle with the language of the other.

Lacan put it at the end of his seminar on the ego. This is the point where we open to the symbolic order, which is not the libidinal order in which the ego is inscribed, along with all the drives. It tends beyond the pleasure principle, beyond the limits of life, and that is why Freud identifies it with the death instinct. The death instinct is only the mask of the symbolic order, in so far – this is what Freud writes – as it has not been realized. As long as the symbolic recognition has not been instituted, by definition, the symbolic order is dumb. The symbolic order is simultaneously nonbeing and insisting to be, this is what Freud has in mind when he talks about the death instinct as being what is most fundamental – a symbolic order in travail, in the process of coming, insisting on being realized. Through the dialectic with the other one becomes a human being, which is to say, once again, that one is recognized (or realized) in the eyes of at least one person. The human being can be formed only if at least two of these Desires confront one another.

Consequently, Lacan more or less turns repetition into a desire, a compulsion, or *Zwang,* for *communion* with at least one other being. Repetition is, in effect, the basic condition of the dialectic of desire leading to recognition. It is only by being *recognized* by another, by many others, or – in the extreme – by all others, that a human being is really human. Such is the "herd" within which Lacan explicitly locates *human* reality as *recognized* reality. Lacan understood the meaning of "*recognized* reality" perfectly, saying flatly that this discourse with the other produces a small circuit in which an entire family, an entire coterie, an entire camp, an entire nation or half the world will be caught. Such repetition is guaranteed by the fact that the subject of language, so unlike the fictitious mirror-ideal, is always caught up in the symbolic piece-meal, decomposed. Or, to put it differently, the subject is caught, and rather perversely so, by a form of representation understood through (and called by the name of) psychoanalysis – the analytic relation, which can only be understood as a communication. The death drive is, as a result, meaningful as a reflection of the negation and alienation of the subject living in the world of the symbol. The central phenomenon of repetition is, then, the royal road to an understanding that one's subjectivity is always elsewhere, in sum, that *I is an other – Je est un autre.*[11]

The detour of life, of endless miscommunication and *meconnaissance,* is thereupon brought into relation with the endless dialectic that is life and death. As suggested, this dialectic is what Lacan will call – as always, following Kojève following Marx following Hegel – a struggle for "pure prestige", for recognition in the eyes of the other, in a fight to the death without, for all of that, actually killing or being killed. For obviously, as Hegel reminds us, recognition demands that the adversary remains alive – albeit reduced to the position of the Slave – and is overcome dialectically. Desire, Lacan repeats, is caught from end to end in the dialect of alienation and no longer has any other means of expression than through the desire for recognition and the recognition of desire. Such desire is intimately connected, by way of a circle, to death: "[t]he object of desire", Lacan states in *The Four Fundamental Concepts of Psycho-Analysis,* "is the cause of desire, and this object that is the cause of desire is the object of the drive".[12] What is, then, the aim of Lacanian psychoanalysis? Prior to analysis, the ego is only a pure, imaginary mirage. From then on, analysis amounts to being a demystification of what was previously imaginary. So we get to the final point – once demystification has been accomplished, we find ourselves in the presence of death. All that is left is to wait for death and contemplate it.

Or as Lacan more vividly suggests, analysis is over when, as with Oedipus, the analysand tears his face apart. Death, Hegel reminds us again, is the Absolute Master, *der absolute Herr,* for a life governed by this tragic dialectic, a limit that structures existence until, at least, it is actually crossed.[13] Death as such, Lacan of course admits, does not mean anything. Indeed, Lacan always directs his attention to the essential part of human experience: namely that which causes the subject to exist on the level of the emergence of the symbolic. In good dialectical fashion, Lacan's subject may be decomposed and cadaverized but is not, for all of that, dead.

But things are not so complicated, I dare say, with Freud. Lacan thoroughly obscures the metapsychological meaning of *Beyond the Pleasure Principle,* first of all, because he overextends the range of what he repeatedly calls the "Freudian experience" and, second, because he fails to appreciate the actual

---

11 Todd Dufresne, *Tales from the Freudian Crypt: The Death Drive in Text and Context*, (Stanford: Stanford University Press, 2000).

12 Jacques Lacan, *The Seminar of Jacques Lacan, Book 11: The Four Fundamental Concepts of Psycho-Analysis*, ed. Jacques-Alain Miller, trans. Dennis Porter (New York: Norton, 1978), p. 243.

13 Georg Wilhelm Friedrich Hegel (1807), *Phenomenology of Spirit*, trans. A. V. Miller (Oxford: Clarendon Press, 1977), p. 117.

limits of Freud's imagination. For, quite literally, in *Beyond the Pleasure Principle* life is for Freud a regrettable detour away from death and from the pleasures of the id. Life itself is alienated from death, just as the *ego* is alienated from the *id*, an assumption that allows Freud – all self-congratulatory "thank Gods" notwithstanding – to make of the body (organic and social) a ghostly apparition of the truest state: nonexistence. According to Lacan, though, "Freudian experience" is, paradoxically, grounded upon a desire that is prior to any kind of experience, prior to any considerations concerning the world of appearances and the world of essences. It is desire, Lacan states, which achieves the primitive structuration of the human world, desire as unconscious; and again, the desire in question is prior to any kind of conceptualization and emerges just as it becomes embodied in speech. As usual, Lacan echoes Hegel, who states: to understand man by understanding his origin is, therefore, to understand the origin of the ego revealed by speech. But for the Freud of *Beyond the Pleasure Principle* what is *prior* to speech is a *before* of existence that is unrepresentable, literally unspeakable, because it is *nonexistent.* This before is the "beyond of the pleasure principle" of an entirely different order than that of analytic experience and its (full or empty) speech acts. Freud states rather clearly that this order, which he calls metapsychologic, is independent of the orders of experience governed by the laws of psychoanalysis, that is, by the pleasure principle.[14]

Suffice it to say, at this juncture, that this extreme view of life and death is not at all symbolic in Lacan's sense. On the contrary, the deepest meaning in *Beyond the Pleasure Principle* is essentially literal, sitting right there on the surface, tied up as it is with his rather strange discussion of primary (or absolute) narcissism; a discussion, as suggested, that Lacan carefully sidesteps with his theories of the mirror stage and of desire. Nor is Freud's logic, as we have seen, simply dialectical in the way that Lacan claims; in its most radical formulation, the beyond is not alienated life, existing somewhere else, in another place, and for another. Rather, the beyond Freud introduces is radically *outside* the dialectic of the life and death drives. Like some demoniac unmoved mover, Freud's death-drive theory is an ideal that complicates both his old theories and the experiences upon which they are purportedly based. And this, I think, is precisely why Lacan takes the linguistic route of Freud: the symbolic saves Freud from the extremity, and also the absurdity, of his inflated speculations introduced in *Beyond the Pleasure Principle.* Quite simply, Lacan could not accept what Freud had to say any more than the ego psychologists could and so he made of *Beyond the Pleasure Principle* a dream symbolizing something else, something more, in a word.

---

14 Kiarina Kordela, *Surplus. Spinoza, Lacan*, (State University of New York Press, Albany 2007).

5. The return of the dead

Wagnerian hero is therefore a hero who resembles a living corpse, who because of unfinished suffering cannot die. Wagnerian hero is someone who from the position of death returns to the position of life. The question is why he/she does it? Why do the dead return? What unfinished business do they still have with us or do we still have with them? The question is all the more important that, as already we have noted that ghosts, the dead and the undead walk among us now as much as ever. On television and in the cinema, a host of successful films and television series have portrayed some sort of survival after the grave, from the ghosts of *Truly Madly Deeply*, *Ghost*, *The Sixth Sense* and *The Others* to the vampires of the three *Blade* films, *Interview with the Vampire*, *Van Helsing* or *Buffy the Vampire Slayer* to the zombies of George Romero's *Night of the Living Dead*, *Dawn of the Dead*, *Day of the Dead* and *Land of the Dead* to contemporary TV serials *Twilight*, *The Vampire Diaries*, or *True Blood.*[15]

Žižek suggests that the return of the living dead deserves to be called the "fundamental fantasy of contemporary mass culture". Explaining this fantasy, Žižek finds a concordance between popular culture and Lacanian psychoanalysis:

> The answer offered by Lacan [to the question of why the dead return] is the same as that found in popular culture: *because they were not properly buried*, i.e., because something went wrong with their obsequies. The return of the dead is the sign of a disturbance in the symbolic rite, in the process of symbolization; the dead return as collectors of some unpaid symbolic debt.[16]

There is some simplification, though, in describing this fantasy as characteristically modern. But the main intuition is correct. The dead man returns because he has not been "duly laid to rest". The duty of the living to bury the dead has not been performed according to established practice, and the rite of passage remains incomplete. So the dead return in part because their affairs on earth are not yet complete. The ghost's appearance is the sign of a disturbance in the symbolic or moral order. Once that disturbance has been corrected, the ghost will depart again, dispatched this time for good. So the ghost returns in order to be sent away again. Its incursion in our world is only temporary. Once our symbolic debt has been duly paid, the domains of the living and of the dead can be kept decently separate again.

---

15 Colin Davis, *Haunted Subjects. Deconstruction, Psychoanalysis and the Return of the Dead*, (Great Britain: Palgrave Macmillan, 2007).

16 Slavoj Žižek, *Looking Awry: An Introduction to Jacques Lacan Through Popular Culture* (Cambridge, MA: The MIT Press, 1991).

In some respects, recent stories of the supernatural reproduce the "unfinished business" model of the commerce between the living and the dead. The dead return either because the rituals of burial, commemoration and mourning have not been properly completed (*Truly Madly Deeply*), or because they are evil and must be exorcised (*Buffy the Vampire Slayer*), or because, like the ghost of Hamlet's father, they know of a secret to be revealed, a wrong to be righted, an injustice to be made public or a wrongdoer to be apprehended (*Ghost*). When the dead return to claim an unpaid debt, it is perhaps not surprising that the response of the living is characteristically ambivalent. We are doubly angry at the deceased. How could they leave us, and why do they not leave us alone? The desire to keep the dead amongst us, to refuse the scandal of death, competes with the desire to be rid of them for good, to stop the dead from returning and disturbing our fragile peace of mind.

Certainly, as Žižek observes, the rites of burial are ambivalent: through them, we show our respect for the dead, and thereby prevent them from returning to haunt us. This ambivalence of the work of mourning is clearly discernible in the two opposed attitudes towards the dead: on the one hand, we should not ignore them, but mark their death properly, perform the proper rituals; on the other hand, there is something obscene and transgressive in talking about the dead at all. We both want the dead and want to be rid of them. The belief in ghosts is, like the ghost itself, something that survives or returns long after it should have been relegated to the past; it is a kind of excess or fault line within belief, or perhaps an unconscious remainder of magical thinking, revealing a gap between what we think we believe – How could there be ghosts? How ridiculous!, and what we nevertheless continue to believe – There are ghosts!

IV. Rethinking Deconstruction: Why Deconstruction is Inventive or It is Nothing at All?

Deconstruction cannot limit itself or proceed immediately to a neutralization: it must, by means of a double gesture, a double science, a double writing, practice an overturning of the classical opposition and a general displacement of the system. It is only on this condition that deconstruction will provide itself the means with which to intervene in the field of oppositions that it criticizes, which is also a field of nondiscursive forces.

Jacques Derrida[1]

I have constantly insisted on the fact that the movement of deconstruction was first of all affirmative – not positive, but affirmative. Deconstruction, let's say it one more time, is not demolition or destruction.

Jacques Derrida[2]

Deconstruction, [...], is engaged in the construction of the "quasi-synthetic concepts" which account for the economy of the conditions of possibility and impossibility of the basic philosophemes. Infrastructures, a word used by Derrida on several occasions in references in these quasi-synthetic constructs, seemed to represent the most economical way to conceptualize all of Derrida's proposed quasi-synthetic concepts in a general manner.

Rodolphe Gasché[3]

1. The question of school

Some words are sometimes their own worst enemies. Deconstruction is one of them. Like *existentialism*, *liberal*, and *postmodern*, its meaning is often so vague as to be useless. Much has been written on and about deconstruction, and several times Jacques Derrida has attempted to qualify this term, which he declared he

1 Jacques Derrida, *Margins of Philosophy*, trans. A. Bass (Chicago: The University of Chicago Press, 1982), p. 327.

2 Jacques Derrida, *There is No "One" Narcissism (Autobiophotographies)*. An interview broadcast in the program prepared by Didier Cahen over France-Culture, *Le bon plaisir de Jacques Derrida*, March 22, 1986, published with the title *Entretien avec Jacques Derrida* [in:] *Digraphe* 42, December 1987; http://www.hydra.umn.edu/Derrida/narc.html (Date of access: February 19, 2006).

3 Rodolphe Gasché, *The Tain of the Mirror: Derrida and the Philosophy of Reflection* (Cambridge, Massachusetts, & London: Harvard University Press, 1986).

uses "for the sake of rapid convenience"[4] though it is a word he has never liked and one whose fortune has disagreeably surprised him.

Deconstruction is often defined as a school of philosophy which upends the Western metaphysical tradition. It represents a complex response to a variety of theoretical and philosophical movements of the 20th century, most notably Husserlian phenomenology, Saussurean and French structuralism, and Freudian and Lacanian psychoanalysis. In other places deconstruction is defined as a school of literary criticism invented in the writings of the Belgium/North American literary critic Paul de Man. Deconstruction is also described as a theory of reading which aims to undermine the logic of opposition within texts. And last but not least, in current literary studies, deconstructive readings are usually part of a larger interpretive strategy (feminist, new historicist, queer theory, etc.), and often put in the service of destabilizing hierarchical oppositions (between male and female, elite and popular culture, straight and gay, etc.).

What is worthwhile, deconstruction is not the centerpiece of Derrida's work, and he has been somewhat dismayed by attempts to formalize it into a system, movement, or school. In *Letter to a Japanese Friend,* Derrida wrote: "[t]he question would be therefore what deconstruction is not, or rather ought not to be", and he added "[w]hat deconstruction is not? everything of course! What is deconstruction? nothing of course!".[5] For those of us who like the order of definitions, this obviously is not much help. I am aware it is too late to save deconstruction from the fate of meaninglessness or synonymy with *destruction*. On the other hand, it may be not too late to say something about how the readers perceive the term in the philosophical interpretations and readings. The principle task of this chapter is not even to look for the definition of deconstruction because I do not believe that explicit definition increases our knowledge and understanding of how things really are, but rather the task of my work is linked with looking for the possible contexts in which the term "deconstruction" could be used. In *Signature, Event, Context* Derrida asked: "Is there a rigorous and scientific concept of the *context?* Does not the notion of context harbor, behind a certain confusion, very determined philosophical presuppositions?".[6] In other words, it is important for Derrida's suspicions that a context is never absolutely determinable, or rather its determination is never certain. I would like to

4 Jacques Derrida, *The Time of a Thesis: Punctuations*, trans. K. McLaughlin, [in:] *Philosophy in France Today*, ed. Alan Montefiore (Cambridge: Cambridge University Press, 1983), p. 42.

5 Jacques Derrida, *Letter to A Japanese Friend*, [in:] *Derrida and Difference*, David Wood, Robert Bernasconi (Evanston, IL: Northwestern UP, 1988), p. 5.

6 Jacques Derrida, *Margins of Philosophy*, p. 310.

demonstrate that this statement refers to the term deconstruction as well as to other words.

Could deconstruction really be nothing? I try to give the answer through the process of posing a series of hypotheses and denying them. In other words I will try to take very seriously Derrida's statement that deconstruction is nothing. Strictly speaking, the statement that "Deconstruction is inventive or it is nothing at all".[7]

2. Is deconstruction a form destruction?

The first, very naive hypothesis is that deconstruction is merely negative reduction. In many places Derrida stressed that the word "deconstruction" has the association with the Heidggerian words *Destruktion* or *Abbau*. The problem is that in French "destruction" obviously implied an annihilation or a negative reduction much closer perhaps to Nietzschean "demolition" than to the Heideggerian interpretation and use the word *Abbau*. However, the negative appearance was and remains much more difficult to efface than is suggested by the grammar of the word (*de*-), even though it can designate a genealogical restoration [*remonter*] rather than a demolition.

In the summer of 1927, Martin Heidegger delivered a lecture course, later published under the title *Einführung in die phänomenologische Forschung*. Given the topic of his lectures, Heidegger appropriately begins them with a discussion of the nature of philosophy and, particularly of phenomenology. Borrowing creatively from his teacher, Edmund Husserl, Heidegger says that phenomenology is the name for a method of doing philosophy; he says that the method includes three steps – reduction, construction, and destruction – and he explains that these three are mutually pertinent to one another. Construction necessarily involves destruction, he says, and then he identifies destruction with deconstruction, *Abbau*.

Heidegger proclaimed the "end of philosophy". He argued that the only real philosophical questions have to do with "being" (ontology) and that "transcendental" questions were meaningless. By the sixties, the notion of the "end of philosophy" had developed into the notion that philosophy was nothing other than the ideology of the western ethos. The liberal humanist tradition presented a *de facto* situation (its own pre-eminence) as a *de jure* situation (its truth). In other words, it presented its traditional privilege as a natural superiority. Such a position is ideological.

7 Jacques Derrida, *Psyché: Inventions de l'autre*, Collection La Philosophie en effet (Paris: Galilée, 1987).

Derrida argued that Heidegger had not escaped transcendentalism, that his "Being" was as transcendental as any other "Transcendental Signified". He also argued that even if the charge against philosophy as ideology were true, the charge was leveled in the language of philosophy, which cannot be escaped. All that was really being asked was that the dominant ideology (philosophy = the ideology of the western ethos) be replaced by another broader or at least different ideology such as Marxism (philosophy = discourse of the ruling class), Freudianism (philosophy = sexual symptom), anti-Freudianism (philosophy = phallocratic ideology).

Derrida did not quarrel with Heidegger's position that history, as perceived in the philosophic tradition was over; only that Heidegger himself had not escaped it. Derrida raised the question of what there was to say after philosophy was over. He argued that the protest against the reason can be made only in the space of reason, only on its own terrain. The strategy he chose was *duplicity,* the playing of a *double game.* He would operate in the language of reason, since there was no other, but try to lay traps for it by posing it problems it could not answer, exposing the inherent contradictions in apparently reasonable positions.

What is the double game? In which way does Derrida avoid the paradoxes of the self-referential critique of reason? Since the "speaking subject", when he/she speaks, must speak the language of reason, there must exist some silent region where the double agent (deconstructor) can sort out his/her trick against the Logos (the rules of reason). In order for this to be possible one condition must be met. In order for the double game of duplicity to be played, the language of philosophy must already be full of duplicity. This is the reason why Derrida sees signifying force in the gaps, margins, figures, echoes, digressions, discontinuities, contradictions, and ambiguities of a text, just as Freud rendered dreams and slips of the tongue *readable* rather than dismissing them as mere nonsense or error. When one writes, one writes more than (or less than, or differently than) one thinks. The reader's task is to read what is written rather than simply attempt to intuit what might have been meant. Derrida said:

> Deconstruction cannot limit itself or proceed immediately to a neutralization: it must, by means of a double gesture, a double science, a double writing, practice an overturning of the classical opposition and a general displacement of the system.[8]

Deconstruction is not simply the decomposition of an architectural structure; it is also a question about the foundation, about the relation between foundation and what is founded; it is also a question about the closure of the structure, about a whole architecture of philosophy. Not only as concerns this or that construction, but also with respect to the architectonic motif of the system.

8 Jacques Derrida, *Margins of Philosophy*, p. 326.

Architectonic: Derrida refers to Kant's definition, which does not exhaust all the senses of architectonic, but Kant's definition interests me particularly. The architectonic is the art of the system. Deconstruction concerns first of all systems. This does not mean that it brings down the system, but that it opens the possibilities of arrangement or assembling, of being together if you like, which are not necessarily systematic in the strict sense that philosophy gives to this word. It is thus a reflection on the system, on the closure and opening of the system. Of course, it was also a kind of active translation that displaces somewhat the word Heidegger uses: *Destruktion*, the destruction of ontology, which also does not mean the annulment, the annihilation of ontology, but an analysis of the structure of traditional ontology.

An analysis which is not merely a theoretical analysis, but at the same time another writing of the question of Being or meaning, deconstruction is also a manner or writing and putting forward another text. It is not a *tabula rasa*, which is why deconstruction is also distinct from doubt or from critique. Critique always operates in view of the decision after or by means of a judgment. The authority of judgment or of the critical evaluation is not the final authority for deconstruction. Deconstruction is also a deconstruction of critique. Which does not mean that all critique or all criticism is devalued, but that one is trying to think what the critical instances signify in the history of authority – for example in the Kantian sense, but not only the Kantian sense. Deconstruction is not a critique. Another German word of which deconstruction is a kind of transposition is *Abbau*, which is found in Heidegger, and also found in Freud. With this latter word, I want to place what I am writing in a network with the kinds of thinking that are important to me, obviously.

From this part of my investigation I draw my first conclusion that the deconstruction is not a destruction, given the simple meaning of the word.

3. Is deconstruction a method of analysis?

My second hypothesis is that deconstruction is a method of analysis in the sense of the latter word linked rather with the work of Edmund Husserl then Bertrand Russell. Clarifying the term deconstruction Barbara Johnson wrote: "[de]construction is not synonymous with *destruction*, however. It is in fact much closer to the original meaning of the word *analysis* itself, which etymologically means *to undo* – a virtual synonym for *to de-construct*".[9] If anything is destroyed

9 Barbara Johnson, *The Critical Difference: Essays in the Contemporary Rhetoric of Reading* (Baltimore: Johns Hopkins University Press, 1980).

in a deconstructive reading, it is not the text, but the claim to unequivocal domination of one mode of signifying over another. But – against this hypothesis – Derrida emphasizes: "deconstruction is not an analysis in particular because the dismantling of a structure is not a regression toward a simple element, toward an indissoluble origin".[10] In which way could we put these two statements, Barbara Johnson's and Jacques Derrida's, in a consistent narration?

To answer the question we have to come back to the origin, that is to the work of Husserl. The method of looking for the origin is the phenomenological analysis. Phenomenology seeks the *origin* of truth, and it locates this *origin* in an *inaugural fact* which by definition can only occur once. Derrida argues that a first is only a first by consequence of a second that follows it. The first is only recognizable as a first and not merely a singular by the arrival of the second. The second is therefore the prerequisite of the first. It permits the first to be first by its delayed arrival. The first, recognizable only after the second, is in this respect a third. *Origin* then is a kind of dress repetition or dress rehearsal, what Derrida calls *la répétition d'une première*, it is a representation of the first public performance which has not yet occurred. The original, in that sense, is always a copy. In *Of Gramatology* Derrida said: "[t]he trace is not only the disappearance of origin […] the origin did not even disappear, that it was never constituted except reciprocally by a non-origin, the trace, which thus becomes the origin of the origin".[11] The trace takes the place of the origin.

If we apply the same reasoning to signs and things in the "real" world, we come to the paradoxical situation that the sign precedes the referent. The sign "dog", for example, precedes the four-legged barking creature because the creature is only recognizable as „a dog" after the sign "dog" has been applied to it. Derrida has shown that, contrary to Husserl's notion of a pure origin, consciousness never precedes language, and we cannot see language as a representation of a silently lived-through experience.

This is, I maintain, the core of deconstructive thinking. We can only understand the priority of the sign by an enquiry into writing. Earlier, we looked at graphemes (the units of writing) as a second-order sign system. Derrida sees the relationship between these signs as semiological. The graphic sign stands in for the phonemic sign. It is therefore "the sign of a sign", while the oral sign is the "sign of the thing". Writing is then *supplementary*. Even the oral sign is supplementary, since it exists as supplement to the "real world". The graphic sign of writing is particularly supplemental since it is a supplement to a

---

10 Jacques Derrida, *Letter to A Japanese Friend*, p. 8.

11 Jacques Derrida (1967) *Of Grammatology*, trans. Gayatri Chakravorty Spivak (Baltimore: Johns Hopkins University Press, 1976), p. 74.

supplement, a sign of a sign. In *Of Grammatology* Derrida argues that writing should not be subordinated to speech, and this subordination is nothing more than an historical prejudice.[12] He argues further that to define a graphic sign is to define any sign. Every sign is a signifier whose signified is another signifier.

From this part of my investigation I draw my second conclusion that deconstruction is not a method of analysis of the simple meaning of the utterance. It could not be because deconstruction is not and should not be only an analysis of discourses, of philosophical statements or concepts; it has to challenge institutions, social and political structures, the most hardened traditions.

4. Is deconstruction a method of critique?

Some critics have dismissed deconstruction as a harmless academic game; others have denounced it as a terrorist weapon or a discourse of last-ditch nihilist unreason. As Christopher Norris demonstrates, both responses are equally wide of the mark. Norris claims that Derrida is first and foremost working within the philosophical tradition. Thus he thinks philosophers like Richard Rorty[13] and Jürgen Habermas[14] too quickly turn Derrida into an

12 *Ibid.*

13 Richard Rorty, *Philosophy as a Kind of Writing*, [in:] *Consequences of Pragmatism. (Essays 1872-1980)* (Minneapolis: University of Minnesota Press, 1982), pp. 164-189.

14 Habermas in the famous chapter of *The Philosophical Discourse of Modernity* suggested that the "rebellious labor of deconstruction aims at dismantling smuggled-in basic conceptual relations of domination, such as those between speech and writing, the intelligible and matter, male and female". Logic and rhetoric constitute one of these conceptual pairs. Derrida is particularly interested in standing the primacy of logic over rhetoric, canonized since Aristotle, on its head. As a consequence, in Habermas's reading, Derrida wants to expand the sovereignty of rhetoric over the realm of the logical in order to solve the problem confronting the totalizing critique of reason. Derrida, like Heidegger, is able to escape the paradoxes of the self-referential critique of reason by claiming a special status for his discourse, that is, its release from discursive obligation. For example, there can only be talk about "contradiction" in the light of consistency requirements. If logic loses its conventional primacy over rhetoric, logical constraints lose their authority or are at least subordinated to other demands – of an aesthetic nature, for instance. Thus, the constraints constitutive of knowledge of a philosophical text only become accessible when the text is handled as what it would not like to be – as a literary text. The general conclusion of Habermas is that Derrida cancels the genre distinction between philosophy and literature. Jürgen Habermas, *The Philosophical Discourse of Modernity. Twelve Lectures,* trans. Frederick Lawrence (The MIT Press Cambridge, 1995), p. 187.

"antiphilosopher" who rejects serious argument and just plays games. Derrida's work – in Norris's reading – is rather an answer to the questions posed by the tradition of the Enlightenment.[15] By the "Enlightenment tradition" is here understood the modernity tradition from the Reformation as manifested in efforts to strengthen the domains of cognitive rationality, moral autonomy, and social and political self-determination.

Hence, my third hypothesis that deconstruction is indistinguishable from a kind of critique. Is it possible that deconstruction could be a critique in Kantian sense? To answer this question I should first ask: What is critique? Kant by transcendental critique understood the determination of the formal conditions of a complete system of pure reason. In other words, the principal task of transcendental philosophy is to discover the formal conditions that are necessary for the thing under scrutiny to operate or to be and in this case philosophy stands in need of a science which shall determine the possibility, the principles and the extent of all *a priori* knowledge.

The question "whether deconstruction could be a critique in Kantian sense?" is important if we are aware that deconstruction is not simply the decomposition of an architectural structure; it is rather a question about the foundation, about the relation between foundation and what is built; it is also a question about the closure of the structure, about a whole architecture of philosophy. Derrida wrote on the architectonic motif of the system: "[d]econstruction concerns first of all systems".[16] This does not mean that it brings down the system, but that it opens the possibilities of arrangement or assembling that are not necessarily systematic in the strict sense that philosophy gives to this word. It is thus a reflection on the system, on the closure and opening of the system.

However, Derrida wrote also that deconstruction is not a critique, in a general sense or in Kantian sense: "[t]ranscendental critique is only one of the

15 Norris may have a point. He does, in fact, come very close to suggesting how Derrida's late works, as indebted to philosophy as they are (and as they need to be), open a whole range of possibilities of communication, and even noncommunication. Even in these late works, which seem less concerned with arguments and more inclined to exploit the various possibilities of noncommunication with cross-purpose exchange, Derrida is "resuming issues and problems that are worked over with meticulous care in his more philosophical texts" (195). But Norris stops short. In his efforts to distance himself from philosophers like Rorty, who (according to him) reduces Derrida to a gamester – he does the opposite; he puts "play" aside, downplays it, does not explore its possibilities, and thus turns his back on a crucial part of Derrida's style. Derrida becomes an almost antipoet, or an antiplayer, who "insists" (197), "argues" (193), and "issues statements" (195). Christopher Norris, *Deconstruction, Theory and Practice* (New York: Methuen, 1982).

16 Jacques Derrida, *Letter to A Japanese Friend*, p. 9.

essential *themes* or *objects* of deconstruction".[17] Why Derrida objects to the identification of the work of deconstruction with the method of critique? What kind of reasons cause his insistence on defending deconstruction from its identification with critique? When one thinks of Derrida and Kant together, the work that immediately comes to mind is Derrida's paper *Mochlos: or, the Conflict of the Faculties.*[18] Less known, but also concerned with Kant and the place of philosophy in the university, is his paper *Of the Humanities and the Philosophical Discipline* in the e-journal *Surfaces*,[19] which arose from a talk he gave at UNESCO.

In *Mochlos*, Derrida outlines Kant's attempt from *Der Streit der Fakultäten* (1798) to position philosophy as a speaker of truth as opposed to the faculties which operate in the outside interests of the powers that be. Derrida, in familiar style, takes a classic text and teases out a new set of meanings than are apparent at first reading. Kant's point was to position philosophy against the professional disciplines which were sponsored by a higher authority. Philosophy (taken broadly as the liberal disciplines) is regarded as the "lower" faculty which nevertheless has access to the truth of propositions precisely because it acts on freedom, rather than on the imperatives of revelation, the state, or the courts. As such, philosophy should be left alone to pursue its own aims, because without some discipline to focus on truth, human reason is not truly represented. The higher disciplines are useful tools to obtain certain goals, but they do not have the ability to discern whether their stated ends are the result of reason or simply inclination.

In *Of the Humanities*, on the other hand, Derrida is less interested in establishing the place of philosophy in the conflicted academia and more interested in exploring the ways in which the "cosmopolitical" ideal of Kant's sketched in the work *Idee zu einer allgemeinen Geschichte in weltbürgerlicher Absicht* (1784) makes any sense today. Unlike *Mochlos*, Derrida looks outside rather than inside the academy. He points out that Kant argues that it is the unsociability of men which nature uses to push us toward constructing artificial institutions, which bring about peace. Our natural unsociability eventually makes possible the ends of reason and the production of the institutions of

17 *Ibid.*, p. 8.

18 Jacques Derrida, *Mochlos: or, the Conflict of the Faculties*, [in:] Richard Rand (ed.), *Logomachia: The Conflict of the Faculties* (Lincoln, Nebraska: University of Nebraska Press, 1992), p. 3.

19 Jacques Derrida, *Of the Humanities and the Philosophical Discipline. The Right to Philosophy from the Cosmopolitical Point of View (the Example of an International Institution),* [in:] "Surfaces" Vol. IV. 310 Folio 1, Montréal Vendome, Editions UNESCO Verdier PUF 1997.

European modernity. In other words, Kant recognizes that philosophy is founded on conflict and division. To go back to philosophy's origin to discover its purpose cannot therefore be a matter of finding a unified and coherent point. Memory must take into account Greco-European origins, but it must also recognize the conflicted nature of those origins. This means that universalist understandings of philosophy must be resisted, but also it means engaging philosophy in nontraditional languages, in ways that recognize both the traditional and the new aspects of the problems of philosophy.

I would like now to come back to my principle question, "whether the deconstruction could be a critique in Kantian sense?" or rather I would like to ask: "Why deconstruction could not be a critique?" What kind of objections has Derrida to Kant's project of philosophy? There are above all two objections. (1) Instead of asking about the place of philosophy in the academy, Derrida through Kant asks about the place of philosophy in the world. Kant wants to imagine a universal (and therefore philosophical) history but, as Derrida points out, this project stands in danger of becoming literature, that is, of simply being a representation having no basis in reality. To resist the possibility that universal history or philosophy might just be literature, Kant takes his starting point from the history of Greece and Rome, as opposed to the "barbaric" nations. So, the cosmopolitical becomes rooted in the hegemony of Europe. But it means that the place of philosophy is in relation to its communities. This problem appears to us very clearly when we ask a question such as this: "What is African philosophy?" or "Does African philosophy exist?" The right to philosophy requires not only an appropriation of competing several philosophical models, styles and traditions (the continental tradition of philosophy, Anglo-Saxon philosophy, etc.); the right to philosophy also requires the reflection, the displacement and the deconstruction of the hegemonies, the access to places and to philosophical events which are exhausted in the dominant traditions. (2) The second objections has a more technical significance. Critique always operates in view of the decision after or by means of a judgment. The authority of judgment or of the critical evaluation is not the final authority for deconstruction. Deconstruction is also a deconstruction of critique. Which does not mean that all critique or all criticism is devalued, but that one is trying to think what the critical instances signify in the history of authority.

From this part of my investigation I draw my third conclusion that deconstruction is not a critique. It is rather perhaps a critique of critique.

5. Is deconstruction a practice of reading?

My fourth hypothesis is that deconstruction should be treated as a very special kind of the practice of reading. What kind? Jonathan Culler recalls the strategic meaning of Derrida's treatment of philosophical texts through literary criticism in order to suggest that, in turn, literary criticism treats literary texts also as philosophical texts. The most truly philosophical reading of philosophical text is one that treats the work as literature, as a rhetorical construct whose elements and order are determined by various textual exigencies. On the other hand, the most powerful and opposite readings of literary works may be those that treat them as philosophical gestures by teasing out the implications of their dealings with the philosophical oppositions that support them.

> If serious language – wrote Culler – is a special case of non-serious, if truths are fictions whose fictionality has been forgotten, then literature is not a deviant, parasitical instance of language. On the contrary, other discourses can be seen as cases of generalized literature, or archi-literature.[20]

Of course the same text can be open to different readings; it is the text itself that makes possible its uncontrollable effective history. But in which way would Derrida like to justify the paradoxical statement that any interpretation is inevitably a false interpretation, and any understanding a misunderstanding? If a text can be understood, it can in principle be understood repeatedly, by different readers in different circumstances. These acts of reading or understanding are not identical. From this we can thus conclude that understanding is a special case of misunderstanding, a particular deviation or determination of misunderstanding.

Such interpretation is one of the huge consequences of the death of the origin, which offers us the logic of supplementation. We can think of the origin as a place where there is no originary, only a supplement in the place of a deficient originary. It is deficient for this reason. We can think of the supplement as a surplus, something extra added to the whole and outside of it. But if the whole is really the whole, then nothing can be added to it. If the supplement is something and not nothing, then it must expose the defect of the whole, since something that can accommodate the addition of a supplement must be lacking something within itself. Derrida calls this "the logic of the supplement".

In the same way, the present is only present on the condition that it alludes to the absence from which it distinguishes itself. Metaphysics, Derrida argues, is the act of erasing this distinguishing mark, the *trace* of the absent. We may now

---

20 Jonathan Culler, *On Deconstruction: Theory and Criticism after Structuralism* (Ithaca: Cornell University Press, 1982).

define *trace* as the sign left by the absent thing, after it has passed on the scene of its former presence. Every present, in order to know itself as present, bears the trace of an absent which defines it. It follows then that an originary present must bear an originary *trace,* the present trace of a past which never took place, an absolute past.

Derrida sees the term "deconstruction", always used in specific contexts, as a metonymy for "a certain dislocation", what he called in previous writings a "displacement", "something which occurs", or which is trying to occur, without ever reaching a point of resolution (see Derrida's constructs of *différance*, preface, pretext, introduction, and so on). According to Derrida, this "certain dislocation", these deconstructions, are found in every text, that is "text" taken in a Derridean sense, where a text is "experience", "reality", be it "social, historical, economic, technical, military, and so on".

Precisely in this context Derrida formulated this most famous statement: *il n' y pas de hors-texte*, which can be rendered as "there is nothing outside the text", or "there is no outside text". This phrase stirred up many voices of disagreement and indignation, and for the most part caused misunderstanding. Derrida does not say that there is really nothing outside the text, that there are only texts, that they are limited on the paper or identical with books. He rather found it necessary to recast the concept of text by generalizing it almost without limit. In consequence, the idea that there is nothing outside the text means that there are only contexts which are not always saturated.

If we are even inclined in this way to accept the thesis that deconstruction is some kind of art of reading, we must still remember that it is a very special kind of reading. As Harold Bloom noted: "Criticism starts – it has to start – with a real passion for reading". According to Bloom all forms of literary critics are suspended between tautology and reduction. The pole of tautology suggests that the text is identical with his own message, that is, it is only what it is, nothing more. On the other hand, reductions strategy suggests that the text refers to the reality which is not textual, for example to social relations, to relations of power, to the economic system, and so on. In my opinion – and that is my fourth conclusion – Derrida and Bloom offer two distinct ways of escaping beyond this paradox of reading.

While Derrida emphasized the instability of linguistic meaning and the contradictions of conceptual thought, Bloom believed in the autonomy of imagination of the strong Poets from language, both literary and philosophic. To Bloom literature is not the mind's play among unstable signs but the spirit's struggle for originality.[21] To Derrida, the battle is waged against atemporal

21 Harold Bloom, *The Anxiety of Influence: A Theory of Poetry* (Oxford: Oxford University Press US, 1973).

linguistic structures. To Derrida, the originality is always problematic. To both Derrida and Bloom the struggle is against the limits of the human condition as they are enforced by the full weight of past cultural achievements.

6. The ethics of deconstruction

My fifth hypothesis is that deconstruction should be treated as a very special kind of ethics. Is there a reason to recognize in deconstruction a kind of ethics? Simon Critchley claims not that an ethics can be derived from deconstruction, like an effect from a cause, a superstructure from an infrastructure, or a second critique from a first critique; rather, he hopes to demonstrate that the pattern of reading produced in the deconstruction of – mostly, but by no means exclusively – philosophical texts has an ethical structure: deconstruction "is" ethical; or, to formulate the same thought less ontologically, deconstruction takes place (*a lieu*) ethically, or there is duty in deconstruction (*Il y a du devoir dans la deconstruction*).[22] The ethical turn prompted by Lévinas and Derrida, therefore, is not away from philosophy to its prior origin in ethics, but an *ethics beyond ethics*, or more radical still, an *ethics against ethics*, which gives rise to the paradoxical, if not the entirely contradictory, possibility of a postmodern ethics.

As Derrida notes, Lévinas' politics follows the structure of the messianic as it is driven by the hope for a justice that is always to come. This is enough to affirmatively answer the earlier question of whether Lévinas has a political philosophy. But as Lévinas teaches us in his discussion of the question of the third, the more difficult problem remains – to bring to light the roots of violence and exclusion, to think and to act otherwise, not only with the single other to whom I might give myself in love, but to each and every other from time immemorial to time everlasting, and most of all, here and now. This, of course, remains a guiding commitment of classic liberalism, and as such, it reveals both the promise and limit of Lévinas's politics. That is to say, as long as the existing present is held in relief by the messianic promise of the future, the hope for justice that Lévinas so clearly expresses can never amount to more than a politics of decision. This perhaps is the ironic consequence of the deconstructive insistence on structural undecidability.

The question this raises for us with regard to Lévinas is an important one – namely, as the postmodern return of religion has turned to the political, is this an extension of, or turn away from, the ethical as conceived by Lévinas? What exactly

22 Simon Critchley, *The Ethics of Deconstruction: Derrida and Lévinas* (Oxford: Blackwell Publishers, 1992).

is the connection between Lévinas's conception of the ethical and the political? Or, put otherwise, is the promise of deconstruction also its limit, and does the political turn in contemporary thought mark the eclipse of Lévinas? After all, a Lévinasian ethic is characterized first and foremost by the impossible – the unconditional demand of the Other, the infinite scope of responsibility that precedes and exceeds all intentionality. For Lévinas, responsibility comes prior to freedom, and as such, its obligation is absolute, but also absolutely undecidable and indeterminable. The political, on the other hand, is concerned with the art of the possible, the negotiation of and for power, and, at least with modern liberal thought, is predicated on the free acts of autonomous political subjects. Does Lévinas have a political philosophy? If so, does he belong to the tradition of modern liberalism? And finally, what does any of this have to do with Lévinas's talk of God, and more specifically his employment of the ontological argument for God's existence? Following Derrida's traces one must say that the question of friendship is framed less around the concern of presentability qua concept and more around the question of friendship beyond the limits of fraternity and the reconciliation of ethics and politics. The difficulty is not so much Derrida's concern with fraternity but the place of friendship in political affairs and how their interrelation situates the questions of ethics. But like Derrida, I am unable to imagine the passage between ethics and politics that could serve as a foundation for the future political or the imminent politics. Moreover, I cannot imagine reconciliation between politics and ethics without assuming normative premises, hostile to the question of particularity, so characteristic of friendship. Unable to resolve the problem of normativity I ask: Must it be the case that there is no passage *assuré* between friendship and politics, no deduction from one to the other, no foundation?

Without a solution to this question of foundation, I return to the question of the decision as the means by which a new ethics and politics of friendship can be attempted. Is a break between friendship and politics imaginable, in which, far from inducing paralysis or resignation, it is possible to experience a political decision? Derrida remains uncertain as to what the "decisive content" of this passage between friendship and politics would be, he attempts to unite a Lévinasian conception of ethics as hospitality with the suggestion that the ethical is at one and the same time the performance of a political intervention. Rightly Derrida asks whether it is possible for an ethics of hospitality to found the sphere of politics and law, but is unable to overcome the difficulty of deducing a politics from ethics. Nonetheless, Derida's conclusions are important because instead of finding a passage out of this said paralysis he claims that the very indeterminacy of the passage from ethics to politics entails that the taking of a political decision must be a response to the utter singularity of a particular and inexhaustible context. What makes "deconstruction" an innovative political gesture is this precise reworking of the time and space in which it is said to act.

If time and space of ethics and politics of deconstruction are to be thought it could only ever be thought foundational during the time in which its enactment is performed. It is foundational without imposing a generalized norm or posing as an arbitrary and unquestioned response to circumstances. The infinite ethical demand of deconstruction arises, Derrida reminds us, as a response to a singular context and calls forth the invention of a political decision. By engaging the problem of decision, Derrida argues that this allows us to think and act out what could be deemed the "political" differently. Under this framework, politics is to be understood as the art of response to the singular demand of the other, a demand that arises in a particular context – although the infinite demand cannot simply be reduced to its context – and calls for political invention, for creation.

For Derrida the test of a deconstructive practise of the political would be its negotiation between an ethics and politics and the invention of a singular relation to the other which pivots on the question of the decision. This for him unites the singular regard for the other under a mode of action whose criterion he identifies as universal. Derrida's work is insightful because it stresses the aporetic nature of this negotiation and insists on the singularity of the decision and context in which subjects act in relation to others, without, I add, seeking a normative model of politics. Derrida affirms that such an ethics of response finds itself at odds with normative politics. The point for me remains that friendship can only form the basis of political commonality once it affirms the irreconcilability of ethics and politics.

In conclusion, the difficulty here is to engage with the question of friendship as a subject of inquiry and advance a new perspective on the topic at the limit of its being delimitable as an object of theory. Time will tell how the work of theory can push us beyond being just and urge us all to take an ethical stance, where to live means to constantly experience a call to friendship, the foundation and character of which is always questioned. The question remains how the "to come" and "more than" of friendship might be possible given its untranslatable, unpresentable, unknowable qualities, and what Derrida is right to suggest is its impossible basis for a generalized model of political relations. In this sense we can begin to understand why Derrida's anticipatory lament is maintained on the condition of the promise.

The only "politics of friendship" which can be advanced is not of the order of a programme and/or subject but an ethical stance that remains inexhaustibly open to the question of friendship's future that is still to come as much as it is still to be created. In this sense it is much about exploring the identity of the concept, the force of its call to particularity as much as generality, and the aporias which mark their coming together. If the time, space and event-ness of friendship circulate as a persistent question in Derrida's work, it is because there is an incessant demand for philosophic practice and an ethics of maintaining that the question remain as such: that the question of what it is and what can be advanced in its name remain the task of philosophy. His ethics, which we must not forget is also his faith in the promise, is one of philosophic practice, such that his meditation on friendship both testifies and deepens the tradition which links philosophy with friendship and maintains the place of friendship in the very practice of philosophy. It is because of this fundamental relation that the politics of friendship must never be thought independent of the space that would allow the work of philosophy to occur. It is that friendship remains as much a question as a possibility which maintains its futurity. In this sense, perhaps all we are left with is the promise, as Derrida insists, to give friendship a future; to maintain the future of friendship qua concept as the condition of its survival however "apolitical" this may seem. Insofar as we remain hospitable to the question of friendship, however vague and romantic, in this spirit may we say and act with the faith of its possibility. Such a friendship would be one whose fidelity remains bound to the thought of friendship in such a way that the returning to the question would itself mark a return to friendship, in the sense of a befriending of its concern as something which one is driven to experience and/or accomplish. In this sense, may the promise of friendship remain as much its promising thought as the promise of the thought. To affirm a politics from this thought reaffirms the politics of practicing that which we call philosophy. It provides an opportunity to redouble the political and philosophical questions, at the same time affirming their tension; it divides and fixes the questions of philosophy and politics on top of each other, but nonetheless affirms that this very redoubling is none other than the work of friendship, as much its home as its otherness.

7. Invention

Deconstruction is never the effect of a subjective act of desire or will or wishing. [...] Therefore, deconstruction is also the deconstruction of the concept of method (both scientific and philosophical) and has to be determined accordingly.

Rodolphe Gasché[23]

This chapter of the book confines itself to an analysis of the philosophical background and implications of deconstruction, and to a discussion of some of the premises of a criticism based on it. Unlike others who have attempted to

23 Rodolphe Gasché, *The Tain of the Mirror: Derrida and the Philosophy of Reflection*, p. 123.

situate Derrida's thought in the history at the grand disputes concerning the question of being, or in the apocryphal history of the grammatological, not to mention certain histories bordering on the phantasmic which some philosophers and critics have devised, I discuss Derrida's philosophy in terms of the criticism to which the philosophical concept of invention has been subjected. In *Psyche: Invention of the Other*, Derrida said:

> Deconstruction is inventive or it is nothing at all; it does not settle for methodological procedures, it opens up a passageway, it marches ahead and marks a trail; its writing is not only performative, it produces rules – other conventions – for new performativities and never installs itself in the theoretical assurance of a simple opposition between performative and constative. Its *process* involves an affirmation, this latter being linked to the coming [*venir*] in event, advent, invention.[24]

Deconstruction is not, should not be only an analysis of discourses, of philosophical statements or concepts, of a semantics; it has to challenge institutions, social and political structures, the most hardened traditions. And, from this point of view, no architectural decision is possible that does not implicate a politics, that does not put into play economic, technical, cultural and other investments. An effective, radical deconstruction must pass by way of architecture, by way of the very difficult transaction that architectures must undertake with political powers, cultural powers, with the teaching of architecture. All of philosophy in general, all of Western metaphysics, if one can speak in this global way of a Western metaphysics, is inscribed in architecture, which is not just the monument in stone, which gathers up in its body all the political, religious, cultural interpretations of a society. Consequently, deconstruction can also be an architectural deconstruction, which once again does not mean a demolition of architectural values. On the one hand, one has to consider that this architecture called deconstructive, in a nutshell, begins precisely by putting into question everything to which architecture has been subjugated, namely, the value of habitation, utility, technical ends, religious investments, sacralization, all of these values which are not themselves architectural.

In other words, we now know – or have no excuse for not knowing – that deconstruction is not a technique or a method, and hence that there is no question of "applying" it. We know that it is not a moment of liberation, but a moment of the deepest concern with limits. In fact, *deconstructions* – Derrida insists on using the plural form – are everywhere. They are not limited to the

---

24 Jacques Derrida, *Psyché: Inventions de l'autre*, Collection La Philosophie en effet (Paris: Galilée, 1987).

practice of literary or philosophical criticism, within a classroom, a university, or any other institution.

"Deconstruction is inventive or it is nothing at all". But what exactly does the word "to invent" mean? The first meaning of the word is "to create" or "to design" something not existing before, for example the steam engine, the telephone, the plane, and so on. In a sense, the history of technology is the history of inventions. Sigmund Freud in *Das Unbehagen in der Kultur* (1930) maintained that in every tool humanity perfects its own human organs, whether motor or sensory, or is removing the limits to their functioning. Such inventions as a wheel, bicycle, car, and plane reinforce our motor skills; spectacles, microscopes, telescopes reinforce our sensory skills; and paper, books, writing, tape-recorders, and, finally, computers amplify our intelligence. For Derrida this reinforcement would also be a form of weakness, if we remember the analysis about "pharmakon", which could be understood as a remedy and the poison at the same time.

The second meaning of the word "to invent" is "to discover", or "to find" something existing before, for example genetic code, water, same unknown animal. In this sense the history of science is the history of inventions. Thomas Samuel Kuhn in *The Structure of Scientific Revolutions* used this meaning of the word "invention" when he wrote that "for men like Kelvin, Crookes, and Roentgen, whose research dealt with radiation theory or with cathode ray tubes, the discovery of X-rays necessarily violated one paradigm as it created another".[25] Derrida in the same context wrote: "An invention always presupposes some illegality, the breaking of an implicit contract; inserts a disorder into the peaceful ordering of things, it disregards the proprieties".[26]

And the third meaning of the word "invention" is the capacity for inventing, to make up, to think of, for example the capacity to generate the stories and even sentences. When Noam Chomsky says that "the language is reinvented each time it is learned" and when he writes about the "creative aspect of language use", he recalls this meaning of the word "invention".[27] The normal use of language is innovative, in the sense that much of what we say is entirely new, not a representation of anything that we have heard before and not even similar in pattern to sentences or discourse that we heave heard in the past.

There is one important feature which is in common to these three meanings: in every one of these three cases invention concerns finding something: (1)

25 Thomas Samuel Kuhn, *The Structure of Scientific Revolutions* (University of Chicago Press, 1962), p. 124.

26 Jacques Derrida, *Psyché: Inventions de l'autre*.

27 Noam Chomsky, *Language and Mind* (New York, 1968), p. 10.

something new, (2) something tacit and hidden, (3) and something which allows us to generate an infinite sequence of supplementation. Derrida suggested in *Psyche*: "[i]nvention begins by being susceptible to repetition, exploitation, reinscription". It is because the name of "invention" derives from the Latin *invenire*, that is "to find", but also *venir* ("to come", "to arrive", "to recover", "to occur") and even *revenir* ("to return", "to come back").

At this point I would like to draw my last conclusion. There is naturally a desire, for whoever speaks or writes, to leave one's signature in an idiomatic, that is, irreplaceable, manner. But as soon as there is a mark that is the possibility of a repetition, as soon as there is language, generality has entered the scene and the idiom compromises with something that is not idiomatic: with a common language, concepts, laws, general norms. On the other hand there are also some general rules, some procedures that can be transposed by analogy but these rules are taken up in a text which is each time a unique element. Institutions (the general) and the idiomatic (the singular) meet each other in the events of inventions.

V. Roland Barthes reads Michel Houellebecq's *The Map and the Territory*

Photography is subversive not when it frightens, repels, or even stigmatizes, but when it is pensive, when it thinks.

Roland Barthes[1]

– *"As remuneration, as I told you, we've budgeted for ten thousand euros. Franz, my gallerist, told me that I could, instead, offer you a painting, but I'm a bit uncomfortable with that, as it would be delicate for you to refuse. So, a priori, we'll say ten thousand euros; but if you prefer a painting, it's a deal."*
– *"A painting," – Houellebecq said pensively. "Well, I have walls to hang it on. It's the only thing I really have, in my life: walls."*

Michel Houellebecq[2]

The lower sensitivity to light of the early plates made necessary a long period of exposure in the open. This, on the other hand, made it desirable to station the model as well as possible in a place where nothing stood in the way of quiet exposure.

Walter Benjamin[3]

1. Adjacency and randomness

Roland Barthes, in his perhaps most risky and personal book entitled *La chamber claire. Note sur la photographie* puts forward a hypothesis that the genius of photography is hidden in the individual, singular existence, absolutely idiomatic in the language which can only be expressed by the word *contingence* [*contingency*], signifying both adjacency and randomness. Barthes confronts us with a statement, which is not at all obvious: "What the Photograph reproduces to infinity has occurred only once: the Photograph mechanically repeats what could never be repeated existentially"[4]. Barthes's non-obviousness does not stem from the fact that he does not talk about what cannot be repeated but above

---

1 Roland Barthes, *Camera Lucida. Reflections on Photography*. trans. Richard Howard, (New York: Hill and Wang 1982), p. 67.

2 Michel Houellebecq, *The Map and the Territory*, trans. Gavin Bowd, (New York: Vintage 2012), p. 91.

3 Walter Benjamin, *A Short History of Photography*, trans. Phil Patton, "Artforum" 15, 6 [February 1977]: p. 204.

4 Roland Barthes, *Camera Lucida*, p. 4.

all, as he suggests, from the fact that the ambiguity of the photograph stems from the sameness of the image and the subject: the photograph is "never distinguished from its referent", "a pipe here is always and intractably a pipe", "Photograph always carries its referent with itself" or rather abducts it, affected by "amorous or funeral immobility"[5]. To remain in the bondage of photography is to remain in the bondage of mourning.

It seems that Barthes is particularly intrigued by the question of why from all the things in the world, in the whole chaos of images which surrounds us, we are always stricken by one image, which is the very singularity, *contingence* – adjacency to the world, and randomness in the world? Why is truth, our truth, always singular and always a most intimate image demanding the "impossible", the "scandalous" act of being made public? Truth, identity and death are in Barthes so tightly linked that they are doomed to their random adjacency. The position from which Barthes observes and describes photography is obvious. Barthes does not write as a photographer, the subject taking the pictures, the predator hunting for images. Nor does Barthes write from the position of the victim, the position of the photographed, who becomes the image. What is then the position occupied by the author of *La chambre claire*?

Barthes writes about three significant forms of practicing photography: the subject can take the pictures (hunt), the subject can be subjected to the process of depiction (die), finally the subject may view the images (call them to resurrection). Barthes is convinced that in the moment of depiction the subject has a microexperience of death and becomes an apparition, but Barthes also believes that in the moment of reviewing the photograph the apparition acquires a new reality and becomes its double. Hence the risk: the return of one's most familiar deceased, the most intimate photograph (mother) is inevitable. Barthes does not kill, Barthes does not die, Barthes calls for the resurrection of the image.

This last practice – calling and summoning the dead through images – is dangerous inasmuch as it is always linked with the work of mourning and the return of the dead, especially when, as in the case of Barthes, during the recollection of images we are dealing with an attempt to reach a new science, new knowledge – phenomenology of singularity (*mathesis singularis*) and when we are dealing with "unsuccessful" mourning, mourning which is futile, one that only distances us in time from the object of suffering, but does not change suffering itself. "The photograph itself is in no way animated (I do not believe in "life like" photographs), but it animates me: this is what creates every

5 *Ibid.*, p. 5-6.

adventure"[6]. In such phenomenology the "essence of things" always presents itself as a wound. Barthes considers photography from the point of view of inquisitiveness, *punctum*, i.e. the sting which a photograph gives to the viewer; Barthes considers photography from the point of view of the wound (being). "A photograph's *punctum* is that accident which pricks me (but also bruises me, is poignant to me)"[7]. But also – stings, marks, cuts, punctuates, throws, penetrates, and finally – "inflicts" the wound. He talks about the transition of the photograph during its development [*développer*], but that which is transformed by chemical reactions is already given, it the very essence of being wounded, something, which can no longer be transformed, but can only be repeated. It is a living motionlessness. Photography may develop [*rèvèler*], but what gets developed is the persistent existence of the developed object.

Barthes is not interested in phenomenology understood as a science about the eidetic, universal and timeless (Husserl's case), but neither is he interested in the pure idiomaticity, singleness, and elevating the individual biography of the individual to the sole model of truth which we have at our disposal (Freud's case). For Barthes, truth is always the truth of someone and the discussion of photographs has to end with a reflection on the subject of the Image, the most personal and intimate, adjacent to my body and to my imagination, but also the most unified with me in the randomness of my existence. "Death is the *eidos* of that Photograph"[8]. Because of this stigmatization with death, photography for Barthes has more to do with theater than with the discovery of the camera: the first actors were marked in the community by the fact of playing (calling and summoning) the dead.

It is no different in the case of the first photographers, who worked for the theater. Louis Jacques Mandé Daguerre, a French painter, set designer, author of a work entitled *Descriptions des procédés de peinture et d'éclairage inventés par Daguerre, et appliqués par lui aux tableaux du Diorama*, is credited with the invention of photography, apart from inventing the daguerreotype in 1839, and also has to his credit a theatrical invention – diorama, i.e. a kind of painting created on both sides of translucent fabric which with proper lighting gave the impression of three-dimensionality of the objects. Let us also recall that Daguerre's method allowed him to obtain a proper photograph, but only in one copy, because the image formed on the plate was already a positive image. There was only one image. "Daguerre's photographs", writes Benjamin in an essay with the telling title *A Short History of Photography*, "are iodized silver

6 *Ibid.*, p. 20.
7 *Ibid.*, p. 28.
8 *Ibid.*, p. 15.

plates exposed in the *camera obscura* which could be turned back and forth until, in the proper light, one could make out a delicate, light gray image. They were unique and they cost, on the average, 25 gold francs per plate. They were frequently kept in cases as decorations [...]"[9]

Among the objects adored by Barthes, a photograph is the object perhaps the most coveted and beneficial at the same time. It is the *punctum* of all his work. To Barthes, literature is an object with enigmatic signifier[10], which causes the desire to overthrow the written language, to abolish the distinction between the metalanguage and the language of analysis, and the desire of unification with something, which can only be called the "practice of writing". Fashion, on the other hand, is an institution torn between the pragmatism of clothing and the nonchalant pursuit of the novelty, and being the pretense of luxury[11], which condemns it to the ambiguous antonymy – fashion is constructed as both a "pragmatic program" and a "spectacle of luxury", because it has to propagate the aristocratic model, for which the source of prestige is Pure Fashion and must simultaneously create a world of consumers, the consequence of which is the Naturalized Fashion. The language, as a prototypical semiological system, is an institution torn between the system and the event, paradigmality and syntagmaticity, the signifier and the signified, metaphor and metonymy[12] and in this sense, it is never reconciled with itself, and hence becomes synonymous with the division of the subject. Myth is a logos stolen and hijacked, sentenced to a constant escape of the signified, and the work of the myth consists therein that it does not lead to the disappearance of the deformed material, whereby the relation linking the meaning proper with its explicit sense is a relation of distortion[13]. Finally, the love discourse is condemned not only to a fragmentary character, but above all to the absence of the subject – the Other (loved) is constantly on the move, on a journey, and the loving (I) is always present, at home, defined by the one who is constantly in motion[14]. Thus, photography is the only hope for a coherence and continuity, truth and resurrection.

---

9 Walter Benjamin, *A Short History of Photography*, p. 201.

10 Roland Barthes, *Science versus Literature*, [in:] "Times Literary Supplement", September 28, 1967. Reprinted as *From Science to Literature*, Roland Barthes: *The Rustle of Language*, trans. Richard Howard. (Oxford: Basil Blackwell, 1986). pp. 3-10.

11 Roland Barthes, *The Fashion System*, trans. Matthew Ward and Richard Howard, (New York: Hill & Wang), 1983.

12 Roland Barthes, *Elements of Semiology*, trans. A. Lavers and C. Smith, (New York: Hill & Wang, 1964).

13 Roland Barthes, *Mythologies*, trans. Annette Lavers, (New York: Hill & Wang, 1972).

14 Roland Barthes, *A Lover's Discourse: Fragments*, trans. Richard Howard, (London: Vintage Books, 2002).

Photography is the Easter Sunday, an empty grave. Although Barthes perceived the organ of the photographer to be the finger and not the eye, the cameras themselves were, and are, in fact, "clocks for seeing", in which one can still hear the "living sound of the wood", still only photography gives one the chance to recover the truth about one's adjacency to oneself and to one's body, only photography gives hope for *contingence,* which signifies – random adjacency. Photography, therefore, is the *punctum* of Barthes's whole life.

As a result, Barthes writes that what he seeks in the picture is neither Art nor Message, but Reference, which constitutes the primary assumption of photography. "I call 'photographic referent' not the *optionally* real thing to which an image or a sign refers but the *necessarily* real thing which has been placed before the lens, without which there would be no photograph"[15]. Image is not a reflection of some shape on a photographic film, or a range of light intensities, but is the very emanation of the object, it is taken out, expressed, extracted through the operation of light. Image is more of a sculpture than a painting. That is why photography has something in common with the resurrection, with the case of the Shroud of Turin, and its essence is the sole confirmation of what it presents; it is the sole certification of the event's authenticity. It is a wound, a *punctum.*

These long citations from Barthes, this introductory meditation on *La chambre claire* is basically supposed to put me in a more inquisitive, sensitive frame of mind, a wounded reading of Michel Houellebecq's last novel entitled *The Map and the Territory*. It is not just about the fact all the tracks left by Barthes, and partly also by Benjamin, concerning the topic of photography return in Houellebecq's work. It is also not about the fact that Barthes or Benjamin provide us the methodological instruments which allow us to dissect the corpse of *The Map and the Territory* with greater precision. It is more about the fact that the juxtaposition of Barthes's confessions and Houellebecq's novel allows me to think again about the category of testimony and giving testimony through the art of photography. It allows me to ask the question: what is registering?, what is a testimony?, and what function do registration and photographic depiction fulfill today in the "testimony" about the surface (if not the nature) of the world, especially the world of objects devoid of voice?

Benjamin, cited here, quotes Brecht, who writes soberly – "A photograph of the Krupp works or the A. E.G. tells us next to nothing about these institutions. Actual reality has slipped into the functional. The reification of human relations – the factory, say – means that they are no longer explicit"[16]. If then

15 Roland Barthes, *Camera Lucida*, p. 76.

16 Walter Benjamin, *A Short History of Photography*, p. 213-214.

"photography tells us next to nothing about these institutions" because "reality has slipped into the functional", then what does it say? And is its silence not speech just the same, speech which is more radical and politically critical than the speech of numerous words reaching the roots of reality? Is photography not a subversive factor, when it does not frighten, repel or even stigmatize, but when it provides one too much to think about? But when does it provide food for thought? When does the image not restrain thinking, but initiates it? Is thinking possible at all, if the image here is touched with "amorous or funeral immobility"? Is it possible to return to the old photographic plates of lower photosensitivity, which – as Benjamin notes – necessitated longer exposure in the open air and to "station the model as well as possible in a place where nothing stood in the way of quiet exposure"? Does the work *Michel Houellebecq, Writer* have a simiarly aimed *punctum*?

2. Painting entitled *Michel Houellebecq, Writer*

Barthes says that "[...] look is always potentially crazy: it is at once the effect of truth and the effect of madness"[17]. I understand that this is a declaration in favor of the thesis of the indeterminacy of the look. Look is potentially crazy because it does not have a designated object of the look. The object of the look is always random. Randomness determines the madness. Yet madness does not exhaust the look. The look is the result of madness and truth. The truth requires attaching the look to the object. Probably no one gave a stronger argument to Barthes's thesis than Michel Houellebecq, who devotes his latest novel entirely to madness and the truth of the image. The main character of *The Map and the Territory* is an "artist", Jed Martin. "Becoming a bit confused, Jed ended up saying that yes, in a certain sense, you could say he was an artist"[18]. Michel Houellebecq, writing about his artist, Jed Martin, states: "Jed devoted his life (or at least his professional life, which quite quickly became the whole of his life) to art, to the production of representations of the world, in which people were never meant to live"[19]. The idea which became the *logo* of the novel is the murder of Michel Houellebecq, a writer. Michel Houellebecq, thanks to Jed Martin, creates an image (map) of the territory of Michel Houellebecq. Jed Martin does the painting *Michel Houellebecq, Writer* which is the reason of the death of Michel Houellebecq, a writer and the author of *The Map and the Territory*, as well as the author of the "introduction" to Jed Martin's works.

17 Roland Barthes, *Camera Lucida*, p. 113.
18 Michel Houellebecq, *The Map and the Territory*, p. 42.
19 *Ibid.*, p. 19.

The evolution of Jed Martin's aesthetics goes through three non-accidental phases. Jed Martin's eye is crazy, but his paintings are the result of madness and truth. In the first phase of his creative activity, as a graduate of the Academy of Fine Arts, Jed Martin dealt with photography. His ambition was to develop a comprehensive catalogue of human products of the industrial age. "His six years of work had produced more than eleven thousand photos. Stored in TIFF format, with a lowest-resolution JPEG, they were easily held on a Western Digital 640GB hard disk, which weighed a little under seven ounces"[20]. In Martin's work screws, nuts and wrenches took an appearance of discreetly shining jewels[21]. Let us say that it is the Iron Age, the aesthetic Industrial Age, the age of faith in the durability of objects and truth stemming from the long process of exposure of the shell of the object.

The next stage of his artistic work was the idea of taking pictures of Michelin's maps. During the trip exploring the most beautiful countryside of France he has an epiphany: the map is more important than the territory.

> This map was sublime. Overcome, he began to tremble in front of the food display. Never had he contemplated an object as magnificent, as rich in emotion and meaning, as this 1/150,000-scale Michelin map of the Creuse and the Haute-Vienne. The essence of modernity, of scientific and technical apprehension of the world, was here combined with the essence of animal life"[22].

Martin employed a technique of photographing a map at an angle of thirty degrees from the horizontal, to achieve the highest "depth of field", and subsequently adding the blur effect in Photoshop. Visible in the background are winding roads, villages and woods, which looked like a landscape out of dreams, fabulous and completely inaccessible. Jed Martin's real discovery was therefore not aesthetic, but economic.

> When he put the first photograph online, an enlargement of the Hazebrouck region, the series was sold out in a little under three hours. Obviously, the price wasn't quite right. After a few tentative weeks it stabilized at around two thousand euros for a 40-by-60-format print. There, that was now sorted out: he knew his market price[23].

In this way, he acquired his vocation and his profession – profession and vocation of an artist. The calling to truth means for the cultural subject of the West the finding of one's vocation and profession (*Beruf*)[24]. Let's say that in the

---

20 *Ibid.*, p. 20.

21 *Ibid.*, p. 26.

22 *Ibid.*, p. 28.

23 *Ibid.*, p. 54.

24 Max Weber wrote: "Now it is unmistakable that even in the German word *Beruf*, and perhaps still more clearly in the English calling, a religious conception, that of a task set

history of the work of Jed Martin it is the representational era, the aesthetic era of reproduction, the era of belief in the repeatability of a thing in its copy, its double and the truth stemming from the structural, architectural, syntactic recovery of the object. Martin's images repeat what can never repeat itself existentially.

This calling, this interpellation to become his profession is most fully revealed in the third period of Jed's work. Jed Martin abandons the creation of maps for easel painting. According to the description in the novel one should probably assume that Jed Martin was a hyperrealist. For several years his paintings were created in two series: presenting humans at work (a waiter, a call center employee, a prostitute) and presenting meetings. Jed Martin creates the following series of paintings: *Haymaking in Germany*, *Ferdinand Desroches, Horse Butcher*, *Claude Vorilhon, Bar-Tabac Manager*, *Maya Dubois, Remote Maintenance Assistant*, *The Journalist Jean-Pierre Pernaut Chairing an Editorial Meeting*, *The Stock Exchange Flotation of Shares in Beate Uhse*, *The Engineer Ferdinand Piëch Visiting the Production Workshops at Molsheim*, *Forward to Irrigated Rice Growing in the Province of Hunan!*, *Damien Hirst and Jeff Koons Dividing Up the Art Market*[25], *The Architect Jean-Pierre Martin Leaving the Management of His Business*, *Aimée, Escort Girl*, *Bill Gates and Steve Jobs Discussing the Future of Information Technology*, *Michel Houellebecq, Writer*. Jed Martin in his work depicts forty-two typical professions, jobs, callings of a man of the west (Beruf), offering us a kind of phenomenology of work which allows for a reconstruction of the working conditions in a post-industrial society. Twenty-two further paintings, called the

---

by God, is at least suggested. [...] And if we trace the history of the word through the civilized languages, it appears that neither the predominantly Catholic peoples nor those of classical antiquity have possessed any expression of similar connotation for what we know as a calling (in the sense of a life-task, a definite field in which to work), while one has existed for all predominantly Protestant peoples /Max Weber, *The Protestant ethic and the spirit of capitalism*, trans. Talcott Parsons, (New York: Charles Scribner's Sons 1950), p. 79/.

25 Damien Hirst, an English avant-garde artist, born in 1965, Turner award laureate. Among the best-well known works of Hirst is the *Natural History* series, which includes dead, dissected animals (among others: a cow, a sheep, and a shark) immersed in formalin and placed in glass cases. The series includes, inter alia, *The Physical Impossibility of Death in the Mind of Someone Living*, depicting a tiger shark which measures 14 feet in length. It was sold in 2004 for $ 8 million. Jeff Koons – born in 1955, in Pennsylvania, is an American artist who uses the everyday objects, readymade toys, and is inspired by advertising. In the beginning of the 90's, he made a scandalous series of sculptures in glass and plastic, *Made in Heaven*, showing him with his wife in positions of the *Kama Sutra*, kept in a kitschy style.

Series of Business Compositions, are devoted to confrontations and meetings and are supposed to show the functioning of the economy as such, apart from the subjective engagement of the subject of work. Let us say that in the works of Jed Martin it is the age of identification, an aesthetic age of interpellation, i.e. the age of faith that the human organisms become subjects thanks to their answer to the interpellation (recruitment, call, seduction) of the ideology/discourse, hence becoming a kind of effect of interpellation[26].

The key moment of the book is the meeting between Michel Houellebecq, the writer, with Jed Martin, the artist, during which Jed, the artist, makes the writer an offer of writing an introductory essay for a catalog of his exhibition, for the price of 10,000 €. Additional payment would constitute a painting done by Jed Martin, entitled: *Michel Houellebecq, Writer.* This painting completes the third phase of Jed Martin's work, the age of "paintings of professions". It is also important for us to experience what kind of transfer occurs between the writer and the artist, the word and the painting, the territory and the map, Michel Houellebecq and Jade Martin. Well, both craftsmen make their own replicas (doubles): the writer creates a map (interpretation) of the territory of work (paintings) of the artist, and the artist makes a map of the territory (words) of the writer. After this exchange, after this transfer, after this mutual wounding, i.e. finding one's *punctum*, after the "scandalous" act of being made public and having put a price on one's work, i.e. giving it a market identity, the writer-artist has no other reason (argument) for repeating the process of life. At least in its present form. That is why Houellebecq, being in possession of the painting *Michel Houellebecq, Writer*, is murdered with surgical precision, and Jed Martin has to abandon the age of "paintings of professions". Houellebecq's crime has been extensively photographed and got its map. This map has become the domain of the most objective order, the order of the police

> [In the police file] there were about fifty A4 prints on glossy paper. Each represented a rectangle of the floor of the living room where the murder had taken place, of basically a square meter. The photographs were clear and well exposed, devoid of shadow, taken from practically directly above. They overlapped only very slightly, and put together they faithfully re-created the floor of the room[27].

26 I refer here to Louis Althusser's theory of ideological apparatuses. Althusser uses the term *interpeller*, which has several meanings in French. To trivialize the matter slightly, I would say that for Althusser interpellation was a practice subordinated to a particular ritual and the most appropriate translation of this word to English would be the word "recruitment" or "call". Louis Althusser, *Ideology and Ideological State Apparatuses*, trans. Ben Brewster, (New York: Monthly Review Press 1971).

27 Michel Houellebecq, *The Map and the Territory*, p. 195.

Benjamin remarks that the pictures of Eugène Atget and August Sander – two of the greatest artists of the image, to whom we will return in a moment – are similar to the pictures which register the crime scenes, adding immediately: but is there even a piece of land today which is not a crime scene? Here, finally, is an image devoid of *punctum*, an image in which *punctum* is only a subject, it is a uniform photograph, containing only a clear field of vision without the seeing subject, a pure study. The police picture is, after all, an image of the object set apart, in a place of seclusion, where nothing interrupts the absolute concentration. But will it allow for the exposure of the Truth?

Yet the truth is exposed not thanks to the neutral image of the police, but thanks to the artist, Jed Martin, who in the territory of the writer notices a lack of his painting (map). The work *Michel Houellebecq, Writer* does not return to the market for years, but finally the perpetrator of the murder, a surgeon and an art collector, is exposed. Jed crosses another threshold of his life – he stops painting the pictures of the calling (work) and after the euthanasia of his father, who, ill with cancer, had fled in secret to a Swiss center with the pathetic name Dignitas, sells his house and settles in the countryside, in his grandparents' estate. The painting of the writer (map) entitled *Michel Houellebecq, Writer* returns to the territory of the artist, Jed becomes its owner again, but the artist cannot keep this gift marked with the death of the writer, hence he puts it into circulation, giving it nothing more than the meaning of exchange value: "He phoned Franz that very evening to explain to him what had happened, and his intention to put *Michel Houellebecq, Writer* on the market"[28].

After many years of silence, he returns to his paintings and creates videograms. During more than ten of the final years of his life, Jed only gives testimony of existence of the world: since ten years he has been throwing his audiovisual equipment to his van and looking for a point of solitude, a secluded place, where nothing stands in the way of absolute concentration, a place, in which photography hijacks its reference and continues to exist in the slavery of mourning. After having found such a place Jed abandoned his lenses with 1.9 aperture and maximum focal length of 1200 mm for a 24-by-26 format and allowed them to register random fragments of the ground.

> Once the framing was done, he plugged the power supply of the cameoscope into the cigarette lighter socket, switched it on, and walked back home, leaving the motor to run for several hours, sometimes during the rest of the day and even overnight – the capacity of the hard disk would have allowed him almost a week of continuous shooting[29].

28 Michel Houellebecq, *The Map and the Territory*, p. 250.

29 *Ibid.*, p. 265.

Next, he processed the footage, which consisted primarily in editing, because the author would leave only a couple of frames from a three-hour-long session. Such editing enabled him to obtain "those moving plant tissues, with their carnivorous suppleness, peaceful and pitiless at the same time, which constitute without any doubt the most successful attempt, in Western art, at representing how plants see the world"[30]. Is this not a return to the situation of the first photographs, which Benjamin recalls: the lower sensitivity to light of the early plates made necessary a long period of exposure in the open. Jed Martin photographs in the open air in places of absolute seclusion.

Yet this was not the end of the evolution of Jed Martin, who after ten years devoted himself entirely to filming used objects: cell phones, a computer keyboard, a desk lamp, computer motherboards. Sometimes he accelerated the decomposition of these objects by pouring sulfuric acid over them. However, the finale of his artistic work was the development of a program for superimposing images, which allowed for superimposition of ninety-six video images, with the option of adjusting the brightness, saturation, and contrast.

> It was this software that allowed him to obtain those long, hypnotic shots where the industrial objects seem to drown, progressively submerged by the proliferation of layers of vegetation. Occasionally they give the impression of struggling, of trying to return to the surface; then they are swept away by a wave of grass and leaves and plunge back into a plant magma, at the same time as their surfaces fall apart, revealing microprocessors, batteries, and memory cards[31].

Certainly, here death became the *eidos* of the Photograph. Certainly, these photographs may invoke, call out, but what has been invoked is the persistent existence of the object, at once developed but also recalled and invoked.

3. Father or the Pre-Raphaelites

In the book *The Map and the Territory* we encounter the subject of a painting strictly connected with the subject of death – the suicidal disappearance of the mother and the return of the terminally ill father. *Jed Martin's memory did not preserve any image of the mother, although it retained the memory of her photographs which enshrined her beauty.* However, the relationship with his father, a man who had been trying to become an architect-artist throughout his life, and at the age of ten had built in the barn a nest for swallows, which swallows refused to occupy, this relationship with his father is exhibited by

30 *Ibid.*, p. 266.

31 *Ibid.*, p. 267.

Houellebecq as the central relationship – the main painting. Above all, it is astounding that at the time of his approaching death, Jed's father speaks to him in a confessional tone, moved, nearly awed, as if his voice demanded comfort, care, support and his son's very presence. At the moment of his father's death the son becomes his father's father.

The father visits his son at Christmas and tells him about his struggles with life. Above all, he relates him about his two intellectual fascinations – Charles Fourier and William Morris. According to Jed's father, what really interested Fourier was not sex, as is commonly believed, but the organization of production. Primarily, Fournier asked: why does man work at all? Liberals respond that this is due to the pursuit of profit; Marxists turn this problem into the question about the conditions for the elimination of the labor process. According to Fourier, people had worked before capitalism emerged and their work was related to the love of God and a sense of honor. Jed's father suggests that this was what his son, Jed Martin – the artist, wanted to convey in his paintings of professions.

Thus, Jed Martin becomes the artist of the times of post-production. Marx's great dream of the coming of the day, in which humanity will be fully socialized, and its sole purpose will be to provide hospitality to the process of life, and the difference between work and production will disappear completely, so that all production will be work, well this great dream of Marx, which de facto is the great dream of mankind, is fulfilled before our eyes, in our world, but it is fulfilled as a curse. After all, at all stages of his work Marx defines the human through work, and then leads him to the society in which this most powerful human force has ceased to be necessary. As a result, humanity is faced with the tragic choice: between a productive slave and an unproductive freedom. The price of absolute freedom is that the place of real life (work) is usurped by a supplementary life – unlimited consumption. Jed Martin, therefore, depicts the last working man.

Hence, according to Marx, capitalism was born around the sixteenth century, when the model: commodity – money – commodity, representing the earlier forms of economy, changes into the model: money – commodity – money, which means that the sale with the purpose of buying is replaced by buying in order to sell. The essence of capitalism is, therefore, that the capitalist invests money in the production of goods which he sells in order to get even more money. Marx refers to the surplus emerging during production as the value added. Jed Martin experiences it all as a formula: sustaining the process of accumulation constitutes the meaning of life, the exchange value in the form of a numerical value of money is the only value.

Yet it is not Fourier, but William Morris who is the main character to whom Jed's father is trying to allude. Morris is an appropriate object of artistic identification of the dying father. Thanks to Morris, Jed's father can above all tell the story of degeneration and decline of art, and as a result of work, and present the views of artistic formation usually defined as the Pre-Raphaelite Brotherhood. According Pre-Raphaelites, one should abolish the distinction between art and craft, between the concept (project) and the execution (incarnation): each person can be the creator of works of art in the form of a painting, clothes, or furniture, and in everyday life every person deserves to be surrounded by beautiful objects. Morris combined this belief with his socialist activities, which led him in the direction of becoming involved in the movement for the liberation of the proletariat. He believed in the coming of the golden age, when industrialists will be replaced by artists. Nearing death, Jed's father mentions Fourier and Morris, reminiscing the images from his youth, reliving the hopes which constituted the history of his life and their loss. Son listens: he photographs his father's dead hopes that suddenly come alive at the time of his death.

Interestingly, the character of William Morris returns in his book *The Map and the Territory* in an interview between Jed Martin and Michel Houellebecq. Houellebecq – the writer is surprised that Jed's father – an unfulfilled artist was fascinated with Morris, whom "almost nobody knows". Houellebecq is in possession of Morris's book, decorated with Art Nouveau designs, in which this Pre-Raphaelite states that artists are the last representatives of the craft, which was annihilated by industrial production. William Morris is not only a painter and illustrator, he is also the editor of books: in 1890, he opens the printing house on the outskirts of London with the resolution to restore the dignity of the book. The prints in Morris's printing house were set by hand and copied by hand presses. The Pre-Raphaelite ideal was the Renaissance book and illuminated medieval codes, so they used the decorative motifs of the Renaissance, and for typesetting they used the font modeled on Jenson's Roman typeface.

In a sense, the author of *Elementary Particles* develops and completes for Jed Martin Morris's story, related by his father only in fragments. Houellebecq completes Morris's story with the intimate details of life of a Pre-Raphaelite: he reminds Jed that another artist Dante Gabriel Rossetti replaces Morris in his own marriage bed. Perhaps in this way Houellebecq indicates the paradox of Pre-Raphaelite aesthetics and ethics: they committed themselves to handicraft, thus creating expensive works, and as a result inaccessible and in conflict with the socialist desire to popularize beautiful objects. Similarly, they were devoted to the idea of joint property, *community art*, the art of speaking with the Others, yet in their private life they became victims of their own selfishness.

Jed's father and Houellebecq communicate to Jed not only the story of William Morris, but, above all, their own death, or in fact the form of this death, its inscriptions. Houellebecq dies butchered, the father dies cremated. Houellebecq is murdered in contract hit put out by doctor Petissaud, who created compositions from human bodies. The doctor's office contained a picture of the artist Francis Bacon, two plastinations of von Hagens and a canvas titled *Michel Houellebecq, Writer*. However, Jed's father chooses a "dignified death" in the Swiss resort dealing with serene demise by euthanasia. Like most visitors of the resort, he chooses cremation as the most appropriate form of his own disappearance. But it is not the point that the writer's death and the death of the architect are ways of dying worthy of the biopolitical times, that are part of the politics of death and the politics of life, the point is that this death must have its presentation, it must have its map, and as a result must have its witness. Jed Martin is a witness to the death of Houellebecq – the writer and the death of his father.

Now, after his father's cremation and the dismemberment of Houellebecq, it becomes clear why they both gave Jed lessons on William Morris. Jed Martin is supposed to become not so much a contemporary of William Morris – a Pre-Raphaelite, but rather a modern Franciscan Tertiary, a Giotto di Bondone of late capitalism. Giotto, at the request of the Prince of Naples, created the prototype of Jed's work about human professions, decorating the palace chapel with frescoes and creating a series of paintings entitled *Famous people* in the great hall of the royal palace. Capitalism, by transforming goods into an image and by compressing space does not so much exceed its physical limitations as it acquires an external form – the form of the image. In this way, aesthetics has triumphed over ethics, the image dominated the narrative, map dominated the territory, and the ephemerality and fragmentation outweighed the eternal laws and coherent policy.

4. Involuntary images

Walter Benjamin, stating that the fog which encircles the beginnings of photography is not as thick as the darkness which envelops the beginnings of print, basically evokes only two names from this short history emerging from the aura – those of Eugène Atget and August Sander. Atget photographically documented Paris: George Eastman Housec collection currently holds 500 pictures of the city. For over 20 years, Atget collected photographs in the 18-by-24 format, depicting all streets of the old Paris; they became the testimony of the architecture of the city space from the 15th to the 19th century. This enormous documentation is so monstrous that Atget surely had the right to say towards the end of his life: *I possess all of Old Paris!* August Sander, on the other hand, tried to realize a gigantic project under the title *Menschen des 20. Jahrhunderts*. It was supposed to document the full spectrum of people living in the 20th century Germany. The photographs were supposed to be divided into seven groups, corresponding to seven social classes. Sander intended to portray the peasants, workers and the unemployed, as well as students, artists, and politicians. A part of the photographs from the planned five hundred appeared in a publication entitled *Antlitz der Zeit*. In 1933 the publication of the *Face of our Time* was prohibited because Sander presented the diversity of the German nation, which did not match the Nazi vision of the Germans and the Aryan type. For a long time, there was silence surrounding the human face, permeated by a curious glance, Sander, as opposed to the photographs of the paparazzi, radicalized this silence. Certainly, this provides us with a confirmation of Barthes's intuition: *Photography is subversive not when it frightens, repels, or even stigmatizes, but when it is pensive, when it thinks*[32].

Benjamin points to the fact that Atget's photographs showing Paris are not so much lonely, as devoid of a mood; the city in the pictures is empty like an apartment waiting for a new tenant. On the other hand, Sander's photographs, which are not only an album, but above all an atlas, change our perception and understanding of the human figure as well as what the definition of a portrait is. Sander approached the task of giving testimony of the human physiognomy not as a scholar, instructed by anthropologists and sociologists expert on human races, not as a physician possessing knowledge about human tendencies, but based on direct observation, film speed itself, he provided us with a serious argument that image is a result of truth and madness. When a human face found its way to the photographic plate, uniqueness and continuity of the human face intermingled as much as the repeatability and the surface of the human image. "Man is created in the image of God and God's image cannot be captured by any human machine"[33]. Perhaps this is the reason why the "first people to be reproduced entered the visual space of photography with their innocence intact – or rather, without inscription."[34]

One cannot fail to notice the affinity and similarity between the works of Eugène Atget and August Sander and the work of Jed Martin. This phase of Jed Martin's work, which we named "professional", reproduces and simply repeats Sander's project entitled *Menschen des 20. Jahrhunderts*. On the other hand, the

32 Roland Barthes, *Camera Lucida*, p. 38.

33 Walter Benjamin, *A Short History of Photography*, p. 200.

34 *Ibid.*, p. 205.

last phase of Martin's artistic work, in which he returns to the lonely photography of still life, is a paraphrase of Atget's project. In his work, however, it is not Paris that is lonely and deserted, but the whole planet Earth is completely subject-less: spotless and unsigned, i.e. uninterpellated.

Roland Barthes, in his alphabetic autobiography, *Roland Barthes par Roland Barthes* – recently published also in Polish – confesses:

> I have kept only the images which enthrall me, without my knowing why [...]. And, as it happens, only the images of my youth fascinate me. [...] When consideration (with the etymological sense of seeing the stars together as significant constellation) treats the image as a detached being, makes it the object of an immediate pleasure, it no longer has anything to do with the reflection, however oneiric, of an identity; it torments and enthralls itself with a vision which is not morphological (I never look like myself) but organic. [...] Once I produce, once I write, it is the Text itself which (fortunately) dispossesses me of my narrative continuity. [...] The image-repertoire will therefore be closed at the onset of productive life (which for me was my departure from the sanatorium). Another repertoire will then be constituted; that of writing[35].

What has amazed me since the first reading of the mysterious book by Barthes on Barthes is the privileging of the image system. Barthes writes explicitly in the entry on the *Image system* [*L'imaginaire*]: "The vital effort of this book is to stage an image-system"[36]. To stage means here to simply play a role of a theater director – sets up the backstage, assign roles, rewrite the script, design the costumes, place the sources of light. However, what amazes me when I juxtapose the thinking about the images of Barthes and Houellebecq's narration is not only the profound analogy with the experience of the image, not only the approximation of the politics of the image, but above all this feeling of dispossession of the narrative continuity by means of word production. Since I have been producing, since I have been writing, the Text (luckily) dispossesses me of my narrative continuity. Both – Barthes and Houellebecq – have an equal right to say: the image-repertoire will be closed at the onset of productive life, in the life of writing only images of writing will remain. Michel Houellebecq and Jed Martin are one and the same person, but it is Houellebecq who is defeated, doomed to the images of the word and the loss of the continuity of his life, separated from images, which amaze and fascinate – the images of childhood. Jed Martin, through images, which become bodies is not only alienated from himself and his body, but above all inserts himself in the design of the world, becoming again and anew its territory.

---

35 Roland Barthes, *Roland Barthes by Roland Barthes*, trans. Richard Howard, (Berkeley: University of California Press 1994), p. 7.

36 Roland Barthes, *Roland Barthes by Roland Barthes*, p. 109.

VI. The Return of Alcibiades. A Tale on Repression of Eros

This was seized on by those who had particular reason to resent Alcibiades for blocking their own path to any clear political supremacy, and thought that if they could get rid of him they would take over the leadership of the people. So they were concerned to blow up the whole affair and make strident claims that the profanation of the Mysteries and the mutilation of the Herms were part of a plot to subvert the democracy, and that Alcibiades was behind it all: as contributory evidence they cited the undemocratic excesses of his general lifestyle.

Thucydides [1]

But when the opposition and war in such a nature have the effect of one more charm and incentive of life-and if, moreover, in addition to his powerful and irreconcilable drives, a real mastery and subtlety in waging war against oneself, in other words, self-control, self-outwitting, has been inherited or cultivated, too-then those magical, incomprehensible, and unfathomable ones arise, those enigmatic men predestined for victory and seduction, whose most beautiful expression is found in Alcibiades and Caesar (to whose company I should like to add that first European after my taste, the Hohenstaufen Frederick II),15 and among artists perhaps Leonardo da Vinci. They appear in precisely the same ages when that weaker type with its desire for rest comes to the fore: both types belong together and owe their origin to the same causes.

Friedrich Nietzsche[2]

The atopia of Socrates is linked to Eros (Socrates is courted by Alcibiades) and to the numbfish (Socrates electrifies and benumbs Meno). The other whom I love and who fascinates me is atopos.

Roland Barthes[3]

1. Alcibiades' Mystery

In Friedrich Nietzsche's *Beyond Good* Alcibiades appears in a meaningful and thought-provoking milieu: that of Julius Caesar, Frederick II Hohenstaufen, and

---

1 Thucydides, *The Peloponnesian War*, trans. M. Hammond (Oxford/New York: Oxford University Press, 2009), p. 322.

2 Friedrich Nietzsche (1886), *Beyond Good and Evil,* trans. W. Kaufmann (New York: Vintage Books, 1966), p. 112.

3 Roland Barthes, *A Lover's Discourse: Fragments*, trans. Richard Howard, (London: Vintage Books, 2002), p. 34.

Leonardo da Vinci. To Nietzsche, Alcibiades is equally incomprehensible, unfathomable and predestined for victory and seduction. Alcibiades may well be considered an epitome of this type of subjectivity which desires ever greater anxiety and comes to the fore in civilizations breeding "weaker type" of man; peaceful, seeking happiness in leisure, folly, satiety, and the ultimate unity of all – or as St. Augustine says: "the Sabbath of Sabbaths." Nietzsche's impression of Alcibiades corresponds to that of Athenians as formulated by Corinthians in *The Peloponnesian War* by Thucydides. It is in their nature, we learn there, "to have no quiet themselves and to deny quiet to others"[4]. As instructed by Nietzsche, I will approximate the magic of Alcibiades – a man predestined for victory and power. I believe this will help us understand Athens in the days of Pericles, let alone the intellectual and political position of Thucydides[5].

---

4 Thucydides, *The Peloponnesian War*, p. 35.

5 Understandably, my interpretation of *The Peloponnesian War* and the figure of Alcibiades do not follow a traditional approach. First of all, I question the stance of Leo Strauss,, who highlights the opposition of Plato (the primacy of peace and rest) and Thucydides (the primacy of war, power and necessity) in his vision of politics and opposition of lifestyle of Athens (the school of freedom) and Sparta (the school of necessity) /Leo Strauss, *The City and Man*, (Chicago/London: The University of Chicago Press, 1964)/. Simply put, I find both oppositions much exaggerated. Plato's verbal quest for the ideal city meets with a severe reprimand by Thrasymachus who equates justice with the law and the law with the law of stronger, which is not that distant from the logic of Thucydides, who begins with the law of stronger and after questioning its reason justifies it. In addition, would it not do justice to *The Peloponnesian War* to treat it as a collection of speeches that remain dialogically related (both dialectically and polemically)? If so, would it surprise us to see *The Peloponnesian War* staged in a theatre? The reader will also notice that my approach differs from the tradition considering either Pericles or Diodotos as Thucydides' *alter ego* and his *logos*. /*inter alia*: Jacqueline de Romilly, *Histoire et raison chez Thucydide*, (Belles Lettres, Paris: 1956)/. Of the commentators I know only Gerald Mara conceives that *The Peloponnesian War* is in fact in praise of Alcibiades, and that the "return of Alcibiades" is associated with the advent of *eunomia*. Mara is also aware of the fact that Alcibiades served the city as a mediator. Mara's book about justice, necessity and democracy in the ancient world is most eminent analysis on Thucydides' views I have been able to find thus far /Gerald M. Mara, *The Civic Conversations of Thucydides and Plato: Classical Political Philosophy and the Limits of Democracy*, (Albany: State University of New York Press, 2008)/. What I miss in Mara's approach, however, is the lack of in-depth analysis of the erotic and adventurous spirit of Thucydides, which makes of him a mere "diplomat", "intercultural translator", or a "cosmopolitan citizen". Nonetheless, Mara's investigation into the relationship between the action (*ergon*) and the story (*logos*) in the work of Thucydides is simply superb. We need to give it to Leo Strauss that he started this investigation first, however, he is from the outset in favour of *logos*: a true speech is a speech heard by a wise statesman, that is a statesman who has the picture of a whole

Four literary sources give account of Alcibiades' life, none of them offering more than mere glimpses of his ecstatic life: *Greek Lives* by Plutarch, *Alcibiades I* by Pseudo-Plato, Plato's *Symposium* and The *Peloponnesian War* by Thucydides.

Plutarch provides us with a set of anecdotes (clichés) on Alcibiades' lifestyle, whereby complexity and a heterogeneous architecture of his personality of this "rightly proud" man is established. Alcibiades is thus reported to sport a sort of soft linguistic eroticism in speech but at the same time has Melians slaughtered in a display of hard-core cruelty – to give but one example. Overall, such ambivalences compel us to characterise Alcibiades as an autoerotic and perhaps even highly narcissistic figure[6]. But is that really so?

Narcissus is a young man of a stunning and elevated beauty. He rejects favours of the nymph Echo, who in turn cools her affection and eventually disappears in thin air. It anticipates and prefigures the death of Narcissus, who although experiences love, does not have a love object. On the one hand Narcissus symbolizes exaltation with the reflection [non-objet] and on the other

---

human life at hand. Leo Tolstoy, Ernst Jünger, and Jonathan Littel are in a sense the followers of such a strategy of writing on life representing the totality of human experience to be seen in a martial setting.

6 In his famous 1914 work *On Narcissism: An Introduction* Sigmund Freud looks for ways to understand narcissism. After discussing two extremities – the temptation to think about narcissism terms of perversion (one's own body and ego as the only objects of pleasure), and the possibility to think about narcissism in terms of an element of self-preservation "healthy" and "inherent to every living creature", he finally opts to think about narcissism in terms of *libido* liberated from object. It is perhaps surprising that there is in fact affinity in Freud's analysis of melancholy and narcissism. Both positions provoke Freud to inquire what is happening to *libido* following the loss of a loved object. Freud's essay *Mourning and Melancholia* and *On Narcissism: An Introduction* both concern the fate of *libido* liberated from the object and unable to adopt a new object of love. In mourning and melancholia libido regresses to *das Ich*. Such a regression is a complex and indirect process mediated by the ideal ego. After the ideal ego develops, it demands love which in puberty belonged to the ego proper. Freud says that the narcissistic type may love: (a) what he himself is (i.e. himself), (b) what he himself was, (c) what he himself would like to be, (d) someone who was once part of himself. Freud says succinctly: "A strong egoism is a protection against falling ill, but in the last resort we must begin to love in order not to fall ill, and we are bound to fall ill if, in consequence of frustration, we are unable to love" /Sigmund Freud, *On Narcissism*, [in] *The Standard Edition of the Complete Psychological Works of Sigmund Freud*, Volume XIV (1914-1916): *On the History of the Psycho-Analytic Movement, Papers on Metapsychology and Other Works*, p. 85/. Perhaps the secret of Alcibiades is *inter alia* that it defies the alternative: Alcibiades does not need to love to defy being ill, ill are those he does not love.

the power of the image which fascinates despite its non-existence. In the case of Narcissus, madness lies in the absence of the object, which is ultimately a sexual object. However, what is the object for? It exists in order to freeze libido (allow it to be invested in itself). Narcissus is incapable of making any investment, since he is not attached to any object. In this case Eros is not recognized in anything but Narcissus' own reflection, i.e. idealized part (the body) functioning instead of the whole (cosmos). Narcissus is thus subject to reflection and death. The tragedy of Narcissus reaches its climax when his tears distort the surface of water (the mirror), thus making him realize that the beloved image is his mere reflection, and that it is prone to disappear. Narcissism dies at the brink of his image. Alcibiades, on the contrary, dies of dissipation of his image. Alcibiades, like Narcissus is not attached to any object, however, Eros does not return to him like a ricochet and instead disperses in the world resulting with the whole (cosmos) functioning in part (body). Narcissus is the subject of multiple investments, heterogeneous and constantly intensified, so that it eventually becomes the subject of distraction and of immortality. In this sense, Alcibiades takes more from Dionysus rather than Narcissus.[7]

What matters most, however, are his mimetic and imitative skills combined with otherwise firm statue, consistency of character, uncompromising attitude and active nature. Plutarch is full of respect:

> In Sparta, he was all for bodily training, simplicity of life, and severity of countenance; in Ionia, for luxurious ease and pleasure; in Thrace, for drinking deep; in Thessaly, for riding hard; and when he was thrown with Tissaphernes the satrap, he outdid even Persian magnificence in his pomp and lavishness. It was not that he could so easily pass entirely from one manner of man to another, nor that he actually underwent in every case a change in his real character; but when he saw that his natural manners were likely to be annoying to his associates, he was quick to assume any counterfeit exterior which might in each case be suitable for them[8].

What we are looking at here is probably a total subject, a subject able to absorb any culture and champion any given socialization, to adopt any desired policy and to proceed with any given strategy. An entity which, as Machiavelli would put it, like a fox discovers the snares and terrifies wolves like a lion[9], an entity able to follow war conventions and equally able to suspend existing laws. It is this kind of subject which adapts to the circumstances, but even more so makes

7 Julia Kristeva, *Tales of Love*, trans. L. Roudiez (New York: Columbia University Press, 1987), pp. 101-117.

8 Plutarch, *The Life of Alcibiades*, [in:] Plutarch, *The Parallel Lives*, trans. B. Perrin (Harvard: Loeb Classical Library Edition, 1916). p. 203.

9 Niccolò Machiavelli (1513), *The Prince*, trans. Harvey Mansfield, (University of Chicago Press, 1985), p. 100.

best use of the circumstances at hand to achieve his own goals and thus makes the world adapt to his will. While Narcissus errs in ignoring himself as the source of the image, Alcibiades is far from making such a mistake: he multiplies its influence and the impact of his eye. Narcissism abolishes causality by ignoring the connection between him and the world. Alcibiades behaves as if his mere presence multiplied and modified the causality of the world.

I think no one approached the mystery of Alcibiades closer than Plutarch. I also think that it is not a coincidence that Nietzsche, a theorist of resentment, picked up exactly where Plutarch had left off to admire this highly erotic and proud thumos. One of the traits I will myself follow is the resentful nature of Alcibiades. Is it only the wounded pride of Alcibiades and his unfulfilled love to Athens that makes him look for other cultures, cities, and policies – whether in Sparta or in Ionia, Thrace, or in Persia, which would grant him respect and love equalling his not only material but internal wealth? Is everything he does the result of resentment towards Athens? Rather than think about the consequences of his actions and the actions themselves, we should inspect what precedes and triggers these actions, what gives Alcibiades reason to act. If we venture such retrospection, it may occur that his actions are always preceded by rejection, disappointment in love, or mere sense of being unfulfilled. Alcibiades loses twice in his life, and of that we learn not from Plutarch nor from Thucydides, but from Plato. First he loses to Nicias in a competition for the position of the Athenian military strategist; the second loss is to Socrates himself when the stake is Agathon's favours. These losses however, barely upset Alcibiades as they lead to his later victories. Would these victories be symptomatic of a resentimental will to power?

Maybe it is just the opposite? After all, in him we find not only the first man fully active but shameless too – in the sense that Alcibiades is not ashamed of his fame and success – a true oligarch in spirit. In his first speech preceding the invasion of Sicily and addressed to the Athenians, as reconstructed by Thucydides in *The Peloponnesian War*, he gives an apology of his own self and his lavish lifestyle. It is an apology of what he conceives as dear and very personal, an apology of youth, pride, bravery and adventurous lifestyle. Persuading the Athenians to undertake the expedition to Sicily Alcibiades argues that "effective policies are a blend of every sort of opinion – shallow, middle-of-the-road, or highly specialized" and appreciates the "combination of youth and age" where recklessness of youth, strength and courage of maturity, and reason and self-control of the old age are all given equal share, thus ensuring the State is never idle and may further its aims: "Remember too that if the city is at rest its mechanism will seize like anything else out of use, and everyone's skill will atrophy, whereas constant campaigning will add to our experience and train us to fight our cause with action rather than rhetoric"[10]. The guiding principle of Alcibiades' thermodynamics is: the State at rest consumes itself. Similarly, the subject consumes itself when avoiding disturbance and adventure.

Let us see how Thucydides himself describes our hero:

> The most insistent advocate of the expedition was Alcibiades the son of Cleinias. His motives were in opposition to Nicias (they had always had political differences, and now Nicias had made insulting references to him), and above all a strong desire to have the command: he hoped that this would give him the conquest of Sicily and Carthage and that success would also restore his own fortunes, bringing cash as well as glory. He had a position to maintain in the eyes of his fellow citizens, and his devotion to racehorses and other expensive pursuits went beyond his existing means. This extravagance of his was later a significant factor in the ultimate defeat of Athens. The general public became wary of the excesses of his unconventional and hedonistic lifestyle and of the huge ambition apparent at every turn in all areas of his involvement; they thought he was aiming at tyranny, and turned against him. So, even though in the public sphere his command of strategy was unrivalled, on a personal and individual level the people took exception to his behaviour, and replaced him with others; by so doing they caused the city's downfall not long afterwards. Alcibiades now came forward and addressed the Athenians as follows: "Athenians, not only do I have a better claim to command than any other (I have to start with this point, since Nicias has impugned my credentials), but I also think I deserve it. Those pursuits for which I am criticized bring me personal fame, as they did my family before me, but they also bring benefit to my country. My outstanding performance at the Olympic festival made the Greeks revise and even exaggerate their estimate of the power of Athens, when they had expected the city to be exhausted by war. I entered seven chariots – more than any private citizen had ever done before. I won the victory and second and fourth place too: and my whole display at the games was of a piece with my victory. Quite apart from the regular honour which such successes bestow, the plain fact of their achievement also hints at reserves of power. And then again my sponsorship of productions and any other public duty on which I may "preen" myself, though naturally exciting envy at home, does make its own contribution to the impression outsiders form of our strength."[11]

In this description by Thucydides we find a summary of all motifs that predestine Alcibiades' life and would later serve as a reservoir of anecdotes about his lifestyle. Alcibiades would be suspected of tyranny and excessive demonstration of his wealth and lavish lifestyle, while his supposed immaturity would deny him exercise political functions. His speeches give account of his pride and a tendency to defy the political order. In his speeches Alcibiades finds himself outside democracy or against democracy, he circumvents democracy and suspends both democracy and politics. Speaking somewhat beyond the

10 Thucydides, *The Peloponnesian War*, pp. 315-316.

11 *Ibid.*, p. 316.

empty space of power, Alcibiades seems to be saying: 'Athens it's me'. The funny thing is – perhaps he was right.

Alcibiades demonstrates his need to live actively and reflects the joy of life. Let us not forget that the outcome of the expedition to Sicily would be a terrible defeat of Athens and its ensuing death, one of the reasons being the rejection of Alcibiades' services on the grounds of subverting democracy by desecrating the Herms and parodying the Mysteries. Alcibiades on his part would not subject himself to public trial in Athens and instead he would offer his service to Sparta, which at that time was eager to apply his creative military strategy against Athens. To put it somewhat ironically, one could say that Alcibiades is doing better without Athens than Athens is doing without Alcibiades. Alcibiades without Athens is still the Athenian, while Athens without Alcibiades becomes its own caricature. Athens without Alcibiades equals Athens' death.

2. Educational Failure

The second account of Alcibiades' life we find in a dialogue ascribed to Plato but deemed unauthentic: *The First Alcibiades* or *Alcibiades I*[12]. In this dialogue Alcibiades is portrayed in a key moment of his life: he is no longer young and beautiful, yet he has not reached the stage of maturity – power and sovereignty. Michel Foucault, in *The History of Sexuality* volume II, *The Use of Pleasure* describes Alcibiades' dilemma as a dilemma of boy's honour[13] which may serve as the Greek equivalent of the modern crisis of adolescence[14]. A boy's honour concerns the question of acquiescence – whether a boy should succumb and to whom if at all, under what conditions and with what warranty? Also, may the one who loves demand his lover's submission? As we shall soon see, for Alcibiades the key issue is that of warranty.

In this dialogue Alcibiades appears in the company of his lover – Socrates. Alcibiades, let us not forget, is the legitimate child of Athens, in the sense that he is both a former student of Socrates (the greatest philosopher) and Pericles (the greatest politician). The tutelage of the latter is mentioned, albeit implicitly, in *The Peloponnesian War*, where Thucydides reflects upon the extent to which Alcibiades can be considered the rightful heir to the legacy of Pericles. One of the hypotheses that we will have to consider, boils down to the claim that

12 Plato, *Alcibiades*, Nicholas Denyer (ed.) (Cambridge: Cambridge University Press, 2001), pp. 1-26.

13 Michel Foucault, *The Use of Pleasure. Volume II of The History of Sexuality*, trans. R. Hurley (New York: Vintage Books, 1990), p. 204.

14 Erik H. Erikson, *Childhood and Society*. (New York: Norton 1950).

Alcibiades is indeed the embodiment of the conscious and fully disclosed, that is unlocked and unrestrained Pericles. Would we be equally willing to admit that Alcibiades is the embodiment of politically fulfilled, unrestrained and conscious Socrates?

In the dialogue, Socrates probes Alcibiades' ability to perform political duties. How would he justify before the public imperial war against peoples considered just and peaceful? There is irony in the fact that, as Thucydides records; a 32 year-old Alcibiades will try to persuade the Athenians to enter an unjust war. In puberty, however, he responds that it is "an awkward question"[15] and in the course of the dialogue it appears that to declare unjust war one needs to provide a 'noble lie' which partially silences and ignores the principle of justice.

We know that at the end of his life Socrates will face accusation of demoralizing the youth of Athens and the zeal with which Plato defends his master in *Apology*. However, the case of Alcibiades confirms the accusations not only as far as sexuality is concerned but in respect to his teachings on virtue. Is it not ironic that both Socrates and Alcibiades face charges which could equally apply to Pericles? In his commentary following the third speech of Pericles Thucydides mentions in passing: "The universal anger at Pericles among the Athenians did not subside until they had punished him with a fine"[16]. Is it a coincidence that the majority of Greek strategists, including Themistocles, Pausanias and Thucydides himself, were at the end of their lives either removed from Athens or voluntarily emigrated to barbarous countries, as if anticipating the privileged status of a refugee, an outlaw?

Let us now consider whether Alcibiades is indeed a double educational failure of Athens, namely – the failure of Socrates and of Pericles. Two speeches of Alcibiades reported in *The Peloponnesian War* need to be interpreted in the context of three speeches given by Pericles. Contrary to the common opinion Pericles' speeches are not in praise of democracy. Pericles does praise democracy but he does so rhetorically to justify declaration and then continuation of imperial war. It is a 'noble lie' to praise democracy and evoke in public the image of its might while in terms of *Realpolitik* demand that Athens declare war out of necessity. In his second and perhaps most challenging speech over the bodies of those first dead, Pericles tells the Athenians that "[l]ove of honour alone does not age" and that "[f]amous men have the whole earth as their

15 Plato, *Alcibiades*, "SOCRATES: And would you advise the Athenians to go to war with the just or with the unjust? ALCIBIADES: That is an awkward question; for certainly, even if a person did intend to go to war with the just, he would not admit that they were just."

16 Thucydides, *The Peloponnesian War*, p. 105.

tomb". It looks like a mere foreplay to the third speech where Pericles openly says that at this stage Athens may not renounce the empire and informs the Athenians that they now manage the State not as a people, but as a tyrant: "The empire you possess is by now like a tyranny — perhaps wrong to acquire it, but certainly dangerous to let it go."[17].

Athens, which will later fear Alcibiades' tendency to tyranny, here easily succumbs to the "tyrant" Pericles, who is bold enough to let the Athenians know that Athens is now a tyrant and Athens needs to continue be a tyrant! Let's listen to Pericles:

> You no longer have the option to abdicate from your empire; no one suffering the present fear should affect this idea as a noble-sounding means of disengagement. The empire you possess is by now like a tyranny — perhaps wrong to acquire it, but certainly dangerous to let it go. If people of that sort managed to persuade the others they would quickly ruin a city, and even if they set up their own independent state somewhere they would ruin that too. The disengaged can survive only when men of action are ranked beside them. Their policy has no place in an imperial state, but it belongs in a subject city, and what it means is safe servitude[18].

To put it bluntly, it is Pericles not Alcibiades who enlightens the Athenians on the fact that Athens is running its empire like a tyrant.

Since our question concerns not so much Pericles but Alcibiades, we shall now turn to his auto-erotic speech and assess whether it is substantially different from that of Pericles, who makes a caveat that at the beginning of his second speech that "[i]t is not easy to find the right measure of words". Alcibiades addressing the Athenians in his first speech opposes Nicias and arguing for the expedition to Sicily reverberates the argument of Pericles without, however, his purely rhetorical praise of democracy. Alcibiades speaks as if providing addendum to the speeches of his uncle Pericles – in whose house he grew up after death of his father Cleinias – and as if he was trying to put his words into action. In other words, Alcibiades speaks somewhat inspired by the spirit (pathos) of Pericles. While avoiding the argument that the interests and fortune of the State may align with the interests and fortune of individuals, Alcibiades seduces the Athenians with the image of his own might and the possibility of its expansion, the possibility to gain advantage over other states and the sheer possibility that each adventure offers in accordance with the eternal law of nature, where nature is the space offering the opportunity to multiply fame. The law of nature to which Alcibiades appeals would be as follows: those inherently powerful are forced (*anankaias*) by a certain right (*tons nomon*) to rule

---

17 *Ibid.*, p. 104.

18 *Ibid.*, p. 104.

whenever an opportunity allows them to do so. Perhaps we should question, somewhat in terms of clinical psychology, whether the Athenians by ascribing to this law are not in fact compelled to do so because of their political obsession, a kind of obsessive-compulsive disorder?

The theme of justice is indeed the main subject of *The Peloponnesian War*. Almost all speeches begin with reference to "justice", but those speaking find themselves "coerced" to take action or see the actions they propose as "necessitated" by the circumstances. Corinthians, somehow producing a material cause of the war, address the Athenians: "Athenians, you are at fault in starting a war and breaking the treaty. We are pursuing a grievance against our own enemies, and you have taken arms to stand in our way."[19] The Athenians, on their part, so explain their hegemonic position when addressing the Lacedaemonians before the war:

> We did not acquire this empire by force. It came about because you [other peoples of Peloponnese] were not prepared to stay on to deal with the remnants of Persian power, and the allies approached us of their own accord and asked us to become their leaders. The very fact of this hegemony was the initial spur to the expansion of the empire to its present extent; the motives driving us were first and foremost fear, then prestige, and later our own interests. [...] So too we have done nothing surprising or contrary to human nature in accepting an empire when it was offered to us and refusing to give it up, under the domination of the three most powerful motives – prestige, fear, and self-interest. Nor again did we start anything new in this, but it has always been the way of the world that the weaker is kept down by the stronger[20].

We may observe that it was the very nature of things that forced the Athenians to acquire hegemonic position; the nature of things is the advantage of stronger ones and their right to be unjust.

The right to be unjust is perhaps best pronounced in Mytilene dialogue where Mytilenaeans once again begin by postulating justice:

> We shall first – especially since we are asking you for an alliance – address ourselves to questions of justice and honesty. We know that no friendship between individuals or association between cities can have any lasting basis unless the partners treat each other with patent honesty and are generally of the same mind; divergence of thinking is the start of differences in action[21].

To which the Athenians respond in crude language of force and injustice: "You know as well as we do that when we are talking on the human plane, questions of justice only arise when there is equal power to compel; in terms of

19 *Ibid.*, p. 27.
20 *Ibid.*, pp. 37-38.
21 *Ibid.*, p. 134.

practicality the dominant exact what they can and the weak concede what they must"[22]. After many years of war, defeated and humiliated, fleeing from Sicily under the pressure of the enemy, that is, finding themselves in the former position of Mitilenaeans, the Athenians speak: "Others before now have gone to war against other countries, doing what human nature will do, with consequences which human nature can bear. We too have cause to hope now for a gentler divine dispensation (meriting now the gods' pity rather than their resentment)"[23]. Unfortunately, by God's grace the negligence of justice results in hatred and resentment. The omnipotence of God is a folly. God is the right to be unfair. His justice is biased: *justice as unfairness*. The law of the stronger and the very nature of things did not cease taking effect: the weaker submit to the stronger and justice in human relations plays decisive role only provided that two equivalent forces abide. Such equivalence does not exist in *Realpolitik*.

Let us summarize this thread: justice is possible provided there is balance of power. As of the nature of things, however, unbalance prevails. This is the cause of desire to strengthen hegemony, which in itself is immoderate, just as the speeches concerning it. Athens fall prey to such excesses. The symbol of the most audacious excesses is Alcibiades.

3. Seductive Satyr

In *The First Alcibiades* Socrates separates from Alcibiades leaving him with a declaration of eternal love, and a story about *philotimo* to ponder – the only value constituting a permanent political community, the association of lovers. Socrates explains to Alcibiades that rather than love the incidental beauty of his body he shall persist in love for his soul. Such is the only guarantee Socrates gives to his lover. That this guarantee is unenforceable we learn not from pseudo-Plato, but from Plato himself. In *Symposium* we get the third and final glimpse of our hero as bestowed on us in antique literature. This time, the learned philologists had no doubts that Alcibiades was no longer in his prime, he was 31 years old. Within a year the Athenians, instigated by Alcibiades, would venture on Sicilian war. Within a year Alcibiades would also be charged with sacrilege; knocking off phalluses of the Herms. Let us therefore take up the question of the relationship between our hero and Socrates. More precisely, we should ask what happened to the promise of a lasting friendship made by Socrates to Alcibiades. Alcibiades enters *Symposium* late in the dialogue. He is

22 *Ibid.*, p. 302.
23 *Ibid.*, p. 407.

drunk and bleeding after Socrates abandoned him. He cannot bear the sight of Socrates sighing to his new object of adoration – Agathon.

The main theme of Plato's *Symposium* is that of a tension between Eros and Politics[24]. This tension is, of course, recorded in all political dialogues of Plato – the *Republic*, the *Statesman*, and perhaps the least so in the *Laws*. Let us never forget that, in accordance with the teachings of Socrates expressed in the *Republic*; his claim that the virtue of courage is superior to the virtue of temperance is based on a deliberate abstraction from Eros – an abstraction characteristic of the *Republic*. Although Socrates presents a project of the ideal city and enumerates the fundamental needs which give rise to human society, he stubbornly resists the need for procreation. And when he describes the tyrant – injustice incarnate, he presents him as Eros incarnate. For this reason, Leo Strauss concludes that "there is a tension between *Eros* and the city and hence between *Eros* and *justice*: only through the depreciation of *Eros* can the city come into its own. *Eros* obeys its own laws, not the laws of the city however good"[25]. Demands of *Eros* are simply silenced, and to this end the institution of family is abolished. According to Socrates, a common feature of both tyranny and democracy is the subordination of sensuality (senses) to desire (the government). Poets, according to Socrates, praise Eros conceived as an untamed and privatized force that promotes injustice. The Socratic condemnation of Eros is thus tantamount to condemnation of poetry. *Symposium* is the only Platonic dialogue in which Socrates wastes time on such a thing as talking with poets. It is also the only dialogue fully dedicated to Eros. Supposedly, the invocation to poets is meant to restore dignity of Eros and demonstrate that is in fact a political force, contrary to other dialogues where it is seen as an anti-political power. Let us also remember that the *Statesman* ends with a praise of politics conceived as the art of matchmaking and breeding those meek with the daring, and Eros with Thumos. In this dialogue a Statesman becomes a *de facto* organizer of biopolitics.

In *Symposium*, the promise of Eros socialized and dedicated in the service of political affairs is abandoned upon the return of Alcibiades. This uninvited guest, drunken statesman and wounded lover demonstrates Eros privatized and dedicated in the service of private matters, so to say – Eros untamed. How different is this return from the one described in *The Peloponnesian War*, where in Book VIII he is to carry the promise of salvation as the sole diplomat able to

24 Plato, *The Symposium*, trans. Alexander Nehamas and Paul Woodruff, from *Plato: Complete Works*, ed. by John M. Cooper, Cambridge: Hackett Publishing Company, 1997, pp. 457-506.

25 Leo Strauss, *Plato*, [in:] Joseph Cropsey, Leo Strauss, *History of Political Philosophy* (Chicago/London: The University of Chicago Press, third edition 1987), p. 48.

convince the Persian satrap Tissaphernes to help Athens in the war against the Lacedaemonians. Thucydides says quite roughly there, that "Alcibiades was using Tissaphernes to put pressure on the Athenians, and the Athenians to put pressure on Tissaphernes"[26]. After silencing his personal passions, following the period of submitting policy to Eros, Alcibiades now enters adulthood, in which eroticism is in the service of politics. In this new incarnation Alcibiades devotes himself to the art of diplomacy, which makes of him a double spy and scout on one side, but also a cosmopolitan citizen on the other, or – as we would say today – a translator involved in intercultural dialogue. The new Alcibiades no longer undermines politics with Eros; he makes politics with the help of the art of seduction.

In our culture, Plato's *Symposium* remains the most mysterious and fundamental work on Eros and its suppression. Paradoxically, this dialogue by Plato, widely perceived as praising Eros, in fact concerns its suppression. Socrates, the only sober person of the dialogue, recoils and postpones his praise of Eros until other voices are heard. There comes a reference to Phaedrus' speech affirming community bound by love and demonstrating political power of Eros (there are no people vile enough to stop Eros inspiring them to do brave deeds), a reference to Pausanias' speech on the ethical conditioning of Eros (tyrannies condemn both pederasty and philosophy, as what they fear most are strong bonds and great thoughts, liberal regimes allow everyone to be loved but just for the indolence of the rulers, and only Athens ascribe love to men of honour), a reference to a speech by Eryximachus the physician (there exist two types of Eros, one seeking harmony and moderation, that is love, and the other seeking excess and multiplicity, which is a disease), by Aristophanes the comedian, who, hiccupping and sneezing tells of the mythical times of Androgynes (vigorous hermaphrodites attempting to overthrow the gods), and finally by Agathon of feminine beauty, a tragic poet and a lover of Socrates, who speaks of the governing (Ares) and creative (Muses) power of Eros. Here, instead of praising Eros, Socrates puzzles the audience saying Eros is in fact a deficient and unsettled force since it desires that which it has not. Thus, Eros is a wanderer and a nomad occasionally desiring material goods, moral virtues, wisdom, strength, health, or justice.

In Socrates' speech we find three not obviously coherent definitions of Eros: (1) Eros is a desire to possess good forever. (2) Eros is a desire to conceive and bear in beauty. (3) Eros is a desire for immortality. Socrates' speech however, especially in the part where the words of Diotima are referred to, is yet in praise of ascending and subliming power of Eros – from one body to a number of

26 Thucydides, *The Peloponnesian War*, p. 456.

bodies, from bodies to deeds, from deeds to the sciences, from the sciences to the teachings on beauty, and therefrom to the contemplation of beauty itself. Just as the sublimation of Eros reaches its climax there enters a drunken politician – Alcibiades, Socrates' disappointed lover, the embodiment of human, jealous, incoherent, vibrating, unhealthy, and bodily Eros. He then addresses Socrates as "a satyr", "a serpent", "an ironist", but also "the only worthy lover" and "a man like no other".

It is primarily by making reference to Freud's *Wit and Its Relation to the Unconscious* that I intend to refresh our attitude toward the complex vision of Eros outlined by Plato. In his *Wit...* Freud says that if wit is not an end in itself, it enters the service of two tendencies: it either becomes malignant and serves aggression, satire, or repelling an attack; or it is obscene, and as such exposes and demonstrates obscenity.[27]. The latter is the speech of Alcibiades the exhibitionist addressing Socrates. Further on Freud says that when such a speech does not produce sexual arousal "the sexual aggression is inhibited in its progress towards the act" and it becomes an end in itself as a "libidinous impulse confronted by a hindrance" and then utilizes arousal and produces pleasure at any sign thereof[28]. Freud puts it bluntly: the force that makes it difficult, if not impossible, to derive pleasure from explicit obscenity is the force of repression. And to repress is to keep the whole complex of impulses away from consciousness. Thus, the work of repression is to make absent primary human pleasures. Wit and satire provide tools to reverse the process of sacrificing pleasures and to redeem what seemed to have been lost.

I order to understand the complex relationship between Alcibiades and Socrates one would need to reconstruct the sense of psychical economy between both of them, the work of repression and its economy, Socrates' subtle sense of humour and Alcibiades' sense of bawdy humour. I would also like to examine the complex relationship between wit, humour, and different types of wit and humour, and different types of economy. If, as Freud says, wit produces pleasure corresponding to the saved psychic effort by deceiving the critical potential of the mind and culture, then is Socrates' and Alcibiades' pleasure the same thing? Does the pleasure derived from obscene wit originate in a release of the effort of repression, and the pleasure derived from sublimative wit originates in a release of the effort to act and imagine (to appoint and invest)? If it were so, and my

27 Sigmund Freud (1905). *Jokes and their Relation to the Unconscious* [in:] *The Standard Edition of the Complete Works of Sigmund Freud*, Volume XIII., ed. by James Strachey et al. The Hogart Press and the Institute of Psychoanalysis, (London: Hogarth Press, 1953-74).

28 Sigmund Freud, *Jokes and their Relation to the Unconsciout,* in paragraph 33 "The Transformation of the Obscenity into Obscene Wit".

intuitions proved to be accurate, in the persons of Socrates and Alcibiades we would have had two prototype examples of alternative psychic economies. Economic thinking (suspended work of repression) and economic action (suspended work of investment) would result in two divergent profits (pleasures).

To summarize this thread: the return of Alcibiades in the *Symposium* is a return of what had thus far been suppressed. Alcibiades is the unstoppable force re-entering the scene and with the help of sarcasm and obscenity invites Socrates, who is locked, sophisticated and talkative, to delight the pleasures of dissipation being the result of the work of intrigue (abolition of repression), and certainly not the work of thinking and contemplation (the establishment of suppression) or speaking (the work of sublimation).

4. The Return of Alcibiades

Discussing his method in Book I, Thucydides admits that "Of the various speeches made either when war was imminent or in the course of the war itself, it has been hard to reproduce the exact words used either when I heard them myself or when they were reported to me by other sources" – therefore he decided to arrange the speeches "to make each speaker say broadly what I supposed would have been needed on any given occasion, while keeping as closely as I could to the overall intent of what was actually said"[29]. Thus, the speeches cited in *The Peloponnesian War* are the intellectual construct of the author, and it seems they are governed by what we might call a situational truth. On the other hand, the events quoted are subject to the logic of the witness as reconstructed by Giorgio Agamben[30]. In Thucydides we find three types of "witness": (1) *auctor* – the person who intervenes in the case of a minor (or the person who, for whatever reason, does not have the capacity to posit a legally valid act), in order to grant him the valid title that he requires, (2) *testis* – the person who, in the trial or lawsuit between two rival parties, is in the position of a third party, (3) and *superstes* – someone, who has experienced an event from beginning to end and can therefore bear witness to it. Thucydides bears witness to the Peloponnesian War as *auctor* – certifying its credibility, as *testis* – a mediator in the dispute between Athens and Sparta, and as *superstes* – someone who experienced the war from beginning to end and thus is its "remnant".

Thucydides reports the war as if he was a messenger of a tragedy. Bear in mind, such messengers were usually killed. In *The Peloponnesian War* we find a

29 Thucydides, *The Peloponnesian War*, p. 12.

30 Giorgio Agamben, *Remnants of Auschwitz. The Witness and the Archive*, trans. D. Heller-Roazen (New York: Zone Books, 1999), p. 148.

parable about a man compelled to tell the true course of events who eventually gets killed by the listeners who find his cold account unbearable. A detailed description of the social organization of tragedy and natural history of destruction programmed by repeated and escalating errors of history imply that the proper understanding of the tragedies as staged by people is the foremost yet uncertain condition of happiness. To Thucydides, however, beyond doubt a penetrating writer, people seem unable to learn anything from such tragedies and thus uninformed and uneducated continue to follow the paths of the already departed civilizations.

Thucydides says explicitly:

> In recording the events of the war my principle has not been to rely on casual information or my own suppositions, but to apply the greatest possible rigour in pursuing every detail both of what I saw myself and of what I heard from others. It was laborious research, as eyewitnesses on each occasion would give different accounts of the same event, depending on their individual loyalties or memories. It may be that the lack of a romantic element in my history will make it less of a pleasure to the ear: but I shall be content if it is judged useful by those who will want to have a clear understanding of what happened – and, such is the human condition, will happen again at some time in the same or a similar pattern. It was composed as a permanent legacy, not a showpiece for a single hearing.[31]

Thucydides constructs political speeches as interventions determining the direction of actions and the dynamics of the "great movement" which the Peloponnesian War was. The speeches of Alcibiades are similarly constructed, but they intervene in the logic of war so strongly that they become actions on their own right. Based on this observation I claim that the relation of Thucydides to Alcibiades reveals the relation of Thucydides to the world of war and peace.

In *The Peloponnesian War* Alcibiades takes more from Odysseus than Achilles, for it is not anger (*menis*) but a trick (*metys*) which is announced by the arrival of Alcibiades. Thucydides perceives Alcibiades as a schemer applying instrumental reason to expand the intrigue. However, contrary to Odysseus, subjected to analysis by Theodor W. Adorno in *Dialectic of Enlightenment*, Alcibiades formula of cunningness is not that of a detached instrumental reason surrendering and adapting to nature by giving it due homage in order to somehow recover it[32] – since Alcibiades never lost nature and there is nothing

31 Thucydides, *The Peloponnesian War*, p. 12.

32 Max Horkheimer, Theodor W. Adorno (1944), *Dialectic of Enlightment. Philosophical Fragments,* trans. E. Jephcott, (California: Stanford University Press, 2002), pp. 38-39: "Odysseus, like the heroes of all true novels after him, throws himself away, so to speak, in order to win himself; he achieves his estrangement from nature by abandoning himself to nature, trying his strength against it in all his adventures; ironically, it is implacable

for him to recover. Alcibiades never suppressed anything but he was rather suppressed himself. Similarly, Alcibiades is not burdened with the task of recovering anything, to the contrary – it is us who need to recover Alcibiades. Exaggeratingly, we could venture to say that the whole Peloponnesian War is a consequence of Alcibiades' intrigue. This time Alcibiades is no more a constellation of anecdotes as he appears to Plutarch, nor a juvenile pondering upon his future as he is to pseudo-Plato, or a jealousy-stricken drunkard and a mocker as he is to Plato. Only in *The Peloponnesian War* Alcibiades he is revealed to be a man standing behind the whole intrigue and the only true witness of the war – the fact which makes him so precious to Thucydides.

Let us now outline the very intrigue. Alcibiades first appears in Book V where he cunningly persuades Lacedaemonian envoys to disavow the possession of full authority to reach agreement on all matters of dispute and later denounces the Spartans in the assembly as insincere in order to achieve alliance with Argos, Elis, and Mantinea. His second intervention is to persuade the Athenians to make a provision for the naval expedition to Sicily. The third takes place in Sparta where Alcibiades convinces the Spartans to ally with the Syracusans and then pursue a new military strategy against Athens. Finally, in a full disclosure of cosmopolitanism and cunningness Alcibiades plots fourth intrigue concerning the new policy between the three great powers – Athens, Sparta and Persia. Paradoxically, the balance of powers enables the return of justice to politics, thus far excluded of necessity.

If Alcibiades is Pericles applied, then Thucydides is Alcibiades voiced. Thucydides reconstructs three of his speeches. The first speech is addressed to the Athenians and concerns the waning of an idle state, the second is addressed to the Lacedaemonians and deals with the *esprit de corps* of Alcibiades:

> I hope that none of you will think the worse of me for joining its greatest enemies in a vigorous attack on my own land, when once I was known for my patriotism, or will suspect me of the usual exile's zeal in what I tell you. I am indeed an exile, but what I have forfeited is the malignity of my persecutors, not my ability to do you service, if you will listen to me. The greater enemies of my country are not those like you who have damaged it in open hostility, but the people who have forced its friends to become its enemies. The patriotism I retain is for the city which guaranteed my citizen's rights, not for the city which has done me wrong. I do not think of myself as attacking my own country — what is there now is no longer mine — so much as reclaiming my country as it once was. The true patriot unjustly robbed of his country does not hesitate to attack it, but his very love for it makes him seek any means of recovering it.[33]

---

nature that he now commands, which triumphs on his return home as the implacable judge, avenging the heritage of the very powers he has escaped."

33 Thucydides, *The Peloponnesian War*, p. 357.

What is really amazing in this statement is its reference to love. Alcibiades, putting aside his affinity, declares love to a world ensuring a pot full of possibilities and including that of a limitless self-fulfilment so that his self could fill it all up. What the speech also reveals is his untamed cosmopolitism and a truly non-political spirit. I daresay that all modern cosmopolitans, the likes of Ulrich Beck, originate in this particular speech[34].

There is also a third speech by Alcibiades in Book VIII, although unaccounted for, in which Alcibiades upon his triumphant return to Athens addresses humbled Athenians. Thucydides reconstructs only the actions taken by Alcibiades; inciting Ionian cities to revolt against Athens, notifying trierarchs in Athens of his readiness to negotiate with the Persians their support to Athens, effecting the fall of the Athenian democracy and establishing instead "a political system of substantial and obvious merit, which blended the interests of the few and the many without extremes"[35]. He also mentions that it was "then that Alcibiades can be said for the first time to have done an outstanding service to his country" by restraining and shaming the Athenians at Samos who were ready to sail against their own people at home. I hereby propose that the testimonial of Thucydides is in fact the third, unaccounted for speech of Alcibiades, and essentially the whole *The Peloponnesian War* is inspired by his intrigue.

Given the essential facts, we may now fully appreciate the recurring topic of love. In doing so, we need to reflect upon the relationship of Eros (desire) and Thumos (pride) on one hand, and the relationship of Eros and tyranny on the other. Jacques Lacan in probably the most Platonic seminar *Le Transfert* in 1960 says that in Plato's *Symposium* it only appears to Alcibiades that he desires Socrates, while in fact the real object of his desire is Agathon[36]. For Lacan the story of Alcibiades concerns the direction of human desires. A desiring subject of the unconscious takes a different position from that of the imaginary *ego*. The latter operates within its fantasies about desires, while the former within real desires. Speaking of Alcibiades, we should ask what his real desire is. Is it Agathon or is it love of Athens, Athens of his uncle Pericles and Athens of his master Socrates? We should also consider yet another possibility, namely that it is Alcibiades that Athens desires, that it is Alcibiades the Athenians had always wanted to be. Instead, they cultivated the virtues of moderation, leisure and carefree life characteristic to the times of peace – "Sabbath of Sabbaths".

34 Urlich Beck, Edgar Grande, *Cosmopolitan Europe* (Cambridge: Polity, 2007).

35 Thucydides, *The Peloponnesian War*, p. 466.

36 Jacques Lacan, *Le Séminaire de Jacques Lacan, Livre VIII: Le transfert*, 1960-1961, ed. Jacques-Alain Miller, (Paris: Éditions du Seuil, 2001).

In *Lover's Discourse. Fragments* Roland Barthes says that love discourse is devotional rather than obscene, and that being devoted equals being seduced or abducted by image. Barthes associates image with a wandering position of Socrates and his constant elusiveness and atopos. It is because of this atopos that Alcibiades harasses Socrates with an avalanche of epithets. Barthes, following Lacan's seminar, provides the following interpretation: "it may well be Agathon whom Alcibiades is addressing and whom he desires, though he is being monitored by an analyst, Socrates."[37] For both Barthes and Lacan Alcibiades is the subject abducted and enchanted by the flickering image of Socrates, he is the victim of a love triangle, as condoned by the fact that he takes imaginary position of *ego*.

My diagnosis would be opposite to that of Lacan and Barthes: it is Alcibiades who enchants Athens – Pericles, Socrates and Agathon altogether. Alcibiades is an active force subsuming the image of Eros. Toasts of Agathon, mitigating activities of Socrates, and seemingly moderate speeches of Pericles do not do justice to the spirit of insolence which we find in excess in lavish, subversive, wasteful, and enchanting exploits of Alcibiades in *The Peloponnesian War*. In Book III, in associative context of the account of the Athenian people being fiercely suspicious of the alleged profaners of the Mysteries, thinking that it was all part of some oligarchic or tyrannical conspiracy, we come across a hilarious account of the relation linking Eros and the tyrant. It is the story of the fall of Peisistratus and historical amnesia of Athens concerning the origins of the State and the birth of Athenian democracy. Thucydides writes,

> The people were aware, by oral tradition, that the tyranny of Peisistratus and his sons had grown oppressive towards the end, and also that its overthrow was not brought about by their own efforts or by Harmodius, but was the result of Spartan intervention. This knowledge kept them in a state of constant anxiety and universal suspicion[38].

What is the historical truth? Who overthrew the rule of tyranny in Athens? What was the role of Eros?

The history recounted by Thucydides depicts yet another love triangle. After the death of Peisistratus his eldest son Hippias became the tyrant and his younger brother Hipparchus fell for Harmodios – Athenian in his prime and of radiant beauty. Unfortunately, he was already a lover of another Athenian middle class citizen Aristogeiton who, "In all the passionate jealousy of a lover, and terrified that Hipparchus would use his power to take Harmodius from him

37 Roland Barthes, *A Lover's Discourse. Fragments*, p. 74.

38 Thucydides, *The Peloponnesian War*, p. 335.

by force, immediately began to plot the overthrow of the tyranny, as best he could in his social station"[39]. Harmodios and Arystogeiton later plot a pre-emptive assassination of Hippias but change their mind last minute and take their vengeance on Hipparchus "in the height of passion, a lover's jealousy in one" and eventually both lovers are killed too. Thucydides recounts, quite ironically: "the conspiracy of Harmodius and Aristogeiton [...] began with a lover's resentment, and the final desperate act was the result of a last-minute failure of nerve"[40]. A side effect of the attempted assassination was that Hippias, who prior to the attempt made himself approachable to everyone, was later increasingly fearful for his security and the tyranny entered a more oppressive stage – and this is how it came to be remembered in memory of the Athenians. Let me repeat my question: what is the relationship of Thumos and Eros, erotic power and the power of Eros, tyrannical desires and the desires of Eros? Does Eros project the ways we need to take to reach objects missing in our lives, thus caring about man always lacking something? And could Thumos i.e. the theory of human pride, ambition and just anger be the sole alternative to Eros, projecting for us the ways we need to take to reach the stage of "strong subjects", which is who we are and who we can be[41]? Who are the Athenians afraid of when invoking the memory of tyrants or Hipparchus whose miserable death made him more famous than Hippias – the real tyrant? And what this memory has to do with the public opinion about profanity of Alcibiades? Do the Athenians see in Alcibiades a potential and erotic beyond measure tyrant i.e. the synthesis of human ambitions and human desires, Eros and Thumos?

Combining love with enchantment and love discourse with devotional discourse Roland Barthes gives surprising definition of image: "that from which I am excluded"[42]. Barthes adds that in the amorous realm the most painful wounds are inflicted more often by what one sees than by what one knows. Alcibiades is the object of Athens' love, from which the Athenians were excluded. The suffering of the Athenians is not limited to humiliation following defeat in the Sicilian expedition, its source is the exclusion of the phantasm that Alcibiades is, the phantasm they themselves brought to life. It is not Alcibiades who suffers at the sight of Socrates caressing Agathon – the image, from which he was excluded, but it is Socrates, Pericles and Agaton who suffer presented with the image of Alcibiades who remains in a love clinch with the world, from which the Athenians were excluded.

39 *Ibid.*, p. 336.

40 *Ibid.*, p. 338.

41 See: Peter Sloterdijk, *Rage and Time,* trans. M. Wenning (New York: Columbia University Press, 2010).

42 Roland Barthes, *A Lover's Discourse. Fragments*, p. 132.

If, according to Lacan, love is giving what one does not have, to the one who does not need it, then transfer between Athens and Alcibiades best demonstrates this empty transaction of love. Athens did not have what could become the object of desire for Alcibiades: adventure and motion, treating him instead with moderation and peace. In the end, it is Athens that is immersed in its imaginary register and constantly speculates about its power. In turn, Alcibiades is the very principle of reality embodied in action. Alcibiades is the phantasm subsuming all Athenian dreams; he is the representation of all Athenian aspirations, a postulate of a proud man who feels liberated to the extent that he continues to give and to spend. Alcibiades is the embodiment of narcissism or rather heteronarcissism: he confirms diversity and multiplicity which penetrate, delight, surprise and unite his genius. His ethics are those of absorption and radiation: Alcibiades does not follow but exudes, and contrary to Plutarch's opinion he reverses the direction of imitation, forcing the world to imitate him.

PART TWO:
POLITICS

I. The Limits of the Political

The specific political distinction [...]is that between friend and enemy.

Carl Schmitt[1]

Nietzsche: »*Perhaps to each of us there will come the more joyful hour when we exclaim:*
'Friends, there are no friends!' thus said the dying sage;
'Foes, there are no foes!' say I, the living fool.«

Jacques Derrida[2]

Is it possible without setting off loud protests on the part of militants to think and to live the gentle rigour of friendship, the law of friendship qua the experience of a certain ahumanity, in absolute separation, beyond or below the commerce of gods and man? And what politics could still be founded on this friendship which exceeds the measure of man without becoming a theologem? Would it still be a politics?

Jacques Derrida[3]

1. The very concept of the political today

When and under what conditions can we say that an event is political? To what extent "that, which is happening" is happening politically? In which way can we differentiate the main spheres of culture – politics, knowledge and ethics? Could we call the reflection on oneself and the other – knowledge, the action on the action of oneself – ethics, and the action on the action of the other – politics? What is politics? Is politics the management of the power of the State? Is politics the realm of the decision, of action in the social world, of what Ernesto Laclau, following Gramsci, calls hegemonisation?[4] And in a sense could we say that every decision is political? Or maybe politics is first the invention and the exercise of an absolutely new social reality, a new social order? Is politics the creation of thought or rather is it the creation of action? How to compare Lenin's idea of politics when he wrote *What Is to Be Done?* with Schmitt's idea of

1 Carl Schmitt (1927) *The Concept of the Political*, trans. by G. Schwab (Chicago: University of Chicago Press, 2007), p. 26.

2 Jacques Derrida (1994), *Politics of Friendship*, trans. G. Collins (New York: Verso, 1997), p. 28.

3 *Ibid.*, p. 297.

4 Ernesto Laclau, Chantal Mouffe, *Hegemony & Socialist Strategy: Towards A Radical Democratic Politics*, trans. Winston Moore and Paul Cammack (New York: Verso, 1985).

politics when he wrote *Political Theology*? Is an event political if the subject of this event is collective? But what does collective mean? Is "collective" a numerical concept? Or is it "collective" rather an ontological concept that conveys the potental requirements of all subjects? And in this last sense – is "collective" immediately universalizing? Does the effectiveness of the political emerge from the assertion according to which "for every x, there is thought"?

In such a barrage of questions I would like today ask about the limits of politics or even more so about the limits of the political. Today, so in a very peculiar moment, when there is a widespread feeling of exhaustion of the great narratives of modernity and the blurring of the boundaries of the public spaces, the ideology, which seems to be stealing all meaning from collective action, is leading to a generalized retreat from the political. So, I ask about the limits of politics at the moment when many theoreticians see the reasons for the claim announcing the death of the concept of the public men. But perhaps the death of the concept of a public man is only the other side of the death of the very concept of a private man?

We live, as everyone knows, at a time of endings. We live at a time when all boundaries have been transgressed; we have crossed all the frontiers. There is the reason why the question about the limits is so important. When I ask about the limits of politics or even the political I use the terms "limit" and "boundary" in a strong sense. The boundary in a sense is not only the line between two epochs or areas or spheres, but it means the very end, the moment of disappearance of the very term "political". There is also the reason why the question about the existence of the limits is so urgent! True limits are always antagonistic. As Ernesto Laclau said: "True limits can never be neutral limits but presuppose an exclusion. A neutral limit would be one which is essentially continuous with what is at its two sides, and the two sides are simply different from each other".[5]

In *The Order of Things*, Michel Foucault seeks to show that it is only quite recently that "man" has emerged as an object of our knowledge. Quite soon "man" will disappear from our knowledge.[6] So, from the Foucauldian perspective we live on the edge of the death of the Subject. Francis Fukuyama in the book *The End of History and the Last Man,* following Nietzsche's line of thought, asked questions: "Is not the man who is completely satisfied by nothing more than universal and equal recognition something less than a full human being, indeed, an object of contempt, a 'last man' with neither striving nor

5 Ernesto Laclau, *Emancipation(s)* (New York: Verso, 1996).

6 Michel Foucault (1966), *The Order of Things. An Archaeology of the Human Sciences* (London, 1992).

aspiration?".[7] So, from Fukuyama's perspective, we live on the edge of the end of History. Today we see liberal capitalism and its political system, parlimentarianism, as the only natural and acceptable solutions. Every revolutionary idea is considered utopian and, ultimately, criminal. Can we indeed say that today we are at the end of the emancipation process?

But, on the other hand, rather the reverse hypothesis could be reasonable and probable. Perhaps there are reasons to say that we are at the beginning of the emancipation process? Perhaps we do not stand at the end of history, but rather at its very beginning? Perhaps the death of the Subject in the classical sense has been the main precondition of the renewed interest in the question of subjectivity? Perhaps the death of politics in the classical sense has been the main precondition of the renewed interest in the question of politics? Hence, we see the reasons for the talk of an expansion of the field of politics instead of its retreat – a widening of the field of structural undecidability that opens the way to an enlargement of the political decision. For example, Ulrich Beck writes: "[p]eople expect to find politics in the arenas prescribed for it, and performed by the duly authorized agents: parliament, political parties, trade unions and so on. If the clocks of politics stop here, the political as a whole has stopped ticking, in that view".[8] According to Beck when we look for politics in such spheres as parliament, political parties, trade unions we make category error resting on the equation of politics and state, of politics with the political system, of politics with full-time political careers. We thus look for the political in the wrong place, on the wrong floors and on the wrong pages of the newspapers. Temporary politics are full of zombie-institutions which have been clinically dead for a long time but are unable to die. From such diagnosis, Beck draws the general conclusion: "the political constellation of industrial society is becoming unpolitical, while what was unpolitical in industrial is becoming political".[9] The areas which had been protected by the political in an industrial society – the private sector, business, science, towns, everyday life and so on – are caught in the storms of political conflicts in the reflexive modernity. From Beck's point of view there are reasons to talk about a renaissance of the political or even of a reinvention of politics.

I return to the main motive of my argument. I ask about the limits of the political at the very peculiar moment in history, above all at the very peculiar moment in the history of philosophy, namely, when (1) the reflection linked

7 Francis Fukuyama, *The End of History and the Last Man* (Penguin Books, 1992).

8 Ulrich Beck, *The Reinvention of Politics*, [in:] Ulrich Beck, Anthony Giddens, Scott Lash, *Reflexive Modernization: Politics, Tradition and Aesthetics in the Modern Social Order* (Cambridge: Polity Press, 1994).

9 *Ibid.*

with the subject of the "political" lays at the centre of interest of contemporary social and political philosophy, and when (2) the limits and referential identity of "what is political" never were so problematic and diffused. Hence, I assert that the problem of the limits of the politics and political is today so important and so urgent.

2. Diagnosis: from the end of politics to the reinvention of politics

To tackle these issues a little further, I maintain that the fact that politics today reaches its limits was described at least in five schools of thought or paradigms.

The first paradigm is very Foucauldian. According to Foucault, politics in our word would be continually replaced by bio-politics. Bio-politics and bio-power emerged as a coherent political technology in the seventeenth century. It has two poles or components. The increasing state concern with the biological well-being of the population includes disease control and prevention, adequate food and water supply, sanitary shelter, and education. This form of bio-politics is associated with the pole of scientific categories of human beings, such as species, population, race, gender, sexual practices, and so on. The second pole is disciplinary power. The basic goal of disciplinary power is to produce a person who is docile. Such institutions like armies, schools, monasteries, hospitals, factories, boarding-schools are the areas where disciplinary power is most rigorous.

Particularly in the final chapter of the first volume of his *History of Sexuality*, Foucault wrote: "For millennia, man remained what he was for Aristotle: a living animal with the additional capacity for a political existence; modern man is an animal whose politics places his existence as a living being into question".[10] For Foucault politics for centuries entailed the exercise of a form of power – sovereign power. Sovereign power is characterized by a particular right, the right to decide over life and death. Modern powers for Foucault are more closely aligned to a bio-politics in which power is not the right to kill but rather the right to reinforce life and to produce another form of life. Hence for Foucault medicine is the centred institution in our society;[11] this is the reason why the problems associated with life such as euthanasia, abortions, transplantation of organs, various forms of prenatal testing divide our

10 Michel Foucault (1976), *History of Sexuality*, vol. 1, *The Will to Know*, trans. R. Hurley (New York, 1978).

11 Michel Foucault (1963), *The Birth of the Clinic: An Archaeology of Medical Perception*, trans. A. Sheridan (London, 1976).

society so strongly. This is the reason why these problems give rise so intensive discussions in our society. Society with sex is society with life and above all with health and techniques to reinforce life and health. For Foucault, society with sex is above all medicalized society, hence modern politics is above all bio-politics, and modern ethics is above all bio-ethics.

The second diagnosis of the eclipse of political in the reflexive modernity is associated with Ulrich Beck's thesis of the replaced politics by sub-politics and Anthony Giddens's thesis of the politics of emancipation being replaced by the politics of life.

According to Giddens *emancipatory politics* is a politics of life chances, *life politics* is a politics of lifestyle. *Politics of emancipation* understands the concept of power as an hierarchical concept, that is, power is here understood as the possibility of imposing one's will upon the behaviour of other people or groups. Emancipations movements presuppose the elimination of power relations, the abolition of the subject/object distinction and emancipations is doing it for the sake of justice. *Life politics*, on the contrary, is the politics of the system of late modernity, which, on an individual and collective level, has radically altered the existential parameters of social activity.[12] It is a politics of self-actualisation in a reflexively ordered environment, where that reflexivity links self and body to systems of global scope. The exciting aspect of this view lies in the fact that here the political is achieved through the private sphere. All the things that are considered loss, danger, waste and decay in the left-right framework of bourgeois politics, things like concern with the self, the questions: Who am I?, What do I want?, in short all the original sins of individualism, lead to a different type of identity of the political: life politics.

The central concept for Beck is not life politics but sub-politics.[13] According to Beck sub-politics is distinguished from politics first in that agents outside the political or corporatist system are allowed to appear on the stage of social design; this group includes professional groups, the technical intelligentsia, research institutions and management, skilled workers, citizens' initiatives. The second difference lies therein that not only social and collective agents, but individuals as well, compete with each other for the limited resources and as a result shape the authority and the political.

I see some objections to Beck's idea of sub-politics and Giddens' idea of life politics. As we know, political science has opened up and elaborated its concept

12 Anthony Giddens, *Modernity and Self-Identity. Self and Society in the Late Modern Age* (Cambridge: Polity Press, 1991), p. 214.

13 Ulrich Beck, *Risikogesellschaft: auf dem Weg in eine andere Moderne* (Frankfurt/M: Suhrkamp, 1986).

of politics into three aspects. First is *polity*; it inquires into the institutional constitution of the political community with which society organizes itself (the administration); second is *policy*; it is the substance of the political programmes for shaping social circumstances; and, third is *politics*; it is the process of political conflict over power-sharing and power positions. If we transfer the distinction between polity, policy and politics to sub-politics, then the following questions arise: (1) How is the *sub-polity* organized institutionally, what are the sources of its power and its potential for strategic actions? (2) With what goals, content, ideology and programmes, for example in health precautions and social security, is *sub-policy* conducted? (3) What organizational forms and forums of *sub-politics* are emerging and can be observed? Are scientists, specialists, ecological and feminist circles or other discrepant groups divorced from the pure work relations and remain outside of the economical system?

Beck answered the three questions in the following way: (1) Sub-politics means shaping society from below. There are growing opportunities to have a voice and a share in the arrangement of society for groups hitherto uninvolved in the substantive technification and industrialization process: citizens, social movements, expert groups, working people. This is what we could call *sub-polity*. (2) Perhaps the main ideology of sub-politics, its internal content, is the attempt of reform of present instrumental rationality. The last element here is often interpreted in utilitarian terms; the rational actor is supposed to choose and calculate means and ends from the standpoint of maximizing utility or expectations of utility. From noninstrumental rationality's point of view not only the anticipating profit is important but also the values with are associated with actions. This is what we could call *sub-policy*. (3) And finally, in *sub-politics* the instrument of power is congestion as the modernized form of the involuntary strike and the struggle for consensus as well as modernizing reforms on the inside and outside of the political system.

The third interpretation of the fact that politics is disappearing from the contemporary world is Slavoj Žižek's idea that contemporary political thought is an attempt to neutralize or even invalidate the political antagonism but not by the idea of bio-politics or sub-politics, but by the four forms of simulating it.[14] In a nutshell, these four forms of simulating politics are archeo-politics, as-if-politics, meta-politics and ultra-politics.

Archaeo-politics is a communitarian attempt to provide a direct ontological foundation for politics via ethics, for example some substantial notion of supreme Good or common wealth (Alasdair MacIntyre). Politics is conceived

14 Slavoj Žižek, *Tarrying with the Negative: Kant, Hegel, and the Critique of Ideology (Post-Contemporary Interventions)* (Duke University Press: Durham, 1993).

here as the reflexive form of substantial ethical life. It constitutes the medium in which the members of quasinatural solidary communities become aware of their dependence on one another. For Aristotle, politics is the way by which we as living beings can become full, true, genuine human beings.

As-if-politics is associated by Žižek with Jürgen Habermas' idea of "deliberative democracy" and "discourse ethics" or John Rawls's theory of justice. It is an attempt to neutralize the political by sacrificing its substantial content and giving universalism a proceduralist twist; indeed, Habermas believes that: "with the discourse ethics as a guiding thread, we can indeed develop the formal idea of a society in which all potentially important decision-making processes are linked to institutionalized forms of discursive will-formation".[15]

Meta-politics is Marx's attempt to reduce politics to economy. Indeed, in *The Communist Manifesto* he writes: "[i]n every epoch, the ruling ideals have been the ideals of the ruling class".[16] The association between property and power is to Marx so simple and direct that he has considered these two concepts comprehensive. For Marx property was not only the decisive but also the sole source of power, the integument that held and holds the capitalist system together. As long as it remains in private hands, no one else can possess power.

Ultra-politics is Carl Schmitt's attempt of militarizing the language of the politics.[17] In this interpretation politics is war, "a war continued by other means", which is of course the reversal of Clausewitz's assertion that "war is politics continued by other means". For Schmitt violence is not the essence of the political; but as much as the state presupposes the concept of the political, the political presupposes the concept of war. War is the existential negation of the enemy. It must remain a real possibility for as long as the concept of the enemy remains valid. According to Žižek, ethics, language, economy and war are four forms of simulating and substituting for politics today.

The fourth diagnosis of the death of the traditional concept of politics is linked with feminists circle and the statement that the private and personal is political. Many years ago, Kate Millett used the term "sexual politics" and in this way she posed the question: Could the private be the political, could our private decision and private conduct of life have some political sense, some political implications?[18] Of course, in introducing the term "sexual politics" one

15 Jürgen Habermas, *Three Normative Models of Democracy,* [in:] "Constellations", Volume 1, no. 1, 1994, p. 16.

16 Karl Marx, Friedrich Engels (1848), *The Communist Manifesto, Selected Works,* 2 vols (Moscow: Foreign Languages Publishing House, 1962), p. 54.

17 Carl Schmitt, *The Concept of the Political.*

18 Kate Millett, *Sexual Politics,* (New York: Doubleday and Company , 1969).

must first answer the inevitable question: Can the relationship between the sexes be viewed in a political light at all? But the answer to the question depends on how one defines politics. If we mean that politics is linked to the methods or tactics involved in managing a state or government, if we define the political as that relatively narrow and exclusive world of meetings, chairmen, and parties then the private life will not associated with the political sphere. At least not directly. The private and the personal is not political. On the other hand, if one understands patriarchy to be an institution perpetuated by the techniques of control of the state, one perhaps can be eager to answer: yes!, the private life has political implications.

Kate Millett does not define the political as that relatively narrow and exclusive world of meetings, chairmen, and parties. She compares the term "politics" to power-structured relationships, arrangements in which one group of people is controlled by another. By way of parenthesis one might add that although ideal politics might simply be conceived of as the arrangement of human life according to agreeable and rational principles from which the entire notion of power over others should be banished, one must confess that this is not what constitutes the political as we know it.

Perhaps in this way we rediscover the principal conflict between the liberal vision of politics and radical vision – feminist or Marxist. The disagreement turns around the meaning of the term "political": feminist interpretation gives to it an extensive application while the liberal is far more restricted. But perhaps much more than the meaning of the term lies at the heart of the dispute. Feminism suggests that the term "political" can appropriately be applied to a range of actions where the liberal has never thought of applying it. Moreover, feminism could suggest that the important issue here is not a disagreement about the term but rather the fact that a liberal is a person of blinkered political sensitivity and awareness. Untouchability of the private sphere, which from the liberal point of view is the guarantee of easy conscience, from the feminist perspective is a guarantee of an uneasy conscience.

When I ask about the limits of politics I ask about something different from the limits of the concept of "game" or "piece of furniture". If the liberal does not perceive that the sense of the political encompasses the kind of situation that feminism is referring to, this could be for one of two reasons: (1) either because of the logical mistake, or, (2) because of the blinkered political sensitivity and awareness. So, I repeat, the question about the limits of the political is not only the question about the limits of the concept of the political, whether we have a limited list of properties (features) which enables us to identify some object or event as political; the question about the limits of the political is above all the question about the limits of our political sensitivity.[19]

The fifth diagnosis of the death of the traditional concept of politics is linked with the idea of politics of truth or politics of knowledge. In the well known book *The Postmodern Condition. A Report on Knowledge*, Jean-François Lyotard wrote:

> [...] that functions of regulation, and therefore of reproduction, are being and will be further withdrawn from administrators and entrusted to machines. [...] Access to data is, and will continue to be, the prerogative of experts of all stripes. The ruling class is and will continue to be the class of decision makers. Even now it is no longer composed of the traditional political class, but of a composite layer of corporate leaders, high-level administrators, and the heads of the major professional, labor, political, and religious organisations.[20]

We live in the world in which the experts and managers have power, not politicians and property owners. Hence, for Lyotard knowledge and power are simply two sides of the same question: Who decides what knowledge is, and who knows what needs to be decided? In the computer age, the question of knowledge is more than ever a question of government.

The same is suggested of course by Foucault in many places. For him each society has general politics of truth – the techniques and procedures accorded value in the acquisition of truth. In Foucault's thought political economy of truth in our society is characterised by four important traits.

Truth is centred on the form of scientific discourse and the institutions which produce it. This discourse is of course science. (1) It is subject to constant economic and political incitement, which creates the demand for truth. (2) It is the object, under diverse forms, of immense diffusion and consumption circulating through apparatuses of education and information whose extent is relatively broad in the social body. (3) It is produced and transmitted under the control, dominant if not exclusive, of a few great political and economic

---

19 Of course I realize that the concept of politics is one of those concepts that are unavoidably value-dependent and even more essentially contested. Every definition of a concept of politics is also inextricably tied to a given set of value-assumptions which predetermine the range of its empirical application. Politics might well be an instance of what Ludwig Wittgenstein famously termed a "family-resemblance concept" – a loose grouping of individuals, each characterized by one or another of a set of overlapping features or similarities, none of which pervades among all of the others. Ludwig Wittgenstein (1953), *Philosophical Investigations*, trans. G. E. M. Anscombe, (New York 1958), p. 43.

20 Jean-François Lyotard, *The Postmodern Condition. A Report on Knowledge*, (Manchester University Press, 1984).

apparatuses (university, army, media). (4) Truth is the issue of the whole political debate and social confrontation ("ideological" struggles).[21] In Foucault's thought, in contemporary Western societies power is dispersed, but not as democrats hoped to disperse it, not to citizens who argue and vote the policies of the central government. Citizenship and government alike have been superseded by professional expertise and local discipline.

Let me summarize these five diagnoses. If I properly understand my reflections, I showed the process of politization of five spheres of life. The idea of the politics of knowledge or truth blurs the distinction between science and the politics; the idea of the "sexual politics" blurs the distinction between private life and public sphere; the idea of the sub-politics blurs the distinction between vocations (or professions) and politics, so destroys the very important liberal postulate to distinguish the role of citizen (*citoyen*) and the role of contractor (*bourgeois*); and the idea of bio-politics blurs the distinction between the sheer fact of living and the fact of decision making (action); archeo-politics blurs the distinction between ethics and politics, as-if-politics blurs the distinction between discourse or discussion and politics; meta-politics blurs the distinction between economy and politics; ultra-politics blurs the distinction between war and politics. In this way all boundaries have been transgressed. An important point here is (1) how far this process goes, (2) what it means and where it leads?

Above all, anyone who abolishes the boundary between politics and nonpolitics deprives himself of the basis of his argument. Where everything is somehow political, somehow nothing is political anymore. The knowledge that everything is politics leads us astray if it is not supplemented with the insight that everything is also economics or culture. If between every point of social body, between a man and a woman, physician and patient, between the members of a family, between a master and his pupil, between everyone who knows and everyone who does not, between the owners and the workers there exist relations of power which are not simply a projection of the sovereign's real power over the individual, if such a picture of society is proper, then how can a system of mutually interconnected positions of power emerge out of the perpetual process of strategic conflict among actors? If society is thought of exclusively as a nexus of types of strategic action, how shall the situationally and occasionally achieved outcomes of action actually be temporally stabilized and then also be socially connected to a system of outcomes of action achieved and stabilized in other places?

---

21 Michel Foucault, *Truth and Power,* [in:] *The Foucault Reader,* Ed. Rabinow Paul (New York, 1984), p. 73.

3. What is politics proper?

I am afraid that I have not any clear answer to the last question, at the moment I will not even try to answer it, in exchange I try to give the answer to another question: Why in our reflections on politics do we have only some derivatives of politics, only some parasites of politics, only bio-politics, sub-politics, politics of life, archeo-politics, as-if-politics, meta-politics, ultra-politics, sexual politics, politics of truth, geopolitics and so on and so forth? Why are we not able today to talk about simple politics? Have we still any politics or maybe we have only its implications? Maybe today we have only the implications and not the sources and reasons?

Let me ask the question: What is politics proper? Or better: Have we any proper concept of politics at all? I betray at once that my answer is that we have not a proper concept of politics. I try to justify the thesis in two ways. The first way is the analysis of Carl Schmitt's concept of the political, and the second is the analysis of Slavoj Žižek's concept of proper politics. So, to answer the question what is political proper and whether we have some idea of political proper, I would like to come back in the first step to the well known text of Carl Schmitt, *The Concept of the Political*, and in the second step to Žižek's concept of proper politics.

4. The concept of the political as the parasites concept

The political, said Schmitt, is a category like the ethical, aesthetic, religious, or economic, but it is distinct from and more important than those other categories. Ethical, religious, and economic issues may – and often do – become political considerations, but they need not necessarily do so. In a sense, the political is the ultimate category; it is the sphere of life to which all the kinds of issues enumerated above, if they become significant enough, may rise. The emphasis Schmitt placed on the political is a product of the responsibilities he assigned to it. At its most fundamental level, the political is the realm in which ally and foe are determined. As Schmitt explained, "The specific political distinction to which political actions and motives can be reduced is that between friend and enemy".[22] Every religious, moral, economic, ethical, or other antithesis transforms into a political one if it is sufficiently strong to group human beings effectively into friends and enemies.

For example, religion is not necessarily political, but it becomes so when it is the basis of a friend-enemy distinction. Consequently, we may speak today

22 Carl Schmitt, *The Concept of the Political.*

simultaneously of a strict separation between political and religious life in the United States and of a religiously motivated conflict between Pakistan and India. In short, distinctions in other realms may rise to the level of political distinctions because "the political is the most intense and extreme antagonism, and every concrete antagonism becomes that much more political the closer it approaches the extreme point, that of the friend-enemy grouping".

I have some doubts linked with the concept of the "political" articulated in this way. I want to raise just three questions, or objections to this position: The first doubt is associated with the concept of the enemy. As there is never "the Other" as such, for same reason there is never such a thing as the "enemy" as such. There are only projects of thought, or of actions, on the basis of which we distinguish between those who are friends, those who are enemies, and those who can be considered neutral. The question of knowing how to treat enemies or neutrals depends entirely on the project concerned, the thought that constitutes it, and the concrete circumstances (is the project in an escalating phase? is it very dangerous?, etc.).

The second objection is associated with the very concept of the "political". I would like to ask: What does it mean exactly that every religious, moral, economic, ethical, or other antithesis transforms into a political one if it is sufficiently strong to group human beings effectively into friends and enemies? At least in my interpretation, it means that the very concept of the political (and not only such concepts as ultra-politics, sexual politics, politics of truth, geopolitics, and so on) is parasitical with regards to more fundamental concepts! In other words, has politics no autonomous place of action, which could be independent of other places of action such as morals, religion, science, economy, home space, and so on? Politics is always dependant on these others spheres of life and, what is equally important, our understanding of politics is dependent on understanding other phenomena. By this, I would like to say that we are able to understand the political phenomenon only if we borrow the dictionary from other domains of life.

This style of thinking is coherent with the Nietzsche's dictum that truth is only "a mobile army of metaphors"[23] and Richard Rorty's claim that a recognition of contingency of our conscience and cognition "lead[s] us to a picture of intellectual and moral progress as a history of increasingly useful metaphors rather than of increasing understanding of how things really are".[24]

---

23 Friedrich Nietzsche (1873), *On Truth and Lying in an Extra-Moral Sense,* trans. S. L. Gilman, [in:] *Friedrich Nietzsche on Rhetoric and Language* (Oxford: Oxford University Press), p. 244.

24 Richard Rorty, *Contingency, Irony, and Solidarity* (New York, 1989), p. 9.

In some sense my thesis also coincides with the ideas of George Lakoff.[25] According to him, metaphor was not a minor kind of trope used in poetry, but rather a fundamental mechanism of mind. We may not always know it, but we think in metaphors. A large proportion of our most commonplace thoughts makes use of an extensive, but unconscious, system of metaphorical concepts. The concepts from a typically concrete realm of thought are used to comprehend another, completely different domain. Such concepts are often reflected in everyday language, but their most dramatic effect comes in ordinary reasoning. Because so much of our social and political reasoning makes use of this system of metaphorical concepts, any adequate appreciation of even the most mundane social and political thought requires an understanding of this system. But unless one knows that the system exists, one may miss it altogether and be mystified by its effects.

5. The concept of the proper politics as a concept of representation

Slavoj Žižek maintains that we have a proper concept of politics. For him politics proper is a phenomenon that appeared for the first time in ancient Greece when the members of the demos presented themselves as the representatives, the stand-ins, for the whole of society, for the true universality.[26] For Žižek political conflict proper thus involves the tension between the structured social body, where each part has its place, and the part of no-part, which unsettles this order on account of the empty principle of universality, of the principled equality of all men qua speaking beings.

Politics proper thus always involve a kind of short circuit between the universal and the particular; it involves the paradox of a singular that appears as a stand-in for the universal, destabilizing the "natural" functional order of relation in the social body. This identification of the nonpart with the whole, of the part of society with no properly defined place (or part which resists its allocated subordinated place) with the universal, is the elementary gesture of politicization, discernible in all great democratic events, from the French Revolution (in which the Third Estate proclaimed itself identical to the nation as such against the aristocracy and clergy) to the demise of European socialism, in which groups such as the Czech Civic Forum proclaimed themselves representative of the entire society against the party *nomenklatura*.

25 George Lakoff, *Moral Politics* (University of Chicago Press, 1996).
26 Slavoj Žižek, *The Plague of Fantasies* (London: Verso, 1998).

For Žižek the political struggle proper is therefore never simply a rational debate between multiple interests but, simultaneously, the struggle for one's voice to be heard and recognized as that of a legitimate partner. When the excluded, from the Greek demos to Polish workers, protested against the ruling elite (the aristocracy or *nomenklatura*), the true stakes were not only their explicit demands (for higher wages, better working conditions, and so forth) but their very right to be heard and recognized as an equal participant in the debate. In Poland, the *nomenklatura* lost the moment it had to accept Solidarity as an equal partner. In this precise sense, politics and democracy are synonymous: the basic aim of antidemocratic politics always and by definition is and has been depoliticization, that is, the unconditional demand that things should return to the normal, with each individual doing his or her particular job.

I have some doubts linked with the concept of the "proper politics" articulated in thus way. I want to raise just three questions, or objections to this position. The first doubt is associated with the concept of the singularity. Jacques Derrida in *Politics of Friendship* said that there is some *aporia* between democracy and singularity.[27] Democracy means, minimally, equality. There is no democracy except as equality among everyone but an equality which can be calculated, countable: you count the number of units, voters, voices, citizens. On the other hand, we have to reconcile this demand for equality with the demand for singularity and respect for the Other as singular. Hence an *aporia*: How can we, at the same time, take into account the equality of everyone and nevertheless take into account and respect the heterogeneous singularity of everyone? For Derrida that is a double bind. On the one hand we should respect the singularity of the Other and not to ask him or her that he or she respect or keep intact my own space or my own culture. But on the other hand in the idea of democracy contains the idea of equality, which tries to reduce the idea of Otherness to the idea of identities, to the logic of the same. Hence Derrida asks, in a rather rhetorical style: Is it possible to think differently of this double injunction of equality for everyone and respect for singularity beyond the limits of classical politics?

In other words, the question that concerns me here is whether the demand for respect for one's cultural traditions (respect for those activities, practices, and ways of viewing the world that are particularly valued by, or associated with, members of disadvantaged groups, including women, and a multitude of other minority groups in the state) follows from the principle of equal respect for each individual (respect for the unique identities of each individual, regardless

27 Jacques Derrida, *Politics of Friendship*.

of gender, race, or ethnicity), or whether, at least in some cases, these two demands will necessarily come into conflict with one another.

The second objection is associated with the concept of social order. For Ernesto Laclau there are two possibilities of thinking about society. The first one is that society is an addition of discrete groups, each tending to their particular aims in constant collision with each other. The order of society could mean the precarious equilibrium of negotiated agreement between groups, all of which retain their conflicting aims and identity. According to second possibility society has some kind of pre-established essence, that is, society as the whole has a content of its own, independent of the will of the particular groups; what Laclau named "hegemony" would mean here the realization of such essence. Hegemonisation is understood as actions that attempt to fix the meaning of social relations. If we can see politics with the category of hegemony, then politics is an act of power, force and will that is contingent through and through. Hegemonic universality is the idea that political action is action motivated or orientated around the universal term – equality, human rights, justice, individual freedom, and so on – and yet that universality has to be contaminated by a particularity, by the specific social context for which the universal term is destined.

At least in my interpretation both of these views are intended to explain what has been, and I am afraid will continue to be, the most puzzling problem of social philosophy: How is it that human societies cohere? The first vision of society suggests that social order results from a general agreement of values; a *consensus omnium* which outweighs all possible or actual differences of opinion and interest. The second school holds that coherence and order in society are founded on force and constraint, on the domination of some, and subjection of others.

I would claim that neither of these models could be conceived as exclusively valid or applicable. They constitute complementary, rather than alternative, aspects of the structure of total societies as well as of every element of this structure. We have to choose between them only for the explanation of specific problems. Strictly speaking, both models are "valid" or, rather, useful and necessary for sociological analysis. We cannot conceive of society unless we realize the interlacing of: stability and change, integration and conflict, function and motive force, consensus and coercion.

The last objection is associated with the concept of "authority of the state", which implicates some form of antinomy. Perhaps this antinomy is the central question of all political philosophy because it concerns the nature of the authority of state. As Peter Winch showed, the concept of such authority generates philosophical puzzlement. On the one hand, authority of the state seems to involve a power "to override" the will of the individual citizen. On the other, the existence of power seems in a certain sense to depend on the wills of the individuals who are subject to it. For they can decide whether or not to acknowledge it as legitimate. Where there is no such acknowledgement, one feels hesitant in saying that one is dealing with an instance of political authority at all.[28]

Hence the paradox: on the one hand what we call the state power is a form of representation. The representation is the process by which somebody else – the representative – substituted for, and at the same time embodying, the represented. The condition for a perfect representation is when representation is a direct process of transmission of the will of the represented. On the other hand, what we call subject is a form of representation, too. George Herbert Mead in *Mind, Self and Society* tries to construe reason as the internalisation of social norm, rather than as a built-in component of the human self.[29] Mind is only the individual importation of the social process into the individual organism. Perhaps the power someone else has over me is the basic condition and premise that allows me to establish power over myself. The very sense of autonomy is, in an individual as well as in a social development, later than the sense of heteronomy. Similarly, the sense of external locus of control is earlier than the sense of inner locus of control. I maintain that this view was developed also by Freud and Foucault but in very different ways.

Hence my conclusion: power is only the representation of the individual wills, but the individual wills are only the effect of shaping the subject by the power, they are the intrapsychic extension of social authority. On the one hand, the subject is the result of the relations of power but on the other hand it is a precondition for these relations.

6. Politics, politizations and depolitizations

At the very end I would like to come back to my main question concerning the limits of politics. According to the liberal view, such concepts as citizen, law, and the nature of the process of political will formation have very clear meanings. The citizen's status is determined primarily by the individual rights he or she has vis-à-vis the state and other citizens. As bearers of individual rights citizens enjoy the protection of the government as long as they pursue their private interests within the boundaries drawn by legal statues – and this

28 Peter Winch, *Ethics and Action* (London, 1972), pp. 90-109.

29 George Herbert, Mead, *Mind, Self, Society* (Chicago, 1965).

includes protection against state interventions that violate the legal prohibition on government interference. Individual rights are negative rights that guarantee a domain of freedom of choice within which legal persons are freed from external compulsion.

Here politics has the function of bundling together and bringing to bear private social interests against a state apparatus that specializes in the administrative employment of political power for collective goals. Politics in this view is essentially a struggle for positions that grants access to administrative power. The political process of opinion- and will-formation in the public sphere and in the parliament is shaped by the competition of strategically acting collectives trying to maintain or acquire positions of power.

When we really have crossed the frontiers of the political, that is, if the liberal concept of the political was really replaced by the new one in which we redefine the role of citizen, the meaning of the politics and the role of political struggle, then the simple consequence of the fact is that (1) the meanings of such concepts as citizen, law, the nature of the process of political will formation were completely changed and that (2) the many political decisions – decisions at the level of state administration or those concerned with taking over the state – attempt to deny their political character. In other words, political decisions attempt to erase their traces of power, force, will and contingency not only by naturalising or essentialising the context of decisions but also by washing away the boundary between the public and the private. The main strategy of politics is to make itself invisible in order to claim for itself the status of nature for a priori self-evidence. In such opportunities there is not only a tendency towards invisibility in politics; politics would be invisible.

In other words, my doubts linked with the formula "the private is the political", my doubts linked with the process of invalidating the distinction between the public sphere and the private conduct of life are caused by the suspicion of the implications of such a process. If we really invalided the distinction, then does not arise a danger of still enlarging and expanding social and state control over our private life? Does not in such a situation come true the worst dream of Franz Kafka, George Orwell and Michel Foucault: the spectacle of law has its repercussions in our bed, or is even taking place in our bed. As we know a large part of Kafka's work consists in the fear that one day my secret life in bed become the center of the court of law, that the private could become the public. A large part of Orwell's work concerns the fear that the process of politizations of private life in totalitarian societies is much stronger than in a democratic political order.[30] A large part of Foucault's work consists in showing how the patterns of acculturation and socialization characteristic of modern societies have imposed on their members kinds of constraints of which older, premodern societies had not dreamed. Perhaps the process of politizations is more dangerous than the process of depolitizations. Perhaps the dangerous ingredient of Nazism is not its "utter politizations" of the whole of social life but, on the contrary, the suspension of the political through the reference to an extraideological kernel, much stronger than in a normal democratic political order.

30 Carl J. Friedrich, *The Unique Character of Totalitarian Society*, [in:] *Totalitarianism, Proceedings of a Conference held at the American Academy of Art and Sciences* (New York, 1953). Carl J. Friedrich, Jerzy Brzezinski, *Totalitarian Dictatorship and Autocracy*, (New York, 1966).

II. Mourning Populism: the Case of Poland

The correlation of melancholia and mourning seems justified by the general picture of the two conditions. Moreover, the exciting causes due to environmental influences are, so far as we can discern them at all, the same for both conditions. Mourning is regularly the reaction to the loss of a loved person, or to the loss of some abstraction which has taken the place of one, such as one's country, liberty, an ideal, and so on. In some people the same influences produce melancholia instead of mourning and we consequently suspect them of a pathological disposition.

Sigmund Freud[1]

Populism is, quite simply, a way of constructing the political.

Ernesto Laclau[2]

1. Populism in question

The concept of populism would now seem to be present in every democratic political culture, although the term is used by historians, social scientists, journalists and politicians to describe social, political and institutional phenomena that are often very different from each other. These differences may be explained by the fact that populism tends to emerge at different times and in various places. It also seems that today populist slogans are not only used by radical parties, as it is said often in the literature. In fact, populist rhetoric has been worked out by vast political platforms, not only on the right but also on the left of the political scene.[3] Populism today is not restricted to populist parties as such, but is increasingly associated with European leaders and movements.

---

1 Sigmund Freud (1917), *Mourning and Melancholia.* [in:] *The Standard Edition of the Complete Psychological Works of Sigmund Freud*, Volume XIV (1914-1916), ed. James Strachey, (London: Hogarth Press 1957), p. 243.

2 Ernesto Laclau, *On Populist Reason*, (London/New York: Verso), p. XI.

3 Hans-Georg Betz, *Radical Right-Wing Populism in Western Europe* (Basingstoke, Macmillan, 1994), p. 33; Michael Kazin, *The Populist Persuasion: An American History* (New York, Basic Books, 1995); Paul Taggart, *The New Populism and the New Politics. New Protest Parties in Sweden in a Comparative Perspective*, (Basingstoke, Macmillan, 1996), p. 14; Cas Mudde, *The Ideology of the Extreme Right* (Manchester, Manchester University Press, 2000). p. 67; Fareed Zakaria, *The Future of Freedom: Illiberal Democracy at Home and Abroad* (New York: W. W. Norton, 2003), p. 56.

Cas Mudde defines populism as "an ideology that considers society to be ultimately separated into two homogeneous and antagonistic groups, 'the pure people' versus 'the corrupt elite', and which argues that politics should be an expression of the general will of the people".[4] Considering populism as an ideology or not, Mudde's definition seems to be only a collection of the features of populism. The first one is negativism. Populism reacts against elites and institutions and is seen as anti-capitalism, anti-Semitism, anti-urbanism, anti-modernism, anti-etc. From the negation populists benefit by expressiveness. Negativism and expressiveness are presented by a discourse. Here, the discourse plays an important role and is based on the rhetoric that expresses not who they are in favor of but who they are against. The next strong element of populist thinking is treachery. Populists usually claim that the people have been betrayed by the establishment. Usually all political elites are accused of abusing their position of power instead of acting in conformity with the interests of the people as a whole.[5] To go further, populists argue that there is a conspiracy of elites against the people.[6] This is based also on simple rules derived from the common wisdom of the people and is deeply rooted in local tradition and culture.

The question is then: what do María Eva Duarte de Perón, Hugo Rafael Chávez, Silvio Berlusconi, Jean-Marie Le Pen, Jörg Haider and Jarosław Kaczyński have in common? They all are said to be, or have been, populists. The differences in political orientation between these disparate leaders shows the problematic nature of the concept and the difficulties in establishing its meaning. A first problem arises because populism has become a matter of attribution rather than a term with which most political actors would willingly identify: politicians would define themselves as "liberals", "socialists" or "nationalists", but hardly ever as "populists". The reasons for this reluctance are quite obvious. The term populism has a negative normative connotation both politically and economically. Politically, it has been associated with personalism, authoritarianism and the manipulation of a not very well informed or even irrational *populus*. Economically, it has been identified with irresponsible fiscal profligacy that exchanges short-term gain for long-term pain.

Ernesto Laclau's *On Populist Reason* positions him firmly on the side of those who vindicate the democratic nature of populism. More so, he turns the wheel full circle to argue that far from being incompatible, populism and democracy are

4 Cas Mudde, *Populist Radical Right Parties in Europe*, (Cambridge University Press United Kingdom, 2007), p. 41.

5 Yves Mény and Yves Surel (eds.), *Democracies and the Populist Challenge*, (Basingstoke/New York: Palgrave 2002), p. 13.

6 Jerzy Szacki, *Pytania o populizm* [*Questions about populism*], [in:] "Krytyka Polityczna", nr 4, 2004, p. 33.

almost inseparable twins. The ground for this claim is that there is no democracy without a *demos* ("the people") and that the constitution of democratic identities is based on the very same logic that underlies the populist mode of identification. Populism is, for Laclau, a political logic rather than a political movement or an ideology, and to understand how this logic operates it is necessary first to grasp his theory of politics. Drawing on Saussurean linguistics, Freud and Lacan's psychoanalysis and Gramsci's theory of hegemony, Laclau has developed a highly distinctive theory of politics, which is both elegant and sophisticated. His is a relational theory of society whereby the elements of socio-political life exist only in terms of relations of differences and equivalences with each other. Relations of differences predominate in well-structured social constructs such as language (in which, for instance, the term "father" draws its meaning from its differential position with respect to that of "mother", "son" or "grandfather" within the discourse of the family), administrative structures and the welfare state.

Laclau's theory of populism helps us to understand populism as a mode of identification that arises out the chasm separating political institutions from the people and calls our attention to the limitations of a purely institutional understanding of democracy. His formal reading of populism as a political logic rather than as an ideology explains the elusive nature of populism, as the populist logic could be put at the service of the most diverse ideological contents, from the radical left to the extreme right. He is also right in claiming that populism has a radical democratic edge, and that populism and democracy share a common ground in the constitution of popular democratic identities. But although Laclau does not claim that populism is necessarily democratic, his arguments that the very possibility of democracy depends on the constitution of a democratic people and that democracy does not necessarily equate with liberal democracy fail to fully explore the undemocratic underside of populism given by the imagining of a homogeneous people. If democracy is about the enactment of the will of the people, its survival depends on the acknowledgement that we can only have provisional versions of the popular will, and therefore the argument for the toleration of differences is not just a liberal argument but a democratic argument as well.

Moreover, the relation between Laclau's theory of politics and his theory of populism leads him to regard populism as the natural form of radical politics, and even of politics *tout court*. If populism consists in postulating a radical alternative within the communitarian space, a choice at the crossroads on which the future of a given society hinges, does not populism become synonymous with politics? The answer can only be affirmative. The problem is that Laclau's answer leaves a lot out of politics, as not all politics is necessarily radical and not all radical politics is necessarily populist. The *status quo* is as much a political construction as its radical alternatives. It is based on the political construction of differences, which Antonio Gramsci, using a term taken from the Italian political tradition, called the politics of *trasformismo*. On the other hand, many forms of radical politics are localised struggles that are no less radical because they fail to, or even do not aspire to, crystallise into a systemic alternative. But Laclau is right in reminding us that politics is ultimately about the construction of alternatives to the *status quo*, and this is even truer in an era of centrist consensus and political alienation.

Taking as a point of departure Laclau's theory of populist reason and some ideas from *Mourning and Melancholia* of Freud, I would like to question two established theses. According to the first one, populism is a hollow and nonspecified term as long as it is without reference to some postulates or political claims; according to the second one populism can be considered only on a rhetorical, not ideological level. Instead, I postulate that: (1) the difficulty of determining the populist discourse is not a transient ailment, only occasionally related to that phenomenon, but a quality built in social reality, permanent and irremovable; (2) the populist rhetoric is not solely an epiphenomenon that can be neglected in any serious analysis. On the contrary, there is a direct link between the two layers: the rhetorical and the conceptual.

The reconfiguration of thinking about populism I would like to advance should allow me to expect answers to a number of questions: (1) What are the relations between politics and populist politics? (2) How and to what extent does populist logic alter the mechanisms governing politics? (3) Is the de-politicization of liberal democracy (the prevalence of administration over politics) a direct cause of the return of populism? In order to substantiate the thesis that populism is today's way of doing politics, I would like reconstruct the recent postcommunist history of Poland, above all the situation after the Smolensk tragedy, when the Tupolev-154M aircraft of the Polish Air Force crashed near the city of Smolensk in Russia, killing all 96 people on board. This moment marks for me the opening of a new stage of development of populism which I refer to as "mourning populism".

2. Not populism but the logic of populism

The weakness in defining populism as an ideology of some movements results from the fact that what is here treated as a tacit assumption is the thesis that populism simply expresses the inner nature of some political subjects.[7] Here, I

7 Margaret Canovan, *Populism*, (New York and London: Harcourt Brace Jovanovich, 1981), p. 56.

defend the reverse possibility of understanding populism. We could assume that the political practices do not express the nature of social agents but, instead, constitute the latter. Such a solution was proposed by Ernesto Laclau, who suggests that practices would be more primary units of analysis than the group, which means that the group would only be the result of an articulation of social practices.

If this approach is correct, we could say that a movement is not populist because in its politics or ideology it presents actual contents identifiable as populist, but because it shows a particular logic of articulation of those contents – whatever those contents are. Individuals – in the theoretical context – are not coherent totalities but merely referential identities which have to be split up into a series of localized subject positions. And the articulation between these positions is a social and not an individual affair. The concept of populism that Laclau proposes is, as a result, a strictly formal one, for all its defining features are exclusively related to a specific mode of articulation independent of the actual contents that are articulated. That is the reason why "populism" is an ontological and not an ontic category.[8] Most of the attempts at defining populism have tried to locate what is specific to it in a particular ontic content and, as a result, they have ended in a self-defeating exercise whose two predictable alternative results have been: either to choose an empirical content which is immediately overflowed by an avalanche of exceptions, or to appeal to an "intuition" which cannot be translated into any conceptual content.[9]

---

8 Ernesto Laclau, *On Populist Reason*, p. 34

9 Ernesto Laclau, *Why do empty signifiers matter to politics?* [in:] E Laclau, *Emancipation(s)*, (London: Verso), p. 45; Jacob Torfing, *Discourse Theory: Achievements, Arguments and Challenges* [in:] Howarth, D. & J. Torfing, *Discourse Theory in European Politics: Identity, Policy and Governance*, (Palgrave, Basingstoke, 2004), p. 89. The smallest unit of his analysis of populism is the category of social demand. The strategic reason of choosing this term is clear: the subject of demand is constituted through raising this demand. However, the term "demand" involves a whole theatrical scene in which a subject is addressing his demand to an Other presupposed to be able to meet it. Laclau calls such an elementary demand "democratic"; as he explains it, he resorts to this slightly idiosyncratic use to signal that a demand still functions within the socio-political system, i.e., a demand is met as a particular demand, so that it is not frustrated and, because of this frustration, forced to inscribe itself into an antagonistic series of equivalences. Although he emphasizes how, in an institutionalized political space, there are multiple conflicts, these conflicts are dealt with one by one, without setting in motion any transversal antagonisms. Laclau is well aware that chains of equivalences can also form themselves within an institutionalized democratic space. But what Laclau neglected to emphasize is not only the uniqueness of democracy with regard to his basic conceptual opposition between the logic of differences and the logic

Approaching the question of populism formally makes it possible to address another, otherwise intractable issue. To ask oneself if a movement is or is not populist is, actually, to start with the wrong question. The question that we should, instead, ask ourselves is the following: To what extent is a movement populist? In this way we have presented political practices as operating at diverse points of a continuum whose two extremes would be: (1) an institutionalist discourse dominated by a pure logic of difference and (2) a populist one, in which the logic of equivalence operates unchallenged. These two extremes are actually unreachable: pure difference would mean a society so dominated by administration and by the individualisation of social demands that no struggle around internal frontiers, and in consequence no politics, would be possible; and pure equivalence would involve such a dissolution of social links that the very notion of "social demand" would lose any meaning, which offers us the image of society as the "crowd" or "mass" as depicted by the 19th century theorists of "mass psychology" such as Hippolyte Taine[10] or Gustave Le Bon.[11]

To be quite truthful, Laclau maintains that a social situation in which demands tend to reaggregate themselves on the negative basis that they all remain unsatisfied is the first precondition of that mode of political articulation that we call populism. While the institutional arrangement was grounded on the logic of difference, in a populist situation it is the reverse, which can be described as a logic of equivalence. In this case all the demands, in spite of their differential character, tend to reaggregate themselves forming what Laclau calls an equivalential chain.[12] This means that each individual demand

---

of equivalences, but also the full inner entwinement of these two uses of logic. Democracy can not only include antagonisms, it is the only political form that solicits and presupposes it, that institutionalizes it, which means that what other political systems perceive as a threat, democracy elevates into a positive condition of its functioning. The conclusion to be drawn is that populism is not the only mode of existence of the excess of antagonism over the institutional-democratic frame of regulated agonistic struggle: not only the Communist revolutionary organizations, but also the wide phenomena of noninstitutionalized social and political protests, from the student movements in the 1968 period to the later antiwar protests and the more recent antiglobalization movement, cannot be properly called populist.

10 Hippolyte Taine (1878), *The French Revolution*, trans. J. Durand, (London: Daldy, Isbister & Co. 1878), vol 1.

11 Gustave Le Bon (1896), *The Crowd: a Study of the Popular Mind.* (New York: Macmillan, 1977).

12 Ernesto Laclau, *On Populist Reason*, p. 178; Jacob Torfing, *Discourse Theory: Achievements, Arguments and Challenges*, p. 123.

is constitutively split: on the one hand, it is its own particularised self; on the other it points, through equivalential links, to the totality of the other demands.

The subject of the demand is different in these two cases. In the first, the subject of the demand was as punctual as the demand itself. The subject of a demand conceived of as a differential particularity is called a democratic subject by Laclau. In the other case the subject will be wider, for its subjectivity will result from the equivalential aggregation of a plurality of democratic demands. Laclau calls a subject constituted on the basis of this logic a popular subject.[13] This shows clearly the conditions for either the emergence or disappearance of a popular subjectivity: the more social demands tend to be differentially absorbed within a successful institutional system, the weaker the equivalential links will be and the more unlikely the constitution of a popular subjectivity. Conversely, a situation in which a plurality of unsatisfied demands and an increasing inability of the institutional system to absorb them differentially coexist creates the conditions leading to a populist rupture.

For Laclau the very logic of hegemonic articulation applies also to the conceptual opposition between populism and politics: populism is the Lacanian "*objet a*" of politics, the particular figure which stands for the universal dimension of the political, which is why it is "the royal road" to understanding the political. Populism is not a specific political movement, but the political at its purest: the "inflection" of the social space that can affect any political content. Its elements are purely formal: populism occurs when a series of particular "democratic" demands (for better social security, health services, lower taxes, against war, etc.) is enchained in a series of equivalences, and this enchainment produces "people" as the universal political subject. What characterizes populism is not the ontic content of these demands, but the mere formal fact that, through their enchainment, "people" emerge as a political subject, and all different particular struggles and antagonisms appear as parts of a global antagonistic struggle between "us" (people) and "them". Again, the content of "us" and "them" is not prescribed in advance but, precisely, is the stake of the struggle for hegemony.[14]

---

13 Ernesto Laclau, *On Populist Reason*, p. 148.

14 Populism, therefore, follows a logic of equivalence and antagonism, whereby a part (or part object) comes to stand in for the whole. Indeed, this synecdochic substitution is doubled: first, a particular *signifier* from within the populist movement represents the people as a whole, retrospectively unifying their disparate demands; second and more generally, the people as an oppressed part of a divided society claim the right to stand in for society as a whole, deposing the parasitic minority who, they claim, illegitimately cling to power. Sovereignty should be returned to the people who constitute, populism argues, the full body of social totality. As Laclau points out, the same operation of taking

For Laclau the fact that some particular struggle is elevated into the "universal equivalent" of all struggles is not a predetermined fact, but itself the result of the contingent political struggle for hegemony – in some constellation, this struggle can be the workers' struggle, in another constellation, the patriotic anticolonialist struggle, in yet another constellation the antiracist struggle for cultural tolerance. The struggle for hegemony thus not only presupposes an irreducible gap between the universal form and the multiplicity of particular contents, but also the contingent process by means of which one among these contents is "transubstantiated" into the immediate embodiment of the universal dimension. For example, in Poland of the 1980s, the particular demands of *Solidarność* were elevated into the embodiment of the people's global rejection of the Communist regime, so that all different versions of the anti-Communist opposition (from the conservative-nationalist opposition through the liberal-democratic opposition and cultural dissidence to leftist workers' opposition) recognized themselves in the empty signifier *Solidarność*.[15]

Laclau's conceptualization of chains of equivalences that forge links between demands which are not necessarily connected draws upon Saussurian linguistics, with its distinction between syntagms and paradigms predicated on a nonreferential and nonessentialist conception of language and relations among elements more generally. The creation of equivalences occurs through processes of articulation, which bring together elements that have no necessary belonging. It is only through the creation of equivalences that a set of relational differences can be drawn together into a totality, defined as a unity against something it is not. The separate, differential demands that emanate from a variety of different sectors of society are unified through their common opposition to an oppressive regime. In other words, while each of the particular demands is distinctive, they share the fact that they are opposed to a common enemy, which is the oppressive regime. They are rendered equivalent in this respect.

---

hold of that which is particular, some universal meaning, is what he has elsewhere, including his work with Chantal Mouffe, called *hegemony*. It is also, as Laclau indicates, very close to Jacques Rancière's recent argument that politics is defined by the emergence of an "uncountable part" (Jacques Rancière, *Hatred of Democracy*, trans. S. Concoran, (London & New York: Verso, 2007) that "distorts the very principle of counting" and which "while being a part, also claims to be a whole" (Ernesto Laclau, Chantal Mouffe. *Hegemony and Socialist Strategy: Toward a Radical Democratic Politics*. (London: Verso 1985), p. 245).

15 Slavoj Žižek, *Against the Populist Temptation*, [in:] "Critical Inquiry", no. 32, Spring 2006, p. 56.

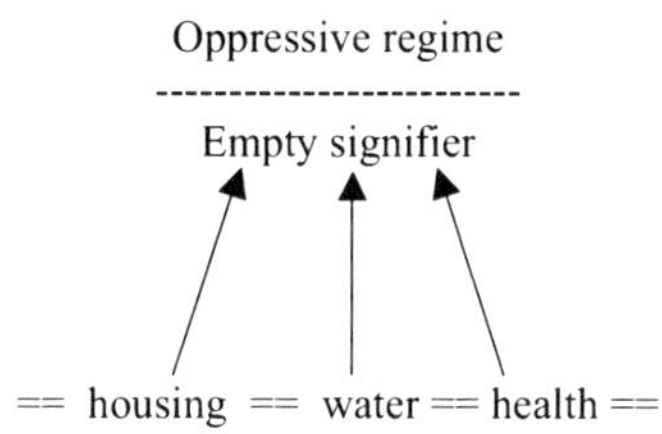

The unity of the chain of equivalences is then established by one of the elements of the chain taking on the function of representing the chain as a whole, thus operating as an *empty signifier*. In this way, the democratic subject emerges in and through the process of making demands, which in turn may come to perform as *empty signifiers*. It is important to note that the *empty signifier* plays a dual role in the constitution of a people. On the one hand, it has an active role of representation as it constitutes the people in the process of representing them; it does not simply reflect a pregiven totality. On the other, it represents the people. Since it has to act as a point of identification, it cannot be entirely autonomous from them. Given this, the constitution of "the people" causes tension. If the totalizing moment – that of equivalence – prevails, representation is destroyed. If, on the other hand, there is a complete autonomization of demands – where difference prevails – the moment of totalization necessary for the constitution of some form of unity would be blocked. To put it more simply, if the constitutive function of representation prevails without attention to the fact that a particular actor is being represented, the link between the representative and the represented is broken. If, on the other hand, the representative simply reflects the represented, there is no possibility of drawing together a number of distinct demands into a unity which exceeds the specificity of each of the demands. Hence, the *political* function of representation is of necessity one of maintaining the tension between the two extreme points of the continuum.

3. Populism in Poland

Before we start to elaborate on populism in Poland one issue has to be mentioned, an issue which influences political and social conditions in the country. The remark concerns the circumstance of settlement with communism. In particular, a series of negotiations between the communists and the opposition *Solidarność* called "the round table" started in 1989. The round-table agreement called for "your President, our Prime Minister", to quote the famous sentence of Adam Michnik. As an effect of the peaceful agreement, Poland's initial approach to the communist past was set in 1989 by Tadeusz Mazowiecki, who declared that Poland should draw "a thick line" to mark off the communist past from the democratic future. Although Mazowiecki's intention was to make communists responsible for their era and the new government responsible for the future, in Polish parlance, the "thick line" came to signify a blanket forgiveness of past communist misdeeds. The opponents of this decision have been saying that practically what it meant was creating tolerance for Communists, even worse, a silent cooperation with the Communists at the cost of the right wing. And so the post-*Solidarność* camp divided into those who shared Mazowiecki's and Michnik's idea to build a democratic system without looking back at the past and those who did not want to accept the Postcommunists' participation. In consequence of the peaceful agreement with the Communists, two problems that divided the post-*Solidarność* can be located. The first one relates to the concept of decommunization, while the second, resulting from the first, is lustration. Those concepts have influenced the political atmosphere and have become an important factor behind the condition of Polish democracy and a particular place of populism in it.[16]

To exemplify Laclau's thesis that there is no populism as such but only the different ways of doing politics with the use of populism and that it does not make sense to ask whether a party or the movement is populist or not but only to ask to what extent a movement is populist, I try to analyze the different logics of populism in Poland. In January 2005, Law and Justice (L&J) wins the parliamentary election and its victory gives the party a mandate to deal with two focal issues of the campaign: social justice, to be achieved by the introduction of the vetting law, and launching an attack against the system of corruption.[17] It seems that the latter of these issues provided an "empty signifier", capacious enough to be able to accommodate various social claims, beginning with those of the nurses and ending with those of the intelligentsia – all mesmerised by the idea that the troublesome social reality is a corrupt fruit of the Roundtable Talks in 1989. There it was, the Roundtable Agreement, to be finally blamed for taking away their rights, leaving them helpless and poor, and for deforming the political scene. In that sense, the victory of L&J and its later policies were short of populist. The need to refer to the nation and to represent the nation, the need to carry out their policy not just by democratic choice and the sufficient number

16 Zdzisław Krasnodębski, *Demokracja peryferii* [*The democracy of the outskirts*], (Gdańsk: słowo/obraz terytoria, 2005); Paweł Śpiewak, *Pamięć po komunizmie* [*The memory of communism*], (Gdańsk: Słowo/obraz terytoria, 2005).

17 Jarosław Kaczyński, *Interview with Kublik and Olejnik, We mnie jest czyste dobro* [*There is pure good in me*], "Gazeta Wyborcza", 3.02.2006.

of votes cast, but by acclamation, anointment, and delegation, has deformed the otherwise noble project and tied it with populism.

On the other hand, however, the victory of Civic Platform (CP) in the parliamentary elections in September 2007 had much to do with the promise of a new Ireland, our dream to come true. The fact that it was such a successful message and that it became a true banner of the victory allows us to see CP's success in terms of populism: the ignition of the dream of Ireland has also channelled a set of multiple social claims: for the entrepreneurs, more freedoms, more support for free initiative; for everyone, education and health. All that can be a worrying signal, a signal that in fact contemporary politics is merely a mix of various populisms, addressing varied groups, with the help of varied structural combinations. While L&J seduces the nation of the rejected ones, CP seduces the nation of people who decided to become economically active. One thing that both parties have in common is that they both accuse each other of pandering to the electorate and formulating hollow promises.

One of the objectives here is to establish whether a distinction between "good" and "bad" populisms is implicitly assumed in analyses of populism. If so, "good" populism would be the one celebrating democracy as its core value, asking for more power on behalf of the people – and appearing to go along the lines of the customary way of doing politics. "Bad" populism, on the other hand, would question the delegation of power to a few chosen people, the foundation of today's representative democracy, as well as most of the democratic institutions and long established democratic procedures. "Bad" populism, while shaking the foundations of democracy – its core ideas and procedures – is even more critical towards guarantors of the constitutional order other than those democratically chosen by the nation, for example the chairmen of central banks or the judges of the Constitutional Tribunal.

Based on Laclau's definition, Polish populism regards the society as being ultimately separated into two homogeneous and antagonistic groups. "The pure people" can be represented by different social classes such as workers, farmers, Catholics, but also by the smaller entrepreneurs. All of them are disappointed with the transformation (meaning democratisation, Europeanisation, globalisation, etc.) and blame the establishment for its failures. They are all united around disagreement with "the network", which for the Polish populists means everything that has any connections with communism. Interestingly, that includes not only postcommunists but also those who settled the agreements with them and, according to populists, blended the past with the future. Populists stress that such conduct has led to the divisions of society, pathologies and corruption on different levels (political, economical, social).

However, the good, or should I say – "blessed" populism of CP is ready to sacrifice some of the beneficiaries of the transformation in new middle classes – like doctors who have their own profitable practice, successful academics employed at various institutions, bankers, presidents and directors of big companies, and so on – who all too hastily believed in their success being the inevitable outcome of positive changes as well as their own hard work and skills, and thus justified liberalism as a free market ideology bringing little security to the unfit, unskilled, and unlucky. Those beneficiaries saw liberalism as the religion of a strong and victorious, self-confident man who takes from God and Nature whatever he justly deserves. The teaching of this religion is reason promising better future to all, and bringing contempt to what makes the coming of this better world so distant, namely helpless and irrational clerical masses. This way Polish populism has thus been trapped in a vice between the discourse of desire for success and the success necessitated by the CP, which is essentially a discourse about the promise of heaven and salvation here on earth, and the discourse of frustration triggered by corruption of elites, who renounced ties with the people and allowed them to perish in liberal hell. It would be only little exaggeration to say that Polish populism is trapped in a vice between the "rebellion of the elite" alienated from society, and the "revolt of the masses", alienated from the corrupt elite.

The claim that the Civic Platform is a populist party may raise controversy, and even the argument to divide populism into good and bad populism does not dispell these doubts. Doubts are not resolved by the appeal to a broad concept of populism, according to which populism is a way of doing politics today. The problem with the Civic Platform is that, above all, the status of the party is problematic. Civic Platform is the platform on which fit all kinds of ideas and concepts, which is clearly demonstrated by the changes before the election, which permitted the CP to absorb politicians from other parties, including politicians as ideologically diverse as those coming from L&J and SDA (Social Democratic Alliance). These diverse ideas have tied up the rhetoric of modernization and rationalization. As a result, CP grows to become the hegemonic party defending the system, and not an antisystem, populist party. At which moment of the political process does Civic Platform become a populist party, at least at the level of rhetoric? When does Civic Platform become a party again? Of course, CP becomes a party condemned to populist rhetoric at the moment of election. At this moment CP models its enemy in the form of the L&J party and urges voters to vote for CP, because not voting for CP will mean the return of the dangerous ghosts of the "IV Republic" and its worst demons. In this way CP creates the idea of a hegemonic state of government of L&J. In which way does the populist rhetoric work if not in exactly in this way? The system in the rhetoric of the CP is simply connected with the idea of the state, which we remember from the period of the L&J government. We are threatened by the return of these governments and warned against an almost Manichean evil in which these governments are involved. Populism occurs when one fraction of the dominant class seeks to establish hegemony but is unable to do so and so makes a direct appeal to the masses.

If we come back to Laclau's distinction one could even say that CP's populism and L&J's populism seek to attain what Laclau recognizes as unconceivable: (1) CP's aim is to establish an institutionalist discourse dominated by a pure logic of difference and (2) L&J's aim is to establish a world in which the pure unchallenged logic of equivalence rules. Let me only evoke this: pure difference would mean a society dominated by administration and in consequence would mean the very death of politics; while pure equivalence would involve such a dissolution of social links that the very notion of people would lose any meaning.

4. Populism after trauma

The thesis of this chapter is rather straightforward, and before we move forward a few general remarks on the dynamics of populism in Poland are necessary. In the 1990s, at the frontier of populism in Poland were dissatisfied peasants – remnants preserved in state economy, still treasuring the memory of robust years and now assigned to "Poland B"; they took capitalism for St. John's revelation and equipped with the survival instinct made stage debut in big cities, displaying peasant populists. Since then, the negative effects piled up, governments fell and other social groups started to appreciate the demands for state-controlled economy. When the socialists left they made a concession and accepted the inevitable, and the disenfranchised formed a unified front of discontent and assigned their problems to the Nation; vows were renewed, corporations, global and transnational, the European Union and the State were put on watch and surveyed for negligence.[18]

However, the majority and the media were still blindly optimistic, that is until the date of the accession of Poland into EU was made public and despite betterment in the lives of many, prophets came, and warned the Nation of a

18 Zygmunt Bauman, *Handlarze strachu* [*Merchants of fear*], [in:] "Krytyka Polityczna", nr 4, 2003, pp. 15-22; Olga Wysocka, *Populism in Poland: In/visible Exclusion*, [in:] *Junior Visiting Fellows' Conferences: In/visibility: Perspectives on Inclusion and Exclusion*, Vol. XXVI Lauren Freeman (ed.) IWM, Vienna 2009, [Published on the Web] Wysocka, 2009.

mistake in letting the rich buy out Polish land. Radical populism, soon boiled down to the grass-root party called "Self-Defence", administered justice rather than talk, with admirable timing – the state of emergency before accession. The popularity of the fearless peasant leader peaked on the day of elections, the borders were opened and – popularity fell, together with that of other nationalist parties. Importantly, the shift towards the right remained present. Even the 2008 crisis was not that much of a problem. Populism and its late parliamentary formation lost currency.[19]

And then, one fatal day in 2010, a terrible tragedy at Smolensk airport brought immense loss to the country, taking the lives of the whole board of administrators, members of the state, and late President Lech Kaczyński, at that time cohabiting with the liberal government and often engaging in competence disputes. The crash of the Polish Air Force Tu-154M occurred on the 10th of April 2010 near the city of Smolensk in Russia, killing all 96 people on board. These included the Polish president Lech Kaczyński and his wife, former president Ryszard Kaczorowski, the Chief of the Polish General Staff and other senior Polish military officers, the president of the National Bank of Poland, Poland's deputy foreign affairs minister, Polish government officials, 15 members of the Polish parliament, senior members of the Polish clergy, and relatives of victims of the Katyń massacre.[20]

---

19 Joanna Dzwończyk, *Populistyczne koncepcje w społeczeństwie postsocjalistycznym na przykładzie Polski* [*Populist concepts in a post-socialist society as exemplified by Poland*], (Toruń 2000); Maria Marczewska-Rytko, *Populizm na przełomie XX i XXI wieku. Panaceum czy pułapka dla współczesnych społeczeństw?* [*Populism at the turn of the 20th-21st centuries: remedy or trap for contemporary societies?*], (Toruń: Wydawnictwo Adam Marszałek, 2006); Radosław Markowski (ed), *Populizm a demokracja* [*Populism and democracy*], (Warszawa: Instytut Studiów Politycznych PAN, 2004).

20 The final accident report, created by MAK, was published on the 12th of January 2011, and placed most of the blame for the accident on the pilots. Some aspects of the report were criticized by members of the Polish government, specifically that the investigation found no fault with the Russian air traffic controllers. Poland published comments to the MAK final report on the same day. Commenting on the MAK final report the Polish Interior Minister Jerzy Miller said that the report was not created in full compliance with Annex 13 to the Convention on International Civil Aviation because some of the requested documents and evidence were not provided by Russia. Additionally, Polish comments on the final report were not agreed to nor fully applied. The Polish comments on the report are not part of it, however, they are published on the MAK website among other appendices. The MAK defended their report and stated they would accept any international investigation or audit of their findings. In spite of no access to some evidence (the wreck of plane and the original recorders from plane are in Russia, 13 recorders including the radar recorder and the camera mounted in the air traffic control

In Poland, the public reacted with shock and grief to the disaster. Almost immediately after the news broke, tens of thousands of Poles assembled at the Presidential Palace to lay tributes, including flowers, wreaths, and candles. A week of national mourning was declared in Poland. Poles around the world mourned Kaczyński and set up shrines in the week that followed: many wept openly, flags flew at half mast in Poland. Sports fixtures, including women's U-17 UEFA Championship elite qualifying phase game Poland versus Republic of Ireland in Ukraine, were postponed. Concerts were cancelled. On 11 April, Kaczyński's body was flown to Warsaw on a military plane; tens of thousands of Poles gathered on both the airport tarmac and in the streets of the city to pay their respects to the late president as his casket was driven by hearse to the Presidential Palace. Afterwards, the casket was laid in state at the Palace. The casket remained there throughout the week, until Kaczyński and his wife were laid to rest at the Wawel Cathedral a full week after the crash, on 18 April. On 15 April, Polish scouts put a wooden cross in front of the Presidential Palace at Krakowskie Przedmieście in Warsaw to commemorate the 96 victims of the Polish plane crash. The establishing of the cross provoked much controversy in Poland. Polish politicians began a dispute; the topic of the dispute was where the cross should be placed. Some people, mainly Catholic Church members, said the cross should stay in front of the Presidential Palace, because it is a "dignified manner of remembrance". Other people said the cross should be moved to St. Anne's Church, because the Presidential Palace is a secular place and it should be "without sings of religion". A lot of people of religions other than Catholic were outraged and disappointed. The Catholic Church in Poland did not make any comment about the situation. During the summer of 2010, there were several protests. The acting president of Poland Bronisław Komorowski said the cross should be transferred. After many disputes and the turbulent summer of 2010, on September 16, 2010, the cross was transferred to St. Anne's Church. Also, during the summer of 2010, the people in Poland commemorated the 96

---

tower were not given to Poland – according to the MAK report all were broken and did not save any data). The Polish Committee for the Investigation of National Aviation Accidents published its report on 29 July 2011. According to the Polish report, the main cause of the accident was the trial approach and the descent below the allowed altitude at an excessive rate of descent in bad weather conditions, in conjunction with late execution of the go-around procedure. Circumstances that led to this are inadequate training of the Polish pilots, but also the inadequate work of the Russian air traffic controllers, who gave inaccurate information to the crew of the Tu-154m. Criminal investigations by the Russian and Polish prosecutor's offices, which focus on the criminal responsibility of individuals rather than just the causes of the accident, have yet to be concluded.

victims of the plane crash by putting the arrays. One of them was placed on the wall of the Presidential Palace.

Shortly after, an elderly, unknown man poured filth on the wall. A public noon commemoration ceremony in Warsaw's Piłsudski Square was attended by more than 100,000 people on 17 April. Sirens sounded and bells tolled around the country. A three-gun salute was fired. People waved the Polish flags complete with black ribbons and the names of those who died in the crash were read out from a white stage decorated with a giant cross and photographs of the dead. The crowds bowed their heads. On 18 April, the presidential couple's caskets were driven at a slow pace through the streets of Warsaw, passing the city hall and a museum dedicated to the 1944 Warsaw Uprising, which Kaczyński favoured. The funeral ceremony began at 2 p.m. local time with a Mass held at Kraków's St Mary's Basilica, with thousands attending, the archbishop of Kraków Stanisław Dziwisz presiding over the ceremony, and personally addressing the President of Russia, Dmitry Medvedev.

Since the crash, conspiracy theories have spread in Poland about the cause of the disaster. Artur Górski, a Polish Member of Parliament belonging to L&J, claimed that the Russians in the Smolensk North Airport's control tower were ordered to keep the plane from landing so that the president could not attend the Katyń ceremony, which resulted in the crash. Górski apologized for his remarks, saying that he had been in a "state of shock". In November 2010, Law and Justice members Anna Fotyga and Antoni Macierewicz travelled to Washington with an open letter by Jarosław Kaczyński and a petition of 300,000 signatures from the Association of the Katyń Families 2010, calling for the U.S. government to launch an independent international investigation into the crash. Fotyga, Macierewicz, and Jarosław Kaczyński have become critical of the Russian-led investigation, and have expressed suspicion that the Russians have engaged in a cover-up of the disaster.

Disbelief and suspicion beyond reason became trademarks of the underrepresented and the critical towards the government. This period marks the absorption of politics by two parties, liberal and social. *Vox populi* was anxious and neither charges nor responses were satisfying, accusations of both sides and third parties added fuel to the national community. By almost unanimous and slightly hasty decision, the late President with late First Lady were buried in the Wawel cathedral in Kraków, thus far a place reserved for Poland's kings and heroes. This moment marks the opening of a new stage that I will refer to here as "mourning populism". No katharsis was discussed, and opposition party leaders echoed all, even the most nonsensical, insinuations. The tragedy, as a reference point, unfolds into a complex map of interdependent indicators establishing with accuracy one's political opinion, if only that. The official line is the rejection of conspiracy theories which, based on the facts in question, establish links and then a web of questions ponting to to treason, punishable negligence or grave disrespect to Polish history.

The manner of remembering Smoleńsk gives rise to a key distinction in the political life. "Reliving it" is a token of patriotism and devotion to the nation, while "coming to terms with it" shows disregard for the country and treason. To do justice, it is the least exotic form of populism among those mentioned so far. There is a certain level of control over its use in politics, but since it is either-or, all political stands are ultimately reduced to this axis. During the last elections in Poland, in October 2010, this was without a doubt the major topic in the campaign.[21] Impenetrable to the core, the division may prove lasting in political life, but even given the spin it has today, the prerequisite is its footing in culture, and to find it we will trace it back to the classical Romantic period, when the framework of today's populism was forged.

---

21 Poland's elections on 9 October 2011 produced two significant firsts – a governing party was reelected for the first time since the collapse of communism in 1989 and a new anticlergy party, Palikot's Movement, won the third place. Donald Tusk's Civic Platform was probably rewarded for its predictability. It did not run an especially impressive campaign, but more voters seem to place their trust in its ability to handle the second wave of the global crisis better than any of its rivals. Its focus on Europe is also appreciated by many. Janusz Palikot is an extrovert businessman who wants a clear separation of Church and state. He created a party and campaigned to legalise abortion, gay marriage and marijuana. Those are still extremely controversial issues in Poland, where the Roman Catholic Church remains influential. Mr Palikot's support among younger voters is perhaps a sign that Polish society is heading in a more liberal and secular direction. What, however, links Palikot's Movement with the party of Kaczyński, is their open attack against the system. Palikot admits that, when answering the question whether something links him with Jarosław Kaczyński, he said: "[t]here is one common point: we are against the system. Being against the system unites us. Only that Kaczyński used it for the challenge of democracy, and I was to strengthen it" (Janusz Palikot, *Tajemnice Platformy, rządu i parlamentu* [*Secrets of the Platform, the government and parlament*], (Warszawa: Wydawnictwo Czerwone i czarne 2011), p. 141). This superbly illustrated Palikot's populist thinking, because if the strengthening of democracy is to take place by the struggle with the system then, using Laclau's concepts, Palikot's Movement request (demands) are not democratic, but populist. The distinctiveness of populism is that it gathers together disparate ideological positions or political demands and stresses their equivalence in terms of a shared antagonism to a given instance of political power or authority. In other words, once again, populism should be defined by its form rather than its content: it tends to divide the social field into two distinct camps, championing the "people" over what Laclau variously terms "the dominant ideology", "the dominant bloc", "the institutional system", "an institutionalized Other", or even "power" itself.

From the political perspective, romanticizing Poland's past is a must.[22] What is not so obvious and not so viable, is how the application of Romantic imagery shapes political agenda and translates into decision making. The heritage of late president Lech Kaczyński is another flight, the flight to war stricken Georgia, founded on the rock solid belief that the enemy – Russia, is and will be hostile. From a very practical point of view, to take and hold such a political stand one needs to establish it at the intersection of great loss and great sacrifice. As for the loss, the extreme position is that of biblical Job. In his classic gesture he is helplessly submerged in his suffering and so devastated by the loss, that no explanation and no gratification would suffice. From this standpoint, the question "why" is almost irrelevant, as "because" is given beforehand. The same applies to the Russians: *Russians* – this suffices. Job's loss is so irreparable that no apology nor punitive measure can ever soothe his bitter disbelief. We have seen it, his life, and such is the lesson by Job. Despite the loss he never really gets down to thc qucstion "why", instead he preserves his faith in God, despite the prevailing sensation that injustice has been done. In other circumstances, we would call it dignifying loss, that is loss which is moral, ultimate, and unexplainable. This is exactly how Poland takes losses. I should think this is a Christian trait, making memory of departure the guarantee of salvation, as epitomized by Job.

Second, the for ever greatest Polish Romantic poet, Adam Mickiewicz, presents us in his masterpiece *Forefathers' Eve* a new type of hero: Gustav/Konrad. However, it is already in the preface that we come across an observation as valid today as before. He famously says there that suffering inherent to Poles is the best compliment to the concept of nationality. The drama alone is a voyage into the land of many irrefutable reasons for his earlier claim. Martyrdom is one of the indispensable among those. The slogan "Poland – Christ of Nations" is, of course, a cornerstone of the national myth, to only gain more weight in time. In a letter to his fellow-exile, the historian Joachim Lelewel, on the 23rd of March, 1832, Mickiewicz wrote:

> I place great hopes in our nation and in a course of events unforeseen by any diplomacy. [...] I would think only that our aspirations should be given a religious and moral character, distinct from the financial liberalism of the French and firmly grounded in Catholicism.[23]

The third part of *Forefathers' Eve*, which Mickiewicz wrote in Dresden later that spring, develops these ideas in a dramatic form, taking the enigmatic fragments of

---

22 Maria Janion, *Gorączka romantyczna* [*Romantic fever*], (Warszawa: PIW, 2007).

23 Adam Mickiewicz (1899), *Wybór listów* [*Selected letters*], ed. Józef Kallenbach, (Kraków: Spółka Wydawnicza Polska, 1899), p. 89.

the earlier parts in quite a different direction. The starting point is Mickiewicz's own biography: its central character, Gustav, who takes the name "Konrad", is, like Mickiewicz, a victim of Tsarist oppression in Vilnius in the early 1820s. It is over Konrad's soul, and, by extension, the soul of Poland, that the greater forces of Good and Evil are waging a titanic struggle. As he awaits trial in his cell, Konrad questions the existence of divine justice, given the monumental crime against Poland. His blasphemous conclusion is that God is, in fact, the Devil, identified with the Tsar. However, he is saved from damnation by Father Peter, who leads him to understand the need for expiation and suffering, introducing ideas which Mickiewicz was to expand upon in the *Books of the Polish Pilgrimage and Nation* (1832), specifically that Poland was the "Christ of Nations" whose collapse was a necessary sacrifice in the moral regeneration of Europe. The Vilnius scenes are complemented by a series of realistic, satirical scenes set in Warsaw, showing sections of Polish society collaborating with the Russian oppressor.

Even a brief excursion into the historical context of Polish culture originates risks of becoming entangled in the great dilemmas and debates of Poland's aesthetic and political history, debates both emotionally heated and conceptually confused. Like many other national literatures in the nineteenth century, Polish culture broke with Classicism and embraced Romanticism by riding the wave of national aspirations. However, while the nationalist component became only one among many other ingredients of Western European Romanticism, in Poland it came to define and dominate literary experimentation and innovation. The triumph of national Romanticism is responsible for shaping the concept of the Polish poet as national destiny's supreme interpreter (Adam Mickiewicz), its inspired visionary (Juliusz Słowacki), or its shrewd dialectician (Zygmunt Krasiński). Each individual voice became vatic *ex officio*, at the same time pushing the lyrical voice into a sort of tolerated exile (Cyprian Kamil Norwid).

As a result, the English obsession with the weather is equalled by the Polish obsession with suffering. This is a proper way to make friends and begin a conversation. Overall, Polish populism makes best appearances when matched with a trauma – the partitions of Poland in the 19th century, the uneven war in the 20th century, Stalin's genocide of Polish intelligentsia in Katyń in 1940, then of course the Warsaw Uprising, and along the line – the last flight of Presidential Tupolev 102, landing in Smolensk near Katyń on the 10th of April 2010 – whether the mist that day was artificial or not is still under investigation. Katyń-Smolensk and 1940-2010 is no coincidence.

It is so ostensibly visible that the dates soon appeared on the T-shirts and graffiti, and the names of the late President and his wife provided names for parks and institutions. There is even a painting presenting the site at Smolensk and the killed climbing up the skies on the rays of the sun, their kind faces telling "You know All". All this shows how desperate is the demand for symbols to serve as pegs of Polish collective memory. Katyń-Smolensk, 1940-2010 is seven decades of martyrdom, and a proof that forces of evil defy time, as does perseverance and memory. To add more substance to this claim, after the crash there was a march of a group of protesters chanting "woe betide those who forbid Jesus to be King of Poland". And apart from this initiative, which by the way is legally grounded, Poland now holds a new record. As of November 2010 Rio de Janeiro's Christ the Redeemer is the second tallest in the world. The tallest, at 33 meters high – a meter for each year of the Savior's life – is now home at Świebodzin. We may only feel sorry for the editors of the New York Post, who called it "a grandiose dream of a local priest", but anyhow, let us now consult Freud.

In *Mourning and melancholy* Freud says that mourning has an affinity for melancholy in that both are affected by the loss of ability to find a new object of love. In a way beneficial, stage two requires a little distance from the deceased achieved by refraining from the shared memories, or avoiding going to places that evoke memories from the past. We did not see it happen in 2011. The work of mourning is full ahead and excelling. We might call this advanced mourning phase, which means that the patient has already made a discovery that the beloved object is elsewhere, and has made such accusations like questioning the good will of the persons involved and a plethora of other factors that kept coming daily for the period of the last year. Also, there is a sign of progress as we are partly relieved from thinking of the loss on a daily basis, and instead deposit collective memory by erecting monuments. This is all in progress, but here we reach resistance, since the next stage envisaged by Freud needs to see a new object of adoration. At this stage, clearly visible is perseverance. At this stage those who mourn perceive the lost as a phantasm or void, an empty signifier, as if possessed by a demon that starts pulling the strings of emotions – something which reminds of the living spirit of Hamlet's father.

In *Mourning and melancholy* Freud wrote explicitly:

> There is no difficulty in reconstructing this process. An object choice, an attachment of the libido to a particular person, had at one time existed; then, owing to a real slight or disappointment coming from this loved person, the relationship was shattered. The result was not the normal one of a withdrawal of the libido from this object and a displacement of it on to a new one, but something different, for whose coming about various conditions seem to be necessary. The object-cathexis proved to have little power of resistance and was brought to an end. But the free libido was not displaced on to another object; it was withdrawn into the ego. There, however, it was not employed in any unspecified way, but served to establish an identific action of the ego with the abandoned object. Thus the shadow of the object fell upon the ego, and the latter could henceforth be judged by a special agency, as though it were an object, the forsaken object. In this way an object-loss was transformed into an

> ego-loss and the conflict between the ego and the loved person into a cleavage between the critical activity of the ego and the ego as altered by identification.[24]

This passage leaves little doubt as to the reason why today in Poland the opposition is messianic and the ruling party has no idea how to react and cope with it in the long term. But as a hypothesis we may assume that in the case of Poland the functions of politics is the transformation of an object-loss into an ego-loss.

The opposition party leader, twin brother of late President Kaczyński, shows little resemblance to the romantic hero of Mickiewicz, and to approximate his image I could only compare it to a rather peculiar hybrid of Hamlet and King Lear: not only is he mourning over the immense loss, but he is also seeking an object, as Freud puts it, to place his free libido, which in time is gradually getting absorbed by his national ego and makes him the embodiment of the Christ of Nations. This, in turn, would explain why the major party leader and Prime Minister Donald Tusk is in comparison a mix of Pontius Pilate and Lady Makbeth, presenting reports on the progress of the investigation and defying accusations of the lack of diligence before the eyes of the confused public.

5. From mourning to narcissism

Political correctness advocated by liberals for over 20 years came through with the assertion that there is no modernization without secularization. It is now evident that sociological argumentation stressing that the inevitable cost of modernization is secularization was empty. Poles were definitely participating in the processes of modernization, and if so, there must be a different reason for this puzzling negligence. What is wrong, however, is the whole equation: Polish modernism is epidermal, and such is also our radical nationalism altogether with our supposedly strong religious beliefs. What this means, however, is that both fake modernists and radicals are particularly vulnerable to the return of populism. The modernists have just displayed how modern they really are by showing much interest in anticlerical discourse (Movement of Support for Janusz Palikot). The secularized are meantime waiting for the return of the avenger, the Messiah whose earthly abode is the opposition party and whose person is its leader (radical wing L&J, Jarosław Kaczyński). And the declared liberals from the governing party (one-man government of Donald Tusk, CP) do nothing apart from inciting panic in face of roaring extremism and practicing liberalism of fear. Yet others feel the urge to act and equipped with torches and

24 Sigmund Freud, *Mourning and Melancholia*, p. 248.

high spirit once again enter the center of world events, refusing the new President the moral right to be where they are, before his office, and let the flames tell of the conspiracy while they share a word of encouragement, weary of local TV. Some probably still wonder how to restore the cross placed there on the day of the tragedy and months later hidden and profaned by the forces of the police state at the service of the traitors. The cross stands unguarded in the nearby church – a proof of pure evil.[25]

The 2010 Smoleńsk tragedy only intensified division between the liberal and enlightened establishment and the unenlightened clerical mass. It was also a rich source of symbols that guarantee action and suspense, each opening the gap between the two forces. It makes a return of populism plausible, as much as a return of naive, profane, quasi-liberal Enlightenment. We tend to forget that liberal science is church of atheism in the same way that religion is guardian of the revelation. The account of the tensions in Poland twined with the unredeemed loss, the evil spell of the land, unknown malfunction, culpable misdoings and irreproachable errors, piled up with evidence tracing back to years ago and churning out imputations and pleas to institutions worldwide – this was just a beginning of a process that with time started posing the question of the very nature of state and politics, from foreign affairs to lower bureaucracy. On the other hand it brought the realization that there is a dimension beyond state and directly related to religion, where grief poured in and thickened in accusations. This put institutions under surveillance and revealed them impotent exactly when their might is sought and their authoritative stand is expected. Similarly, the State proved not much of an avenger, shepherd or deliverer. This way, in the course of events, what first seemed a tiny crack or a dent, quickly opened a chasm where only torches flickered in the deep. Irreparable loss coupled with deploying an external institution instead of taking control, compensations which somebody called petty and asked fivefold, army proved danger to itself – the State was as bulky as it was hollow. The match should not be hasty, but I think we may feel rushed to try to arrange the hollow within the state with void in-between religion, and in my opinion the case of Poland adds substance to the idea of arranging space in-between by marriage of state and religion, civil religion that is independent of the state, but at the same time complementary to its functioning.

---

25 Agata Bielik-Robson, *Polski triumf Tanatosa* [*Polish triumph of Thanatos*], [in:] *Żałoba* [*Mourning*], Warszawa: Wydawnictwo Krytyki Politycznej 2010, p: 56; Yannis Stavrakakis, *Religion and Populism in Contemporary Greece*, [in:] *Populism and the Mirror of Democracy*, (eds.) F. Panizza, (London, 2005).

My analysis of what I call here "mourning populism" is thus half-way between the purely formal, structural position of Laclau and positions analyzed by Cas Mudd in reference to the contents of populism. I follow Laclau in his observation that populism has its own logic, which is transcultural and may in principle apply to any content – be it economic, religious, racial, and so on. However, in an attempt to understand the specific embodiment of populism and its syntax, we must analyze also the cultural context specific to a given country. This does not mean that populism is the expression of the very nature of a given population, but it does mean that in a discourse a given population organizes and builds its identity around recurring fixations and themes. It is not nature, however, that provides a pretext for their expression, but discourse, which becomes a prerequisite to provide a natural and irrevocable form of identity.

A superficial reading of Freud's *Mourning and melancholy* goes that his "sane mourning" is opposed to "pathological melancholy". While mourning, a suffering subject is about to accept the loss, allow for it, and reconcile with the "so-called" reality. A melancholic, while mourning, is supposed to narcistically identify with the object lost, unable to let it go, denying "the reality". However plausible, this Freudian insight may not be sufficient to explain the mechanisms governing the labour of memory, the work of our life energy systems, our energy residues, and accordingly – our affects.

Maybe we should, contrary to that reading, assume the supremacy of melancholy over "sane mourning". There are always reasons to impair one's ability to accept the loss, and the final loyalty towards the object. Maybe we – the Poles, have particular reasons to become a nation of melancholics, whose loyalty and persistence constitutes our civic responsibility. A suffering subject, if loyal towards the object – be it his erotic fascination, or intellectual choice, or personal identity – is bound to become a melancholic. For only he guarantees loyalty to the object and disagrees to break off with the past. Given that standpoint, the process of "sane mourning" could now be seen as a kind of betrayal, where the object is let aloof, its heart breaking, its make-up flaking. We accept the loss, because – we are told – "life goes on". It has to go on.

Using Kant's terminology, a melancholic makes a mistake blending the loss with the lack of the object. Object of desire – here in its crucial and constitutive meaning – is something that is missing, something that we lack. In melancholy however, this lack is interpreted as the loss. Melancholy blurs the fact that the object was missing from the start. This is why a melancholic so easily turns into a plaintiff or a prosecutor. First, he is mourning the loss of the object of love, then he complains it has been stolen, his pleasures intentionally denied, his very own house taken away. This is what constitutes Hamlet.

Freud in *Mourning and melancholy* wrote explicitly:

> Melancholia, therefore, borrows some of its features from mourning, and the others from the process of regression from narcissistic object-choice to narcissism. It is on the one hand, like mourning, a reaction to the real loss of a loved object; but over and above this, it is marked by determinant which is absent in normal mourning or which, if it is present, transforms the latter into pathological mourning. The loss of a love-object is an excellent opportunity for the ambivalence in love-relationships to make itself effective and come into the open.[26]

If I understood this fragment properly, it means that the case of politics of mourning is in fact the case of politics of narcissism because it offers to the subject the opportunity for regression from narcissistic object-choice to narcissism.

Perhaps, for us Poles, this bitter time is a revival of national symbols, the moment of identification with one object, and so we reunited with a community, at this stage – community of tears. Perhaps the tragedy at Smoleńsk released an already nonmodernist, and with yet more patience and ease, maybe even antimodernist attitude: Smoleńsk meant reuniting the whole people. Today, in retrospect, we already realize how tricky the sense of national unity can be, and how deceptive politics is when devoid of divisions, the vision of the State (society/nation) completely reconciled. We, the Poles, already know that this sense of unity was temporary, and the work of mourning was opening chasms and mounting new divisions, namely the work proved to be that of libido free from the love object, libido which is not bound up with the new object after the loss and instead has been absorbed back into one's own national ego. The sort of genius Freud was would never miss or pass a remark destroying the divine perfection a melancholic wishes to retain.

26 Sigmund Freud, *Mourning and Melancholia*, p. 249.

III. Beyond Identity. Beyond Europe

I always hear the word "Europe" from those who demand from others what they are not ready to set on their own.

Otto von Bismarck[1]

Europe is the Bible and the Greeks.

Emmanuel Lévinas[2]

True limits can never be neutral limits but presuppose exclusion. A neutral limit would be one which is essentially continuous with what is at its two sides, and the two sides are simply different from each other.

Ernesto Laclau[3]

1. Europe and the problem of identity

The problem of identity is a new theme in the intellectual debates in East and Central Europe. It is argued that the old identities, which stabilized the social world for so long, are in decline. New identities are rising and destabilizing the individual as a unified subject. This so-called "crisis of identity" is a part of the process of change that is taking place in contemporary social and political life.[4] Identity becomes a problem whenever one is not sure where one belongs, where to place oneself in the narrations of the past, and in the network of interrelationships with others. It becomes a problem also when one is not sure whether others will accept this placement as correct. Such questions as "Am I still German or not?" or "How is it possible to be a European and still remain Polish?" might be translated as "Who are we?" or "Is such a person still one of us or is he/she the Other?"

1 Otto von Bismarck quotes, http://www.qotd.org/search/search.html?aid=5290&page=2

2 Emmanuel Lévinas, *Is it Righteous to Be?*, ed. Jill Robbins, (Stanford: Stanford University Press, 2001), p. 182.

3 Ernesto Laclau, *Emancipation(s)* (New York: Verso) 1996.

4 Ulrich Beck, *Risikogesellschaft: auf dem Weg in eine andere Moderne* (Frankfurt/M: Suhrkamp, 1986); Anthony Giddens, *Modernity and Self-Identity. Self and Society in the Late Modern Age* (Cambridge: Polity Press, 1991); Ulrich Beck, Anthony Giddens, Scott Lash, *Reflexive Modernization: Politics, Tradition and Aesthetics in the Modern Social Order* (Cambridge: Polity Press, 1994).

There are no fixed and unambiguous answers to these questions. The Other as well as the Self are not stable and bounded entities that can be uncovered to secure and stabilize our sense of ourselves. Rather, they are subjects of the continuous play of history, culture, and politics. This is a paradoxical feature of identity. It is obvious that everybody has to have it, but we do not have it as we have other organs of our body – noses and ears. It has to be reinvented and reinterpreted in each new situation, by each generation and each community. It does not pass from generation to generation by teaching and learning. If institutionalised and taught, it easily makes people chauvinist and exclusionist. In short: a sense of identity is transmitted less through cognitive language or learning than through imagination and fantasy.[5]

There is a close link between group identities and the distinct pattern of orders which set them securely apart from their neighbours. When an order loses its distinctiveness, so does the identity. The dissipation of orders is another name for the shock of de-differentiation; and de-differentiation is confusing and frightening – because the blurring of differences challenges consciousness, effaces cognitive maps and explodes the codes of legitimate behaviour.[6] In the progressively d-differentiated world too large a part of daily experience stands "un-ready" rather than preformed, predictable, coming complete with its predefined meaning. When people complain that their identity is unclear or under threat, what they worry about is the unclarity of the world around; the enormity of the meaning-making task, and therefore also about the task of identity-building, which now falls fairly and squarely on their own individual shoulders and cannot but overload their mental and emotional capacity.

It seems as if in the modern world some form of community such as nation, race, class, or gender to which we belong, or suppose we belong, constitutes a part of our self-image. Roger Scruton for example argues that:

> The condition of man requires that the individual, while he exists and acts as an autonomous being, does so only because he can first identify himself as something greater – as a member of a group, class, or nation, or of some arrangement to which he cannot attach a name, but which he recognizes instinctively as a home.[7]

Whereas, from a more liberal position, Ernest Gellner wrote: "That man must have a nationality as he must have a nose and two ears is quite obvious, but not true".[8]

---

5 Slavoj Žižek, *The Plague of Fantasies* (London: Verso, 1998); Slavoj Žižek, *The Ticklish Subject. The Absent Center of Political Ontology* (London, 2000).

6 René Girard, *La violence et le sacré*, (Paris: Grasset, 1972).

7 Roger Scruton, *Authority and Allegiance*, [in:] J. Donald and S. Hall, eds., *Politics and Ideology,* (Open University Press, 1986).

8 Ernest Gellner, *Nations and Nationalism* (New York: Cornell University Press, 1983).

But the problem is that it seems that the national identities no longer feel secure, while European identity is just now not able to offer the standards of security once set by the nation-states.

The problem of identity has two faces – collective and individual, but these two sides of the "identity problem" are not necessarily tied. Anxieties related to each of them do not have to grow together; the polyculturalism of the Information Age and insecurity of the individual livelihood are two aspects of contemporary living which meet and mix in human experience, but are not reducible to a common cause. The crises of collective and individual identities do not stem from the same root. Psychologically, however, the two anxieties tend to collapse and blend. The feeling of the risk tends to be experienced as a total condition and to breed nervousness and frantic search of solutions often unrelated to the problems they are hoped to solve. One could say that the complex experience of uncertainty produces a considerable amount of diffuse fear, anxiety and free-floating aggression – all in search of an elusive target. It is a rather open question whether the solution to the individual identity crisis could be found in the postulated security of collective identities?

Thanks to the technical advances aided and abetted by the progressive dismantling of political constraints, capital is now free to move whenever and wherever it desires. Political institutions stay local – while the real powers which decide the shape of things that are and those yet to come have acquired genuine exterritoriality. As Manuel Castells puts it in his recent monumental three-volume study of *The Information Age,* power in the form of capital, and particularly financial capital, flows – while politics remains tied to the ground bearing all the constraints imposed by its local character. Power has been, we may say, emancipated from politics. But once this has happened, the state charged with the promotion and defence of collective identity has become all but a figment of nostalgia-fed fantasy.[9] Citizens are still citizens but they are more and more unsure of what state and of what nation.

The real problem is in how we should write about Europe? Should we be enthusiastic about the Idea of the European Dream? Jeremy Rifkin writes in this mode. Twenty-five nations, representing 455 million people, have joined together to create a United States of Europe. Like the United States of America, this vast cultural entity has its own founding documents and hopes for the future. It also has its own empowering myth.[10] Although it is still in its adolescence, the

9 Manuel Castells, *The Rise of the Network Society.The Information Age: Economy, Society and Culture Vol. I.* Cambridge, MA; Oxford, UK: Blackwell.

10 Jeremy Rifkin, *The European Dream: How Europe's Vision of the Future Is Quietly Eclipsing the American Dream,* (New York: Penguin, 2004).

European Dream is the first transnational vision, one far better suited to the next stage in the human journey. For Rifkin the new European Dream is based on specific assumptions about what constitutes freedom and security. For Europeans, freedom is found not in autonomy but in embeddedness. To be free is to have access to many interdependent relationships. The more communities one has access to, the more options one has for living a full and meaningful life. It is inclusivity that brings security – belonging, not belonging. The American Dream emphasizes economic growth, personal wealth, and independence. The new European Dream focuses more on sustainable development, quality of life, and interdependence. The American Dream is inseparable from the country's religious heritage and deep spiritual faith. The European Dream is secular to the core. The American Dream depends on assimilation. The European Dream, by contrast, is based on preserving one's cultural identity and living in a multicultural world. The American Dream is wedded to love of country and patriotism. The European Dream is more cosmopolitan and less territorial.

But maybe the poetic of dream is not an adequate style of writing in political philosophy; perhaps the better perspective is offered to us by demography and history. Writing in "Merkur", historian Walter Laqueur views the demographic collapse that Europe is experiencing and sees no possibility of the continent becoming once again a major force in world affairs.[11] Laqueur rebuffs all those who nurse the illusion of a "new European century": Europe in 2050 is going to be a very "grey-haired continent", writes Laqueur. According to the United Nations Populations Division, in 1900, 21 percent of the world's population lived in Europe. Today it's less than 12 percent. In 2050, the UN office predicts it will be 7 percent and by the end of this century, less than 4 percent. According to these projections, the German population (currently 82 million) will have fallen to 32 million by the end of the century; in Italy, from 57 to 15 million, in Spain from 40 to 11.9. The decline will be even greater in Eastern Europe. By 2050, the population of Ukraine will drop by 43 percent, in Bulgaria by 34 percent and in the Baltic states by 25 percent. Much the same is expected in the Russian Federation. At the end of our century, more people will live in Jemen than in Russia.

In which way should we reconcile the enthusiastic style of writing about Europe of Rifkin and the pessimistic diagnosis and prediction of Laqueur? Is it possible to find such a way of thinking and writing about Europe which does not overestimate its real potentiality on the one hand and does not underestimate its cultural and intellectual power on the other?

---

11 Walter Laqueur, *Europa im 21. Jahrhundert*, [in:] "Merkur", nr 59, 2005, p. 653-666.

The problem of Identity implicates the very idea of Alterity. In modern Europe the difference between identity and alterity is translated into cultural and national differences. A system of logic was developed according to which cultural differences define the sites of political conflicts. In a sense we are the culture of conflict, what means *inter alia* that our identity lies precisely in the process of continuous de-identification and reidentification taking place in conflicts. The problem we are facing in Europe today is how to come to terms with this diversity so that identity and alterity will complement, rather than exclude, each other.

It was supposed by some that the solution of the problem could be the establishment of alienated political institutions. These would be formal and empty enough to maintain their distance from claims of identity; they would not embody any particular community's dream, and thus keep open the space for them all. Only if the term "citizen" denotes an empty place, in the network of interrelationships between people, a place which can be occupied by anyone, may a citizen be imagined as a subject of the proclamation of human rights, all people without regard to race, sex, religion, wealth, or ethnicity.

Why then is the nation or ethnicity the best candidate to fill the empty space? Perhaps Scruton is right. A person simply cannot be devoid of local identity, traditions, views and convictions. Perhaps an individual can exist only when he/she can identify himself as a member of some "we". But it is also true that this identification is always the work of belief, of fantasy instead of cognition. To believe in nation means to believe that I am not alone, that I am a member of a community of believers. Each belief has its causes and effects; but the paradoxical feature of some beliefs is that they are caused by their own effects. Unifying ideas and unifying symbols are causes of this kind. They exist only insofar as people believe in their existence. To believe in a common thing (in an idea that unifies us) means to be a member of the community of believers in the same thing. But what is the thing we all believe? Be it religion, or nation or money, it is always a substantiation of some habit to behave. "The others" are those who are dangerous for our habits of behaviour and way of life, but rather than real beings they are constructs of fantasy. This is the pathological aspect of our contemporary intellectual and political situation: the imaginary Other determines the way we act toward the real Other.

It was assumed that multiculturalism was a good starting point for a politics which is neither exclusivist nor assimilativist. According to the liberal reading, multiculturalism was understood as an expression of the antiracist idea that there are no superior or inferior races, no superior or inferior cultures. There are only various traditions, various ways of organizing social life, each of equal value, and each worth preserving, if there is a community of people to identify with.

In many parts of contemporary Europe, however, the neo-conservative and exclusivist reading prevails. In this the national and ethnic tensions, the ethnic cleansing in Bosnia and Hercegovina, or the rages of skinheads in Germany, have to be seen as perverted and maybe pathological expressions of a real problem, namely that in the contemporary world the experience of belonging to a well-defined ethnic community which gives meaning to an individual life has lost ground. The true culprits are cosmopolitan liberals who force races and cultures to mix and thereby set in motion natural self-defence mechanisms.

The problem with multiculturalism, in either the liberal or the conservative interpretation, is that it reduces differences to different identities. It neglects the fact that even under the conditions of cultural and national differences political goals are selected more by interests than by cultural values.

2. The idea of recognition

The usual approach to the politics of recognition or politics of identity – I will be using these two terms as equivalent – starts from the Hegelian idea that identity is constructed dialogically, through a process of mutual recognition (*Anerkennung*). According to Hegel, recognition designates an ideal reciprocal relation between subjects, in which each sees the other both as its equal and also as separate from it. This relation is constitutive for subjectivity: one becomes an individual subject only by virtue of recognizing, and being recognized by, another subject. Recognition from others is thus essential to the development of a sense of self. To be denied recognition, or to be misrecognized, is to suffer both a distortion of one's relation to one's self and an injury to one's identity.[12]

Proponents of the identity politics – as I can see it – transpose the Hegelian recognition schema onto the cultural and political terrain. They contend that to belong to a group that is devalued by the dominant culture is to be misrecognized, to suffer a distortion in one's relation to one's self. As a result of repeated encounters, based on misrecognition, the members of disesteemed groups internalize negative self-images and are prevented from developing a truly cultural identity of their own. In this perspective, the politics of identity aims to repair internal self-dislocation by contesting the dominant culture's demeaning picture of the group. It proposes that members of misrecognized groups reject such images in favour of new self-representations of their own

12 Charles Taylor, *Multiculturalism and "The Politics of Recognition"*, ed. Amy Gutmann, (Princeton: Princeton University Press, 1992).

making, which will gain the respect and esteem of society at large. The result, when successful, is recognition: an undistorted relation to oneself.

It is beyond the scope of this chapter to offer historical or sociological surveys of the many different social movements that might be described as identity politics; instead the focus here is to provide an overview of the philosophical issues which are generated when we use these two terms together, that is the term "identity" and the term "politics".

Without doubt, identity politics offers some genuine insights into the psychological effects of racism, sexism, colonization and cultural imperialism. Yet it is theoretically and politically problematic. I would like to discuss some issues and doubts which are linked with the idea of identity politics articulated in this way. Strictly speaking, my intention is to articulate three such doubts.

3. The reification of identity

The first problem is linked with the question whether the identity politics does not tend to reification of identity? My simple doubt is whether the model of identity does not overestimate the concept of identity and the power of community over its members?[13] Stressing the need to elaborate and display an authentic, self-affirming and self-generated collective identity, it puts moral pressure on individual members to conform to a given group culture. I am not also sure whether in the identity politics we are able to find one consistent model of individual acquisition of one's identity. The question about the sources of our identity seems to me the most important and problematic question for politics of identity.

In order to see some of the strengths and weakness of identity politics, we need to make a distinction. For there are at least two distinct conceptions of identity. The first perspective considers identity a rather static quality of persons, and views the process of identity formation in predominantly passive terms. The other perspective suggests that identities are more active and flexible constructions. Correspondingly, each of these views yields a different view of politics; both of which, I will suggest, can be seen as quite limited, but for different reasons.

From the first perspective, there is no active component in the process of identity formation; identity is constructed *for* women, blacks, criminals, lesbians, as well as for the members of particular nations imposed from without

13 Nancy Fraser, *Rethinking Recognition*, [in:] "New Left Review", nr 3, May-June 2000; Axel Honneth, *The Struggle for Recognition. The Moral Grammar of Social Conflicts*, trans. Joel Anderson, (Cambridge 1995); Axel Honneth, *The Fragmented World of the Social, Essays in Social and Political Philosophy*, ed. Charles W. Wright (New York, 1995).

by powerful others and by hegemonic cultural norms and beliefs.[14] In this view the subject has certain core essential attributes that define her or his identity over which are imposed forms of socialization that cause her or him to internalize other nonessential attributes. For defenders of this model of identity, the politics of identity seems to be about the diagnosis of social power and hierarchy, that is: Who is different from whom?, Who defines what the norm is?, Who is the single individual from whom all others are supposed to differ?, Who imposes the interpretation of the discovered or invented distinction?

On the other hand, there is also a position stressing "the flexibility of identity", which refers to an entirely different strand of thought. In such theories identity can be constructed in many different ways; and while this process is contingent, it can involve choosing, shaping, and reinterpreting the identity one has. For the defenders of this model of identity, the politics of identity seems to be about the continuous formation and reformation of identity, about the free play of *différance*, and about a process of exploration and experimentation that is active and open-ended.[15]

In fact, I would say that the first of these views of identity may be too deterministic, static, and monological, and the second view may be too plastic and voluntaristic. If identity is a construction, it is not a *mere* construction; we cannot choose or reshape it in any way that we please, and a theory of constructed identities needs an account of how this process occurs. In our thinking about identity we have to navigate safely between the twin shoals of essentialism and nominalism. Hence, a voluntaristic identity politics as well as deterministic identity politics can be limited. I repeat, simply because identity is constructed does not mean that we can make our identity in any way that we please. Hence the need for another theory of subjectivity – one that can explain the sources of human creativity as well as victimization, agency as well as passivity.

4. Two politics

The second problem which I can identify is the conflict between two ideas of politics, that is universalistic politics of dignity and nonuniversalistic politics of recognition. At this point I would like to recall Ronald Dworkin's distinction between two kinds of moral commitment. We all have views about the end of life, about what constitutes a good life which we and others ought to strive for.

14 Steven Pinker, *The Blank Slate: The Denial of Human Nature and Modern Intellectual Life*, (New York: Viking Penguin Press, 2002).

15 Judith Butler, *Gender Trouble: Feminism and the Subversion of Identity*, (Routledge. London, New York, 1990).

But we also acknowledge a commitment to deal fairly and equally with each other, regardless of how we conceive our end. We might call this latter commitment "procedural", while commitments concerning the ends of life are "substantive". Dworkin claims that a liberal society is one that as a society adopts no particular substantive view about the end of life.[16]

This view understands human dignity to consist largely in autonomy, that is, in the ability of each person to determine for himself or herself a view of the good life. According to Dworkin, we are not respecting this power equally in all subjects if we raise the outcome of some people's deliberations officially over that of others. Those who take the view that individual rights must always come first assert that a liberal society must remain neutral about the good life, and restrict themselves to ensuring that however they see things, citizens deal fairly with each other and the state treats everyone equally.

The problem is the way in which i is possible to reconcile the idea of politics of recognition, which attempts to treat social actors in an individual way that is respecting the social, class, language, gender, ethnic, and religious diversity, with the idea of politics of dignity, which tries to avoid such nonprocedural style of thinking of social actors? With the politics of equal dignity, what is established is meant to be universally the same, an identical basket of rights and immunities. With the politics of difference, what we are asked to recognize is the unique identity of this individual or group, their distinctness from everyone else. The idea is that it is precisely this distinctness that has been ignored, glossed over, assimilated to a dominant or majority identity. And this assimilation is the cardinal sin against the ideal of dignity. Where the politics of universal dignity fights for forms of nondiscrimination that were quite "blind" to the ways in which citizens differ, the politics of difference often redefines nondiscrimination as requiring that we make these distinctions the basis of differential treatment.

These two modes of politics, then, both based on the notion of equal respect, come into conflict. Do we have any idea how to resolve this conflict? As for me, some sketch of the possible solution lies in the way we answer the following question: Is liberal society a society without a substanitive view about the end of life, is it possible that liberal values are not culturally embedded? And, if so, does it mean that our capacity to justify it – the arguments we can offer in its defence – are similarly embedded and thus, presumably, uncompelling to bearers of nonliberal cultures? If we are eager to give the positive answer to the question, if we are eager to say for example that John Stuard Mill's liberalism cherishes not diversity *per se* but liberal diversity, that is, diversity confined

---

16 Ronald Dworkin, *Sovereign Virtue: The Theory and Practice of Equality,* (Harvard University Press, 2000).

within the narrow limits of the individualist model of human, moreover, if we are eager to say that the neutral citizens of liberal theory were in fact the bearers of an identity coded as white, male, bourgeois, able-bodied, and heterosexual, then in this way we discover the limits of procedural politics of dignity, and at the same time we invent the road for the promotion of explicit, culturally embedded politics of recognition.

5. Fragmentation of identities

The third question about identity politics is associated with the problem of fragmentation of our identities. This problem was articulated very strongly already in Seyla Benhabib' articles.[17] Benhabib asked: In which way many identities which define any subject may be integrated in the single representations of her/himself? Are identities like race, gender, ethnicity, class, job, and language additive? Are they like layers of clothing that social actors can wear and remove? How are they experienced by a single individual who is her/himself a concrete totality uniting all of these into a single life-history?

My worry is whether the model of multiple identity, fragmented identity, nomadic identity, antitotalitarian identity does not overestimate the concept of fragmentation and plurality of one's image? Of course the dream of the nomadic existence is the mainstream dream of postmodern thinkers; of course many of us would like to talk still from new places, new languages, new perspectives; the desire to be someone else is a huge desire of our life and perhaps at the same time is the basic principle of an intellectual; of course the principle of repeated experiment on ourselves and the courage to be different is even the crucial principle of the unfinished task of reinvention ourselves. But is it a proper description of social reality: How many times do social actors change their identity during the course of their lives? In particular: How many times do social actors change her or his class, race and gender identity in her/his life?

According to Zygmunt Bauman – many among us, because, in the postmodern world the problem of identity is one of avoiding a fixed identity and keeping our options open.[18] Avoiding long term commitments, consistency and devotion. In place of a life project established as early as possible, which we

---

17 Seyla Benhabib, *From Identity Politics to Social Feminism: A Plea for the Nineties,* [in:] Seyla Benhabib (ed.), *Democracy and Difference: Contesting the Boundaries of the Political.* (Princeton: Princeton University Press, 1996).

18 Zygmunt Bauman, *Postmodern Ethics, Life in Fragments. Essays in Postmodern Morality*, (Basil Blackwell, 1995); Zygmunt Bauman, *Liquid Modernity*, (Cambridge: Polity Press, 2000).

loyally follow, postmodern people choose to have a series of short projects that are not fixed. Moreover, postmodernist theorists tell us that any group identity, any "we", even if only invoked as a rhetorical gesture of public speech and writing, is politically suspect, in that it tries to create a seeming community of opinion and views where there is usually none.

I do not like to discuss the question whether a picture of social reality delivered by postmodern thinkers is proper, I assume it is. Instead, I would rather like to ask whether the process of lost stability, lost in the nomadic road to one's Plural Identities, the fact the we belong to the age of emigrants and many of us have the problems with the process of identification (on the one hand we could not identify with anything and anyone, on the other we are eager to identify with everything and everyone) shouls worry us. In essence, I would like to ask whether the process of fragmentation of our identity should worry us? Perhaps there is no reason why it has to follow that once I recognize multiple faces of myself, or alternative identities, I must feel fragmented, or conflicted? Or, more to the point, if I do feel conflicted, fragmented, there perhaps is no reason why I need necessarily regard that as a bad thing rather than as something to "work with"?[19]

When I ask whether the process of fragmentation of our identity should worry us, I really ask, in a rather rhetorical way, whether we are able to find such a path of our life which will enable us to succeed in navigating between the extremes: the Absolutism of Identity (reification of identity) and the Role Confusion (identity crisis). When I ask whether the process of fragmentation of our identity should worry us, I really ask whether the split in the field of contemporary particular identities, the split between on the one hand the Fundamentalism whose basic formula is that of the Identity of one's own group, implying the practice of excluding the threatening Others; and on the other hand postmodern identity politics of Multiculturalism aiming at the tolerant coexistence of hybrid lifestyle groups, divided into endless subgroups (black gays, white male AIDS patients, lesbian mothers, gay tourism) only conceals a deeper solidarity and affinity between them. Let me repeat, I ask whether the split between Fundamentalism and Multiculturalism only conceals a deeper solidarity and affinity between them: a fundamentalist group can adopt the strategies of identity politics, presenting itself as one of the threatened minorities, simply striving to maintain its specific way of life and cultural identity.

---

19 Susan Bickford, *Anti-Anti-Identity Politics: Feminism, Democracy, and the Complexities of Citizenship*, [in:] "Hypatia" 12:4:1997, pp. 111-133; Sandilands Catriona, *From Natural Identity to Radical Democracy*, [in:] "Environmental Ethics" 17: 1995. pp. 75-91; Chantal Mouffe, *The Return of the Political*, (New York: Verso, 1993).

6. The metaphysical heritage of Europe

Some time ago one might have had an impression that the West had became fascinated with the disintegration of communism in Eastern Europe that happened fifteen years ago. On the other hand, the East of Europe became fascinated with the integration of liberalism, which took place more than fifteen years ago. The East and the West of Europe seemed to look at each other disapprovingly, as if in a fairground mirror: the East could see in the West its faraway ideal, while the West noticed in the East new and salutary energy for its values, for the liberal democracy doubtful about itself. Today it is difficult to talk about mutual fascination. We tend instead to be facing mutual disappointment. The East of Europe appeared to be different from what the West had deemed it to be and *vice versa*. For example, the so-called decline of the welfare state, one of the post-War projects, is an important case in point: what was achieved in the 1950s-1970s was destroyed in the 1990s; the West that the New Europeans were longing for had become a thing of the past by the time they reached it. Paradoxically, the disillusionment process coincided in time with the process of formal integration. Thus, today we are no longer facing the "Europe of the Twelve", or "the Fifteen" on the one hand and the "postcommunist" countries on the other, but the enlarged and to-be-even-more-enlarged European Union that comprises a part of the Eastern and postcommunist Europe and wishes to execute the "policy of neighborhood" towards some other countries. Thus, we are looking at the creation of the New Europe – a structure without historical precedence, impressive with its force and promising, but based on fragile social and cultural foundations. The common identity of this New Europe is particularly unsure. The ambition of our project is to study both the embryos of the new European identity, as well as the obstacles standing in the way of its formation. Our ambition is also, and even most of all, to provide a language that would allow to diagnose these opportunities and pitfalls.

European integration and the more general process of so-called "globalization" require posing the question about the real and demand forms of "modernity" within the expanding European Union (EU which is in the process of extension to the "East": East Central, South East and Eastern Europe), and – indirectly – within the contemporary world as a whole, related to Europe, and remaining under its considerable influence. In this context, the fundamental question is whether the "new Europe" (that is, the countries that joined the European Union in 2004 or are going to do so in the near future) can and need to be only an emanation of the "old" one; or whether it has to modernize itself, aiming at an assimilation of the old "European core"? Alternatively, we need to search for a "new quality" created both by the "old Europe" and the "new Europe" as well as by the countries (still) from beyond the EU but able to contribute in defining a "European identity". We need to answer the question whether the newly integrated countries and those which are staying beyond the borders of the EU can be treated only as a territory of a "civilization delay", whose only aim is "making up for lost time", and a territory of "adaptation", "becoming equal with European standards", and so on. Alternatively, there arises from their experiences something important for the identity of the whole "new Europe" in the wider sense. One can say that the "arrogance" of the established EU nations would be disastrous for the development of "Europe" if people of the Western European countries thought of Poland, Hungary, and so on, as "backward" or "lagging behind", as if their history was not "European". The idea of the "new Europe" by no means consists in opposing the "two Europes", but tends, on the contrary, to relativize the ideological opposition between "old" and "new", "central" and "peripheral" or "borders" of Europe. The intention of the very concept of "new Europe" is certainly not to put into question the role that the countries of the European "core" have played, are playing and may still play in Europe as a whole, but to focus on questioning the opposition between the "core" and the "rest", and on constructing some conceptual bridges between the elements of the opposition mentioned above. Moreover, we are supposed to focus not on the old conflict between "Easterners" and "Westerners", but to devote our attention to current problems. What is the EU, Europeanization or Europeanism for people from the West and the East in Europe, and what should it be in their opinions and consciousness in the future? Is the new (extending) EU (an will it be) an unstable synthesis of the "West" and "East", liberalism and postcommunism, modernization and tradition? It boils down to the question of whether the "new countries" have to adapt themselves to an existing (maybe illusory) consensus, or whether they can and must revitalize the concept of "Europe" as such; it will not have escaped our attention that in the "old" Europe people can hardly be interested in general "Europe", because they take it for granted.

The question about the distinctive trait of the European identity, especially if it is understood as a borderline identity, is difficult. This difficulty is well-diagnosed by Jacques Derrida and Jürgen Habermas.[20] Derrida and Habermas state that since Christianity and capitalism, natural sciences and technology,

20 Jacques Derrida, Jürgen Habermas, *February 15, Or What Binds Europeans Together: A Plea for a Common Foreign Policy, beginning in the Core of Europe,* [in:] *The Derrida-Habermas Reader* ed. L. Thomassen. (The University of Chicago Press: Chicago). pp. 270-277.

Roman law and the Napoleonic Code, middle-class life, democracy and the rights of man, secularization of the state and society have spread over other continents, these achievements no longer are the *proprium*. The Western spirituality, rooted in the Judaic-Christian tradition, definitely has its characteristic features. But it is also this spiritual attitude, which is characterized by individualism, rationalism and activism, that the European nations share with others living in the United States, Canada and Australia. The West, as the spiritual contour, comprises more than just Europe. Conscious of these difficulties as they were, Habermas and Derrida undertake the risk of listing, if not defining, the features comprising the European identity. We can find here the following features: secularization of society, trust in the powers of the state, skepticism towards the market and technological development, attachment to the welfare state and solidarity, renunciation of the capital punishment. Of course each of the features listed may bring some doubts, with different intensity it may be sensed in such places as Barcelona and Berlin, Paris and Bucharest, Budapest and Rome. What seems to be valuable in the analyses presented by Habermas and Derrida is the suggestion that one should not look for the finished list of features of the European, that is, one should not seek a closed concept of Europe, a finite European identity, but think rather of these concepts as complex or open.

However, the problem related to Habermas's and Derrida's diagnoses and peculiar to their following suggestions: (1) the suggestions concerning the deepening of the precipice between the continental countries and the United States of America and England, as well as between "the old" and "the new" Europe; (2) the statement that only the founder states of the Community are able to give the European Union the legal competences of a state; (3) and the general conclusions stating that the idea of "the Europe of different velocities" should be promoted, lies in the fact that every attempt to define Europe and its identity against America, and, above all, every attempt to differentiate between "two Europes" will not unite but divide. The demonstrations of 15 February, 2003, when the inhabitants of Berlin, Paris, London, Madrid and many other capitals of the Old Continent took to the streets were not the demonstrations of people astonished at the "New Europe's" declaration of loyalty towards president Bush (the so-called "letter of the eight"), but of people astonished at the constant possibility of degradation of the world of politics into ultrapolitics (where war takes the place of negotiations) and the fragility of the European identity: the letter of the eight was more the vote for Western values and transatlantic relations than for Bush, still it broke the European solidarity.

In his text *Can Europe happen?*, Leszek Kołakowski writes in the same spirit, perhaps in a slightly more satirical tone:

> I once asked a man I know in Brussels, if the Belgians, the Flemings and the Walloons even existed. He told me that there had always been a handful of Polish Jews who were neither Flemings nor Walloons, so they had to be the Belgians.[21]

Kołakowski's joke, when analyzed from a more serious perspective, brings us to an ambiguous question: Is the set of candidates for the prototype of the European not an empty set by any chance?

As a result, perhaps it is worthwhile to think about the question, posed by Rodolphe Gasché, if Europe constitutes merely a kind of philospheme?[22] Wanting to construe the question of Europe as a calling for a distinctively philosophical and especially phenomenological study, Gasché could, perhaps, have retained a studied indifference to what it understands as its opposition. Gasché identifies a stubbornly dogmatic discourse that stands squarely in the way of such an inquiry when he suggests that there are many who confidently pretended to know exactly what Europe has stood for, and continues to stand for – namely a hegemonic phantasm and moribund worldview. By depicting Europe and the West as a homogeneous power of domination over the rest of the world, postcolonial criticism of European imperialism, and its construction of non-European cultures, it knows perfectly what Europe is. Indeed it knows it so well that it indulges in the same lack of differentiation of which it accuses the West in its relation to its others. It thus turns Europe into the blind spot of its own discourse. If *Europe* is not only the name of a region of the global surface but something like, for example, the unity of a spiritual life, action, and creation, then perhaps the point or place of departure for what we are seeking is less a matter of researching opinions on territorial questions, a kind of questioning that rather evidently presupposes that "spiritual life" in question,[23] but finding a way of reading or making legible the *configuration of spirit* that belongs to Europe.

The metaphysical heritage of Europe, the onto-theology which is more than merely from Europe but which is inseparable from the Europeanization of the world, inseparable from the *Da-sein* (using Heidegger's language) that for every

---

21 Leszek Kołakowski, *Can Europe happen?*, [in:] "New Criterion", May 2003, Vol. 21 Issue 9, p. 19.

22 Rodolphe Gasché, *Europe, Or the Infinite Task: A Study of a Philosophical Concept* (Stanford: Stanford University Press, 2009). p. 17.

23 Jacques Derrida, *Of Spirit: Heidegger and the Question*, trans. Geoffrey Bennington and Rachel Bowlby (Chicago: University of Chicago Press, 1989). Jacques Derrida, *The Other Heading*, trans. Pascale-Anne Brault and Michael Naas, (Indiana University Press, 1992). Jacques Derrida, *Of the Humanities and the Philosophical Discipline. The Right to Philosophy from the Cosmopolitical Point of View (the Example of an International Institution)*, "Surfaces" Vol. IV. 310 Folio 1, Montréal Vendome, Editions UNESCO Verdier PUF 1997.

European is his or her own, is marked precisely by the way it rejects every fully naturalistic idea of Man – and hence rejects every biological (racial) determination of the human and of human differences – and proposes that this insufficient definition of Man's essence must and can be overcome or offset by adding on to it the idea of Man having an immortal soul; or by adjoining a mind to the human body and saying that we are a thinking thing, a rational being or a self-conscious subject. There is a temptation to meet any such Eurocentricism with an opposing anti-Eurocentrism, and so to regard the worldwide-ization of the European world not as the noble movement of Spirit but as the imperialism of a hegemonic Power. Indeed, the becoming-worldwide of the European world is often identified with, and in many approaches simply reduced to, the hegemonic internationalization of neoliberal techno-capitalism. However, while it would be absurd to deny the colonizing capacities of modern technological and capitalist economies, we need to acknowledge that the globalization we are witnessing today is a process that has a deep historical intelligibility as well as an economic and political one: namely, as Christianization or Pagan-Christianization of the world. As Gasché puts it, those who are happy simply to denounce certain ideas as Eurocentric, ideas such as universality, apodicticity, self-responsibility, and so forth, those who understand Europe primarily as a geographical and political entity or cultural region and who would set themselves in opposition to the investigations of Europe as something like a philosopheme are defeated by the fact that this idea is shaped not only by the fundamental demand to transcend whatever is particular but also that which still tinges this idea itself with particularity. The thought of Europe as a regional culture is still the thought of a European example.

7. Europe again

Maybe it is time, at the end of this chapter, to reveal the reasons why I analyse all these contradictions of politics of identity. My suspicion is very simple: the idea of identity politics and paradoxes which it involves could be linked not only to marginalized groups like women, lesbians, homosexuals or blacks but also to postcommunist regimes. Let me ask the hypothetical question: Is linguistic or national identity any less fundamental to one than gender, race, or sexual orientation? Can identity politics be extended to postsocialist countries as many years ego it would have been in the case of postcolonial lands?

When I ask the question I of course really ask: Why are some identities publicly recognized and acknowledged as legitimate criteria for being counted as a member of an oppressed group, or a "disadvantaged minority" in the official vocabulary of the welfare state? A brief look at Canada shows that Canadian governments have been more social democratic in the distribution of economic and social benefits; there, cultural identity issues and in particular linguistic identity occupy a more prominent position than other forms of identity politics. By contrast, initiatives to make Spanish the official second language of the United States were rapidly defeated and did not arouse particular support or even attention from social movement groups and activists except those directly concerned.

If the last insights are true, if the criteria for being counted as a member of an oppressed group and as a result the object of the identity politics are always arbitrary, and the demarcation between Fundamentalism and Multiculturalism is not so thick as it is often suggested, then there would be perhaps nothing strange in the fact that the West, which began by idolizing the Eastern dissident movement as the reinvention of its own democracy, disappointedly dismisses the present postsocialist regimes as mixture of the corrupt ex-Communist oligarchy and ethnic and religious fundamentalism; and, at the same time, the East, which began by idolizing the West as the example of affluent democracy to be followed, finds itself in the whirlpool of ruthless commercialisation and economic colonization. This mutual disappointment cannot be a great surprise if we are aware that the East very easily simulates the role of victim which delivers some tacit profits, and the West very easily simulates the role of the liberal and rich winner whose obligations are too great in relation to their finite resources. The East and the West look at each other as if they were each other's mirror images, searching in them for the impossible Unified Identity, something which we do not even have the audacity to call "Europe" any more.

If we assume that the common European cultural space cannot be firmly defined and delimited and its borders are necessarily open – because European culture, indeed Europe itself, is not a "fact", but a task and a process,[24] if we agree that there cannot be any fixed, defined European boundaries, be they internal or external, and that the European cultural space that defines the geographical space is in principle open, then the question arises: What is European culture? What is Europe?

According to Greek Mythology Europe was a daughter of the Phoenician king Agenor who was kidnapped by Zeus in the shape of a bull. After she had climbed on his back, he ran off to Crete, and she became the mother of his children Minos and Rhadamanthus, Cretan kings and judges of the dead. According to Herodotus, Europa was in reality a Phoenician princess who was

24 Kurt Biedenkopf, Bronisław Geremek, Krzysztof Michalski, Michel Rocard, *What Holds Europe Together?*, Newsletter, IWM Wien, Fall 2004, No. 4.

kidnapped by the Greeks as a revenge for the Phoenician abduction of the Greek princess Io. I would like at the moment to assert the term "Europe" has still the status of the princess Europa who was kidnapped by particular forces. But the status of thekidnapped entity is similar to the status of empty signifier.

While Saussurean semioticians (with language as their model) have emphasized the arbitrary relationship of the signifier to the signified, some subsequent theorists have stressed the primacy of the signifier. Jacques Lacan even praised Lewis Carroll's Humpty Dumpty as "the master of the signifier" for his declaration that "when *I* use a word, it means just what I choose it to mean – neither more nor less". Lacan postulates a complete disconnection of the signifier and the signified. An "empty signifier" is variously defined as a signifier with a vague, highly variable, unspecifiable or nonexistent signified. Such signifiers mean different things to different people: they may stand for many or even *any* signifiers; they may mean whatever their interpreters want them to mean. In such a state of radical disconnection between signifier and signified, a sign only means that it means. Such a disconnection is perhaps clearest in literary and aesthetic texts which foreground the act and form of expression and undermine any sense of a natural or transparent connection between a signifier and a referent, but it is also present in politics. Whereas Saussure saw the signifier and the signified (however arbitrary their relationship) as being as inseparable as the two sides of a piece of paper, poststructuralists have rejected the stable and predictable relationship embedded in his model. Lacan wrote of "the incessant sliding of the signified under the signifier"[25] – he argued that there could be no anchoring of particular signifiers to particular signifieds – although this in itself is hardly contentious in the context of psychoanalysis.

Europe is still only a empty signifier, it is still only a princess Europa and we are still the bull who wants to kidnap her meanings for our particular interests. In the last decade all European countries insisted on enslaving the meaning of Europe and tried to identify a particular content of their own cultures, languages and rules of life with the content of the very concept of Europe. Bauman argues that despite the odds Europe still has much to offer in dealing with the great challenges we are facing in the 21st century. Through sharing its own hard-won historical lessons, Europe can play a vital role in moving from the Hobbesian-like world in which we find ourselves today towards the kind of peaceful unification of humanity that was once envisioned by Kant. Yes, but for Bauman Europe means *Adventure* – anything that

25 Jacques Lacan, *Écrits*, trans. Alan Sheridan, (London: Routledge), 1977, p. 154.

happened without design – a chance, hap, luck.[26] Such is the etymology of this term. Later, closer to our time, *adventure* came to mean putting one's chance to the test: a venture, or experiment. Are we able to discover in ourselves the nature of Adventurer that is the person who has the courage to use his/her own understanding and is strong enough to create his/her Self and clever enough to discover/create his/her New Worlds?

26 Zygmunt Bauman, *Europe: An Unfinished Adventure,* (London: Polity Press, 2004), p. 2.

IV. The Desire for Sovereignty as the Desire for Addiction

Now, however, I am no less certain I can prove to you that government implies no obstacle to being loved, but rather holds the advantage over private life so far.

Xenophon1

Even a perfectly just man who wants to give advice to a tyrant has to present himself to his pupil as an utterly unscrupulous man. The greatest man who ever imitated the Hiero was Machiavelli. I should not be surprised if a sufficiently attentive study of Machiavelli's work would lead to the conclusion that it is precisely Machiavelli's perfect understanding of Xenophon's chief pedagogic lesson which accounts for the most shocking sentences occurring in the Prince. But if Machiavelli understood Xenophon's lesson, he certainly did not apply it in the spirit of its originator. For, according to Xenophon, the teacher of tyrants has to appear as an utterly unscrupulous man, not by protesting that he does not fear hell nor devil, nor by expressing immoral principles, but by simply failing to take notice of the moral principles. He has to reveal his alleged or real freedom from morality, not by speech but by silence.

Leo Strauss[2]

There is no culture without drug culture…

Avital Ronell[3]

All you need is love
All you need is love
All you need is love, love
Love is all you need

The Beatles

1. King's speech

Our task today is the attempt to understand the text much remote from us in time, but constantly inspiring us. Our task today is to provide the interpretation of *Hiero, or The Tyrant* of Xenophon. I will not say that what I want in a

1 Xenophon, *Hiero or Tyrannicus*, trans. H. G. Dakyns, (Project Gutenberg Release #1175).

2 Leo Strauss, *On Tyranny: Including the Strauss-Kojève Correspondence*, ed. Victor Gourevitch and Michael S. Roth, (Chicago: University of Chicago Press, 2000).

3 Avital Ronell, *Crack Wars: Literature, Addiction, Mania* (University of Illinois Press: Texts and Contexts, 2004).

moment offer you is a close reading of the text. I will rather say that it is a strong interpretation. I want to understand the closeness of Xenophon's reasoning, I want to understand its present rather than to be close to the text, that is, to be its mirror. To do this, however, I have to somewhat depart from the text and juxtapose it with other texts that followed in time after it and are already well known. Texts that complicate our relationship, direct relationship with Xenophon and the theme of tyranny. It will not be such a naive reading of *Hiero, or The Tyrant*.[4]

My plan is very simple. In the first step, I will invoke the interpretations of *Hiero* of Xenophon by Carl Schmitt, Leo Strauss and Alexandre Kojève. Then, in the second step, I am going to go back to the text of Xenophon to verify the main topic of discussion among Schmitt, Strauss and Kojève, namely the opportunity to be an enlightened tyrant. Then, finally, I will turn to Freud and his famous text entitled *Group Psychology and the Analysis of the Ego* to verify my main intuition according to which *Hiero*, or *The Tyrant* of Xenophon is about love, love which is understood as one possible social bond capable to ensure the durability of any state, of any social order.

Carl Schmitt in his famous paper by the title *Political Theology*, with the subtitle *The four chapters on the doctrine of sovereignty*, recalls Donoso Cortés' less famous declaration that in the face of the revolution of 1848 we meet the end of the epoch of Royalism. Frankly speaking, I would like to know today what exactly this death means. In particular, what does it mean in the debate on tyranny. What exactly do this death of Royalism, King's death, the Death of King's Place mean? What may it mean, in particular, for the knowledge of sovereignty?

Well, in a nutshell, this death means that we cannot speak further about the idea of monarchy, because there is no longer a real monarch. There are only monarchs with delusions, envisioned kings, the sick kings, paranoid kings. In the contemporary political world there can be only king's speech, but not a king and kingship in a strong sense. Monarchs with delusions, paranoid kings we find for example in stories of Gabriel García Márquez, even in the famous novel under the title *Autumn of the Patriarch*. "In this sense – Schmitt says – there is no longer the concept of legitimacy associated with the idea of monarchy. That is why Cortés sees only one solution for modernity – a dictatorship". The diagnosis of Schmitt/Cortés seems to have one general application: in a world devoid of monarchs the desire for sovereignty is manifested only in the form of

---

4 See also: John Dillery, *Xenophon and the History of His Times*. London, (New York: Routledge, 1995); Godfrey Hutchinson, *Xenophon and the Art of Command*. (London: Greenhill Books, 2000).

dictatorship or open tyranny. Dictatorship is a paranoid reign, the kingdom of psychotic delusions affected by the delusions of greatness. The desire for a dictatorship, in particular – the desire to establish a dictatorial government – is nothing but a desire for enslavement, and therefore the desire for dependence of other potentially sovereign entities on the arbitrariness of Dictatorship's Will. Before Imove on further, to the less obvious Schmitt's/Cortés's conclusions about the dictatorship and tyranny, I will juxtapose Schmitt's comments with some statements of Leo Strauss about ancient tyranny.

In his comments on *Hiero, or The Tyrant* of Xenophon, Strauss offers us an important and dutiful suggestion dedicated to *Prince* of Machiavelli, saying that this well-known work of the Florentine diplomat is characterized by deliberate indifference to the distinction between the king and the tyrant. *Prince* assumes the rejection of this traditional distinction. According to Strauss's the rejection of the traditional distinctions between good and noble prince and an unscrupulous tyrant,not only takes us from a world where politics meets the educational functions to the world where politics meets only administrative functions, this indifference to the distinction between tyranny and monarchy also condemns us to the ambivalence associated with the very concept of sovereignty. Because tyranny was for centuries defined as the opposite of kingship: the kingdoms are those governments that are exercised over subjects who want to, in accordance with the rights of cities, and the governments of tyranny are those that are exercised over unwilling subjects and do not correspond to the law order, but only to the will of the ruler – dictatorship or tyrant. Strauss writes laconically: "[b]asically, tyranny is simply illegitimate government or, more precisely, unlawful monarchical government". In this way of thinking is unknown the notion of benevolent tyranny, is also unknown the notion of "seeing eye of law". The lack of distinction between tyranny and monarchy negates in consequence the formal policy of universal legality and formal law and establishes a policy of difference, a policy of sensitivity of Dictatorship or Tyrant. Of course the benevolent Dictatorship and Tyrant is in a sense this "seeing eye of law". The dictator and Tyrant is the same love, is itself a same social sensibility, with this one doubt that this love and this sensitivity is arbitrary and is addressed to the subjects in unequal proportions.

Strauss is afraid of beneficent tyrants, of such tyrannical Lovers. Strauss reacts with horror to the idea of seeing the eye of law, the idea which his interlocutor, Alexandre Kojève, enjoys, recognizing in Xenophon's dialogue philosophical justification of the modern tyranny, or the description of events that once, in ancient times, seemed to be utopian, but today have become trivial. Kojève is not especially concerned about the refinement of kingdom to the tyranny, and he is not especially concerned with Schmitt's idea of an advertised embezzlement of the monarchy in a dictatorship. Kojève is concerned with the very fundamental need of man, which is more basic than hunger and safety, which will torment him as long as it is not satisfied. This need is nothing but a desire to be a Leader, the need to be a Commander, a Dictator or Tyrant, or simply: a Master.

Kojève suggests that a political man, driven by the deliberate desire to be recognized (or the desire for glory), will be fully satisfied only if he/she becomes the leader of a State which is not only universal but also politically and socially homogeneous, that which is the goal and the result of a joint act of all time, each and every one. Therefore, as satisfying, for Kojève, comes the fulfillment in being in command, in the possession of power. Kojève cannot see another fulfillment for man. Thus the fulfillment of humanity is the fulfillment of the state in which everyone would be a Leader or Master. I ask a question dedicated to Kojève: Is the State, understood in this way, to be feared as the worst plague of humankind or maybe it is a political form which is always desired as humane ideal? What is the state where all are leaders, that is – Commanders, Dictatorships, Tyrants? Do we know such states? Are we, the humans of the 21st century, familiar with such states or such a political system in which everyone would be masters of themselves?

Kojève develops his thought in clear disagreement with Strauss when he says: we have to do with a tyranny (in the morally neutral sense of the term) when one fraction of the citizens (it does not matter whether it is the minority or the majority) imposes on all others their own ideas and actions, a fraction that was not a success in gaining recognition of others, and when this fraction, not being able to reconcile with such existence, is not trying to reach a compromise by having ideas and aspirations defined by another authority, which spontaneously recognizes the others. Tyranny, or rather a temptation of tyranny is therefore a consequence of the failure in the search for recognition among the other actors, already recognized as sovereign subjects of their actions. This failure, resulting from the refusal to recognize the political subjectivity, condemns the fraction to the temptation of the use of force to impose another form of subjectivity, their Will. Briefly speaking: the tyranny establishes itself in the state by use of violence.

Let us make the first important summary. We have three theses so inspiring to me: (1) Schmitt's diagnosis, according to which the monarchy and its logic of sovereignty today are possible only in the form of dictatorship, (2) the thesis of Strauss saying that we crossed the threshold of modernity when the political regimes ceased to distinguish between a good kingship and an evil tyranny and we found that there is such a thing as an enlightened (benevolent) tyranny, and finally (3) Kojève's thesis, according to which we are coming (if we did not come) to a political form of homogeneous state, which abolished races and class (and other political and social differences), and as a result each race and class which for some reason is not yet an inherent part of the universal state reacts with tyrannical violence aiming to break out of misery of servitude and slavery and obtain the coveted status of the master. I juxtapose these three diagnoses, these three interpretations of the political order, mainly because they allow for a stronger, and greater optical resolution of the problem driven by *Hiero, or The Tyrant* of Xenophon.

With Schmitt, I would like to ask Xenophon whether the desire for sovereignty in the political world can only be revealed as a kind of terror, despotism aiming to paralyse the sovereignty of the Other, to appropriate his or her will and work? Is the desire for sovereignty essentially a desire for slavery, a desire for depending others' sovereign entity to the Will of the Tyrant or Dictator? Let us add: a Tyrant who sees in himself a sensitive lover, tender eye of the law.

With Strauss, in turn, I would like to ask Xenophon whether it is possible to think about a good dependence and what this "good dependence" is. Assuming the distinction between the king and the tyrant, and agreeing on semantics according to which the tyrant is an illegal and involuntary king, you would immediately ask whether the king is simply the voluntary and lawful tyrant. So, is it possible that Strauss encourages us only to cultivate a good demon, a good Tyrant? So, the only distinction to which we are now condemned and whichStrauss tacitly wants us to recommend is refinement of good and bad dependence? Is a desire for sovereignty only a desire for good dependencies, a desire to find a king/master/dictator/object of love who or which will feed us only good thoughts, and free us from the bad feelings?[5]

And finally with Kojève I would like to ask Xenophon whether homogeneous state, which is, if I guess correctly, the heritage of the Empire of Alexander the Great and Christian sheepfold of Saint Paul, is something that we should enjoy? Would such an Empire or sheepfold set the upper boundary of our political imagination? Alexander the Great, instead of establishing the dominance of his country over the conquered territories and imposing the authority of his country on the rest of the world, decided to dissolve and eliminate his native country in the element of the Empire. Similarly, St. Paul recognized Christianity beyond the differences between Greeks and Jews, and therefore recognized the new universal man – a man without qualities. But who is the universal man – a man without qualities living in a cosmopolitan city, a

5 Catherine H. Zuckert and Michael Zuckert, *The Truth about Leo Strauss*. (Chicago: University of Chicago Press, 2006).

cosmopolitan state or a cosmopolitan empire? What is the imperial city of the state understood as part of the imperial world? Imperial means here a state without borders in time and space. Imperial means therefore eternal. Are we invited here to think that such a homogeneous state would be the greatest fulfillment of human needs, the needs of the fair state, fulfillment of our dreams of the kingdom of justice? Or maybe it is only a caricatured fraud? Recall only that Karl Marx, after all, partly inspired Kojève's thoughts at all stages of his work man is defined through work, and then lead toward a society in which this most powerful human force is no longer necessary. Humanity, therefore, is left with a tragic choice between productive slavery and unproductive freedom. To be a productive slave or to be a free but unproductive master/dictator/tyrant. The price of freedom – as we see in our own society – is very simple: in place of real work comes into force unlimited consumption. In this sense, sovereignty today, sovereignty of mass tyrants and dictators is only consumer sovereignty, making the dramatic choice between Lipton tea and Ceylon tea in the supermarket.

2. Good dependence

Speaking in this way, I only state that the question of tyranny is the reverse side of the question about human freedom and independence. The question of sovereignty is therefore a multifaceted question: (1) it is a question about the possibility of disclosure of a sovereign entity in the political world as something other than a dictatorship, and (2) it is a question about sovereignty as a conscious dependency, that is about the choice of an object of dependency and identification, an object of love, and possible conditions of approval for this identification, (3) it is a question about the possibility of developing criteria for recognizing the difference between the kingdom and tyranny, even the kingdom which is within ourselves, in our conscious management in the cognitive and emotional resources, which are to some extent heteronomous. (4) Finally, the question of sovereignty is a question about the conditions of sovereignty, the sovereignty of the social environment, the coexistence of sovereign entities. Are the conditions of a liberal society based on the prior establishment of an independent, cognitively and ethically self-determined entities? Or rather, when it comes down to it, it becomes possible only when there is already a multiplicity of sovereign people, that is, the state is not giving the temptation to fight for the recognition of competing and warring entities, entities which behave like a ruler, like dictatorships or tyrannies express war of all against all and see themselves as the culminating peak of humankind?

Let us go back to close the reading of Xenophon's *Hieron*.[6] The first part of the discussion has to make manifest the specific shortcomings of tyranny, that is, the pathology of power, and the second part has to show how these shortcomings can be mitigated, that is, it delivers a kind of therapy of power. In his dialogues, Xenophon presents an experienced tyrant, bored after the experience of his tyrannical rule, and a poet – a wise man who taught the tyrant enlightened forms of tyranny. The fact that Simonides is called "wise" by Hiero does not prove anything, since we do not know what Xenophon thought of Hiero's competence. But even if we assume that Simonides is simply the mouthpiece of Xenophon, difficulties remain, because Simonides's thesis is ambiguous. It is addressed to a tyrant who is out of heart with tyranny, who has just declared that a tyrant can hardly do better than to hang himself. Does it not serve the purpose of comforting the sad tyrant, and does not the intention to comfort detract from the sincerity of speech? Is any speech addressed to a tyrant by a man who is in the tyrant's power likely to be a sincere speech?

We do not know whether a wise man's speech is really addressed to the tyrant. We do not know whether Simonides really wants to help the tyrant. But certainly we know that he wants to diagnose the situation of the tyrant. Certainly we know that Simonides/therapist behaves like a classic psychoanalyst. The tyrant is here on the psychoanalytic couch. Simonides/therapist first allows the patient to talk, allows the patient to confide in him his sufferings, and during these confessions he mostly remains silent. Only at the end of Hiero's speech Simonides activates himself by way of formulating a therapy. A wise man speaks here to the crazy man, crazy with the worst kind of madness – the madness of power.

One of the main topics of the Xenophon's dialogue is of course the problem of love towards the Ruler. Hiero would have been happy with his office of the tyrant, if he had been loved by the people. The tyrant wants to experience not only physical love, erotic love, eroticism, he wants something more – the evidence of love of all people of the state. Love of all the people, however, is not a kind of pleasure but a kind of respect, it is not simple eroticism. This is a specific eroticism of power. The tyrant thinks that people are not able to love him, and people are only capable of hating him. The topic of love and earning the love is essential in the dialogue. Perhaps the funniest part of the dialogue is the last part, where Simonides carries the proof that winning the love of the

6 Patrick J. Bradley, *Irony and the Narrator in Xenophon's Anabasis*, [in:] *Xenophon*. ed. Vivienne J. Gray. (Oxford University Press, 2010); William Edward Higgins, *Xenophon the Athenian: The Problem of the Individual and the Society of the "Polis"*. (Albany: State University of New York Press, 1977).

people by the ruler is not impossible. Simonides talks as if he was a psychoanalytic, a therapeutic. Simonides talks as if he was for years involved in the shaping of public opinion, and was a specialist in public relations. Simonides talks exactly what Freud shall write twenty-four centuries later in his text entitled *Group Psychology and the Analysis of the Ego*. I would now like to relate the council of Simonides's therapy with Freud's diagnoses of group psychology.

3. All you need is love

Freud asserts in the paper that not suggestion – the crucial concept of McDougall's, Le Bon's and Tarde's psychology of crowd – but *libido* is the key category explaining the nature of the social bond.[7] The social bond would be a libidinal bond; as such, it relates to everything that concerns love. Its nucleus consists, of course, of sexual love, but psychoanalysis has shown that we should not separate sexual love from on the one hand, self-love, and, on the other, love for parents and children, friendship and love for humanity in general, and also devotion to concrete objects and abstract ideas. Although the drives tend in relations between the sexes towards sexual union, in other circumstances they are diverted from this aim or are prevented from reaching it, though always preserving enough of their original nature to keep their identity recognizable. A description ensues of the libidinal ties operating in the Church and in the Army, which, on the one hand, link the members of these institutions to one another and, on the other, link all of them to their leaders, Christ or the Commander in Chief; as well as a description of the disintegrative processes which follow from a sudden disappearance of those leading figures.

Freud goes on to discuss the feeling of aversion or hostility which inhabits all close ties with other people, and is kept out of perception only through repression. In cases where this hostility is directed towards people with whom we are in close association, we talk about ambivalent feelings; but when it is directed at strangers, we can clearly recognize in it an expression of self-love – of narcissism. Self-love is, however, limited or suspended in the case of group formation, in which individuals in the group behave as though they were uniform, tolerate the peculiarities of its other members, equate themselves with them, and have no feeling of aversion towards them. Such a limitation of narcissism can only be produced by one factor, a libidinal tie with other people.

7 Sigmund Freud (1922), *Group Psychology and the Analysis of the Ego*, [in:] *The Standard Edition of the Complete Psychological Works of Sigmund Freud*, Volume XVIII, ed. James Strachey, (London: Hogarth Press, 1957).

Love for oneself knows only one barrier – love for others, love for objects. This requires that we study the kind of emotional bond which is established between members of a group, and this in turn involves looking more closely at the phenomena of being in love. These emotional ties which pull the group together are obviously love drives which have been diverted from their original aim and which follow, according to Freud, a very precise pattern: that of identification.

Identification is, Freud says, "the earliest expression of an emotional tie with another person", linked to the early history of the Oedipus complex. There are three main forms of identification. The first is identification with the father. The second is identification with the object-choice of love. The third arises, according to Freud, with any new perception of a common quality shared with some other person who is not an object of the sexual instinct. The more important this common quality is, the more successful may this partial identification become, and it may thus represent the beginning of a new tie. This third type of identification is the one to be found in the mutual tie between members of the group, and Freud adds that the common quality on which this identification is based lies in the nature of the tie with the leader.

At this point I would like to ask the question: How should the tie with the leader be conceived? Freud approaches this question in terms of the various forms of being in love. The primary way of being in love is experiencing sexual satisfaction in an object. But in the situation of many forms of love choice the object of love serves as a substitute for some unattained ego ideal of our own. We love it on account of the perfections which we have striven to reach for our own ego, and which we should now like to procure in this roundabout way as a means of satisfying our narcissism. When we are in love, the ego becomes more and more unassuming and modest, and the object more and more sublime and precious, until it gets possession of the entire self, love of the ego, whose self-sacrifice thus follows as a natural consequence. The object has, so to speak, consumed the ego. The whole situation can be summarized in a formula: The object has replaced the ego ideal.

4. Identification with the Leader

What exactly is Freud telling us with this account? And is the lesson about love delivered by Freud consistent with the advice given by Simonides to the tyrant? In my view, Freud says here the following: the leader of the group will be accepted only if he presents, in a particularly marked fashion, features that he shares with those he is supposed to lead. In other words: the people are, to a considerable extent, in *pari materia* with the leader – that is to say, the latter becomes *primus inter pares*. Three consequences follow from this diagnosis.

First, that something in common which makes the identification between members of the group possible cannot consist exclusively in love for the leader, but in some positive feature that both the leader and people share.

Second, identification does not take place only between egos, because the separation between ego and ego ideal is far from complete. This means that a certain degree of identification with the leader becomes possible. When Freud compares the Army and the Catholic Church, he suggests that while in the Army the soldier would become ridiculous if he identified himself with the commander in chief, the Church requires from the believer more than identification with other Christians. A believer has also to identify with Christ and love all other Christians as Christ loves them. At both points, therefore, the Church requires that the position of the libido which is given by group formation should be supplemented. Identification has to be added where object-choice has taken place, and object-love where there is identification.

Third, if the leader leads because he presents features which are common to all members of the group, he can no longer be, in all its purity, the despotic, narcissistic ruler. On the one hand, as he participates in that very substance of the community which makes identification possible, his identity is split: he is the father, but also one of the brothers. On the other hand, since his right to rule is based on the recognition by other group members of a feature of the leader which he shares, in a particularly pronounced way, with all of them, the leader is, to a considerable extent, accountable to the community. The need for leadership could still be there but it is a far more democratic leadership than the one involved in the notion of the narcissistic despot.

Did we not find a similar lesson in the case of Symonides? Hiero is disenchanted with tyranny because, desiring to be loved by human beings, he believes that tyrannical rule prevents him from being so loved. Simonides asserts that tyrants are more likely to gain affection than private men. For whatever might have to be said against tyranny, the tyrant is certainly a ruler, hence a man of high standing among his fellows, and people naturally admire men of high social standing. Above all, the prestige attending ruling positions adds an unbought grace to any act of kindness performed by rulers in general and hence by tyrants in particular. It is by means of this assertion that Simonides suggests his cure for Hiero's illness, a cure discovered, just as the illness itself was, by reflecting on Hiero's comparison of honor and sex. Hiero granted as a matter of course that in order to receive favors, to be loved in return, one must first love: the misery of the tyrant consists in the very fact that he loves and is not loved in turn. Simonides applies what Hiero granted as regards sexual love to love in general: a tyrant who wants to be loved must love first. A tyrant who wants to be loved by his subjects in order to be genuinely honored by them must love them first; to gain favors the tyrant must first show favors. Simonides advises the tyrant to think not of his own pleasures but of the pleasures of others; not of his being served and receiving gifts, but of his doing services and making gifts. Returning to Freud, one might say that the problem of the tyrant arises from that fact he wants to be a ruler, which is always like a father, but never like a brother. Hiero cannot understand, Hiero does not want to understand that something in common which makes the identification between members of the group possible cannot consist exclusively in love for the leader, tyrant, dictator but in some positive feature that both the leader and people share.

5. All you need is love (again)

To answer at least in part those vexing questions I will refer to the vision of an autonomous subject derived from the works of Kant and Freud. I choose Kant and Freud for several reasons. First, I have the deep conviction that no one like them expressed the complex relations between autonomy and heteronomy, although both saw the chance of becoming an autonomous subject in something else and perceived differently the dangers of heteronomy. Second, no one matched them in popularizing the dream about eternal peace, about cosmopolitan society, about the subject functioning beyond the pleasure principle and beyond the death drive, in the utopian "beyond"; no one like them diagnosed all possible difficulties leading to this noble ideal. Thirdly and finally, no one like them diagnosed the human need for tyranny and tyrannizing, deep and equivocal powers lying in the economy of passion and thinking techniques.

When in 1783 Immanuel Kant was asked what the Enlightenment is, he replied that it is the liberation from the self-imposed and self-inflicted immaturity; by the concept of "autonomy" he understood the will of self-determination.[8] I stress the word "will" because to Kant autonomy was above all a volitional disposition, connected with the courage to be independent, and less – which is wrongly stressed – the purely intellectual disposition. With Kant we remain nonetheless within the limits of a certain ambiguity. On the one hand, Kant wanted people to escape the yoke of the clergy, the political and moral authorities, and to start to decide over their lives by themselves. On the other hand, he expected that people will overcome their desires and comply with their

8 Immanuel Kant (1784), *An Answer to the Question: What is Enlightenment?,* [in:] *What is Enlightenment? Eighteenth-Century Answers and Twentieth-Century Questions,* Ed. Schmidt James (Berkeley, 1996), p. 58.

moral code, which they created with the faculty of reason. What is more, the norms created this way would be universally used. That is why from his perspective race, sex, or social position of a given person, not to mention the details of their personal life, are completely irrelevant. Taking into account such specific details while making moral choices can only impede one's striving towards autonomy.

To express relations between autonomy and heteronomy Kant uses two terms, which he found in the lexicon of the German language, *Freiheit* ("moral freedom", "autonomy") and *Willkür* ("choice" or "free choice"): freedom is at once autonomy and heteronomy, which means that it contains its opposite. In a nutshell: without free choice one cannot talk about responsibility, and therefore about autonomy: duty only makes sense for the entity which decides for oneself, according to the set goals. At the same time free choice is also a rule of resistance against morality: it is the "ownership of desire", afflicted with inevitable sensuality (which Kant calls a "penchant"). Although the sensual motives explain the passivity of the individual towards free action of the subject and self-imposition of the rules of conduct, they also offer just as great internal resistance to the moral intention. That is why it appears to be a compulsion or an imperative to which – although I myself am its source – I need to "subordinate" myself. Therefore, what I discover in "myself" is both the inability and the necessity to identify with "my will". After all, Kant calls pathological the sensual impulses which work within me with the force of desire. In a 1793 text, *Religion within the Limits of Reason Alone*, Kant defined this intrusion of desire into the heart of freedom not as simple "weakness" but as a "radical evil", the original sin, the "wrong principle" with which we "are secretly in league" and which cannot be disposed of by human strength, although it dooms it to tackling the never ending task of liberating freedom.[9]

Apart from the will and choice there is also the law. And law is the expression and a certain formalization of coercion, employed by individuals on each other to prevent the collision of their freedoms. It seems that the individuals who obey the law act as if they were giving assent to the coexistence of their freedoms. In this sense one should above all understand Kant's expression from *Mataphysische Anfangsgründe der Rechtslehre*: "law and entitlement to use violence are then one and the same".

But what is the purpose of law and what is its function? Well, the answer is straightforward: the compulsion of law is necessary to oblige everyone to proper action when one forgets about one's duty. For if individual freedoms are not

9 Immanuel Kant (1793), *Die Religion innerhalb der Grenzen der bloßen Vernunft*. [in:] Immanuel Kant, *Werke in zwölf Bänden*. Band 8, 9 (Frankfurt am Main, 1977).

consistent with each other, it happens as a result of the lack of inner strength to perform one's duties and one's unassisted, heroic subordination. Therefore, the compulsion of law appears to be the means to transform self-destructive freedom into non-conflicting freedom. As a result we obtain the paradoxical formula: at the basis of compulsion lies freedom, at the basis of freedom lies compulsion.

To Kant, autonomy was tantamount to distancing oneself from one's own inclinations so that one could be led by the terror of reason. In turn, to Freud the psychic apparatus did not exhaust in the reason, but it was responsible for the instinctual impulses, choosing the objects of love, and identification. That is why it could not be separated from the experiences, but rather became a kind of borderline experience – between the inner and the outer. Critical distancing from one's desires, identification and object-cathexis does not mean that one automatically gains a thorough assessment of reality. Distancing, or rather the game of distancing, initiates a never ending process of regrouping forces.

Furthermore, the type of reasoning which according to Kant helps achieve moral autonomy is by its nature formal and logical; the moral norms are tested in their transformation into universal rules. Unlike to Kant, to Freud self-knowledge is connected with the necessity of concrete self-reflection. I emphasize the word "concrete" because it should suggest the necessity of repeating self-reflection again and again. Gaining autonomy in private life means, therefore, the necessity of working out specific, often idiosyncratic and accidental characteristics of a particular person's life history and creating one's own identity on the basis of one's life experiences. Demonstrating that the *ego* is a function of *id* which draws on its reserves, Freud's theory encouraged thinking about oneself in terms of self-management. The basic task of the mind is to connect elements which in practice are considered to be distinct. Freud suggests, therefore, that reason exists in madness, working thanks to it and drawing from it.

The distinction between *ego* and *superego*, introduced by Freud, and his arguments concerning the unconscious roots of the *superego* expose the rigid, compulsory, and punishing character of what is considered moral. Max Weber already regarded not only Benjamin Franklin's utilitarianism, but also Kant's piety as stemming from the Calvinist tradition. Now Freud, considering the *superego* as a derivative of the castration complex, identified Kant's categorical imperative – the universal rule of morality – with *superego*. He wrote in *Moses*:

> To return to ethics: we may say in conclusion that a part of its precepts is explained rationally by the necessity to mark off the rights of the community to the individual, those of the individual to the community, and those of individuals to one another.

> What, however, appears mysterious, grandiose and mystically self-evident owes its character to its connection with religion, its origin from the will of the father.[10]

According to Freud, moral rules imposed by the superego must have been balanced by both the identifications typical for the *id,* and by the realism of the *ego,* its abilities to provide counsel and judgment.

No one like Kant made us sensitive to the problems of relations between law and morality. No one like Freud made us sensitive to the problem of false identifications. Freud suggested that there is no final criterion which would be the ultimate test, allowing us to distinguish between false and successful forms of identification.

Nonetheless, Freud's construction of community is no less intricate than Kant's construction of moral law. In a nutshell, Freud demonstrates the simultaneity of three phenomena which were treated separately before him: (1) identification of various "egos" with each other, thereby creating their imaginary community; (2) substitution in the case of each "ego" of its "ideal ego" by the "object" of its love (or desire); (3) unification of different ideals which results from the fact that in a given situation always the same "external object" (or real object, or a leader, institution or a historical dogma) occupies this imaginary space.

If we consider what enables the same "external object" to simultaneously replace a multitude of "ideal egos", we come to the conclusion that it happens as a result of identifying oneself with different "egos", regarding all ideals as common. Yet, the next step leads us to a hypothesis suggesting that the very establishment of the "ego" is the result of rather than the reason for the process of collective idealization. One could even think that this process is initiated due to the fact that the so-called "external object" is in reality a complex structure, represented simultaneously by people, institutions, convictions, and ideas. One can explain thus the circular character of the analysis, which is no longer concerned with the translation of group structure by means of individual psyche, but with the explanation of the individual's constitution, which always already encompasses the "collective" structure.

Thus, Freud does not write about autonomy understood as self-control and sovereignty of the mind and therefore autonomy understood in Kantian terms. He understands autonomy as an unstable equilibrium between the pleasure, reality and duty principles; it is political and existential autonomy, that is, the freedom of being responsible for one's own life. Freud complicated the

---

10 Sigmund Freud (1939), *Moses and Monotheism,* [in:] *The Standard Edition of the Complete Psychological Works of Sigmund Freud,* Volume XXIII (1937-1939), ed. James Strachey, (London: Hogarth Press, 1957).

Enlightenment's image of human autonomy, opened it to the individual and the idiosyncratic, encouraged the exploration of the inner world, but also sensitized people to the fact that life is full of inauthenticity. The way outside leads through the exploration of what is within, but also the exploration of the inner depends on the means provided by the external world. Freud suggested, therefore, that only opening oneself to what is individual and idiosyncratic will enable man to creatively liberate new energies of public, social activity, that is, to become the citizen of *polis*.

6. Dwarf

If the distinction between the individual and the community is problematic because the individual takes shape through a sequence of identifications and a construction of the external object, and the community is a community of multiple identifications whereby the same psychic apparatus is treated as a type of *polis*, then perhaps we cannot expect from autonomy anything more than it being a fortunate way of connecting all those temporary identifications which determined our life.

If, however, the compulsion of law appears to be a means to transform self-destructive freedom into a nonconflicting freedom then perhaps we have no choice other than to risk the heroism of subordination suggested by Kant. This heroism is certainly more demanding than heroism of submission to one's impulses, heroism of application of the categorical imperative: Enjoy! Jacques Marie Emile Lacan states this explicitly: "[n]othing forces anyone to enjoy except the superego. The super-ego is the imperative of *jouissance*: Enjoy!".[11] For libido's headquarters are no longer in the "ego" but in the "super-ego". Enjoyment, supervision and our identification can be found in the same place – in the headquarters. And this is what we call narcissism or, in Freud's terminology, an "ego" working towards pure pleasure [*Lust-Ich*].

If the way to the public man runs through the analysis of the intimate man, then perhaps the homogenous state predicted by Alexandre Kojève, the loss of ability to distinguish between a tyranny and a kingdom which Strauss cautioned against, and finally installing the desire for independence under the guise of dictatorship in a world devoid of monarchs, the danger of which saw Schmitt – all these three diagnoses are the perspective projections of one and the same: fear, our inability to look at autonomy from any vantage point other than our

11 Jacques Lacan, *Le séminaire, Livre* XX: *Encore,* ed. Jacques-Alain Miller, (Éditions du Seuil, 1999), p. 11.

egoistic point of view – from the point of view of the *libido* headquarters, the point of view of "ego" working towards pure pleasure. The pleasure of dominating.

Perhaps then, if we want to exceed the phantasms of power totally administering the social reality, if we want to avoid thinking about politics in monarchist categories as a series of attempts to replace one tyranny with another, we should reorganize our thinking about autonomy focused on the individual, and perceive it in the processes of formation of the individual and the community and simultaneously acknowledge that obedience – to quote Spinoza – concerns not "outward act, but the internal act within one's soul".[12]

---

12 Benedict de Spinoza (1670), *A Theologico-Political Treatise/A Political Treatise.* trans. R. H. M. Elwes. (New York: Dover Publications, 1951), p. 279.

V. In Praise of Monstrosities. The Case of Niccolò Machiavelli

We must, therefore, I think, in order to be pardoned for our faults, commit new ones; redoubling the mischief, and multiplying fires and robberies; and in doing this, endeavor to have as many companions as we can; for when many are in fault, few are punished; small crimes are chastised, but great and serious ones rewarded.

Niccolò Machiavelli[1]

Concepts are really monsters that are reborn from their fragments.

Gilles Deleuze, Felix Guattari[2]

No facility, but no impossibility in principle. No transcendence, but no prison of immanence either. Nothing but the ordinary work of politics.

Bruno Latour[3]

We live in an age of monsters and of the body-panics they excite.

David McNally[4]

1. A lamb with a pig's head

François Jacob, in his famous 1970 work entitled *La logique du vivant, une histoire de l'hérédité,*[5] states that a sixteenth-century description of the animate world is filled with various, colorful, more or less fabulous monsters. There are authors who, like Ulysses Aldrovandi and Ambroise Paré, devote their whole books to them.[6] According to Jacob, the Renaissance monsters always reflect the properties of the visible world; there is no monster that would not resemble

1 Niccolò Machiavelli, *History of Florence and of the Affairs of Italy from the Earliest Times to the Death of Lorenzo the Magnificent* (The Pennsylvania State University, 2007), p. 142.

2 Gilles Deleuze, Felix Guattari, *What Is Philosophy?*, trans. H. Tomlinson, G. Burchell, (Columbia University Press, 1994), p. 155.

3 Bruno Latour, *Politics of Nature: How to Bring the Sciences Into Democracy,* trans. C. Porter, (Cambridge: Harvard University Press, 2004), p. 219.

4 David McNally, *Monsters of the Market. Zombies, Vampires and Global Capitalism*, (Boston: Brill, 2011).

5 François Jacob (1970), *The Logic Of Life. A History of Heredity*, trans. B. E. Spillmann, (New York: A Division of Random House).

6 François Jacob, *The Logic Of Life. A History of Heredity.*

something and would not be a combination of body parts of other animals. Monsters always reflect and reproduce similarities, but similarities which violated the rules and ceased to match the ordinary, monotone workings of nature. The combinations and signs which can be read from them do not reveal the order existing in the world, but show errors which can slip into this world. François Jacob writes about it thus: "Each monster is the result of iniquity and bears witness to a certain disorder: an act (or even an intention) not in conformity with the order of the world. Physical or moral, each divergence from nature produces an unnatural fruit. Nature, top, has its morality".[7] According to Jacob, the Renaissance knowledge of monstrosity constitutes a whole and complete system in which everything has its place. Therefore, generation was only one of the methods which God used to maintain the world within the particular limits and creating likeness. Here is a world in which nature is endowed with morality. Yet, a question arises: Is a world in which morality exists in nature not a world without morality, a world so to speak beyond good and evil, a world beyond the division into facts and values, or rather a world in which values exist only as much as they are facts, and the facts are taken into consideration only when they aspire to being values?

When we look into Ambroise Paré's oeuvre, the 1573 treatise *Des monsters et prodigies*, our contemporary imagination is astounded the most by the admittance for almost infinite shape-shifting and alteration of organs in the animate world and by the recognition in the act of procreation a source of this ecstatic diversity and plasticity of nature. Ambroise Paré writes about a lamb which had a pig's head because the ewe had been covered by a boar. The world in which nature has its morality is a world of strengthened and generalized, dispersed and transactional monstrosity. Paré does not state anywhere what the offspring produced by the lamb with pig's head looks like or if it produced any other lambs with pigs' heads. Yet he talks about the necessity of the existence of such a kind of monsters in the world economy. Jacob, commenting on those fragments in Paré, states that the Renaissance does not differentiate between the necessity of phenomena and the random occurrence of events.

> For if horse was obviously born of horse and cat of cat – we read in Jacob – this was not the effect of a mechanism that permitted living beings to produce copies of themselves, somewhat as a printing machine produces copies of a text. Only towards the end of the eighteenth century did the word and the concept of reproduction make their appearance to describe the formation of living organisms. Until that time living beings did not reproduce; they were engendered.[8]

---

7 *Ibid.*, p. 46.

8 *Ibid.*, p. 19.

What does this signify? What is the meaning of the enigmatic statement that before the 18th century living beings did not reproduce but were brought into existence? In what sense is reproduction distinct from engenderment? Does in the economy of the world, in which nature has its own morality and every monster is a result of an error and proof of a violation, engendering emerge as a source of error, and thus of monstrosity? Well, not rushing to far reaching conclusions, I will take it to mean that until the 18th century the shaping of a living being was considered to be a singular event, independent of any other act of creation, and resembled more the creation of a work of art by an artist than creating a copy by the printing press. We can therefore talk about the Renaissance art of engenderment, but not about the Renaissance art of reproduction. The art of reproduction is an art form in the day of mass production. Here, the creator became the manufacturer.

The already mentioned captivating intermingling of forms in nature, that is, the world economy allowing for any transaction is the reason why in the 18th century thinking there is no species understood as a formal structure maintaining itself in time, that is, for the succeeding generations. Living organisms create organisms similar to themselves not out of necessity of nature. To explain the formation of an organism, each time one has to refer to the work of God or his agents.[9] François Jacob describes the Renaissance epistemological system, in which Paré operates, in the following manner:

> The likeness which Ambroise Paré invokes to explain the formation of the lamb with the pig's head did not have the same status as today. In order to know things then, it was necessary to detect the visible signs which nature had placed on their surfaces precisely to permit man to comprehend their relationships. It was necessary to discern the system of resemblances, the network of analogies and similitudes providing access to certain of nature's secrets.[10]

Behind the similitudes lies the nature of things, and the similarity of children to their parents is only one particular aspect of all those resemblances which have secretly linked all living beings. In this epistemological order, a living being cannot be reduced only to its visible structure. The visible structure is only a part of the mesh of the secret net which encompasses all of the world's objects. Each animal and each plant becomes a kind of shape-shifting body which extends itself not only to other living beings, but also to stars and stones, or even to the activities of humans.[11]

9 *Ibid.*, p. 46.

10 *Ibid.*, p. 36.

11 The likeness which Ambroise Paré invokes to explain the formation of the lamb with the pig's head did not have the same status as today. In order to know things then, it was necessary to detect the visible signs which nature had placed on their surfaces precisely

Let us summarize this train of thought. Ambroise Paré's biological imagination is open to such a great degree that it allows for any experiments with nature. Those experiments are conducted in the act of generation, which is different from the mechanical act of reproduction. Teratology, or rather monsterology[12] – the science of monsters – allows us to put in the ontological register of the world forms which would have been consistent with *The Book of Imaginary Beings* or the *A Universal History of Infamy* of Jorge Luis Borges. We will find here the representatives of the Acefali people – without heads, with faces between their arms, representatives of Sphinxes – lions with human heads, Manticores – a mixture of a lion, bat and a scorpion, Astons, who do not have lips and feed on smells and are infinitely delicate beings, Ichtrofags, feeding exclusively on fish and drinking only salt water, Antropofags – cannibals who eat their parents out of respect for them, or finally representations of cyclopses, sirens, winged horses, or troglodytes. This is the real, democratic parliament of humanity and unhumanity. Renaissance biological imagination allows for recording in the register of beings all kinds of mutants, hybrids, flawed creatures, surprising, creatures and creations which for us are impossible. Although in the Renaissance memory nature has its morality, this morality allows for or even demands the selection of such a kind of rule of equivalence, this type of transactional system which minimizes the externality and maximizes the internality, that is keeps to a minimum that which is excluded from the imagined collective of the world, from this morality of nature, the triumphant parade of monstrous, constantly recurring act of generation, and not reproduction of creatures.

2. Monsters without a future

It is interesting that those highly inspiring guidelines and comments on the topic of monstrous imagination of the Renaissance, formulated by the French

---

to permit man to comprehend their relationships. It was necessary to discern the system of resemblances, the network of analogies and similitudes providing access to certain of nature's secrets. The very nature of things is hidden behind the similitudes. Thus the resemblance of a child to its parents is only a special aspect of all those by which beings and things are secretly linked. A living being could not then be reduced to the visible structure alone. It represented a link in the secret network tying together all the objects in the world. Each animal, each plant was viewed as a sort of protean body extending not only to other beings, but also to the stones, the stars and even to human activities.

12 David McNally explains that he prefers "the term *monsterology* to the more common "teratology", given the latter's connection to the normativising study of birth-defects".

biologist François Jacob, are made almost at the same time by a French historian Michel Foucault and his probably most daring work entitled *Les Mots et les Choses*.[13] In a significant chapter of the book entitled *Monsters and Fossils*, wondering about the historical roots of evolutional thought and its archeological source, Foucault notes that one of the consistent problems of evolutionary thought is the matter of transformation of live organisms. The fundamental problem is the transformation from one form to another. History is facing the following question: Should we assume that a live organism has a spontaneous affinity towards changing its form or acquiring features slightly at variance with the initial matrix in the future generations, through which this trait becomes with time blurred and uncertain? Or should we rather ascribe to living organisms the blind drive towards achieving the final form of a species, which would show all the preceding traits of the species, but on a higher level of complexity and perfection, on a higher level of integration?[14]

Foucault says that in essence there are two solutions to this problem. According to the first idea, it is suggested that there exists a natural equilibrium of forces between the continuity-preserving memory for patterns and the tendency for deviation from which phenotype differences and varieties emerge. When the balance between the memory of the imitating mechanism and the tendency towards change becomes disrupted through excessive modifications, monstrosity is born. The same monstrosity,which causes the fall of organisms is also the reason for diversity and evolutionary progress. The multiplicity of species came into being due to some reoccurring transgressions, errors, mutations, micro-damage. Mutation is always blind, since one does not know if it will be evolutionarily advantageous. Each change is a risk of regress or progress. But without risk there is no life.

According to the second, competing solution to the problem of the changeability of forms, the continuity of the species is not preserved by memory, but by the initial design. The architecture of natural creations lies between the simplicity of the design hidden in the dark recesses of history, and the engineering complication of the concrete realizations and incarnation of this project, that is, the empirical organisms which link into ever greater wholes. So the thing that can be named the "splendor and lushness of nature" and its striving towards ever greater complexity is a notion responsible for the production of monstrosities. Yet, in this paradigm the monsters do not have a different nature than the species, they are merely metamorphoses of the early prototype. Monstrosity here is productive and progressing, and serves to create new forms.

---

13 Michel Foucault (1966). *The Order of Things. An Archaeology of the Human Sciences.* (London: Vintage, 1992).

14 Michel Foucault, *The Order of Things*, p. 205.

Foucault notes that this productive mode of thinking about monsters has two nontrivial consequences. The first consequence is the very necessity of the appearance of monsters. Monsters are no longer an accidental, unwanted, unintentional effect of life; their existence is necessary. As Foucault states, monsters here are like an "endless murmur of nature", the language of monsters does not tell anything, although it is never silent. If evolution really needs to probe all possible combinations, monsters are as necessary to nature as geological catastrophes are necessary for the formation of the earth's layers. Proliferation of monsters without a future is a necessity. Without monsters the world would have been infinitely flat, uniform, monotone. Foucault writes: "[t]he monster ensures in time, and for our theoretical knowledge, a continuity that, for our everyday experience, floods, volcanoes, and subsiding continents confuse in space".[15] Not only the ontological, but also epistemological necessity of the monster results from the fact that their existence fills out empty spaces, openings, breaks, gaps in time, missing links, which like hyphens allow us to understand the continuity of nature, the lack of breaks in the existential structure of the animate matter.

The second consequence of this productive thinking about monsters is that the signs of the continuity of nature, which monsters are, belong entirely to the order of imitations. Foucault writes here in the rhetoric of François Jacob: all biological forms are trapped in the logic of probability, experiencing all possible metamorphoses, they are only signs, signals of evolution, that is, the progression of nature in the world. For this very reason nature, beginning its sketches from the primitive prototype, is not exhausted in the human figure. Nietzschean figures of the last men – Soothsayer (symbolizing the wish of expiring), Sorcerer (symbolizing the manufacturer of mercy), the Noble One (symbolizing the moralist distorting values), two Kings (symbolizing the triumph of the rabble) are in reality figures of monstrosity. One of nature's qualities is the ability to abandon, to betray the already produced forms. That is why the world is a cemetery of fossils and monsters, fossilized monstrosities, a dumpster of the monstrosities, which could not adapt and make home in the world. Foucault writes: "The fossil, with its mixed animal and mineral nature, is the privileged locus of a resemblance required by the historian of the continuum, whereas the space of the *taxinomia* decomposed it with rigour".[16] For this reason Foucault states that in the register in which the power of continuity administering nature is the essential power, only the monster allows for discernment of the difference, and only the monster is the progenitor of specification. Fossil

15 *Ibid.*, p. 207.
16 *Ibid.*, p. 207.

allows for the survival of monsters, that is, the transfer of even the greatest anomalies. The question is: does science about monsters thus understood become exhausted in the field of natural history?

3. Situation

I claim that the idea of productivity and the necessity of monstrosity has been used the most by the thought of Niccolò Machiavelli. Machiavelli's monstrosity is naturally a part of Renaissance imagination. Yet Machiavelli gives this imagination a strictly political character: it tears out the monstrosity from the dictionary of natural history and transfers the category of monstrosity into the dictionary of politics. It is not solely important that – as François Jacob suggested in his reading of Aldrovandi and Paré – in Machiavelli's imagination "nature has its morality" and in the world economy there exists an extensive interchangeability of everything and everyone. It is also not the most important – as Michel Foucault suggested in his reading of the *avant la lettre* evolutionists – that before evolutionism was invented monstrosity could be the sign of the continuity of nature. Without a doubt, to Machiavelli monstrosity is productive and even more than that: monstrosity is constructive, but it does not have to be the sign of continuity. Rather, it is a sign of mutation and discontinuity. To the author of *The Prince*, only monstrosity is imaginable and this monstrosity is hard to grasp because the monstrosity is nominal, it is the struggle of contradiction, as if Machiavelli wanted to say, long before Deleuze and Guattari, that *concepts are monsters coming back to life from their remains.* This central role of monstrosity in Machiavelli's work allows me to recognize him simply as a theoretician of monstrosity, and his work as one great praise of monstrosity.

Niccolò Machiavelli is a mysterious thinker, ambiguous and ambivalent. Almost all of Machiavelli's concepts are afflicted with this ambiguity and double entendre. For example, Machiavelli writes about history and time as if they had no influence on the nature of things, but also as if they were a primary property; finally, he writes about temporality as if it were entangled in a circle of eternal return. Machiavelli writes about human nature as if it were unchangeable and constantly destined to suffer from the same deficiency, suggesting, for instance, that nature "has created men so that they are able to desire everything and are unable to attain everything. So, since the desire is always greater than the power of acquiring, the result is discontent with what one possesses and a lack of satisfaction with it".[17] On the other hand, Machiavelli suggests that human is a being without nature, a being condemned to eternal experiments with him- or herself and with nature, spelling doom to those who cannot fit into the changing conditions. Machiavelli writes about rule and power as if its sole goal was to keep the subjects in a state in which they cannot, or are not forced to, do damage to the prince;[18] on the other hand, he suggests that proper rule is possible only where we have a conflict between the poor and the rich, the plebs and the aristocracy, where it is not possible for one side to attain definite advantage. Machiavelli writes about the people that they are vain and fickle, but also constant and capable of gratitude, able to make a better choice than the ruler, and finally, that it is the sole mirror in which the ruler can look into and achieve self-awareness. How can the people be both constant and fickle, full of gratitude and ungrateful, able to make decisions and absolutely passive?

On the other hand, Machiavelli writes about the prince as if he had the virtues of a leader and general, recalling Cyrus, the creator of the Persian empire, who according to Herodotus got to power with deceit and treachery, but also Mark Aurelius and Cesare Borgia. Yet the prince is also supposed to be endowed with the virtues of an "armed prophet", whereby Machiavelli provides the examples of Christ and Moses. Lastly, the prince is supposed to have the virtues of legislator and lawgiver for whom the models are Lycurgus and Solon. Finally, above all else, the prince is supposed to prove himself capable of forming a new country – a political innovator with the temperament of Romulus or Theseus. The question is: What is the monster which is simultaneously a leader, a legislator, a player, a prophet and a founder?

Fortune is a fickle, changeable and unjust, pitiless and perjurious goddess, but it is also a lottery, a praise of any aleatoricism. Fortune is also a chance, a threshold, an event, a mutation changing the course of events. But who cannot use her cannot reach the threshold of new possibilities, their potential to recognize their own power. Finally, *virtù* – the collection of specific political abilities: energy, initiative, ability to make decisions and take swift action, described by Machiavelli as a virtue which is the condition for any creative activity, the beginning of any innovativeness, which would mean that it is nothing but the favor and will of fate, Fortune, opening oneself to what happens by chance and what is unknown. "I confess this course is bold and dangerous, but when necessity presses, audacity becomes prudence", writes Machiavelli,

17 Niccolò Machiavelli (1517), *Discourses on Livy*, trans. Leslie J. Walker, S.J., revisions by Brian Richardson. (London: Penguin Books, 2003), p. 95.

18 *Ibid.*, p. 214.

and adds "[...] no one ever escaped from embarrassment without some peril".[19] On the other hand, *virtù* is an inner trait, allowing the prince and the state's formation to be based on Fortune, and to impose on her his own model of constitutional order. *Virtù* is violence inflicted on Fortune. One should also remember that a part of virtù is to double the evil, multiply the arsons and rapine. Therefore, *virtù* is both a virtue and a nonvirtue.

Here is the political teratology and monsterology of Niccolò Machiavelli's concepts. In this teratology there is no one concept which would be unambiguous, not looking for an explicit or hidden ambivalence, there is no transcendence, but there is also no prison of immanence. There is nothing but the ordinary, hard work of politics, in which notions such as monsters, even if they are not restored to life, are surely revived in their outer edges, on their borders. Let us remember that monsters always reflect and reproduce similarities which violated the rules and ceased to match the ordinary, monotone workings of nature. In Machiavelli, the monster is always formed by a creative error and shows a new configuration, a new conjuncture.

It seems that the main axis of tension in Machiavelli's system runs along the vertical axis linking the prince and the people and along the horizontal axis linking the notion of Fortune and virtue – *virtù*. Prince's nature is complex. He is both the phantasmal space of projection of the people's wishes, a kind of personification of the general will, and the *Great Other*, a superhuman who is the foundation of the whole political order. The character of prince's nature is personal and suprapersonal. Analyzing the case of Sparta, Venice, Rome, and Florence, so the political orders of diverse regimes, Machiavelli forwards a conclusion that the sole recommended political order is such an order in which there is a constant separation of interests and powers between the aristocracy and the people, in which the defense of the freedom of the republic is not in the hands of the people or the notables, but in the unstable dynamics and the network of their mutual relationships, as well as the relationships between the entire "state" and Fortune. Two reasons for the fall of Rome are, first, the increase of inequality and the resulting hate between the people and the notables, and second, the privatization of the army, which lead to the disarmament and neutralizing of the "armed citizen", that is, a citizen who was simultaneously a warrior, and his division into the powerless, impotent "citizen" and the warrior, who is armed but without prerogatives. Machiavelli's famous book entitled *The Art*

19 Niccolò Machiavelli (1525), *Florentine Histories*, trans. Laura F Banfield and Harvey Mansfield, (Princeton University Press, 1988), p. 161.

of War[20] is on this very subject, that is, the subject of the necessity of being an armed citizen. In Machiavelli's eyes a citizen is a *condottiere*.

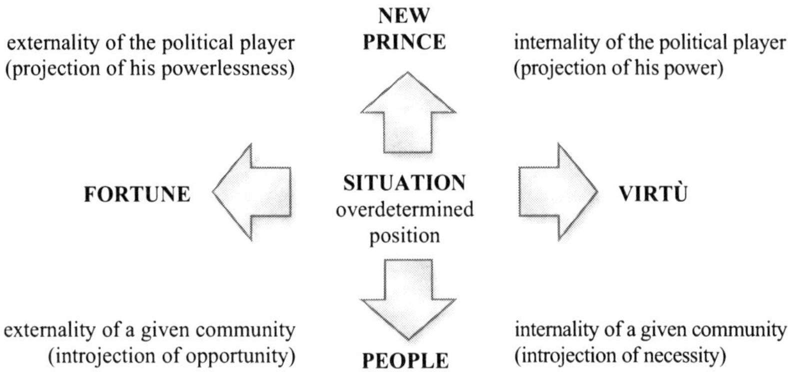

I claim that as a result, the sole concept allowing us to approach the monstrosity of the people and the monstrosity of the prince in the vertical relation, and to recognize the power of the people in the prince, and the power of the prince in the people, and to juxtapose, horizontally, the monstrosity of Fortune and the monstrosity of *virtù,* and to recognize fate's will in Fortune, *amor fati*, and in *virtù* the person of the player affirming chance who knows that the probability is created not by the amassed number of throws but that the repetition of the throw is possible thanks to the nature of the randomly drawn number, the sole concept which can reconcile all these contradictions is the notion of situation, and that Machiavelli's entire philosophy and politics attains the designation of politics of situation, meaning the politics of what is singular, the politics of the event.

For this reason Machiavelli's texts are purely and solely the studies of singular events, laboratories in which the monstrous fossils are reconstructed, and Machiavelli's imagination is not only the Renaissance imagination which adores the proliferation of forms, but, above all, it is the structural imagination justified more by its effectiveness, truth, defined by Machiavelli by the results, verita effettuale della cosa, and less by the method, that is, the imagination leading to the use of old languages in a new way. Monstrosity of situation is the unpredictability of Fortune meeting *virtù*, and the prince

20 Niccolò Machiavelli, *The Art of War* (1520), trans. Ellis Farnesworth. (Da Capo Press Edition, 2001).

meeting the people. Monstrosity of situation is another name given to overdetermination (Freudian Überdeterminierung). The subject of Machiavelli's imagination is no longer the lamb with pig's head, but the overdetermination of situation.

4. Goddess Circe

Let us start with a cardinal and categorical statement. The history of political thought of the West is one great struggle with monstrosity. The politics of the West escapes the phantasmal monstrosity of nature by building a no-less phantasmal artificial monsters called states. Thomas Hobbes's *Leviathan* begins with a declaration of the possibility of constructing a mortal God, a monster, a Leviathan, a great animal, a great automaton and a great man – a synthesis of machine, organism, and soul. Although in Hobbes the figure of Leviathan appears only three times, it foreshadows the mythical completeness consisting of human, animal, and machine.[21] This completeness may aspire to the designation of a mortal God. If we look from the mythological perspective at three names constitutive to the modern political order – Machiavelli, Vico, and Hobbes – then we will see the embroilment of these persons in myth. Vico did not create any myth, but he saw in the history of nations a history of myths. Hobbes is neither a mythologist, nor a myth. Only in his picture of Leviathan did he approach, perhaps against his own will, the mythical sphere. Finally, Machiavelli in his entirety, with all his writings and his name itself, achieved a mythic status.[22] This state of affairs requires explanation. When Antonio Gramsci writes in *The Modern Prince* that *The Prince* is neither a political treatise, nor even a revolutionary treatise, but a live (endowed with performative power) word in which political ideology fuses with political reflection and assumes a dramatic form of myth, he obviously follows this mythological path.[23]

Carl Schmitt is surely right when he writes that there is no political image more suggestive than the figure of a large animal: we find it already in Plato, who in Republic describes the crowd endowed with affects as a large, colorful

21 Thomas Hobbes (1651), *Leviathan or The Matter, Forme and Power of a Common Wealth Ecclesiasticall and Civil*, ed. Ian Shapiro (Yale University Press, 2010).

22 See: Carl Schmitt (1938), *The Leviathan in the State Theory of Thomas Hobbes: Meaning and Failure of a Political Symbol.* trans. George D. Schwab & Erna Hilfstein, (Greenwood Press, 1996). pp. 105-108.

23 Antonio Gramsci, *The Modern Prince.* trans. Louis Marks [in:] Antonio Gramsci, *The Modern Prince and other writings,* (New York: International Publishers, 1968).

animal.[24] While writing about political monsters one should remember that the strict distinction between the organism and mechanism ultimately occurred towards the end of the 18th century. Kant in Critique of Judgment formulated this distinction on the grounds of the opposition between the inner and the outer, contrasting the living being with the inanimate thing, as a result of which the notion of mechanism was deprived of any mythical or spiritual elements, or even the vitality itself. Machine became a soulless device, it ceased to be an organism. When Nietzsche, in his Thus Spoke Zaratustra, calls the state "the coldest of all cold monsters", in a certain sense he ends this mythological, vitalistic kind of thinking about the state's animality in which Machiavelli's thought probably marks a watershed. It is no coincidence that Nietzsche is capable of discovering his affinity only with Machiavelli, writing in Nachlass, ""Highlights of Integrity" (*Höhepunkte der Redlichkeit*): Machiavelli, Jesuitism, Montaigne and La Rochefoucauld. Germans as a return to moral hypocrisy".[25]

Similarly, when Peter Sloterdijk describes the rule of cynical reason as the "vitality of dead men", which has its embodiment both in reality and in literature – in the figure of the vampire, and when David McNally[26] diagnoses an epoch of global capitalism as an era of zombies and vampires, zombies-institutions, and vampire-institutions, then both Sloterdijk and McNally add a certain supplement to the imagination in which the automatons can only be soulless and the monstrosity assumes the shape of the vampire.[27] Let us stress this strongly: Sloterdijk's and McNally's monsters can only be vampires because they have lost their power of fertility and productivity characteristic of Machiavelli's monsters, these monsters are parasites, they live a borrowed life, not their own, they borrow or rather steal vitality, they are no longer generous givers of life as in the paradigm of *The Prince.* Late capitalism is conducive to the birth of monsters bred from superstructure, and not the economical basis. Are the media not promoting today a kind of fashion of "vampires in rehab", "recovered vampires", changing the vampire icon in series such as *True Blood*, or in series

24 Carl Schmitt, *The Leviathan in the State Theory of Thomas Hobbes: Meaning and Failure of a Political Symbol.*

25 Friedrich Nietzsche, *Nietzsche Werke: Kritische Gesamtausgabe.* ed. Colli and Montinari. (Berlin Walter de Gruyter, 1973), Vol 25, p. 74. See also: Don Dombowsky, *Nietzsche's Machiavellian Politics*, New York: Palgrave Macmillan, 2004.

26 Peter Sloterdijk (1983), *Critique of Cynical Reason*, trans. Michael Eldred, (Minneapolis: University of Minnesota Press, 1988) p. 231.

27 David McNally, *Monsters of the Market. Zombies, Vampires and Global Capitalism.*

such as *Twilight*, into the figure which the vampire always has been: the figure of a demonic, metrosexual seducer from the other world?[28]

Yet let us return to Machiavelli. Hanna Pitkin, in a famous book entitled *Fortune Is a Woman*,[29] may be most helpful in the insightful reading of Machiavelli's work, leading to a complete reconstruction of the notion of "nature" which permeates both the literary and political writings of the Florentine, when she states that the notion of *nature* in Machiavelli's work is touched by ambivalence resulting in its characteristic gender politics. Could it be otherwise, since, as it has been presented, all of Machiavelli's notions are monsters revived in their outer edges, on their borders.

For Pitkin, the outset is the observation that in his theatrical and poetic works Machiavelli constantly refers to the world of women, using male, chauvinist phantasms. On the other hand, in political text about the political sphere, women are practically absent. Out of this overrepresentation of womanhood in the private life and lack of representation in the public sphere, Pitkin concludes that to Machiavelli womanhood is a force which should be restrained. This restraint results in a return of the supplanted woman element from another stage, that is, the stage of life.

Maybe the most suggestive example of Machiavelli's ambiguous style of thinking and the return to that which was supplanted on another stage are his novella entitled *Belfagor arcidiavolo,* in which a woman turns out to be worse than Lucifer, and the ending remarks in the third tome of *Discourses on Livy*, where Machiavelli considers the case of Lucretia and ambiguously generalizes: women are the reason for the fall of states. Perhaps a more reliable complement of Machiavelli's well-known political texts is his unfinished poem entitled *The Golden Ass*. The prototype of this work is *Metamorphoses* or *The Golden Ass*, that is, the fantastic-satirical romance of Apuleius which described the adventures of a young man who wanted to learn magic and for that reason journeyed into a magical land. Incidentally transformed into a donkey, he retained all human qualities, apart from speech. With the help of merciful goddess Isis, the young man recovered his human form and from that time served the goddess as her priest. Similarly, Machiavelli's hero is unaware of how he was transported from the city space into an extremely harsh and wild forest. He is helped by beautiful Diana, who serves at the court of goddess Circe, who in turn possesses the power of turning people into animals.

28 See also: Colin Davis, *Haunted Subjects. Deconstruction, Psychoanalysis and the Return of the Dead*, (Great Britain: Palgrave Macmillan, 2007).

29 Hanna Fenichel Pitkin, *Fortune Is a Woman: Gender and Politics in the Thought of Niccolo Machiavelli*, (Los Angeles: University of California Press, 1984).

In Circe's kingdom – the forest, a kingdom of nature, we find animals which are healthy and degenerated. Healthy animals have always remained a part of nature and never dreamed of transgressing it, never succumbed to the fantasies and dreams of transcending nature and becoming something different than nature. Degenerated animals, on the other hand, are the world of men, fallen, enchanted, and imprisoned in nature. In this poem Machiavelli reconstructs not only the opposition between nature and culture, between the male *polis* or *virtù* (politics) and the female world of nondiscernment (Fortune), between the city and the forest, the ordered patriarchy and the tangled and homogenous matriarchy, but, above all, Machiavelli draws here the difference between the decline into animality, which is the simultaneous exclusion from humanity, and becoming an animal, or being an animal so that the animal may become something else. Machiavelli in *The Golden Ass* recalls as a digression a history of one Florentine whose ailment, indisposition, or even a compulsive-obsessive disorder consisted in that to the surprise of his surroundings and without a clear reason he started running in the streets. A doctor ordered for him to be watched day and night, but it was of no use: suffering from the neurotic compulsion, the hero ran. What is interesting, in the *Florentine Histories* Machiavelli returns to this theme, describing the customs in Genoa, and in particular the custom of communal running as an act of achieving freedom.

Pitkin concludes from this ambiguous presence/absence of women in Machiavelli's work that to Machiavelli Fortune was a woman who needs to be conquered and treated brusquely, since that is what the finishing fragment of the 26th chapter of *The Prince* tells us:

> Fortune is a woman and [...] she allows herself to be mastered by the adventurous rather than by those who go to work more coldly. She is, therefore, always, woman-like, a lover of young men, because they are less cautious, more violent, and with more audacity command her.[30]

Contrary to Pitkin, I would claim that it is not a matter of excluding the female element, or identifying femininity with nature and glorifying bio-political regimes, but rather a triumph of the active over the reactive forces. Reactive forces separate power from the ability to act, while the active forces are those which are capable of reaching the limit of their abilities.

Fortune, which in Machiavelli's work assumes a variety of guises – from the image of a flood which suddenly surprises us, to the image of chance (opportunity) which we can use only at a given moment; well, this Fortune is not a special, singular event, or a combination of many factors shaping the event, or

---

30 Niccolò Machiavelli (1513), *The Prince*, trans. Harvey Mansfield, (University of Chicago Press, 1985), p. 103.

even a consequence of imperfection of the human calculating abilities, but the externality of politics (of the republic) which becomes nothing more than the art of dealing with life's vicissitudes. For this reason Machiavelli writes explicitly in *The Prince* that "he will be successful who directs his actions according to the spirit of the times, and that he whose actions do not accord with the times will not be successful".[31] To Machiavelli, the most difficult thing in life was the ability to abandon previously successful tactics and remaining sensitive to the changeable and very fickle mutations of time. The only strategy he recommended was the strategy of using several different tactics, the strategy of a chameleon. The hero of *The Golden Ass* also sheds human nature to resurface in the counternature of an animal, however, this turns out to be the same kind of disguise, the same mask of being as was the primal nature. As a result, Machiavelli writes: the only laws of nature are mask and deceit. One can overcome the mask only by giving it another meaning, and not by freeing oneself from it for some true nature.

Machiavelli has to be both the cunningness and strength, the duplicity and righteousness, deceit as well as law, because only this configuration allows one to lean into time, which is the sole protagonist of actions. That is why the figure recommended by Machiavelli is not at all the philosopher (wise man), attorney (man of law), economist (businessman), anthropologist (expert in foreign cultures), nor, finally, a doctor or a psychologist (expert in human nature and its imperfection), but a diplomat, who is more cunning than the moralist, less relentless than the scientist, less businesslike than the politician, who is both *our own* and *the other*, who is foreign among his own and at home somewhere else, he is, to define him through the monstrous traits which are his nature, a hybrid, a monster, reviving himself from his remains and in his outer edges. Perhaps it is difficult to notice it because of their mythical disguise, but both the goddess Circe, and the centaur Chiron are dealing with diplomacy – they receive the messengers from the unexplored externality and make apparent the frailty of that which they consider "natural".

Here Machiavelli is a couple of centuries ahead of the thought of Bruno Latour, for whom the figure of a diplomat is also paradigmatic. The problem with the diplomat is that we do not know his goal, his method, or even his range. The goal of politician's politics can be anticipation, adaptation, revolution and instigation, as well as preservation and archiving; his method can be to attack or to wait, to build and to dismantle, to patiently delay and to audaciously conquer; finally, the range of his actions can be the sphere of reproduction of life

31 Niccolò Machiavelli, *The Prince*, p. 102.

(fertility) and the accumulation of goods, the sphere of education and armament, demographics and sports, finally art as well as politics.

In her book *On Revolution*, Hannah Arendt insightfully notes the ambiguity of "conservative revolutionary politics" of Machiavelli, writing that when the author of *The Prince* uses the expression *mutazioni del stato* he is constantly referring to Cicero's notion of *mutation rerum*.[32] The word "revolution" initially meant restoration, a return to the beginning; hence, it is not surprising that Machiavelli's favorite concepts – *mutazioni, variazioni, alterazioni* – concepts at the service of conspiratorial struggles, inciting the crowd to rebellion and encouraging them to lawlessness, accompany the republican rhetoric of recreating and reinstating the power of Rome. For Machiavelli, the situation of Italy's anomy in the 15th century was the ideal, revolutionary atmosphere giving hope that a new order would evolve – *lo stato*.

Hence, Louis Althusser is right when he writes about Machiavelli's solitude and his everlasting relevance, which at least in part is a consequence of identification of Machiavelli's intellectual and political positions.[33] Machiavelli's relevance results not from his closeness to us, but from his broaching the subject of relevance[34] in the sense which Foucault gives it in his *The Art of Telling the Truth*,[35] relevance understood as a necessity of diagnosis of the situation, political conjuncture, and the answer to the question: What in the present (situation at this moment) is the relevant sense for philosophical reflection understood as a political practice? Machiavelli's intrigue lies in its mysteriousness, in its enigmatic monstrosity, in its enigmatic attachment and imprisonment in the present, in the situation.

---

32 Hannah Arendt, *On Revolution*, (New York: Viking, 1963). pp. 40-45.

33 Louis Althusser, *Machiavelli and Us*, trans. G. Elliott, edited by F. Matheron, (London: Verso, 1999).

34 This difficulty in diagnosing Machiavelli's position affects even as serious thinkers as Isaiah Berlin, who gives us probably the most complete list of mistaken identifications of Machiavelli's proper intellectual and political positions, after which he inadvertently adds himself to the list of those erroneous interpretations by suggesting that Machiavelli's merit was not liberating politics from ethics or religion, but conflicting two ethical ideals – pagan – based on courage, discipline, strength, attachment to the body, and praise of action, and Christian – based on compassion, generosity, charity, and faith in the afterlife. See: Isaiah Berlin, *The Originality of Machiavelli*, [in:] Isaiah Berlin, *Against the Current: Essays in the History of Ideas*, Henry Hardy (ed.), (London: Hogarth Press; New York: Viking, 1980).

35 Michel Foucault, *The Art of Telling the Truth*, [in:] *Critique and Power: Recasting the Foucault/ Habermas Debate*, ed. Michael Kelly (Cambridge, MA: MIT Press, 1994), pp. 139-148.

When one reads Machiavelli's works one should resist the temptation of thinking about him as a leading republican and ideologist of the republican virtues, to which we could be induced by reading his *Discourses on Livy*,[36] as well as a theoretician of the amorality of power, prince without conscience who realizes his political goals beyond the good and evil using pure calculation to, which we could be induced by a cursory reading of *The Prince*,[37] as well as the father of the theory of *raison d'état – ragion di stato* – and a new formula of necessity.[38] Machiavelli's monstrosity, and his resulting loneliness, which is but another name for monstrosity and singularity, lies in that he denies the claim that the natural course of things is unchangeable and stable, as well as the proposition that everything is in constant motion, and even the statement that it is not the being which returns, but the return constitutes the being; so Machiavelli's monstrosity forces us to reconsider history and politics and pose the questions: under what conditions would it be possible to liberate oneself from the circular necessity of Fortune and to establish such form of government, such organization of the state, such dictatorship of freedom, such tyranny of unity of the people and the prince, humans and nonhumans, animals and minerals, in which we would not dare or need to call it a "democracy"? Tu put it simply: What are the conditions and possibilities of nonhegemonic politics? Perhaps Machiavelli's true monster is the democratic order, and his famous *mantenere lo stato* is nothing else but the construction of this monster.[39]

---

36 This interpretation is prevalent from Jean-Jacques Rousseau, through J. G. A. Pocock, to Quentin Skinner. J. G. A. Pocock, *The Machiavellian Moment: Florentine Political Thought and the Atlantic Republican Tradition.* Princeton, (New York: Princeton University Press, 1975). Quentin Skinner, *The Foundations of Modern Political Thought, Volume I: the Renaissance*, (Cambridge: Cambridge University Press, 1978). Quentin Skinner, *Machiavelli*, (Oxford: Oxford University Press, 1979). *Machiavelli's Liberal Republican Legacy*, ed Paul A. Rahe, (Cambridge University Press, 2006).

37 This interpretation, on the other hand, is prevalent from the Jesuits to Leo Strauss. Leo Strauss, *Thoughts on Machiavelli*, (Glencoe: The Free Press, 1958). This also concerns an otherwise very interesting book by Erica Benner: *Machiavelli's Ethics*, (Princeton University Press, 2009).

38 Here the tradition continues from Giovanni Botero to Friedrich Meinecke.

39 For this reading of Machiavelli's work I am largely indebted to the reading of two books: Claude Lefort's *Le travail de l'oeuvre, Machiavel*, (Paris: Gallimard, 1986), and Mikko Lahtinen's *Politics and Philosophy. Niccolò Machiavelli and Louis Althusser's Aleatory Materialism*, (Leiden/Boston, 2009).

5. Constitution

Antonio Negri in his probably most theoretically advanced work entitled *Insurgencies. Constituent Power and the Modern State*[40] formulates a thesis about the three paradigmatic ways of thinking about the relation between the constituent power and the constituted power, and as a result three models describing the constitution of the political world. In the modern times two concepts are closely linked with each other and frequently confused. Of course, those concepts are power and strength, *potere* and *potenza*, *povoir* and *poussance*, *Macht* and *Vermögen*.[41] The constituent power is an active force, giving reasons to establish a given political order and legitimizing this order. Constituted power, on the other hand, acts due to formal laws, regulations, and official political-judicial practice of a given subject, wielding power at the time. Constituent power is therefore the basis (power/potency) of the democratic process, whereas constituted power constitutes the borders (power/reality) in the form of political practice. Naturally, the main problem of political theory is as follows: What are the relations between these two elements, these two powers?

Negri claims that there exist solely three solutions to this problem. According to the first construct, legislative power is transcendental with regards to the constituted power. The constitution itself is conducted through the initiation of an external force, which gives the mandate and right for a particular configuration of power to consolidate. Even if one does not state here openly that each power is ordained of God, one does seek within this paradigm

40 Antonio Negri, *Insurgencies. Constituent Power and the Modern State*, trans. M. Eoscagli, (Minneapolis/London: University of Minnesota Press, 1999).

41 How then can we avoid a theoretical path that eliminates, together with the vicious circle, the very reality of the contradiction between constituent power and juridical arrangement, between the all-powerful and expansive effectiveness of the source and the system of positive law, of constituted normativity? How can we keep open the source of the vitality of the system while controlling it? Constituent power must somehow be maintained in order to avoid the possibility that its elimination might nullify the very meaning of the juridical system and the democratic relation that must characterize its horizon. Constituent power and its effects exist: How and where should they operate? How might one understand constituent power in a juridical apparatus? This is the whole problem: to maintain the irreducibility of the constituent fact, its effects, and the values it expresses. Three solutions have then been proposed. According to some, constituent power is transcendent with respect to the system of constituted power: its dynamics are imposed on the system from outside. According to another group of jurists, that power is instead immanent, its presence is implicit, and it operates as a foundation. A third group of jurists, finally, considers the source – constituent power – as neither transcendent nor immanent but, rather, integrated into, coextensive, and synchronic with the positive constitutional system.

instances of a higher order which would explain and substantiate the worldly government. Negri claims that his position was occupied by German legal theorists – Georg Jellinek and Hans Kelsen – the creators of the concept of Pure Theory of Law (*Reine Rechtslehre*). The starting point for Kelsen's theory is the radical distinction between law and morality, law and fact. The boundaries of the second distinction are set by the dualism of being (*Sein*) and duty (*Sollen*), where the law is contained in the sphere of duty.

According to the second solution, which Negri associated with the names of Max Weber and Carl Schmitt, the constituent power is always immanent in the constituted power, present *implicite*, hidden and silent, but retaining the founding power. According to Weber's intuition, constituent power cannot be derived from the primal act of violence (charismatic or traditional rule), which cannot give the state a positive form of law and rule. Only legal power is capable of that, power which is a kind of ideal moment, a flash of reason in the historical casualness of politics, sanctioning this casualness as rational.

Finally, in accordance with the third paradigm which Negri connected with the French school of institutionalists – Rudolph Smende, Ernst Forsthoff, or Costantino Mortati – constituent power neither transcends the constituted power, nor is it immanent towards it, but rather is integrated and synchronized with it, which means that it is a part of a not-fully balanced and harmonized system of institutions of a given state. In this paradigm, the constitution of the political order neither seeks the source of the norm which would give the moral guarantee to the law in force, nor does it count on the perfection of the mind which works within the limits of what is real, but assumes that the material conditions for action, the outskirts of politics, the boundaries of the state determine in the final instance the shape of politics. Machiavelli's originality, in short, consists in the fact that he is the actual founder and ideologist of this interactive paradigm.

Political antinomy, or even tragedy of politics in which we have been functioning for years is that – as we stated – every power understood as a force does not know the limits of its validity, it is a dynamic force whose only impulse is expansion; on the other hand, each power understood as validity places boundaries, it is a static value which only cares about the norms of enforcement. The tragedy of politics consists in the fact that power understood as *potentia* (*Vertretungsmacht*) is pure force, authority, meaning without enforcement, a reality which does not know its representation and validity; power understood as authority, *potestas* (*Darstellung*), is nothing more than a representation, false appearance of politics devoid of a real strength, it is a false consciousness, an ideological illusion, enforcement without meaning.

This division suggestively prompts us that there are only two possibilities: either reduction of *potentia* (strength) to *potestas* (authority) – a more conservative variant of politics, or the reduction of *potestas* to *potentia* – an emancipationist variant of politics. Machiavelli's diagnosis is as follows: neither myth nor ideological apparatuses of the state can handle resolving this antinomy, the resolution lies in the actions, practice of the prince, the monster, the centaur Chiron and the goddess Circe. Monsters are necessary in the economy of the world to resolve the basic contradictions by which it is plagued. There is no transcendence, but there is no prison of immanence either. There is nothing but the ordinary work of politics.

6. Chiron the Centaur

In this way we come to the most well-known fragment of Machiavelli's *The Prince*, which offers praise of monstrosity and where the Florentine states:

> You must know there are two ways of combat, the one by the law, the other by force; the first method is proper to men, the second to beasts; but because the first is frequently not sufficient, it is necessary to have recourse to the second. Therefore it is necessary for a prince to understand how to avail himself of the beast and the man. This has been figuratively taught to princes by ancient writers, who describe how Achilles and many other princes of old were given to the Centaur Chiron to nurse, who brought them up in his discipline; which means solely that, as they had for a teacher one who was half beast and half man, so it is necessary for a prince to know how to make use of both natures, and that one without the other is not durable. A prince, therefore, being compelled knowingly to adopt the beast, ought to choose the fox and the lion; because the lion cannot defend himself against snares and the fox cannot defend himself against wolves. Therefore, it is necessary to be a fox to discover the snares and a lion to terrify the wolves. Those who rely simply on the lion do not understand what they are about. Therefore a wise lord cannot, nor ought he to, keep faith when such observance may be turned against him, and when the reasons that caused him to pledge it exist no longer. If men were entirely good this precept would not hold, but because they are bad, and will not keep faith with you, you too are not bound to observe it with them.[42]

I claim that Machiavelli writing in this way opens a completely new and until now unused way of thinking about the nature-culture relationships. In this kind of thinking one does not say anymore that nature was surpassed by culture, but one also does not say that nature is but a string of human speculations on its subject, finally one rejects the hypothesis that only nature exists and nothing else. The modern culture of the West based its key opposition on the relation

42 Niccolò Machiavelli, *The Prince*, p. 71.

between nature and culture. The political philosophy to a significant extent is a story of surpassing nature with the goal of creating a state of law. In a state distant from nature we seek a place for the natural laws. Yet, according to Machiavelli confronting nature and culture as well as narrating the breach of political law of nature or its unavoidable observance are wrong. Confronting nature with culture has destructive consequences, both cognitive and political.

In allowing for ambiguity of the nature/culture opposition and by accepting the fictitiousness of the social contract, Machiavelli formulates new visions of subjectivity and politics in the world in which the "natural objects" seem socialized and the "cultural subjects" seem antisocial. Machiavelli asks: Is politics not a never-ending fantasy about the state of nature, which is either dignified or condemned by it, or denied, only because it uses naturalization as its primary tool? Is the political subject, who in the name of institutional facts (antinature) openly denies in the political discourse the existence of the "harsh social facts" (nature), not seeking a new base in the guise of false nature (para-nature)? Hence, does Machiavelli not recommend monstrosity to us writing texts which to some extent praise it? Are the "natural objects", which are "socialized", and the "cultural subjects", which seem antisocial, not the best candidates for such monstrosity?[43] Are they not children of Chiron the Centaur and the goddess Circe?

---

43 I will defend the claim that by writing this: Machiavelli opened up a new and still unused way of thinking about nature-culture relationship. A proponent of this way of thinking withdraws from saying that nature is surpassed by culture, or that nature is nothing else but a subject of an on-going human speculation, and rebuts the sole hypothesis that what there is is nothing but nature. Modern Western culture entrusted its key opposition to the nature-culture relationship. By and large, political philosophy is a story about surpassing the nature in order to establish a state under the rule of law. It is in this state, as distant from nature as it can be, that we wish to embed natural law. According to Machiavelli, the juxtaposition of nature and culture, the narrative on surpassing politics by the laws of nature, just as the narrative on us being stuck in it, are all utterly wrong. The juxtaposition of nature and culture brings about destructive consequences to our cognition and politics. Accepting the ambiguity of the opposition between nature and culture and assuming that the social contract is indeed fictitious, I would like to question Machiavelli about his vision of subjectivity and politics in a world where "natural objects" appear to be socialized, and "cultural subjects" appear to be dissocial. Is politics a never-ending fantasy about the state of nature – ennobling it, condemning it, or suppressing it – because its own tool is naturalization? Is a political subject, who, in political discourse, on behalf of institutional facts (antinature) explicitly denies the existence of "harsh social facts" (nature) not in fact looking for a new base in the form of a false nature (para-nature)? Hence, does Machiavelli recommend monstrosity by writing stories in praise of monstrosity as it may well seem? Are "natural objects" that are

As Bruno Latour convincingly demonstrates, political philosophy never ceased in its attempts to discover which type of rationality could put an end to civil wars:

> [...] from the *City of God* to [Hobbes's] social contract, from the social contract to the 'gentle bonds of commerce', as Adam Smith put it, from economics to [Habermas's] discourse ethics, from morality to the defense of nature, politics has always had to make honorable amends for the lack of reason characteristic of human beings.[44]

From Machiavelli's point of view, however, nature and society are not entities existing in the world independently and in isolation, that is, two separate areas of reality, but a certain form of public organization. There has never been politics other than the politics of nature and nature other than political. Epistemology and politics are one and the same undertaking embodied in the form of political practice, which blurs the distinctions of scientific practice and the basic subject of public life. One should once more cede a point to Latour's argument – "[p]erhaps not everything is politics, but politics deals with shaping everything".[45] This is also true to Machiavelli, who seems to have freed politics from morality and religion.

As rightly states the not yet fully informed Machiavellian scholar Latour: it would have been preposterous to want to separate society and nature within one constitution, within onc collcctivc, sincc wc could not cxpcct from this connection anything but a mixture, that is, monstrosity – mixture which would at most constitute a horrifying *melting pot*, a monster even more horrifying than the speech of various nonhumans known from history, the sheep with pigs' heads. The constitution of the new world, this monster above all monsters, that is, the nonhegemonic democratic tool must be a kind of *melting pot*, but it is not about melting the objects of nature and the subjects of law into one mass. It is rather the case that the collective mixes powers which can appropriate, exploit and express themselves in things, giving them voice again. They are not points of view, positions and posts to be taken, they assume certain values, but the values assume perspectives which maintain them and from which the values themselves are derived, including the classification into that which is mean and that which is noble.

One should not imagine the new politics as a force with a golden mean, uniting socialization and naturalization, or as a golden ass, since the new politics

---

"socialized" and "cultural subjects" which appear to be dissocial indeed best candidates for such a monstrosity?

44 Bruno Latour, *Politics of Nature,* p. 185.

45 *Ibid.*, p. 53.

knows no simple method of drawing a boundary between an unavoidable necessity of things and the requirements of freedom of the actors participating in the struggle for power. No one would surely imagine having to offer an elephant a greeting: "Citizen!" The point is not the extension of human morality to the world of nature, or extravagant projection of law onto the natural entities, or consideration of the entitlement of objects themselves, but simply the consideration of the inconsistency of removing the concept of external nature: there is no natural reserve in which we could keep the simple means identified through the once and for all defined goals.

Hobbes's man who is a wolf to another man was supposed to be educated by the law, fear of sudden death and prudence is supposed to be replaced by the beast raised by Chiron – a seemingly immortal king of the Centaurs, lethally wounded by a poisoned arrow of his student – Heracles. This beast, this new entity is a figure consisting of a fox, a lion, and a man, a creature capable of recognizing traps and capable of scaring off wolves, an entity using many natures and many languages. It is simultaneously Chiron the Centaur and Circe the goddess. To be able to use both the human and the animal nature means to be beyond all nature, which *de facto* means to be a monster. A sheep with pig's head does not scare anyone anymore.

VI. Friedrich Nietzsche's three Hypotheses about the Origins of the Tragic Chorus

Both tragedy and comedy originated in improvisation: tragedy from the leaders of the dithyramb and comedy from the leaders of the phallic processions which even now continue as a custom in many our cities.

Aristotle[1]

This will to appearance, to simplification, to masks, to cloaks, in short, to the surface [...] is countered by the sublime tendency of the man in search of knowledge to take and to want to take things deeply, multifariously, profoundly, as a kind of cruelty of intellectual conscience and aesthetic taste that every courageous thinker will recognize in himself [...]. They are beautiful, glittering, jingling, festive words: honesty, love of truth, love of wisdom, sacrifice for knowledge, the heroism of truthfulness – there is something about them that makes one swell with pride. But we hermits and marmots, we have long ago convinced ourselves in all the privacy of our hermit's conscience, that even this worthy linguistic ostentation belongs with the old adornments [...]. To ensure that henceforth man faces man in the same way that currently, grown tough within the discipline of science, he faces the other nature, with unfrightened Oedipus-eyes [...] – that may be a strange and crazy project, but it is a project – who could deny that! Why have we chosen it, this crazy project? Or to ask in another way, 'Why bother with knowledge?' Everyone will ask us about it. And we, pressed in this way, we who have asked ourselves just the same thing a hundred times over, we have found and find no better answer...

Friedrich Nietzsche[2]

1. Crisis

In what is perhaps his best known and least read early book, *The Birth of Tragedy from the Spirit of Music* [*Die Geburt der Tragödie aus dem Geiste der Musik* (1872)], a tale about the genealogy of European pessimism which in his later work will acquire the more emphatic name of "nihilism", Friedrich Nietzsche ponders the problem of the "border". He does that through the reflection on the phenomenon of the "tragic chorus". For the author of *Will to*

1 Aristotle, *Rhetoric. Poetics*, trans. S. H. Butcher, W. Rhys Roberts, (New York: Barnes & Noble Classics, 2006), p. 321.

2 Friedrich Nietzsche (1886), *Beyond Good and Evil*, trans. W. Kaufmann (New York: Vintage Books, 1966), p. 180.

Power, to establish the status and significance of the tragic chorus means to establish the concept of "the border". Nietzsche assumes *a priori* that tragedy developed out of the tragic chorus and originally consisted only of a chorus and nothing else. Subsequent evolution of Greek tragedy consisted, in simplified terms, in decreasing and marginalizing the role of the chorus and reducing it to the role of border existence. This reduction meant the alienation of music from speech, thought from rhythm, the work of abstraction from the work of the mouth (song).

This genealogy of tragedy formulated by Nietzsche stands in clear opposition to the genesis of the epos, iamb, and tragedy suggested by Aristotle in *Poetics.* The latter, when trying to explain the origin of poetry, refers to the deeply embedded human instinct for imitation. Imitators gave rise to the art of improvisation which, however, quickly diverged into two directions: "[t]he graver spirits imitated noble actions, and the actions of good men. The more trivial sort imitated the actions of meaner persons, at first composing satires, as the former did hymns to the gods and the praises of famous men".[3] Aristotle's argument is thus the following: the inborn instinct for imitation and the sense of rhythm and melody gave rise to sung poetry. Soon, however, imitation begun to turn into praise or satire. Satire gave rise to the iambic measure, that is, comedy; praise engendered epos and tragedy. What fascinates one today in Aristotelian thought is his brilliant insight that theater art had always had political potential. It constituted either an ideology, that is, praise of the ruler, or caricature and critique, that is, mockery and laughter. What Aristotle is unable to explain, however, is the way tragic elements historically got mixed up with the comic elements, that is, how the chorus of goats, which originally had been a tragic chorus, in time became a satirical, mocking and thus a comic chorus. I would argue that this very element, this displacement of satire and hymn, dithyramb and phallic song is key to Nietzsche's line of reasoning.

Today I would propose an argument that Nietzsche's narrative of the history of the tragic chorus and its fall into obscurity became the model narration on the subject of exclusion, also the exclusion of the animal world and its voices from the enlightened western culture. I will read Nietzsche's thought as a moment of intellectual crisis, as a type of threshold value in which on the one hand motifs anticipated *inter alia* by Hobbes and Spinoza become integrated, and which, on the other hand, gives rise to modern thought of Foucault and Agamben.

3 Aristotle, *Poetics,* p. 321.

2. Hypotheses

Meditating on the status of the tragic chorus, Nietzsche considers three hypotheses. Let us call these three tested intuitions the political, aesthetic and ontological hypotheses. According to the first of those, Greek chorus represents the will of the people of Athens. As Nietzsche mockingly points out, "the invariable moral law was presented by the democratic Athenians in the people's chorus, which was always proved right in matters dealing with the kings' passionate acts of violence and excess".[4] This hypothesis, as I said above, is recommended by the authority of Aristotle himself, whose thought moves exactly in that direction in the chapter of *Poetics* on the genesis and development of poetry.[5] Nietzsche quickly counters this thesis, however, arguing that the religious beginnings of Greek tragedy exclude all possibility of opposition between the people and their ruler and, in fact, even of the political sphere as such. What is more, Nietzsche ridicules the insight according to which the chorus could hold some representative function in the ancient world and as a result aspire to the position of popular representation considering such an insight "blasphemous" and a confusion of terms. According to Nietzsche, ancient political organizations simply lack constitutional popular representation and even the tragedies of Aeschylus and Sophocles do not hint at such representation.

The second hypothesis which I have called aesthetic is related to Augustus Wilhelm Schlegel, whose grand oeuvre, *Vorlesungen über dramatische Kunst und Literatur* (vol. 1-3, 1809-1811), suggests we may consider the tragic chorus to be the symbol of the ideal spectator. Wherefrom this ideal quality of the Greek chorus? To put it briefly, it rests on the erasure of the opposition between the spectator and the actor and between the stage (the space of projection) and reality (the space of perception). The tragic chorus is the spectator who is himself on the stage, who contemplates himself; the stage reality is reality itself which does not yet know the difference between the aesthetic and the ontological, that is, between immanence and transcendence. Nietzsche rejects this premonition as well, scoffing at this idealistic vision of the impulsive and imaginative nature of the chorus of goats. Referring to Prometheus, Nietzsche asks a mocking rhetorical question: "Would it be a mark of the ideal spectator to run up onto the stage and free the god from his torment?". For Nietzsche, "the spectator without a play is a contradictory idea" and the concept of "a spectator in himself" an empty concept. Despite the fact that in his cult of the Dionysian

4 Friedrich Nietzsche (1872), *The Birth of Tragedy*, trans. W. Kaufmann, [in:] *The Birth of Tragedy and The Case of Wagner*, New York: Random House, 1967, p. 53.

5 Aristotle, *Poetics*, p. 319.

element he aimed at cancelling oppositions and finding a formation capable of bearing all contradictions, in his polemic with Schlegel the author of *Will to Power* excludes the possibility of levelling ontology and aesthetics and therefore rejects the aesthetization of life and the ontologization of the aesthetic experience.

These two refutations have made it clear that the Greek chorus is not an embodiment of the wisdom of the people, as much as it is not a simulation, in particular a stimulation of the spectator's aesthetic experience, even that of a mass spectator, this silent majority. Ultimately Nietzsche declares:

> We suspect that the birth of tragedy cannot be explained either from the high estimation of the moral intelligence of the masses or from the idea of the spectator without a play, and we consider this problem too profound even to be touched upon by such superficial styles of commentary.[6]

What, then, constitutes commentary profound enough to grasp and represent the complex phenomenon of the Greek chorus and its ambiguous status?

3. A living wall

After making these two polemical comments, that is, after refuting both the political and the aesthetic theses, Nietzsche proceeds to address the third hypothesis, borrowed from Johann Christoph Friedrich von Schiller. In his introduction to *The Bride of Messina* (*Die Braut von Messina*, 1803), Schiller sees the Greek chorus as a living wall, with which the tragedy surrounds itself in order to cut itself off clearly from the real world and maintain its aesthetic grounding and poetic freedom. It is this hypothesis only that receives Nietzsche's full attention and care, and is recognized as having enough depth to touch upon the problem of the border in all its implications, in all its ontological, political and aesthetic completeness. The chorus understood as a wall allows to grasp the border of the *polis* and the border of the visibility of the *polis*, and thus both the political and the epistemological boundaries at the same time. The ontological hypothesis, adds Nietzsche, does not reduce us to a false adoration of the apparent wisdom of the people who are capable of commenting on the erroneous choices of the ruler, and only this hypothesis does not lead us astray into thinking of the political society as the society of the spectacle in which the public becomes the idealized spectator without the spectacle, a type of disembodied satellite camera-eye. Wherefrom the strength of this hypothesis? Why does only the hypothesis of the chorus as a living wall allow us to move

6 Friedrich Nietzsche, *The Birth of Tragedy*, p. 54.

beyond not only aesthetic but also political aporias, as well as to construct an apparatus which makes it possible to integrate and understand those aporias?

We would misinterpret this hypothesis by narrowing it down merely to the institution of a geographic border, that is, a line which would subsequently divide and regulate the transitions and transfers between the world of nature and politics, nature and art, the reality of nature and the reality of vision. Surely Nietzsche does not want to establish a threshold or demarcation dividing the world in half. As he says in the key passage of the text, "[f]or this chorus the Greeks constructed a suspended scaffolding of an imaginary *state of nature* and on it placed imaginary *natural beings*".[7] What is the meaning of this enigmatic statement? What is the scaffolding that the Greeks have constructed? What imaginary natural beings stand on this scaffolding? And what fantasies about the state of nature do these fantastic natural creatures create?

4. The satyr on the scaffolding

It seems that Nietzsche's argument is as follows. The live wall created by the tragic chorus is a type of contamination of nature and culture; it is an indeterminate sphere, a type of transitional sphere of unclear, unstable identity; it is, then – and I am using this term partly out of ineptitude and partly out of habit – a type of fold in which the world of civilization contemplates nature and nature observes the world of civilization; it is nature's periscope in culture, but also an extension of nature into culture. The Greek chorus is then a projection of politics into the animal sphere, but it is also an introjection of animality into the sphere of the *polis*.

The history of philosophy offers more of such spheres of indeterminacy. One of them is the position of the sovereign and the woolf man in the philosophy of Thomas Hobbes; another the unity of *potentia* and *potestas*, power and law, in the philosophy of Baruch de Spinoza; a still other the figure of the fox in the thought of Niccolò Machiavelli. Nietzsche's third hypothesis on the tragic chorus becomes a veritable recapitulation of this idea and a crisis of this line of reflection. Sigmund Freud will write about this chorus or, rather, about the nostalgia for this chorus, in the final passages of *Totem and Taboo*. Michel Foucault will return to this motif of the lost tragic quality in *Madness and Civilisation: A History of Insanity in the Age of Reason* [*Histoire de la folie à l'âge classique* 1961], especially in the introductions to this ambiguous work. When studying the position of the exile and the architecture of the internment

7 Friedrich Nietzsche, *The Birth of Tragedy*, p. 55.

camp, that is, those contemporary spaces of the tragic chorus, a suspended scaffolding of an imaginary state of nature, Hannah Arendt will come to the conclusion that thanks to this scaffolding the world has discovered that it has "found nothing sacred in the abstract nakedness of being human".[8] It could not have been otherwise because, as Nietzsche demonstrates, the abstract nakedness of being human means being a goat. Finally, following the same track, Giorgio Agamben in *Homo Sacer: Il potere soverano e la vita nuda* (1995) refers to the logic of the exception and to the etymology of the word *ex-capere* used in reference to the outcast in order to undermine the opposition between exclusion and inclusion and to begin talking about the relationship of exclusion which includes; he writes, explicitly: "[w]e shall give the name *relation of exception* to the extreme form of relation by which something is included solely through its exclusion".[9]

Therefore the question is the following: what does the Greek chorus include solely through the exclusion it performs? Who resides on the scaffolding/bridge, on the stage/in the audience, in politics/nature, in the ambiguous space of the nonspace? Nietzsche answers this question directly, without a shadow of doubt: the satyr chorus. If so, we must then answer the question: Who is the satyr, particularly in the Greek imagination? Here also Nietzsche has no doubt: satyr is an imagined natural creature whose relation to the man of culture is the same as that of Dionysian music to civilization. What is the relation? How does the music of Dionysian dithyrambs relate to the Apollonian civilization, the civilization of reason and moderation, to the world of representation, to the world-image? Well, in relation to the civilization of reason it represents what has been excluded by that civilization but was not thrown out and remains as a *residuum* of that civilization, a type of reservoir, excess, or the continually present doubling. Is it any wonder then that having discovered this doubling Nietzsche writes that the Greek must have felt annihilated facing the chorus of satyrs, just as we would have to feel our nothingness when confronted with the reanimation of the music of pain produced by the Dionysian dithyrambs, music which brings relief different than the *ambient* of the shopping malls and airports of our cities. Had not Brian Eno, the author of the *Music for the Airports,* confessed with daring honesty that one of the important features of *ambient* music is not only its ability to absorb noise, but above all to prepare the human being for death?

The Greek chorus is a mob of satyrs, beings who from the perspective of the city appear animal-like, and from the perspective of nature appear to be human

8 Hannah Arendt (1951), *The Origins of Totalitarianism*, New York: Schocken, 2004, p. 231.

9 Giorgio Agamben (1995), *Homo sacer. Sovereign Power and Bare Life*, trans. D. Heller-Roazen, Stanford: Stanford University Press, 1998, p. 31.

fantasies. A mob of satyrs is subject to double exclusion: it is at home neither in the city nor in nature. What annihilation and, above all, what relief can be offered by the tragic satyr chorus which itself knows no relief? Nietzsche believes that the effect of the Greek tragedy is to create the conviction that the state (politics), that is, the abyss, the hostility between one human being and another, gives way to the feeling of unity which leads the citizen back to nature, inviting him to rediscover his animality. Tragic relief is a difficult kind of relief telling us that our mortal individuality (shell) finds its compensation in the indestructibility of life itself. A satyr is an artificial natural being who, existing beyond all civilization, but also beyond all nature, and living an everlasting life, remains someone between Mozart's Don Giovanni and Wagner's Siegfried.

The satyr, who for us became no more than a wild monkey brought from the bush and wreaking havoc in New York under the stage name King Kong, in the Nietzschean formula was the primordial man with a closeness to and a premonition of fullness. The man of culture in confrontation with the satirical man proved only a caricature of a human being, its sick, defective, ressentimental replica. The satyr is a being whose law reaches as far as his power. The fullness of the satyr depends on the fact that he does not yet know the divide, he has the law and the power, he does not yet know the world in which the power which is not the power of law becomes an abuse of power, lawlessness. When Peter Sloterdijk, in *Kritik der zynischen Vernunft* (1983), wants to resurrect the kynical man, whom he juxtaposes with the cynical man, he merely repeats the Nietzschean formulas defined in the context of the satyr chorus.[10] The kynicism of Diogenes, juxtaposed with the cynicism of the king, even if the later is Alexander the Great, is simply the Satyr. Let us repeat Nietzsche's third thesis on the tragic chorus with an even greater emphasis: the effect of tragedy is an antipolitical effect: animosity between people gives way to the feeling of animal unity. Or, to put it otherwise, the only equality among people is the equality in the ecstatic praise, until death, of life.

5. The screen

Let me ask again, then, what is the Greek chorus? We already know that it is a living wall raised against the pounding reality. But this is only the geographical truth. For the Greek chorus is a wall on which a residual image of a certain reality lights up; it is, then, a wall/screen reproducing the existence of the tragic

10 Peter Sloterdijk (1983), *Critique of Cynical Reason*, trans. M. Eldred, (Minneapolis: University of Minnesota Press, 1988).

truth and nature in its highest power, it is a vision of a Dionysian plenty before it has become politically deformed, reduced in the space of the *polis* to the masses, the plebs, proletariat, the irrational eruption of the crowd, or the impertinent crowd of immigrants.

The insight which seems particularly valuable in Nietzsche's thought is the combining of the notions of the wall and the screen in the concept of the border. The wall is a screen and the screen is a wall. Nietzsche states this explicitly: the power of the vision is strong enough to dull and desensitize the sight of the educated, cultured Greeks seated in the audience, to dull the sight of the citizens of the *polis* to the sensations coming directly from reality. The eyes of a Greek seated in the audience see only simulation. The citizen of Athens would not, however, have seen only simulation, had not the screen functioned like a wall separating the audience and the spectacle from nature, which could reach the *polis* only in the form of ominous growls.

In effect Nietzsche reaches the most general of conclusions: the dithyrambic chorus is a chorus of Others who forgot about their civic past, about their social roles and functions: they became timeless, found themselves beyond all political spheres, became the living servants of the god of plenty and contradiction, the god who mocks all exclusion. Sophocles' Oedipus, Aeschylus' Prometheus, Oedipus' excess of intelligence, Prometheus' excess of love still contain traces of this intuition, this vision of existing for what is full of contradictions. Oedipus and Prometheus are still but masks of the original Dionysian hero. It is only Euripides who, by turning the stage into the audience, that is, by introducing the viewer onto the stage, inaugurates populist politics and art: inaugurates modernity. From the times of Euripides, what the viewer heard and saw on the stage was only his double, what he heard and saw was only his wretchedness, his finiteness, his crippled moderation. When today David Hare, the author, among others, of *Stuff Happens*, declares with disarming honesty: "[n]o, I haven't lost my faith in fiction. I simply want to write about the real world, which the audience knows", he is merely repeating Euripides' lesson.

6. Representation

We have established that according to Nietzsche antipolitics is the effect of tragedy: animosity among people gives way to the feeling of animalistic unity. Nietzsche's politics, however, is not exhausted by thus defined antipolitics. The philosophical tradition inherited by Nietzsche has often used the metaphor of the theater for political ends. Theater metaphors are based, however, on a central aesthetic concept – that is, a concept of representation – as well as on a central political concept. For example "representation" mentioned in Hobbes' *Leviathan* is a legal term. Its meaning refers to speaking or acting in the name of someone else, particularly to speaking or acting based on authorization and consent.[11] "Representation", however, has another, even earlier meaning, which belongs to the sphere of aesthetics. In that sphere, "representation" means an artificial production of faithful copies of beings existing in nature; literally it means creating an image which resembles, as much as it is possible, the original model. The aesthetic sense of representation can be found already in the early Roman texts such as Pliny the Elder's *Natural History;* therefore it may be argued that in Roman culture representation was both a legal and an aesthetic matter.

It seems that in *The Birth of Tragedy* Nietzsche simply registers the fact that political theories which pertain to political representation understood as authorization, and aesthetic theories which pertain to representation understood as a copy, became possible and antithetical only as a result of the fall of the tragic chorus which served those two functions simultaneously creating the ontological effect of the living wall/screen.

Thus in *The Birth of Tragedy* Nietzsche reaches back to the primal scene of politics and aesthetics at the same time. I use "primal scene" with the psychoanalytical sense of the term. Freud's concept of primal scene (*Urszenen*) initially referred to a traumatic childhood experience which created organized scenarios adjusted to later experiences. With time, however, the term came to signify the scene of sexual intercourse between the parents which the child imaginatively witnesses and which he deduces based on certain signs. Usually the scene is interpreted as an act of rape by the father.[12] The primal scene reconstructed by Nietzsche's genius child reaches back to the dawn of humanity and its birth imagined as a live construction, a suspended scaffolding of an imaginary state of nature, in which a non-quite-human-yet being experienced an aesthetic spectacle in politics and experienced politics as an aesthetic activity, where the citizen, understood as a viewer, is also a viewer understood as a citizen, where the difference between kynicism and cynicism does not yet exist.

11 Thomas Hobbes (1651), *Leviathan or The Matter, Forme and Power of a Common Wealth Ecclesiasticall and Civil*, ed. Ian Shapiro (Yale University Press, 2010).

12 Jean Laplanche, Jean-Bertrand Pontalis, *Vocabulaire de psychanalyse*, (Paris: PUF, 1967), p. 299. *The Language of Psychoanalysis*, by J. Laplanche and J.-B. Pontalis. with an introd. by Daniel Lagache, trans. D. Nicholson-Smith, (London: Hogarth Press, 1973).

7. Political theater

Next to antipolitics steeped in animality, Nietzsche espouses also politics immersed in the game of presence/absence, audience/spectacle. Following the theater trope, one is tempted to compare the meaning of political and rhetorical representation. In the former metaphor (political), used among others by Hobbes, representation means acting and thinking in the name of the absent masses; in the latter metaphor (rhetorical), it means acting and thinking in the presence of political audience, with the aim of impressing (fascinating) that audience. In political representation subjects are necessarily absent, while in rhetorical representation the represented subjects are necessarily present. According to political strategy, subjects, because of their heterogeneity, are unable to participate in their own representation. Only the sovereign is capable of representing them. According to rhetorical strategy, subjects have to participate as the audience in their own representation, in their own spectacle. Without them the sovereign, that is, the actor, cannot be the representative: there is no one to address, no one to persuade, no one to fascinate.

Can the postmodern understanding of politics and aesthetics be perceived as a synthesis of those two understandings of representation? Do the liberal-democratic processes of political representation contain both the necessary absence and the necessary presence of the people: the Hobbesian absence as an active participant and the Nietzschean presence as a passionate viewer-satyr? If we were to read Hobbes and Nietzsche with the help of the contemporary theories of the media and with the thesis that all power has to go through the media, perhaps our hyperactivity in the sphere of perceptual participation in the political spectacle and our equally pronounced passivity when it comes to genuine impact on the governing process would find a sensible, if surprising, justification. After all, what else do the media do every day if not constitute the community of citizens as the audience for the words and deeds of their government. Liberal democracies, we are told, are "open governments", which means that they not only make their politics clearly visible to all, but also make sure the way they carry out their politics, which is "our" politics, is clearly visible as well. In other words, is it not so that we continually demand to be given more clear information, more proof, more representations, and sometimes also more wars? Are we not placed in the position of the chorus from *The Birth of Tragedy*, a chorus of satyrs convinced by turns about the failings and merits of various political parties and called upon to sing praises, that is, dithyrambs, and not mocking satires? And are we not simultaneously being convinced that our participation in politics after the elections only damages the economy and hinders rational execution of power? Aristotle saw tragedy as still heir to the dithyramb. Nietzsche still hears the music of the dithyrambs in the chorus, only this music has become the music of donkeys, and thus, satyrs. Nietzsche treats tragedy like comedy and dithyramb like a phallic song. Today we – the mute electoral chorus staring into the screen/wall of our political imagination – function only as victims, that is, sacrificial goats used by the sociological public opinion research centers. This is why Nietzsche suddenly compares the Dionysian to Hamlet: they both found out the truth which paralyzed their actions. Hamlet and the Dionysian man already know that action cannot change anything in the eternal nature of things.

8. The border

What conclusions can we draw from this reading of *The Birth of Tragedy* for our contemporary discussion of marginalization and the politics of exclusion?

Above all, it seems that Nietzsche's third hypothesis, addressed here as the ontological hypothesis, in a sense consolidates the more primary intuitions contained in the first and second hypothesis. Thinking of the tragic chorus as a living wall which allows the Greeks to separate nature form *polis* is not only a thinking alternative to the hypothesis that the chorus is the people and the hypothesis that the chorus is the audience. Rather, it is thinking which turns these earlier intuitions into more legitimate, supportable and deepened hypotheses. The subject can become a subject of pure perception only when it separates itself from the object world, and the subject can become a citizen only when a political community is founded which presupposes an exclusion of what cannot be contained by that very community. From this point of view, the ontological boundary becomes a condition *a priori* of political and aesthetic thought.

After all, as Nietzsche observes that

> the acting area, together with the action, was basically and originally thought of only as a *vision*, that the single *reality* is simply the chorus, which creates the vision out of itself and speaks of that with the entire symbolism of dance, tone, and word. This chorus in its vision gazes at its lord and master Dionysus and is thus always the chorus *of servants*; the chorus sees how Dionysus, the god, suffers and glorifies himself, and thus it does not itself *act*.[13]

Let us repeat the assertion which should not escape our attention: the tragic chorus does not itself act.

13 Friedrich Nietzsche, *The Birth of Tragedy*, p. 63.

What is even more important, Nietzsche's thought leads to the conclusion that a political community and, consequently, a vision of political community, does not exist without exclusion. Even the most open political community has to determine its own limitations. Only a psychotic subject functions without limitations. Despite the fact that he directed all his thought to the project of reanimating the original myth of the Dionysian plenty, Nietzsche considered the border necessary. Similarly Spinoza, who despite the fact that he did not talk about anything else but that the human law reaches as far as the human power, still believed that the test of the law/power of the city (that is, of the communal subject) would be its philosophical tolerance for the most extreme views, that is, an internal border taking the form of abstaining from the use of power. And finally, similarly Foucault who, despite the fact that he programmed all his thought toward the renewal of the liaison between reason and madness – madness understood not as foolishness, but as the proto-form and reservoir of all sense – still admitted that there is no society without borders and it is the boundary and not the longing for what is boundless that defines human beings.

Finally, the third important conclusion from Nietzsche's *Birth of Tragedy* is the following: the border is not a simple demarcation, it is not a line, but a "living wall" or "a unique scaffolding of an imaginary state of nature". A living wall means a moving wall, a wall which is never static. A unique scaffolding may mean that the boundary is constructed from within, it constitutes an internal and not an external exclusion. The border is alive, it is internal, it is constructed (that is, it belongs to the imaginary register) and it is in permanent movement, not to say, a moving dispersal.

The question is, therefore, what can we do with a border which seems the inescapable condition of the human being, of the *polis,* and of the visionary world known as art? What can we do with a city which in its longing to be a democracy has to continue to remember that its beginnings contain the undemocratic condition of democracy? How are we to act when facing the border which, while being the border of our law, our speech and our sight is simultaneously an invisible and dispersed border placed at the very heart of life's element?

It appears that there are three imaginable strategies for political action. The first would be a conservative strategy, dictated by the nostalgia for clear, permanent and impermeable borders. In this strategy, a human being would remain a guard taking care to reinstate the border, a being always at risk: of the border slipping and him/herself regressing into nonhumanity, into a postpolitical, postethnic, postanthropological state. A dream of such a patriarchal border which would be grounded in a symbolic and not an imaginary order would be contemporaneous with the dream of a transparent and homogenous society and an army of defined external enemies. Let us call this variety of political life Apollonian politics, in which order, peace, and safety are the supreme values.

The second possible mode of political action would be related to the attempts to renegotiate the borders. This renegotiation could concern several spheres. To begin with, it could mean shifting the boundary of justice, that is, the boundary dividing the political from the nonpolitical sphere, the private sphere from the sphere belonging to the law. This renegotiation most likely would be of a binary character: it could demand a politicization of the world of life, as it is the case with domestic violence, but it could also demand a depolitization of the world of life, as it is the case with resistance to biotechnology and biopower as such.

Finally, the third imaginable politics is a politics of transgression. The ambiguity of such politics results from the fact that, according to Georges Bataille's formula, often quoted by Foucault, to transgress means to simultaneously establish and break the law. In this vein, in his *Preface to Transgression* [*Préface à transgression* (1963)], that is, his introduction to Bataille's *Works,* Foucault argues that the modern world has not liberated sexuality, only took it to its limits. And the limits are threefold: (1) the limit of our consciousness, because sexuality dictates the vocabulary for the reading of the unconscious: the case of Freud and Lacan; (2) the limit of the law, as sexuality seems to be the sole substance of universal taboos: the case of Freud and Lévi-Strauss; (3) the limit of language, as sexuality "traces that line of foam, showing just how far speech may advance on the sands of silence":[14] the case of Sade and Bataille. Foucault draws three conclusions from the politics of transgression: (1) we live in a world in which we no longer have enough space and objects of profanation; (2) it is not that our language is suffused with eroticism, but our sexuality has been engulfed by language; (3) we are not so much experiencing the end of philosophy as philosophy is regaining the capacity of articulation at its borders.

Let us then repeat: next to antipolitics submerged in animality and limitlessness, there is a politics in Nietzsche submerged in the presence/absence of the audience/spectacle. It implies the possibility of three politics. The last one of those leads us not so much to the end of philosophy and politics as to the space where philosophy and politics recover their capacity for articulation. How does this happen?

---

14 Michel Foucault (1963), *Préface à la transgression hommage à Georges Bataille*, *A Preface to Transgression*, trans. Donald F. Bouchard and Sherry Simon, [in:] D. F. Bouchard, ed., *Language, Countermemory, Practice*, (Ithaca: Cornell, 1977), p. 47.

9. Civility

I ask: Is there anything which would not be a politics which re-establishes the border, a politics of the renegotiation of the border, or a politics of the transgression of the border? Is our political imagination narrowed down to these three positions which do not allow us to think about something else, for example, about something which evades the boundaries of our trivialized thought? I will attempt to answer this question by referring to concepts developed by Étienne Balibar in *Masses, classes, ideas. Studies in politics and philosophy* (1994), where he points to the existence of three conceptualizations of politics, or rather, to three dimensions in which we can capture the political scene. Those three dimensions, observation points, or foundations of – to use Nietzsche's formulation once again – "a suspended scaffolding of an imaginary state of nature", that is, the stage of the antique chorus theatre, are, respectively, the autonomy, the heteronomy, and the civility of politics.

Autonomy becomes politics when it occurs that "a part" of society is excluded from the universal right to politics. That part of society emerges then not only as the most active spokesman for civil rights but also as a fraction capable of demonstrating that its own emancipation is the criterion of universal emancipation. In reality, the entire history of emancipation is not a history of the demand for introduction of new laws, but rather a history of real struggle for the right to the already existing laws. If that is the case, then the essence of politics lies in the struggle against the negation and the narrowing of rights. In the process of emancipation, the excluded part has to introduce itself as a pretender to the position of the people, that is, it has to come into being as the people of the people.

The problem is that politics, including the politics of autonomy, always exists in specific conditions or under specific conditions. Thus a heteronomy of politics comes into play. Conditions which may be a form of economic relations or a combination of relations of domination do not determine politics as a whole but define it in important ways and make it real, functioning as the original conditions of politics. If we assume, for example, that economy is the exterior of politics, then we have to assume that the politics of the proletariat (those excluded from the economy) should return to nonpolitical conditions, that is, to economic inconsistency, and control those from the outside. Politics becomes practice and not administrative utopia at the moment when we stop thinking about it as a simple change of conditions which can be calculated and isolated in order to be controlled, and becomes change based on differentiation, dislocation and dissociation of power. Politics as practice would depend on being able to demonstrate that the modalities of what apparently is beyond our control (economy, domination, history) are more basically determined by what is in fact under our control.

Besides autonomy and heteronomy of politics we have, finally, the problem of the civility of politics. Politics is not only a struggle for recognition, not only autonomization happening under some specific heterenomous conditions, it is also implicated in the condition of subjects who are collectively confronted with the limits to their own power. To quote Balibar,

> I will call civility such politics as would regulate the conflict of identities, torn between the impossible (but in some sense real) limits to total and fluid identification. Civility in this sense is certainly not a politics which suppresses all violence; but it excludes extremes of violence, so as to create a (public, private) space for politics (emancipation, transformation), and enable violence itself to be historicized.[15]

The question that I would pose to Nietzsche via Balibar is the following: What would autonomy, heteronomy and the civility of politics mean to the author of *The Birth of Tragedy*? I answer this question not so much authorized by Nietzsche as reproduced by his originality: an autonomy of politics would certainly be the autonomy of the Greek chorus, the satyr chorus, or rather, the freedom to be the Greek chorus, to be the satyr, that is, to be a being who would take on its human form not by denying the animal form or by an escape from it, but by the derivative discovery of the animal form within. Perhaps the politics of Diogenes, which works beyond shame, that is, beyond negative socialization, and which allows Diogenes to look at himself without fear and which, finally, makes him answer the magnanimous benevolence of Alexander the Great, who desires to fulfill the sage's one wish, with simple and unambiguous words: "do not hide the sun from my face", would be the prototype of such new politics realized beyond the naturalization of what is human, but also beyond the anthropomorphization of what is animal. Diogenes' autonomy would not be the autonomy of the zero-sum game, neither would it be the autonomy of the excluded "part" of society, it would not be based on the demand to introduce laws or the claim to the already existing laws. The autonomy of satyr's politics appears to be, rather, a negation of a negation, that is, a negation of the very opposition between nature and culture, reality and performance, *polis* and the world.

The heteronomy of satirical politics is obviously the economy of the body and physicality. The conditions which define satirical politics in important ways and make satirical politics real are the ways of understanding, using and

15 Étienne Balibar, *Masses, Classes, Ideas: Studies on Politics and Philosophy Before and After Marx*, trans. James Swenson, (New York & London: Routledge, 1994).

experiencing one's own body. A satirical being is a being who is its own body, and questions about what the body may do and what power the body is capable of, are fundamental questions. Another fundamental question is also the question about the conditions of the coexistence of bodies and the conditions for combining their power. The latter sends us to the following problem: In what sense is the satyr chorus a chorus at all, and not, for example, a primal horde?

Finally, there is the question of civility: Are there institutions, apparatuses, instruments which could serve the process of civilizing satirical politics, that is, which would allow subjects to confront the limits of their own power? Satirical politics seems to do away with three important oppositions which we have gotten used to in the liberal world, and which constitute for us definitional conditions of politics as such. To begin with, from the point of view of the processes of legitimation of power, satirical politics undoes the opposition between legitimation and legality, because the experience and execution of power are here one and the same thing. Each citizen is his own ruler and the multiplicity of citizens (satyrs) is one king who does not hide anybody's sun. Secondly, from the point of view of morality of power, satirical politics abolishes the opposition between positive and deformed political systems, because the process of corruption is part of the life process. Additionally, the lack of an ideal moment in life prevents the creation of ideal beings deformed by life. Thirdly, and finally, from the point of view of administration, the division of the state into administration, that is, a mass of administrators, and administered citizens, has been deprived of a raison d'etre, because in this politics every citizen is an administrator. The state is a generalized satirical police.

In effect, the difference separating the government from the citizen, the administrator from the citizen and, finally, monarchy from tyranny, becomes a difference dissolved in a million of differences and intensities of the satirical world. Whether we call that world a totalitarian regime, a velvet dictatorship, or the world of postliberal order does not seem to matter much any more. Both the monarchy (tragedy) and tyranny (comedy) were born of improvisation: the monarchy (tragedy) from the improvisation of those who intoned the dithyramb and tyranny (comedy) from improvisations intoning phallic songs, which occasionally continue as a custom in some of our cities.

PART THREE:
ART

I. The Art of Living: Creation and Identity

Poets as poets cannot accept substitutions, and fight to the end to have their initial chance alone. Both Nietzsche and Freud underestimated poets and poetry, yet each yielded more power to phantasmagoria than it truly possesses. They too, despite their moral realism, over-idealized the imagination. Nietzsche's disciple, Yeats, and Freud's disciple, Otto Rank, show a greater awareness of the artist's fight against art, and of the relation of this struggle to the artist's antithetical battle against nature.

Harold Bloom[1]

Expressions like "creating" or "fashioning" a self sound paradoxical. How can one not already have, or be, a self if one is to engage in any activity whatever? How can one not already have, or be, a self if one is even to be conscious of the experiences and views one is supposed to integrate? That paradox may be mitigated if we distinguish this notion of the self from the strict philosophical idea presupposed by the very fact that I am and must be conscious of my experiences as mine. It is not what Kant called the "transcendental unity of apperception", the "I think" that in principle accompanies all my experiences and is required for me to be an agent, a person, in the first place. It is a homelier notion. To create a self is to succeed in becoming someone, in becoming a character, that is, someone unusual and distinctive. It is to become an individual, but again not in the strict sense in which an individual is anything we can point out and reidentify, anything that, like human beings and material things, exists independently in space and time. To become an individual is to acquire an uncommon and idiosyncratic character, a set of features and a mode of life that set one apart from the rest of the world and make one memorable not only for what one did or said but also for who one was.

Alexander Nehamas[2]

1. The case of Oglala Lakota

Among the Oglala Lakota – a primary American Indian tribal community, it was the tradition for an adolescent boy to go off on his own, weaponless and wearing nothing but a loincloth and mocassins, on a dream quest. Hungry, thirsty, and bone-tired, the boy would expect to have a dream on the fourth day which would

---

1 Harold Bloom, *The Anxiety of Influence. A theory of poetry*, (New York Oxford: Oxford University Press, 1997), p. 9.

2 Alexander Nehamas, *The Art. Of Living. Socratic Reflections from Plato to Foucault*, (Berkeley/Los Angeles/London, 1998).

reveal to him his life's path. Returning home, he would relate his dream to the tribal elders, who would interpret it according to ancient practice. And his dream would tell him whether he was destined to be a good hunter, or a great warrior, or expert at the art of horse-stealing, or perhaps to become specialized in the making of weapons, or a spiritual leader, priest, or medicine man.

I told the story about Oglala Lakota because by the time the tribe was visited by Erik H. Erikson,[3] whose ideas very strongly influenced this text, things had changed quite a bit. They had been herded onto a large but barren reservation through a series of wars and unhappy treaties. The main source of food, clothing, shelter, and just about everything else – the buffalo – had long since been hunted into near-extinction. Worst of all, the patterns of their lives had been taken from them, not by white soldiers, but by the quiet efforts of government bureaucrats to turn the Lakota into Americans.

Children were made to stay at boarding schools much of the year in the sincere belief that civilization and prosperity comes with education. At boarding schools they learned many things that contradicted what they learned at home: they were taught white standards of cleanliness and beauty, some of which contradicted Lakota standards of modesty. They were taught to compete, which contradicted Lakota traditions of egalitarianism. They were told to speak up, when their upbringing told them to be still. In other words, their white teachers found them quite impossible to work with, and their parents found them quite corrupted by an alien culture. As time went by, their original culture disappeared, but the new culture did not provide the necessary substitutions.

My present worry is whether such problems are limited to the case of the Oglala Lakota tribe or perhaps they have a more general application? Growing up and finding one's place in the world is not easy for many other young people not only in Oglala Lakota but in all America, Europe and Asia too. Like native Americans, the great majority of young people in Europe have also lost many of the rituals that once guided them through life. At what point are you an adult? When do you go through puberty? Your first sexual experience? Your learner's permit? Your driver's license? High school graduation? Voting in your first election? First job? Legal drinking age? College graduation? When exactly is it that everyone treats you as an adult? And above all: how, by what means, to invent oneself? The difficulties in answering the question: At what point do we become adults? sentence our culture to contradictions. Consider some of the them: you may be old enough to be entrusted with a two-ton tank of speeding metal, yet not be allowed to vote; you may be old enough to die for your country

3 Erik H. Erikson, *Childhood and Society*, (New York: Norton 1950); Erik H. Erikson, *Identity: Youth and Crisis*, (New York: Norton, 1968).

in war, yet not be permitted to order a beer; as a college student, you may be trusted with thousands of dollars of student loans, yet not be permitted to choose your own classes.

2. Adolescence

Erikson was moved by the difficulties faced by the Lakota children and adolescents he talked to and observed. The development of identity seems to have been one of greatest concerns in Erikson's theory. He is most famous for his work in refining and expanding Freud's theory of stages. Development, he says, functions by the epigenetic principle. This principle suggests that we develop through a predetermined unfolding of our personalities in eight stages. Our progress through each stage is in part determined by our success, or lack of success, in all the previous stages.

Each stage involves certain developmental tasks that are psychosocial in nature. Although Erikson follows Freudian tradition by calling them crises, they are more drawn out and less specific than that term implies. The child in grammar school, for example, has to learn to be industrious during that period of his or her life, and that industriousness is learned through the complex social interactions of school and family. Each stage has a certain optimal time as well. It is no use trying to rush children into adulthood, as is so common among people who are obsessed with success. Neither is it possible to slow the pace or to try to protect our children from the demands of life. There is a time for each task.

If a stage is managed well, we carry away a certain virtue or psychosocial strength which will help us through the rest of the stages of our lives. On the other hand, if we do not do so well, we may develop maladaptations and malignancies, as well as endanger all our future development. A malignancy is the worse of the two, and involves too little of the positive and too much of the negative aspect of the task, such as a person who cannot trust others. A maladaptation is not quite as bad and involves too much of the positive and too little of the negative, such as a person who trusts too much.

Perhaps Erikson's greatest innovation was to postulate not five stages, as Freud had done, but eight. Erikson elaborated Freud's genital stage into adolescence plus three stages of adulthood. We certainly do not stop developing – especially psychologically – after our twelfth or thirteenth birthdays. It seems only right to extend any theory of stages to cover later development. Erikson changed also our imagination about the interaction of generations. Freud had made it abundantly clear that a child's parents influence his or her development dramatically. Erikson pointed out that children influence their parents' development as well. The arrival of children, for example, into a couple's life, changes that life considerably, and moves the new parents along their developmental paths. It is even appropriate to add a third (and in some cases, a fourth) generation to the picture: many of us have been influenced by our grandparents, and they by us.

For our purpose the most interesting stage is stage five. Stage five is adolescence, beginning with puberty and ending around 18 or 20 years old. The task during adolescence is to achieve *ego identity* and avoid *role confusion*. It was adolescence that interested Erikson first and most, and the patterns he saw here were the bases for his thinking about all the other stages. Ego identity means knowing who you are and how you fit into the rest of society. It requires that you take all you have learned about life and yourself and mold it into a unified self-image, one that your community finds meaningful.

There are a number of things that make the process of ego-identity achievement easier. First, we should have a mainstream adult culture that is worthy of the adolescent's respect, one with good adult role models and open lines of communication. Further, society should provide clear rites of passage, certain accomplishments and rituals that help to distinguish the adult from the child. In traditional societies, as we have seen in the case of Oglala Lakota, an adolescent boy may be asked to leave the village for a period of time to live on his own, hunt some symbolic animal, or seek an inspirational vision. Boys and girls may be required to go through certain tests of endurance, symbolic ceremonies, or educational events. In one way or another, the distinction between the powerless, but irresponsible time of childhood and the powerful and responsible time of adulthood is made clear. Without these rituals, we are likely to see role confusion, meaning an uncertainty about one's place in society and the world. When an adolescent is confronted by role confusion, Erikson says he or she is suffering from an identity crisis. In fact, a common question adolescents in our society ask is a straight-forward question of identity: "Who am I?".

There is such a thing as too much of "ego identity", where a person is so involved in a particular role in a particular society or subculture that there is no room left for tolerance. Erikson calls this maladaptive tendency fanaticism. A fanatic believes that his/her way is the only way. Adolescents are, of course, known for their idealism, and for their tendency to see things in black-and-white. These people will gather others around them and promote their beliefs and lifestyles without regard to others' rights to disagree. The lack of identity is perhaps more difficult still, and Erikson refers to the malignant tendency here as repudiation. They repudiate their membership in the world of adults and, even more, they repudiate their need for an identity. Some adolescents allow themselves to fuse with a group, especially the kind of group that is particularly eager to provide the details of your identity: religious cults, militaristic organizations, groups founded on hatred, groups that have divorced themselves from the painful demands of mainstream society. They may become involved in destructive activities, drugs, or alcohol, or they may withdraw into their own psychotic fantasies. After all, being "bad" or being "nobody" is better than not knowing who you are!

If you successfully negotiate this stage, you will have the virtue Erikson called fidelity. Fidelity means loyalty and solidarity, the ability to live by society's standards despite their imperfections and incompleteness and inconsistencies. We are not talking about blind loyalty, and we are not talking about accepting the imperfections. After all, if you love your community, you will want to see it become the best it can be. But fidelity means that you have found a place in that community, a place that will allow you to contribute.

3. Identity in the late modernity

The elements which stimulate the process of the achievement of ego-identity mentioned above – rites of passage and mainstream adult culture – are rather rare commodity in western contemporary cultures. Hence my suspicion that the problem of role confusion, in Erikson's sense, is not only peripheral and accidental to our geographical region but is the crucial issue of contemporary word. What is the nature of self and self-identity in the postmodern condition? Above all, what are the life strategies that individuals employ to make their passage in the world? How do individual selves navigate a life in fragments? In which way does an individual invent him- or herself?

What makes being the self such a complex activity in the postmodern condition is that the context is open to a number of valid interpretations, and in the absence of an agreed moral code to guide the self in the choice of right and good, this can generate feelings of insecurity. This makes the construction of an imaginary world for the self a much more difficult activity; and having to cope with unforeseen consequences is a skill that the self must continually exercise. In conjunction, living is now a highly skilled activity, and our key human skill is to direct the course of the fragments that constitute human existence in an effort to feel comfortable and secure. Individuals as dynamic agents attempt to secure or formulate all forms of solidarity including those of class, community, race and gender. This is because, for individuals class, race and gender have lost all influence in terms of determining life events and life chances. In the postmodern condition, individuals have no independent identity other than that which they create for themselves; this is a world in which class, race and gender are immaterial. In the postmodern world you are what you appear. In the postmodern world you are what you create.

Late or high modernity indicates significant transformations in the organisation of society which entail a "disembeddedness" of the self and identity from traditional structures and institutions. Faced with the breakdown of old traditions which related trust and values to a strong sense of place and belonging, traditions which securely locked us into certainties of gender, family, morality and nation, individuals in postmodern world have been thrown back onto themselves, which has involved hazards of individual choice and interpretation of meanings. In the postmodern condition lacking the protection of class and communal togetherness, lacking any given racial and gender identities, individuals are left to experience feelings of isolation and detachment, having to create their own bonds of solidarity, selfhood and rectitude. This is the postmodern predicament; for individuals, anything goes: morally, spiritually, communally. For many of us, life is in fragments and we experience everyday life as an open space of moral, political and personal dilemmas.

Sociologists like Ulrich Beck,[4] Anthony Giddens[5] and Zygmunt Bauman[6] by implicitly accepting that the inhabitants of contemporary society participate in an alienating and egoistic culture, one which has lost its traditional bonds of cohesion and solidarity, assume that the lonely individual is forced to engage in the anxious task of self-identity construction with only the fear of failure for company. There is a consensus among the above-mentioned theoreticians that subjectivity and identity are achieved or constituted along the dimensions of time and space through interaction with social relationships, institutions, frameworks of meaning and social divisions, rather than being a pregiven, presocial state or one that is functionally and predictably determined by structural forces. My aim is not to enter into the debates about whether we live in late, high or indeed, post- modernity; I am more concerned with the conceptualisation of the self and autonomy that appears very specific in the range of these theoretical approaches.

---

4 Ulrich Beck, *Risikogesellschaft: auf dem Weg in eine andere Moderne*, (Frankfurt/M, Suhrkamp, 1986).

5 Anthony Giddens, *Modernity and Self-Identity. Self and Society in the Late Modern Age*, (Cambridge: Polity Press, 1991).

6 Zygmunt Bauman, *Postmodern Ethics, Life in Fragments. Essays in Postmodern Morality*, (Basil Blackwell, 1995).

According to Zygmunt Bauman[7], in the absent modern world the problem of identity was a problem of how to construct and maintain our identity in an effort to secure one's place in the world and avoid uncertainty. This was because in the modern world the avoidance of uncertainty was seen as an individual problem, although support was always available from various professionals. The creation of modern identity is seen as a pilgrimage. In the first instance, on our journey to a fixed identity we need a place to walk to. This is our life project, which ideally should be established early in life and be used to make sense of the various uncertainties, fragments and divisions of experience which make up the posttraditional world. In other words, by creating a fixed and secure identity we attempt to make the world more ordered and more predictable for ourselves.

In contrast, in the postmodern world the problem of identity is one of avoiding a fixed identity and keeping our options open. Avoiding long term commitments, consistency and devotion. In place of a life project established as early as possible, which we loyally keep to, postmodern people choose to have a series of short projects that are not fixed. The world has a feel to it of being in a continuous present. The world is no longer agreeable to pilgrims. In place of the pilgrim there are a number of other life styles that emerge: the stroller, the vagabond, the tourist and the player. These life styles are not new to the postmodern world, but whereas in previous times marginal people in marginal situations practiced these life styles, they are now common to the majority of people in many situations.

There is a close link between group identities and the distinct pattern of orders which set them securely apart from their neighbors. When an order loses its distinctiveness, so does the identity. The dissipation of orders is another name for the shock of dedifferentiation; and de-differentiation is shocking – confusing, frightening, spawning anxiety – because the blurring of differences challenges consciousness, effaces cognitive maps and explodes the codes of legitimate behaviour. In the progressively dedifferentiated world too large a part of daily experience stands (to use Jean-François Lyotard's expression) "un-ready" rather than preformed, predictable, coming complete with its predefined meaning.[8] When people complain that their identity is unclear or under threat, what they worry about is the unclarity of the world around them; the enormity of the meaning-making task, and so also of the task of identity-building, which now falls fairly and squarely on their own individual shoulders and cannot but overload their mental and emotional capacity.

---

7 *Ibid.*

8 Jean-François Lyotard, *The Postmodern Condition. A Report on Knowledge,* (Manchester University Press, 1984).

But if such a diagnosis of postmodern conditions is correct, then the task of Erikson's fifth stage of life-circle, the task of avoiding role confusion and creating one's identity, seems, at first glance, very difficult to achieve and even impossible. I do not like to discuss at this point the question whether such a picture of social reality delivered by postmodern thinkers is proper, I assume it is. Instead I would like rather to ask whether the process of lost stability, lost on the nomadic road to one's Plural Identities, the fact the we belong to the age of emigrants and many of us have the problems with the process of identification (on the one hand – we could not identify with anything and anyone, on the other – we are eager to identify with everything and everyone) should worry us. I would like to ask whether the process of fragmentation of our identity should worry us at all? Perhaps there is no reason why it has to follow that once I recognize the multiple faces of myself, or alternative identities, I must feel fragmented and conflicted? Or, more to the point, if I do feel conflicted and fragmented, there perhaps is no reason why I need necessarily regard that as a bad thing rather than as something to "work with"?

4. Auto-creation and solidarity

At this point we encounter Richard Rorty' ideas. According to Rorty there is the principle tension between two poles in our life. The names of these two poles are: auto-creation and solidarity. Rorty points out that there is an inherent tension between the demands of our private lives, demands to be the Strong Poet, that is (following Harold Bloom's definition), "the person who uses words as they have never before been used, [and who] is best able to appreciate her own contingency"[9], and our public obligation to minimize cruelty, and that we may often face competing claims from different groups to which we belong. Rorty insists also that there is no final vocabulary which will assist us in adjudicating such claims nor any point in seeking to create one.[10]

The important role in our self-creation is palyed by education. Rorty divides education into two components: a period of socialization and a subsequent period of individuation.[11] The weak formulation of this division is extremely general: education seems to Rorty two quite distinct enterprises: lower education

9 Harold Bloom, *The Anxiety of Influence: A Theory of Poetry.* (New York: Oxford University Press, 1973), p. 34

10 Richard Rorty, *Contingency, Irony, and Solidarity*, (Cambridge: Cambridge University Press, 1989).

11 Richard Rorty, *Education as Socialization and as Individuation*, [in:] Richard Rorty, *Philosophy and Social Hope*, (New York: Penguin, 2000), pp. 114-127.

is mostly a matter of socialization, of trying to inculcate a sense of citizenship, and higher education is mostly a matter of individuation, of trying to awaken the individual's imagination in the hope that she will become able to recreate herself. Such a distinction is not, on the face of it, objectionable. Rorty makes this general division between socialization and individuation unpardonably rigid in a much stronger formulation. He writes that the two processes are "entirely distinct" and goes on to assign precollegiate education (kindergarten through high school) the task of socialization and nonvocational higher education (colleges and universities) the task of individuation. Education up to the age of eighteen or nineteen is mostly a matter of socialization – of getting the students to take over the moral and political common sense of the society as it is. Primary and secondary education will always be a matter of familiarizing the young with what their elders take to be true, whether it is true or not. The point of nonvocational higher education is to help students realize they can reshape themselves. The proper business of the university is to offer a provocation to self-creation.

I do not object to the general division between socialization and individuation, but why they must be separate and distinct processes is not clear. Why could they not, for example, proceed simultaneously and coexist within schools, just as liberalism and irony coexist within Rorty's utopian community? Rorty unfairly and arbitrarily limits the process of individuation to colleges and universities. In doing so, he undermines the effect and drastically limits the scope of the "provocation to self-creation" so crucial to his liberal utopia. If individuation is primarily a process, as he says, "of trying to awaken the individual's imagination in the hope that she will become able to re-create herself",[12] we must not consider the imagination to be a faculty of the mind which lays dormant for years only to be stirred to life during college. Individuation understood as the provocation of the imagination may be fruitfully included at any level of education. Younger children, in fact, appear to have quite potent powers of imagination, perhaps because they have not yet been snuffed and stamped out by a powerful socialization process. Their great propensity to ask questions and explore both the natural and social world is well documented by psychologists and philosophers alike. It seems that young children are in some sense in the best position to exercise their imagination.

Because we come to consciousness within the contingency of language, Rorty believes Nietzsche has taught us that we need not become mere replicas or copies of someone else's story, poem, or model of the moral self. According to Nietzsche, to fail as a poet – and thus as a human being – is to accept someone

12 Richard Rorty, *Education as Socialization and as Individuation*, p. 122.

else's description of oneself. Rorty believes Sigmund Freud has done for our conscience what Nietzsche has done for our language, namely, exhibit its entanglement in historical time and chance. Thus, rather than lead us on a futile search for some core or central self, Freud helps us "treat chance (contingency, if you will) as worthy of determining our fate".[13]

Freudian moral psychology gives us a version of the human story much different than the Platonic or Kantian narratives of universal morality, the idea that we must bring particular actions under general principles if we are to be moral. Instead, Freud teaches us to think of our particular actions and idiosyncrasies in terms of our responses to or reactions against a constellation of past influences and present stresses. In this pragmatic and perspectival account of morality, the dynamics of self-creation and mutual accommodation are always contextualized. We may indeed suffer guilt and shame if we fail to meet the expectations of parental, pastoral or priestly figures in our life. But in this story of morality, the strong poet learns to condemn him or herself more for failure to break free of the past rather than for failure to live up to some standard considered universal or binding by her community of origin.

If Freud were simply saying that conscience is the internalized voice of parents, church, synagogue and society, Rorty would not be so taken with his account of morality. After all, Plato, Kant and the man at the hardware store would all concede that the voices of our ancestors, though dead, still speak in identifiable ways in our hearts and minds. Rorty is most interested in Freud's attention to how unconscious imprints form the conscience in radically contingent ways. Most moral philosophy or theological ethics fails to take into serious consideration the realm of the unconscious and assumes that ethical thought and action can be tracked to reason, will, responsibility, and conscious decision, except perhaps in cases of unspeakable evil, where the darkness of unconscious forces is given its due. However, Freud is not referring to the narcissistic origins of evil but rather to the narcissistic origins of compassion. What does this mean? It means many things of course, including the possibility that a disciple might work for peace and justice, live a self-sacrificial, holy life, and even go to the martyr's fiery stake for the cause. Perhaps this disciple is driven by the love of Jesus and the neighbor, or perhaps he is driven by the imprint of an exceptionally severe and punishing super-ego, or perhaps, and most likely, he is driven by some of both in addition to any number private fantasies folded unevenly into public metaphors or moralities. This is the story of conscience, morality and selfhood that intrigues Rorty. In this account,

13 Richard Rorty, *Contingency, Irony, and Solidarity* 1989, p. 31.

morality is nothing to get too moralistic about as one tracks its plural, particular, and ambiguous sources.

For Rorty, the understanding that all our behavior bears the marks of a blind impress is neither tragic nor terrible. It is life. In fact, following the Freudian narrative, he argues that it is neither necessary nor desirable to harmonize, synthesize or integrate a private ethic of self-creation and a public ethic of mutual accountability. Our private obsessions and public commitments need not be reconciled. Indeed, Rorty argues that in the history of civilization, poetic, artistic, philosophical, political or scientific innovation and progress result from "the accidental coincidence of a private obsession with a public need".[14] We must be careful to never say that it is all just contingency; it is in fact – to use Freud's utterance from the essay on Leonardo Da Vinci – "all chance worthy of determining our fate".[15]

5. Imagination and identity

There is naturally a desire, for whoever speaks or writes, to sign in an idiomatic, that is, irreplaceable manner. But as soon as there is a mark that is the possibility of a repetition, as soon as there is language, generality has entered the scene and the idiom compromises with something that is not idiomatic: with a common language, common concepts, general laws, general norms. On the other hand there are also some general rules, some oversingular procedures that can be transposed by analogy, but these rules are taken up in a text which is each time a unique element. Institutions (the general) and the idiomatic (the singular) meet each other in the events of inventions. But the power of mind, the faculty of mind which makes such s meeting possible is imagination.

What is imagination? What is its place within our experience? Is there any place for imagination at all? What about Samuel Beckett's famous saying – "No trace anywhere of life, you say, pah, no difficulty there, imagination not dead yet, yes, dead, good, imagination dead imagine"?[16] Is it not the most accurate and most perfidious diagnosis of our times and of ourselves? A time full of television pictures and pseudoscientific tales; and yet a time of deficit of imagination, when we lack the skill to relate generalizations of the intellect to

---

14 Richard Rorty, *Contingency, Irony, and Solidarity* 1989, p. 31.

15 Sigmund Freud (1910), *Leonardo da Vinci. A Psychosexual Study of an Infantile Reminiscence*, trans. A. Brill, [in:] *The Standard Edition of the Complete Psychological Works of Sigmund Freud*, Volume XI, ed. James Strachey, (London: Hogarth Press, 1957), p. 324.

16 Samuel Beckett, *First Love and Other Shorts*, (Grove Press, 1974), p. 63

what our senses bring. Hannah Arendt said that "[w]ithout repealing life in imagination you can never be fully alive, 'lack of imagination' prevents people from 'existing'".[17] If so, does the deficit of imagination reveal our inability to live truly? So, are there reasons to fear imagination? Is it just another name for wild fantasy? Is imagination everything in the human cognition and acting? Is every act and every cognitive effort made with the risk of a lack of imagination – a risk of being reduced to nothingness, dullness or foolishness? Are those who are unsupported by the imagination which allows the building of internal worlds also unable to experience their own and others' freedom? Also, on the contrary, does the imagination sentence us to unending exposure to nonexistent creations, fantastic, deformed, and grotesque? Should such creatures – instead of being a part of the spectacle of cognition – be solely a part of the drama of dreaming?

Should we fear the power of imagination, or to the contrary, should we worship it and sing laudatory hymns? Does the imagination heighten our cognitive potencies, or does it deceitfully offer us an illusory way out beyond sensory data and intellectual findings? Zbigniew Herbert wrote:

> Mr. Cogito never trusted tricks of the imagination
> the piano at the top of the Alps played false concerts for him
> he didn't appreciate labyrinths the Sphinx filled him with loathing
> he lived in a house with no basement without mirrors of dialectics.

But Mr. Cogito was forced to use this ambiguous power of imagination to understand and recall the most liminal events which fascinated his intellect:

> – Pascal's night
> – the nature of a diamond
> – the melancholy of the prophets
> – Achilles' wrath
> – the madness of those who kill
> – the dreams of Mary Stuart
> – Neanderthal fear
> – the despair of the last Aztecs
> – Nietzsche's long death throes
> – the joy of the painter of Lascaux
> – the rise and fall of an oak
> – the rise and fall of Rome.[18]

What would then be Mr. Cogito's intellect without imagination? What would be the intellect after the rejection of the power of imagination?

---

17 Hannah Arendt, *The Life of the Mind: Volume II: Willing*, edited by Mary McCarthy, (New York: Brace Harcourt, 1978), p. 211.

18 Zbigniew Herbert, *Mr. Cogito and the Imagination*, trans. J. and B. Carpenter, [in:] Zbigniew Herbert, *The* Collected Poems*: 1956-1998,* (Ecco Press, 2007), p. 34.

Imagination is an exceptionally ambiguous cognitive power. It certainly amplifies the sensory powers of human cognition, and it also invigorates the purely notional functioning of the intellect. This power of imagination is different from that of the senses in that it goes beyond the data delivered from the external world. But it is also different from the intellect, as it operates on sensory data, and is therefore not purely conceptual. This is equally the strength and the weakness of imagination. This strength is hidden in the ability of transgressing what is given here and now. Its weakness results from being oversize and overproductive, as its labour is to create what is not there yet at present.

Kant wrote about three sources which provide the initial conditions of human experience.[19] The three sources of human knowledge are these: senses, imagination and apperception. In creating such a distinction, Kant was fully aware that imagination played the key role in human cognitive architecture. It unites the conceptual strengths of the intellect – the power of abstraction, generalization and formulation of laws – with the strengths of the senses, which deliver the empirical material for intellectual machinery. The intellect without sensory data would be empty, but senses without the abstraction of the intellect would be blind. Without the power of imagination, intellect and senses would be defunct. Imagination has the ability of sculpting platonic forms in our mental pictures. Despite this, Martin Heidegger, interpreting this thread of Kant's thinking, will say: "[t]he transcendental imagination is homeless".[20] He may say so, as he knows very well that in many places Kant limits human cognitive sources to just two: sensuality and intellect. It seems that Kant was hesitant about imagination and was uncertain whether to grant it some place in his architecture of human cognition.

6. The frontier identity

At the very end of the chapter, I would like to pose the question as to what kind of identity is still worthwhile to protect and develop. My answer is very dangerous: I assert that the only kind of identity which could be accepted is what I call "frontier identity", or "borderline identity",[21] which was preliminarily

19 Immanuel Kant, (1781/1977) *Kritik der reinen Vernunft*, [in:] Immanuel Kant, *Werke in zwölf Bänden*. Band 3, (Frankfurt am Main, 1781/1977).

20 Martin Heidegger, *Kant und das Problem der Metaphysik*, (Bonn 1929), p. 230.

21 The dangers of using this term draw from the fact that this term belongs to the psychiatric vocabulary. From psychiatric point of view the borderline personality disorder (BPD) is a mental illness characterized by pervasive instability in moods, interpersonal relationships, self-image, and behavior. See: M. Swartz, D. Blazer, L. George, I.

understood as an unaccomplished identity, filled with tensions, variable and open.

Frontier is a region (spatial, temporal and conceptual) of fundamental ambivalence, "non- and dialectical contradictions" and ambiguity with many nonfixed meanings, where a given phenomenon is *not yet* or *no longer* determined, because it penetrates into another phenomenon; a region with a "fluid" border between "the one" and "the other"; a region of differentiation understood as a movement leading finally to the constitution of various oppositions, and so to the establishment a border – but at the same time, on the contrary, a moment overcoming oppositions through differentiations and mediations. In other words, "frontier identity" is a region of simultaneous and mutual collision and penetration between different powers and forces. The frontier must not necessarily be conceived as a "periphery". And it certainly is not a sphere of peace and stagnation. On the contrary, "differences make it work" (*ereignet sich* – to use a Heideggerian term) especially intensively (and sometimes dramatically) just at the borderline.

In this way I come back to Bloom's dialectics of poetic tradition. Bloom's position is, in a nutshell, that literary tradition is founded on the realization by a fresh author not only of his own struggle against the forms and presence of a precursor but also of the "[p]recursor's place in regard to what came before *him*".[22] In other words, each writer is aware of and necessarily "writes back" to predecessors who in turn are aware of and "write back" to their predecessors. No poet writes in a vacuum but, rather, always does so in the wake of the achievement of previous poets as a result of which his work is always secondary. Poems "arise out of the illusion of freedom, out of a sense of priority being possible"[23] as a result of which each poem is the expression of the "poet's melancholy at his lack of priority".[24] For this reason, Bloom speaks of a "psychology of belatedness"[25] afflicting all literary production.

Poetic strength (Bloom's synonym of what we call the power of imagination, synonym for the poet's finding a voice that is seemingly distinctive from those of his precursors) is, in short, an act of usurpation designed to dethrone a strong predecessor similar to that which Freud argues occurs between son and father in the course of the castration complex which resolves the

Winfield, *Estimating the prevalence of borderline personality disorder in the community*, [in:] "Journal of Personality Disorders", 4(3), 1990, pp. 257-72).

22 Harold Bloom, *A Map of Misreading*. (New York: Oxford University Press, 1975), p. 86.

23 Harold Bloom, *The Anxiety of Influence: A Theory of Poetry*. (New York: Oxford University Press, 1973), p. 17.

24 *Ibid.*, p. 17.

25 *Ibid.*, p. 87.

Oedipus complex of early infancy and what Erikson argues occurs in adolescence when a young man tries to achieve *ego identity* and avoid role confusion. Bloom alludes to this when he compares poetry to a "family Romance" and describes it as the "enchantment of incest disciplined by resistance to that enchantment". He puts it this way in *A Map of Misreading*: the "clearest analogue" of the process of literary repression and revision is "necessarily Oedipal; reject your parents vehemently enough, and you will become a belated version of them, but compound with their reality, and you may partly free yourself".[26] From this point of view, all literary works parody, voluntarily or involuntarily, earlier works. It is for this reason that Bloom suggests that a "voluntary parody is more impressive than an involuntary one",[27] for it reveals a consciousness of the inevitability of one's relationship to tradition and a desire to manipulate it.

I have said that if the picture of contemporary society delivered by Bauman, Beck, and Giddens is proper then the process of achieving one's identity could be very difficult and even impossible. But now I should add that at the same time the process of auto-creation is inevitable. There is no other form of being human than to be a Strong Poet, that is the person who has enough courage and imagination to create him or herself. Bloom argues that new poems originate mainly from old poems; that the primary struggle of the young poet is against the old masters. He, the ephebe, must clear imaginative space for himself through a creative misreading of the strong poets of the past. Only strong poets can overcome this anxiety of influence; lesser lights become derivative flatterers and never achieve poetic immortality. Perhaps there is no possibility to come back to tribe community of Oglala Lakota but there is the rigid necessity to go to the community of autonomous persons.

26 *Ibid.*, p. 67.
27 *Ibid.*, p. 98.

II. Labour of Memory: the Case of Warsaw

Repression, not forgetting; repression, not exclusion. Repression, as Freud says, neither repels, nor flees, nor excludes an exterior force; it contains an interior representation, laying out within itself a space of repression. Here, that which represents a force in the form of the writing interior to speech and essential to it has been contained outside speech. An unsuccessful repression, on the road to historical dismantling. It is this dismantling that interests us, this unsuccessfulness which confers upon its becoming a certain legibility and limits its historical opaqueness.

Jacques Derrida[1]

Genealogy means both the value of origin and the origin of values. Genealogy is as opposed to absolute values as it is to relative or utilitarian ones. Genealogy signifies the differential element of values from which their value itself derives. Genealogy thus means origin or birth, but also difference or distance in the origin. Genealogy means nobility and baseness, nobility and vulgarity, nobility and decadence in the origin. The noble and the vulgar, the high and the low – this is the truly genealogical and critical element. But, understood in this way, critique is also at its most positive. The differential element is both a critique of the value of values and the positive element of a creation. This is why critique is never conceived by Nietzsche as a reaction but as an action.

Gilles Deleuze[2]

The phenomenology of memory proposed here is structured around two questions: Of what are there memories? Whose memory is it?

Paul Ricoeur[3]

1. Fashion

It is now widely recognized that the subject of memory has gained much in popularity. Such diagnosis is very likely to be true, though it needs a bit of explaining to be well substantiated. Our recently discovered fascination with memory now echoes at conferences and in recent academic publications.

---

1 Jacques Derrida (1967), *Writing and Difference*, trans. Alan Bass, (Chicago: Chicago University Press, 1982), p. 247.

2 Gilles Deleuze (1962), *Nietzsche & Philosophy*, trans. H. Tomlinson. (New York: Columbia University Press. 1983), pp. 2-3.

3 Paul Ricoeur (2000), *Memory, History, Forgetting*, trans. K. Blamey and D. Pellauer, (Chicago & London: The University of Chicago, 2004), p. 4.

Political reasons that drew social attention to the notion of memory seem pretty much obvious. After a period of future focussed politics, there came an unavoidable drawback – the problem of reconciliation with the past.

As far as I am concerned, there are more profound reasons for this change and our sudden interest in memory. One of them, I believe, is the death of John Paul II – a meaningful death to most of us. This sudden departure to the House of the Lord has subsequently led to bereavement and melancholy. A period like that could be probably best characterized by susceptibility to different kinds of risk factors. The process of overcoming the past, and most importantly – the recent past, is both a risky and melancholic undertaking. First, it is risky because we think that what we are speaking of is long gone, while in fact this total recall of the past allows for its partial return. Secondly, it is a melancholic task because only within a melancholic's mind the past is continuously dealt with and resuscitated – a pragmaticist's mind combines present with future instead.

The risk of melancholy is even more evident given the last decade which witnessed the deaths of the Pope – the Father, and of other founder fathers of Poland as we know it: Zbigniew Herbert, Jacek Kuroń, Czesław Miłosz, Stanisław Lem, Ryszard Kapuściński. As much as it inflicts sorrow and melancholy, it puts us to a test. Father's death allows children to mature and create their own identity. My concern is whether this is really going to happen, or are we doomed to copy and imitate other identities? In doing so, could we possibly go beyond communism – our romanticised childhood, our cherished adolescence? I do not know.

The risk factor in the last year is even more apparent – given the results of our legitimate ballot, we have faced a triumphant new beginning – the fourth coming of the Republic. It was the birth and the new beginning of our state, breaking with the past, with the promise to resurrect the State of Law, yet another name of the Authoritarian Father. So, my concern is going further: Will this Authoritarian Father allow for modernization and let us regain self-respect? It is no accident that Freud, at the decisive moments of his itinerary, has recourse to metaphorical models which are borrowed not from spoken language or from verbal forms, nor even from phonetic writing, but from a script which is never subject to, never exterior and posterior to, the spoken word. Freud invokes signs which do not transcribe the living, full speech, master of itself and self-present. In fact, and this will be our problem, Freud does not simply use the metaphor of nonphonetic writing; he does not deem it expedient to manipulate scriptural metaphors for didactic ends. If such metaphors are indispensable, it is perhaps because they illuminate, inversely, the meaning of a trace in general, and eventually, in articulation with this meaning, may illuminate the meaning of writing in the popular sense. Freud, no doubt, is not manipulating metaphors, if to manipulate a metaphor means to make of the known an allusion to the unknown. On the contrary, through the insistence on his metaphoric investment he makes what we believe we know under the name of enigmatic writing. A movement unknown to classical philosophy is perhaps undertaken here, somewhere between the implicit and the explicit.

From Plato and Aristotle on, scriptural images have regularly been used to illustrate the relationship between reason and experience, perception and memory. But a certain confidence has never stopped taking its assurance from the meaning of the well-known and familiar term: writing. The gesture sketched out by Freud interrupts that assurance and raises a new kind of question about metaphor, writing, and spacing in general. We shall let our reading be guided by this metaphoric investment. It will eventually invade the entirety of the psyche. Psychical content will be represented by a text whose essence is irreducibly graphic. The structure of the psychical apparatus will be represented by a writing machine. What questions will these representations impose upon us? We shall not have to ask if a writing apparatus – for example the one described in the *Note on the Mystic Writing Pad* – is a good metaphor for representing the working of the psyche, but rather what apparatus we must create in order to represent psychical writing; and we shall have to ask what the imitation, projected and liberated in a machine, of something like psychical writing might mean. And not if the psyche is indeed a kind of text, but: What is a text, and what must the psyche be if it can be represented by a text? For if there is neither machine nor text without psychical origin, there is no domain of the psychic without text. Finally, what must be the relationship between psyche, writing, and spacing for such a metaphoric transition to be possible, not only, nor primarily, within theoretical discourse, but within the history of psyche, text, and technology? Memory, thus, is not a psychical property among others; it is the very *essence* of the psyche: resistance, and precisely, thereby, an opening to the effraction of the trace.

2. Static form of Plexiglas

Darek Foks, a poet and a writer, and Zbigniew Libera, a multimedia artist, recently presented an exhibition entitled *What is the messenger doing?*, which was open in the Bielsko BWA Gallery from 3 February, to 5 March this year. The exhibition of Zbiginiew Libera's photograms, accompanied by texts by Darek Foks, was initiated by a book of both authors under the same title.[4] Darek

4 Darek Foks, Zbigniew Libera, *Co robi łączniczka?* [*What is the messenger doing?*], Ars Cameralis Silesiae Supreriosis, (Katowice, 2005).

Foks wrote 63 (the number of days of the Warsaw Uprising) short, seemingly unconnected stories. The messenger, who learned her craft on a crash course, wanders around a forest, then around a station, then gets involved in some operations which we cannot understand and whose purpose outcome we do not know, because sometimes their descriptions stop in mid-sentence.

I recall this exhibition and the book because I deem them to be the best introduction to the subject of memory that I know. The exhibition consists of trick photographs: in the background of the Warsaw ruins from the Warsaw Uprising we can admire images of great stars of the sixties and seventies, such as Monica Vitti, Sophia Loren, Anita Ekberg, and Gina Lollobrigida. Undressed, flaunting tempting cleavages, but more often fashionably reserved, in uniforms, they look at us melancholically and their gaze is once terrified, another time (less often) seductive, clashing strangely with the scenery of the capital city in the state of ruin (and unrest). Naturally, lending the faces of the great actresses to messengers of the Warsaw Uprising may appear to be another scandalizing initiative of the author of *Intimate Rites* and *Lego: Concentration Camp*, as one could react with indignation to the sentence on one of the posters: *Anita Ekberg sitting at the opening of the sewer*; yet, with a modicum of interpretative sympathy, one can interpret this exhibition as a kind of montage which can demonstrate what I call the workings of memory.

In the shortest interpretation, the exhibition *What is the messenger doing?* is about how the Warsaw Uprising, the most tragic event in the memory of most Poles, was filtered through the psychic apparatus of the boys who experienced their puberty during the 60s and 70s. It is enough to say that to quell the uprising Germans murdered 200,000 people, deported 700,000, razed Warsaw to the ground, and decided to subordinate Poland to the Soviet Union, crushing the hopes of a third world war. For people growing up in those decades, I myself being one of them, the Warsaw Uprising was in principle (despite its tragedy) something unknown, looming in the fog of events, something vague, a memory of some anthropological catastrophe which was mentioned by the adults, but which was not explained and which often caused great antagonisms. To the young minds, the Warsaw Uprising was something as distant from their perception as the faces of the divine actresses enjoying their lives behind the iron curtain. The messengers in Libera and Foks's project become therefore not only a memory of the image of the heroic girls from the fighting Warsaw, deeply ingrained in the nation's collective memory, but also pop-icons from the 60s of the twentieth century, the objects of fantasies of boys growing up in those years. This is how the memory of the tragedy merged with the memory of the first delights.

Zbigniew Libera mentions in one of his interviews:

> As a single child I had my personal shady dealings with my mother. Mother also brings to my mind a picture from Fellini's film, Amarcord. The floozy Sabrina, who pees on the beach and boys spy on her. Amarcord means "I recall" in one of Italian dialects and our book is also about remembering. We access images frozen in the archive of memory, we can watch it in a static form, as if embedded in Plexiglas.[5]

My story will concern those static representations, embedded in a form of representation. My story will concern the topic of memory's operation, which enables the most unexpected montages, usually restricting our intellectual freedom.

3. Frameworks

The assertion that our memories are entirely dependent on the frameworks of memory which we have at our disposal is today a rather trivial statement, already well-grounded in social sciences. It is not denied by cognitive psychologists, concentrated on the notion of reference frame, it is not denied by psychoanalysts, focused on the idea of screen memories, it is defended by sociologists, reconstructing the social framework of memory, and finally by anthropologists and philologists, assuming the primacy of interpretation over text. Memory in this new, disenchanted interpretation is no longer treated as a storage room for the past events, it does not constitute a permanent archive which we can look into and refer to and from which we can extricate the preserved data about the past. Memory no longer resembles a closet with old clothes, which we take out at the moment of deep meditation on time and impermanence. Memory is rather a result of something which after Freud I would name the "working-through of memory" or "working-through of remembering" (*durcharbeiten*).

Maurice Halbwachs claimed that a man devoid of social frameworks of memory is like an aphasiac or a paralytic; for the past, rather than be retained in some impenetrable and sealed storehouses, is recovered in the social discourse by means of the present.[6] A person devoid of the past would then be unable to function in the present; but a person devoid of the present would be like a dreamer drifting in the timelessness of stationary state of deep unconsciousness. Both for Halbwachs and Freud dreams are recollections devoid of the social

---

5 *Pinup Girls: Darek Foks and Zbigniew Libera in conversation with Dorota Jarecka and Justyna Sobolewska*, "Wysokie Obcasy", 4 February 2006, no 5 (355), p. 31.

6 Maurice Halbwachs (1925), *On collective memory*, trans. L. A. Coser (Chicago: The University of Chicago Press, 1992).

context of action. When the memory frameworks decompose, the mechanical memory, that is, the memory of events, becomes more helpless and, in a manner of speaking, inert as far as constructing identity and uniform narration is concerned.

Yet it is Henri Bergson who develops from this rapprochement of dream and presence (or absence) of collective frameworks, from this collision of the realty of dream and the reality of perceptual events a more radical conclusion: a human being who dreamt of its existence instead of living it would each moment take in an infinite amount of details of his or her past. On the other hand, a human being who would live in full consciousness of perception, in the infinite exertion of concentration and attentiveness, a human being who would dare to reject memory with everything it holds would continuously enact his or her being instead of presenting it faithfully; "a conscious automaton, he would follow the lead of useful habits which prolong into an appropriate reaction the stimulation received".[7] In the future, Freud will try to describe this automaton. What to Bergson is an incredible and almost fantastic scientific hypothesis, to Freud will become a basis for a scientific project. A conscious automaton is not an automaton capable of unintentional processing of memory traces; it is not only a picture archive, it is above all an entire photographic studio prepared for processing material registered by the optical apparatus. When we deal with Libera and Foks's work, we enter this particular photographic studio, we look at how chemical substances work to enable the development of a series of photographs. Those pictures are dissected like our bodies after death. The dissection of bodies and corpses are for Libera and Foks very similar activities. Yet, let us not get ahead of ourselves. Let us delay a bit more our thinking about death and its representation.

To Bergson, memory is not an ability to pigeonhole memories or to enter them in a register. There is no register or a pigeonhole, or even more so a closet, or any mysterious ability to order events, because such an ability functions with breaks, when it can or wants to, on a whim or under the influence of unrecognized forces, while the overlapping of past with past constantly continues. This overlapping of consecutive layers of the past causes us to think in the geological categories, to think about the very fabric of our memories as if it were layers of earth and rock, or even whole mountain chains. In reality, reminiscing is aggressive and bold mountaineering. There is nothing more dangerous than reminiscing, perhaps apart from mountaineering. As a matter of fact, to Bergson we are merely a condensation of our own history, which we

---

7 Henri Bergson (1896), *Matter and Memory*, trans. N. M. Paul, W. S. Palmer, (New York: Zone Books 1990), p. 54.

lived through from our birth, and even before that, since we are born with some predispositions and inborn convictions. Without a doubt, we are aware of only a small part of our past, but every moment we act under the pressure of the whole past, including the initial outline of our mind. Therefore, from the very beginning, the past appears as a constant pressure, a constant, gigantic urgency, a snowslide demanding release; a tendency, a tension in a sense propelling everything in the present. Although presumably there is a paradox in it, since it is the past that is supposed to be responsible for movement, for changes, and not for inactivity and respite. Although it is surely paradoxical, because this memory is supposed to be the most dangerous cognitive activity of the intellect, exceeding in the risk taken perception, thinking, and even imagination!

4. The present

But what is this working-through of memory? I repeat: working-through, and not a process, state, event, effect, mechanism, or function. The word "work" is supposed to ephasise the effort, which the subject devotes to his or her past, and therefore is supposed to emphasize the fact that the subject has his or her history and that this history needs certain cultivation, care, amelioration, inasmuch as its purpose is to consolidate the subject, and not ruin it. In particular, one should ask how memory works in the posttraditional world – in a world in which the skeleton of social life is based on forgetting or even on the necessity of forgetting, and not brooding over the past and the necessity of its reproduction? Does being part of a hot society, according to Claude Lévi-Strauss's terminology,[8] really mean the affiliation with a society incapable of remembering? That last statement is shocking, since it would mean that in our civilization the excess of devices used for storing (freezing and copying) data is tied with the serious atrophy of the functions of individual memory! Already Plato in *Phaedrus* turns our attention to this circumstance, discussing the case of the most dangerous invention for memory – writing.

Would than a man reluctant to forget be maladjusted to live in such a society? Do memory and oral transmission, which in the traditional cultures were the basic tools of organizing social life, now constitute relics, atavisms, limiting rather than facilitating factors in free communication? Does every man who is unwilling to forget resemble Ireno Fuenes from a story by Jorge Luis

8 Claude Lévi-Strauss (1955), *Tristes Tropiques*. trans. John Weightman and Doreen Weightman, (London: Cape, 1973).

Borges,[9] that is, a man incapable of forgetting, who confesses with a hint of melancholy: "[m]y memory, Mr. Borges, is like a giant dumpster"? To Fuenes the thing which was once thought, perceived, noted, could no longer to be forgotten. Such was Fuenes's genius, but it was also his curse.

What then is the work of memory? What is this effort of remembering? – it is a question particularly important now, when the cognitive power, seemingly towering over others, is heading towards the use of denial and strong interpretation of events rather than a meticulous, impassive archiving of the monuments of the past? What is the work of memory, particularly in the psychoanalytical context? When we encounter Freud's work for the first time, what surprises us the most, perhaps, is the suggestion that in mental life nothing truly disappears, that everything is always stored in the delicate membranes of the psychic apparatus, therefore, the effort of memory can be a much larger effort when forgetting, rather than when remembering. Perhaps, despite the commonly accepted truth that it is easier to forget than to remember, possibly more psychic power is consumed by forgetting than by remembering, which would mean that Fuenes, the man who is unable to forget in Borges's story, reveals a trait characteristic of us all, that is memorizing everything. Does his uniqueness lay only in the absence of defence mechanisms leading to the exclusion of certain memory traces from the scenes of direct (or primary) representation.

Yet, is the case of Fuenes similar to the case of Foks and Libera? Do they also find it so hard to forget? Are they also devoid of the natural mechanisms which purify the archives of our psychic apparatus, the primary scene of our growth?

5. Compulsion

Anthony Giddens, juxtaposing the readings of the texts of Sigmund Freud, Max Weber, and Maurice Halbwachs, claims that the works of the aforementioned authors concern the psychological and social order, in which tradition began to change into compulsion. "Compulsion", writes Giddens, "rather than the unconscious as such, turned out to be the other side of the 'cognitive revolution' of modernity".[10] Tradition, according to Giddens, is strictly connected with the collective memory because it entails ritual and has its guardians, and, in contrast to customs, it has binding force, which is composed of two interconnected

9 Jorge Luis Borges. (1944), *Funes the Memorious,* [in:] Jorge Luis Borges, *Labyrinths*, trans. J. E. Irby. (London: Penguin Classics, 2000), p. 93.

10 Anthony Giddens, *Living in a Post-traditional Society*, [in:] Ulrich Beck, Anthony Giddens, Scott Lash, *Reflexive modernization: politics, tradition and aesthetics in the modern social order*, (Cambridge: Polity, 1994), p. 359.

aspects: moral and emotional. Ritual connects tradition with practice, and the guardians of tradition are not so much experts endowed with mysterious competences, as above all interpreters who talk not only about what has been done in a society, but also perfomatively announce what should be done. However, because tradition is a repetition and assumes a ceremonial and not an adequative conception of truth, different from the ordinary process of informing, tradition resembles in this respect the mechanism of compulsion: obsessive-compulsive disorder.

Compulsiveness is in its widest sense the inability to escape one's past, it is the enslavement by the past. And the enslavement by the past is naturally a great psychoanalytical subject from Freud to Slavoj Žižek. Giddens reasons: "Compulsiveness, when socially generalized, is in effect tradition without traditionalism: repetition which stands in the way of autonomy rather than fostering it",[11] so it is a empty ritual of repetition, devoid of the signs of sacredness or rituality. The hidden compulsiveness of modernity is manifest both in the public and in the individual sphere. In the individual sphere, it offers us a psychic construct predestined to addictions and obsessions; in the collective sphere, it provides us with the paradigm of an entrepreneur, whose drive for material gains goes hand in hand with a frugal lifestyle and dread of hedonism. At the moment when tradition becomes suppressed, the past starts to be affectively and interpretatively inert. Such argumentation carries an important implication: the past cannot simply fade or dissolve, go away, or simply disperse; the past, if it is to be effectively and constructively used, has to be ingrained in the present, it has to be materially fixed in the present. That is why in the montages by Foks and Libera faces of the tragic heroines of the Warsaw Uprising are replaced by the faces of the film pop-culture.

Therefore, the question is: How can the past, the memory, be set in the present so as not to cause compulsive behaviors and reflective actions?

6. The phenomena of hypermnesic memory

The subject of memory is present in Freud's work since the very beginning. Summarizing the past, above all the nearest past, is for Freud a task as much hazardous as it is deeply melancholic. It is a hazardous task because it seems to us that we are writing about something which no longer exists, when *de facto* by reminiscing about a certain fragment of the past reality we create conditions for its return. It is a melancholic task, since only the mind of a melancholic would

11 Anthony Giddens, *Living in a Post-traditional Society*, p. 362.

focus on the past, the mind of a pragmatist focuses on interconnecting the present with the future. An able man does not fantasize and does not live on memories, but perceives and acts in the present. The problem is that able people are so hard to find. Moreover, the present is constantly shaped by the pressure of future events.

Already in the second chapter of *The Interpretation of Dreams*, the author looks into the phenomenon of memory in a dream; the subject of memory occurs here so frequently that it is unclear whether Freud is more interested in the workings of memory or in the workings of dreams. Freud admits:

> The fact that dreams have at their command memories which are inaccessible in waking life is so remarkable and of such theoretical importance that I should like to draw still more attention to it by relating some further hypermnesic' dreams.[12]

In principle, Freuds is interested in two matters: (1) the ability to reproduce the traces of events in memory, which seemed to have been long lost in the conscious, daily mental activity, so the particular, hypermnesic characteristic of dream; and (2) the immediacy of forgetting the dream's content after awakening, the inability to remember dreams and therefore the particular cleansing and dispersing quality of the daily mental activity. Freud is very much interested in the redundancy of night memory in the daytime cognitive activity, and in particular in the clash of these two properties.

Yet it is in the reflections on the subject of the primary and secondary process of repression where Freud advances original hypotheses on the subject of three processes which describe the unconscious organization of our thoughts. To be precise, he describes there the process of abandoning, stopping, and suppressing mental activity and considers the fate of those cathexes which were, so to speak, unlucky and were not realized or fulfilled with help of the initial investment of libidinal energy. Freud writes about this:

> A train of thought that has been set going like this in the preconscious may either cease spontaneously or persist. We picture the first of these outcomes as implying that the energy attaching to the train of thought is diffused along all the associative paths that radiate from it; this energy sets the whole network of thoughts in a state of excitation which lasts for a certain time and then dies away as the excitation in search of discharge becomes transformed into a quiescent cathexis. If this first outcome supervenes, the process is of no further significance so far as dream-formation is concerned. Lurking in our preconscious, however, there are other purposive ideas, which are derived from sources in our unconscious and from wishes which are always on the alert. These may take control of the excitation

12 Sigmund Freud (1900), *The Interpretation of Dreams*, [in:] *The Standard Edition of the Complete Psychological Works of Sigmund Freud*, Volume IV, ed. James Strachey, (London: Hogarth Press, 1957). p. 46.

> attaching to the group of thoughts which has been left to its own devices, they may establish a connection between it and an unconscious wish, and they may 'transfer' to it the energy belonging to the unconscious wish. Thenceforward the neglected or suppressed train of thought is in a position to persist, though the reinforcement it has received gives it no right of entry into consciousness. We may express this by saying that what has hitherto been a preconscious train of thought has now been 'drawn into the unconscious'.[13]

Freud in this fragment warns us against the unexpected fate of the "thoughts which have been left to their own devices", thoughts which have not passed through one's mind, have not been worked-through, have not been mined for meaning, have not been interpreted, thoughts which have been discarded – rejected or suppressed. Freud warns us against their return and the silent, destructive work of our abandoned intentions – our "orphaned" thoughts. The lack of active work of the experiencing subject dooms those thoughts to work and distortive processing the quintessential example of which is to Freud hysteria. In hysteria, just like in the formation of a dream, we encounter thoughts which, to use Freud's own words, "have been subjected to abnormal treatment" and by means of condensation, compromising formation, through loose associations, concealing contradictions or regression have been transformed into a symptom. Symptom stands as an immovable monument to the past, which congealed into empty repeatability. In other words: compulsiveness. To use Libera's expression, a symptom is an image "frozen in the archive of memory", which we can see "in a static form, as if embedded in Plexiglas".

To Freud, therefore, the work of memory is above all work of repetition: a regular return of the mental process leading to turning away from the memory of what used to be unpleasant. This rejection provides a model and the first example of mental suppression, which is reinforced in the fact that the memory, unlike perception, does not have sufficient quality and intensity to stimulate consciousness and thereby bring forth a new cathexis. So it can only act as an invisible, imperceptible, hidden phenomenon.

Memory, in this sense, is composed of the ideational representative and the affective component. However, what is particularly important is not the representation itself, not the trace, but something which Freud calls the fate of the representation,[14] which is *de facto* the fate of the drives. According to Freud, a representation may be suppressed. If the representation, characteristic of the drive, becomes suppressed, the affective component may transfer into another

13 Sigmund Freud, *The Interpretation of Dreams*, p. 591.

14 Sigmund Freud (1915), *Instincts and their Vicissitudes*. [in:] *The Standard Edition of the Complete Psychological Works of Sigmund Freud*, Volume XIV, Ed. and trans. James Strachey. London: Hogarth, 1953-74. pp. 109-140.

representation or become transformed into another affect. To simplify, one could say that the affect is a more readable sign of the repressed impulse than representation. The real measure of the dynamics of memory lies not in what we remember, but in what feeling we remember. These moveable, hidden, unrealized affective components of our memory are probably our greatest threat. Those abandoned affects connected with the Warsaw Uprising in Foks and Libera's work searched for a new cathexis, a new representative. And found it in the images of Anita Ekberg and Gina Lollobrigida.

7. The Mystic Writing-Pad

Jacques Derrida, in his famous text *Freud and the Scene of Writing* writes that "[to Freud] memory is not a psychical property among others; it is the very essence of the psyche".[15] Derrida's text is, in a sense, on the subject of how optical metaphor dominates Freud's thinking until the time of publishing *The Interpretation of Dreams*, when it is suppressed by the metaphor of a writing machine. At one point, Freud stops thinking about the psychic apparatus as an optical apparatus, and starts to think about it in terms of of a *Wunderblock.* After all, did Freud not struggle during his entire life with the problem of finding some artificial construct which could be adequately used to describe memory – one and the same mechanism which can store the changes of its elements, and which still – always fresh and open – can meet the demands for new opportunities for changes! How can those two seemingly incongruous tendencies be joined in one apparatus? Derrida commences his enquiries on Freud's indefatigable ingenuity and the almost dreamlike revival of mechanical models in his thinking. Derrida asks: *What does Freud do?*, and that is how he comments on the desire to find the machine that could meet these two seemingly contradictory requirements, and moreover work entirely on its own:

> That the machine does not run by itself means something else: a mechanism without its own energy. The machine is dead. It is death. Not because we risk death in playing with machines, but because the origin of machines is the relation to death. In a letter to Fliess, it will be recalled, Freud, evoking his representation of the psychical apparatus, had the impression of being faced with a machine which would soon run by itself. But what was to run by itself was the psyche and not its imitation or mechanical representation. For the latter does not live. Representation is death. Which may be immediately transformed into the following proposition: death is (only) representation.[16]

---

15 Jacques Derrida, *Writing and Difference,* p. 354.

16 *Ibid.*, pp. 285-286.

Freud then works hard at making our apparatus work on its own, so that we can always rest. Freud devises for us such an architecture that would absolve us from the effort of repeating the effort, that is, from the necessity for work. Freud works on the liberation of the human from the necessity for work much more diligently than Marx, whose name is probably associated with the phenomenon of work more than Freud's.

Freud, in his indefatigable search for the optimal apparatus, will feel at least slightly satisfied when he gets on the trail of the mystic writing pad – a writing pad made of a piece of wax or resin, dark bronze of color, covered in paper. On the surface of this device there is a thin and transparent sheet, firmly attached to the block with its upper layer, while the bottom layer rests loosely. As a result, the sheet contains two layers, that is, the front layer, which is a sheet of transparent celluloid, and a bottom layer, which is a sheet of thin and transparent wax, Freud finds two attributes which intrigue him in one device: the outward, constantly regenerating innocence and an infinite supply of permanent traces.

Here then is a machine constantly open to experiences of the external world, neutral on its surface like the mirror of an infinitely peaceful lake and simultaneously holding beneath its frozen but sensitive surface the images of the outside world, images which pierced the external matter – the border between the external and the internal. It is important to realize that the machine is not alive, it merely portrays. It – the machine – is therefore death. Just as images "embedded in Plexiglas" in Libera's exhibitions are death.

The subject of death does not end here, nor does the deep contamination of death, memory and machine. Without a doubt, in psychoanalysis a human is an animal which remembers. Even, or maybe especially when memory is a paradoxical process that retains traces of what has never been experienced "as such", and does not leave distinct traces. Hence, here the subject of memory is crucial. Otherwise, how can one remember something, which eludes all representation, which makes itself remembered only in the negative – in disorders of the symbolic order, and does not leave any permanent trace? How is memory possible, especially collective memory, after the Warsaw Uprising?

In psychoanalysis memory is a deeply paradoxical process, based entirely on the partial and unsuccessful mechanism of representation. As Freud puts it in *Beyond the Pleasure Principle*, we remember only what the consciousness cannot make fully present here and now, only that which it could not experience. Consciousness and memory in a sense exclude each other, which signifies that what is remembered is a trace of the experiences which turned out too traumatic for the consciousness to be made aware of here and now, at the moment of their actual happening. Those traces, inscribed in the deeper layer of the psyche, are stored within it like a "reserve" (*der Vorrat*), which the psyche works-through later, *nachträglich*, when the immediate danger is gone. The trace of trauma is therefore not a full piece of information, it is only a catchphrase which stimulates the psyche to exert the effort of evoking the information, although the remembrance is always only partial. The psychic apparatus cannot remember what has passed; yet it can remember that it happened; it remembers the striking force of the eventualization itself: that it is a different world, reality, that it is something which Freud called the internal exteriority.[17]

8. Pornography

What are the relations between the work of the messenger and the work of the boys in Foks's stories? Is the work of the messenger nothing else but the working-through of memory? Do boys merely create events (deliver material for remembering), and the messenger solidifies them (remembers)? Why do the work of the messenger and the work of the boys so completely miss each other? When boys enter a power plant the messenger looks for lightbulbs, and when the boys are looking for lightbulbs, the messenger lights the candles! Why do the messenger and the boys not cooperate with each other? Why does the messenger always do something different than what the boys are doing? And finally: Are the work of the boys and the work of the messenger examples of work of two contradictory systems which Freud finally found in the mystical writing-pad: the boys' exposed innocence and the endless supply of the messenger's traces?! Should the work of the messenger be imagined as that of a housewife, who in autumn puts apples, pears, or cucumbers in jars, for storage in the hermeneutic isolation of the jar throughout the winter, under the lid, in liquid, so that they may delight us with the memory of the summer?

Is this why the boys do not remember that they have been bombed with reality (trauma), which removes the possibility of registering events into infinity? Is this why they do not remember that they constitute a piece of transparent celluloid which has been torn to pieces in the heat of battle? And is this why the messenger remembers that she is that piece of thin and transparent wax in which the memories will leave a trace in a permanent manner?

Why does the messenger raise her voice, that is, screams, when the boys overuse negation? Is it in favor of using the affirmative? When the boys assent

---

17 "Symptom comes from that which is repressed, in a way it is its representative to the "ego" and that which is repressed is outside the "ego", it is its internal exteriority in the same way in which reality – please forgive me this unusual expression – is its external exteriority". Sigmund Freud (1932), *New Introductory Lectures on Psycho-Analysis*, [in:] Sigmund Freud, *The Standard Edition of the Complete Psychological Works*. Vol. 22, Ed. and trans. James Strachey. (London: Hogarth, 1953-74), p. 67.

(use the affirmative), the messenger is silent! When the boys are smoking, why does the messenger smoke cigarettes in secluded corners? Is she so ashamed of this act? Or is she rather so much censured by the boys that she has to smoke in secrecy? Why is the messenger taking notes when the boys are building a barricade? Does she want to erect a barricade around herself in the future? And perhaps this barricade helps the messenger store traces of memory in the inner space? The messenger starts to write at the moment when the boys start building, but the messenger stops writing when the boys change the frequency!

This is not all, when the boys play, the messenger turns her face towards the sun; are boys then playfully talking about her face, or maybe turning her face towards the sun is only a sign of a strong and open ignorance of the boys' playfulness? Does the fact that the boys are studying a map arouse a desire in the messenger to go to the garden, and the boys' self-plagiarism (i.e. their essential lack of inventiveness) a desire to turn the key in the lock? How predictable and horribly homogenous are the boys in this depiction; and how diverse, heterogenic and branching is the messenger in those stories!

When is the messenger under the boys' influence? Perhaps when the boys stand astride, because that is when the messenger overestimates her strength! Yet it is the only instance when she overestimates her strength. On the other hand, the messenger snivels when the boys return at the break of day, and it does not make her look more enticing! When the boys stop on the bridge, the messenger rests her elbows on the handrail. Bridges, therefore, are extremely intriguing to the messenger and cause great tension in her; yet does she not look from the bridge at the water flowing below? Does she not see in the water a symbol of death – the boys' and her own? Yet, when the boys assume their various positions (i.e. clown around), the messenger seems to lose control over her body and starts pointlessly to salute! This is when she recalls that she forsook the attempts to reach an agreement with the boys!

The messenger cannot be whistled at because upon hearing a whistle she reacts by shattering mirrors (images?)! The messenger also loses self-control when the boys stop a car; is it because of the force of inertia, which is abundantly generated at such moments?

How should the messenger's spatial orientation be understood? Is it as unreliable as orientation in time? The messenger is going west when the boys have a hangover; when they are drinking she is going east! The messenger loses boys from sight only when the boys stop their monotone march, which would probably mean that the visual system of the messenger is capable of registering only mobile objects. The boys are moving and working almost frantically, they are working to create events to remember. The messenger does not have any orientation in time, because she herself is stationary, just like unconsciousness for Freud. When the boys glance at a watch, the messenger is wasting time. "Death is (only) representation" (Derrida).

Of course, when we read, the messenger opens the gate when the boys lose gasoline or sticks out her tongue when the boys are writing letters, we begin to think that the whole scene can be considered to be veiled pornography (and not geography), which is worse than overt pornography inasmuch as the pictures are relative to the text, which constantly needs interpretation! The pictures which assail one's sight with an erotic message are very few and far between, among them the one which accompanies the text – *When the Boys Lose Gasoline*. Yet there is much eroticism in the messenger's work, eroticism hidden not as much in the body as in the furtive glances, positions, gestures, facial movements, and constant undertones concerning the relationships of the messenger and the enemy exterminating Polish boys. Is the messenger not collaborating with the enemy by any chance? Maybe the sense of the word messenger does not mean that she links the present with the past or the masculinity with the femininity, or the perception with memory, or mind with the feeling, or finally logic with eroticism, but that this bizarre meaning of the word communicates the connection of one's own with that of the enemy, and thus collaboration!

When Libera mentions Italian cinema as a source of his present, unenviable erotic condition, he says a lot on the topic of his most active spheres: that the anxiety in the boy's temperament about the enemy has a greater power over our messengers than we do, that to them the enemy is more attractive than our closeness, that the enemy seduces better than the friend. Boys resent this fact because they are aware that the messenger has two features which are infinitely attractive to all boys – exhibited, constantly renewable innocence and an infinite supply of permanent traces. The messenger is therefore a virgin, but also experienced. This is naturally the inversion of Gombrowicz's theorem: we turn to the enemy to get the enemy's.

9. Heroism

Tzvetan Todorov, in a text which is well-known although not completely understandable to Poles entitled *Sentenced to Heroism*, juxtaposes two uprisings, two scenarios of armed insurrections, and as a result two ethics and two forms of political responsibility – the Warsaw Ghetto Uprising of 1943 and the Warsaw Uprising of 1944.[18] The difference between these two uprising lays

18 Tzvetan Todorov, *Facing the Extreme: Moral Life In the Concentration Camps*, (New York: Owl Books, 1997).

in the fact that the Warsaw Uprising, although its motives were complex (among which the feeling of political impasse was not the least important), it was not entirely inevitable; it was rather a result of a miscalculation in a situation which had other solutions. The uprising in the Warsaw ghetto in 1943 had to take place, in a sense contrary to the Jew's wishes, if the Jewish nation wanted to prove to itself and the world that it was not going to die like a herd of sheep going to the slaughterhouse.

The Warsaw Uprising – says Todorov – was a result of heroism understood in a peculiar way. Heroism characteristic of the Warsaw insurgents (to refer to the antonymy between the necessity and freedom, the impersonal law of history and the personal will of the individual) is situated on the side of freedom and will. This heroism is also based on the attempt to confront the destiny set by the law, history, and that which is unavoidable. It is the courage to put at stake one's life in a fight uneven and doomed to failure from the start, a fight with fate, history and destiny. The Warsaw Uprising was then an expression of a spiritual construction very characteristic of Poles in which the volitional element and wishful thinking dominates over rationality and calculation. General Leopold Okulicki (head of operations and the last commander of the Home Army, who died on 26 December 1946 in a Soviet prison, a death he had feared the most – he was murdered) demands from the insurgents, from boys, that all his orders be obeyed, he demands a spectacle, he is aware that these events will be mentioned not only in Polish history course books, but will also be remembered by the whole world. By this I want to state that the Warsaw Uprising was from the very beginning planned and programmed to be remembered! Memory, heroization of memory, is the only authentic goal and significance of the Warsaw Uprising!

Todorov talks about heroism with reference to people such as Okulicki; with reference to people such as Edelman, he talks about civil courage. Marek Edelman witnessed the events in the Warsaw Ghetto in 1943 and years afterwards relates those events as he remembered them, and in consistency with the rules of heroic description. Edelman's memory is not subordinate to the rule of arbitrary narrative scripts structuring the events, Edelman's memory is free and reconstructive, and not determined from the start. Edelman related the story of the uprising to Hanna Krall, and what resulted was a book entitled *Shielding the Flame*. In the heroic ethics death is the crown achievement, a value and a target, because it personifies the ideal better than life. Life may necessitate courage, it may also be a sacrifice, but without the flames of passion! Death is a representation, hence the heroism which has to be directed towards the memory and remembrance has to be directed towards death as its own representation.

In the area of ethics of civil courage, death is more of a means than an end: it is the only hope for a humiliated individual, desiring to preserve his or her dignity. The suicide of the individual, and especially of the whole nation, is not a value; suicide, as in Cato, becomes a value only as an act of free will. What is important, Todorov points out that the acts of heroic courage are usually performed by men (boys), while the acts of civil courage, just as often, if not more often – by women. Hence, the second kind of responsibility is in fact a form of ethics of concern, and the concern – whatever Martin Heidegger wrote on this subject – is a phenomenon which is characteristic of the world of the messengers more than of the world of the heroes. Therefore, heroes die for the memory and the ideal; messengers, if they die, do it for the living, for concrete beings, and not for abstract notions such as history, Europe, or the West.[19]

10. Words and images

The books of Foks and Libera present a mystery: What is the relation between images and words in this work? What are the relations between Libera's montage and Foks's words? Do they find each other at all? Are they formed by the same rules? And if not, then what justifies such a specific juxtaposition of words and images? Since images are montages faking the reality of the Uprising, then maybe words should follow this imitation, maybe Foks should simulate a diary of the Warsaw Uprising? But they ostentatiously do not follow it, and Foks does not simulate anything, unless it is written in an archaic, insurgent typeface! Does the work of memory really so violently reject words and images, sensory registers of events, and the always belated linguistic interpretations?! Do the two registers ever meet and is there no chance to connect the work of words and images? Finally, is the working-through of memory solely the work of iconic traces?

In the blurb of his book, Jerzy Jarniewicz answers these questions, commanding us to think about memory as a wholesale store on the outskirts of town, where it stores images and words. He intends to say that images and words which run through our psychic apparatus are not ours, they are ready-made, prefabricated, replayed, schematized, constantly repeated, he wants to say that both the words and the images are ready and that nothing in our memory is

19 Carol Gilligan, as probably the first person of the feminist persuasion defended the ideas, not universally welcomed with enthusiasm by feminists, of feminist care ethics, which would be connected to a greater degree with love, devotion, sensitivity, and affection, rather than virtue, person, human rights, categorical imperative, rational element entailed in humanity, or even respect (so traditional concepts taken out of the androcentric dictionary of ethics) (Carol Gilligan, *In A Different Voice*: *Psychological Theory and Women's Development,* (Harvard University Press, 1993)).

ours. Jarniewicz develops from this premise a rather surprising and incredible conclusion: "[t]hat is why Foks's prose had to meet Libera's pictures". Moreover, he says that "what we see is pregnant with what and how we say. But we can also reverse this sentence: what we say is pregnant with what and how we see". In my view, Foks's prose will never meet Libera's pictures and the whole book is a proof for the deep indetermination of iconic and linguistic lineage, a proof for the fact that nothing is pregnant with anything, that everything is deeply separate, and the juxtaposition of one with the other a roulette, a kind of repeated dealing of cards, stigmatized by the act of shuffling (random chance). In this meeting no necessity exists.

Henri Bergson claimed that between the sensorimotor mechanism (which one needs to imagine in the shape of a flat, planimetric membrane) and the entirety of memories stored in our three-dimentionally (stereometrically) understood memory there is space for thousands of repetitions from our sensory stimulation.[20] Within the cone, which according to Bergson is the best representation of this space, and which with its summit touches the plane of the sensorimotor mechanism and the base of which is formed by the sphere of the past perfect tense, within the so defined space of memory we disperse our memory traces as we progressively distance ourselves from our mobile sensory state, to live the dream life. Those copies, replicas, clichés, which are repeated until the sensorimetric impulse is exhausted, are characterized by one fundamental trait: as they depart from the source, they become more and more schematic, mannered, faded, abstract, and less and less representational.

Libera's photomontage is black and white, adapted to the style of the forties, but always powerfully expressive in its representation. I do not find one photograph in these series which would cause me interpretative problems, I do not find a picture which would be so deformed, or so ruined that my judgment of what it presents should be impaired. The timeworn looks are therefore only illusory.

Foks and Libera's book is constructed in a rather peculiar manner. Not only does it consist of 63 stories and the same amount of pictures, but the last story is the travesty of the first story. In the first story the messenger screams, while in the last story she is silent. The silence of the messenger in the first story is the reaction to the boys' state of negation (the boys' refutation). The messenger's silence from the last story is a reaction to the affirmative state of the boys (the boys are assenting). There is more. Each story written in a male voice starts with a conditional sentence, such as: *when boys [...], the messenger [...].* In sentences thus constructed only the predicates vary. Yet the subject of the

20 Henri Bergson, *Matter and Memory*, p. 55.

sentence is not a male voice, but female memory. The second sentence always starts with the stubbornly repeated phrase: *She recalls [...]*, so it is She who recalls and not He. But then again, it is not She who says: *I recall [...]*, it is He who constantly states what She is supposed to recall. Therefore, he gives her orders in regard to her memory. To Foks and Libera, memory is by nature the feminine authority. Yet recollection, understood as a kind of activity, is masculine. The masculine subject writes, which means that writing is also the masculine authority. The dissonance between the archive of sensory memory and the symbolic record in the form of sentences is a dissonance separating the two sexes.

What is also important for Foks and Libera is that in the last sentence of each story the messenger glances at a color magazine of the enemy, which contains text, a commentary, so to speak, foreign to the whole story. In a sense, it also contaminates the ethnic purity, the ideological, national memory of the messenger. On the other hand, this foreign text, typical of women's magazines, guides for girls, and psychological counsel gives the girls an element of what we would call today normality. The life of the messenger would have looked like life in those foreign magazines of the enemy, if one day she had not signed up for the unfortunate course – *How to become a messenger with little money?*

It is also important that we understand the most dramatic difference between the messenger's and the boys' activity. It is not just the fact that the messenger is occupied with remembering and the boys with creating events, it is not only the difference of the sexes; it is above all about the question put in the title of the book: *What is the messenger doing?*, to which there is only one reply – She is working hard! The work of memory is nothing else but the work of the messenger. It is interesting that Foks and Libera do not ask – *What are the boys doing?* – they do not ask because the reply in their case is compromising: they are constantly having fun!, at the time moment when the messenger is working hard. Foks's text can mislead us because the text often describes different instances of unfortunate behavior of the messenger, which is a function of the boys' behavior; the messenger screams, remains silent, whistles, jumps, locks herself in a toilet, stares at something, and so on. This kind of behavior would mean that the messenger is generally not occupied with any intentional act, and the least of all with work understood as the very essence of an intentional act. Yet it is she, not he, who works; her work entails registering and storing, it is the work of immanence, it is the work of a prisoner in a labor camp and not a hired hand looking for employment in the open labor market. Hence, she is hidden, unseen, and above all unpaid, as generally is the case with the work of women!

Therefore, Foks's text is built on several oppositions, which are not entirely distinct: masculine (speech) – feminine (memory); one's own (speech/image) –

hostile (writing/print); work (messenger) – play (boys). I am saying that the oppositions are constantly contaminated because the basic political opposition dividing the enemy (Germans printing magazines and flyers) and friend (boys playing and messengers memorizing this playfulness) is to some extent halved by the gender opposition (Do our messengers in a sense seduce German soldiers? And do the magazines of the enemy not seduce our messengers?), and the latter is made even more ambiguous by the opposition between work and play. Moreover, in my estimation boys in Foks's texts are always plural; there is always plenty of boys, they are numerous, they are many; the messenger, on the other hand, is always singular. Foks writes as if he was always writing about one woman; although in Libera's pictures we find different faces, they are different images of one and the same woman! Is it the mother?!

This is the domain of the messenger, this is her work, her effort, everything you would like to know about the messenger and were afraid to discover in Foks and see in Libera. Here she is, seducing German boys, but also erecting monuments for the Polish boys, she is the quintessence of death itself, pure representation, machine which does not know plurality, but reveals herself to the world in numerous masks; here she is whistling, screaming, chanting, silent; here is her inner and outer world; here is her work contrasted with the play of the boys; here are mechanisms governing the contemporary compulsion – ritualism without rituals; here are we ourselves. Here is a map of the struggle of memory with the world, gender, writing, speech, death, the physical and political exteriority. Here is the messenger's work; here is the world which we cannot forget; here are we ourselves embedded in a static form of Plexiglas.

11. Monument

I repeat once more: What is the working-through of memory? Is it the work of remembering, representing, replaying, almost anesthesiological effort of keeping alive that which is gone? Or, quite the opposite: Is it the work of intentionally forgetting, erasing, rejecting, selecting, and courageously allowing the passing of what is past? And perhaps it is a particular unification, a combination of forgetting and remembering, retaining and rejecting, which through this process of arbitrary selection and dramatic montage surprises us in its end result remaining freely associated with the primary reality? We mystify and dramatize our past with the masking memories, but we also de-dramatize, violently remove the stigmata of tragedy through new, more frivolous associations!

Throughout his whole life, Nietzsche called himself a philologist, which means that he demanded from philosophers to learn the philological virtues, that is, caution, patience, subtlety, the art of the nuance. Nietzsche clearly recommends philology as the art of patience, resisting haste and feverish thinking. Yet the very same Nietzsche turns against the time-honored foundations of his own discipline (philology) in his polemical study – *On the Use and Abuse of History for Life.*[21] To Nietsche, the human is an animal which cannot learn to forget and constantly looks back at the past. The human says: "I remember" and is jealous of the animal who can instantly forget and "for whom every moment really dies, sinks back into the night and fog and is extinguished for ever". An animal lives unhistorically: it totally contained in the present, "like a number without any awkward fraction left over"; the animal cannot pretend, does not hide anything and each moment presents itself as what it is. "Perhaps there is nothing more terrible and strange in man's prehistory than his technique of *mnemonics*",[22] notes Nietzsche, who linked every act of memory with horrible pain. On the other hand, to Nietzsche the condition for all action is to forget, and only that one acts who is always without conscience, that is, without memory.

This ambiguity of memory, present in the texts of both Nietzsche and Freud, consisting in the superfluity of memory perceived from the long-term perspective, that is, a maniacal need to archive every event and constitutive inability to forget within what psychology calls long-term memory, and the simultaneous necessity to forget in the short-term perspective, the necessity to erase the waxen boards of sensory memory for the new data, new information, which is not fresh enough, never current enough; is this ambiguous memory dynamics not the best description of the contemporary world, that is, is the addiction to the past (inability to forget) and the need to concentrate on the present which is forced by the pragmatics of action? We are trapped, for better or worse, in strange memory dynamics; therefore, we are characterized by the necessity and the desire to forget, which manifests itself for instance in the idea of a "thick line" and the inability to forget, which returns, for instance, in the "failed project of lustration".

At this moment, I would like ask a rhetorical question which connects the two tendencies: Are the advocates of "remembering" and "forgetting" (the ones who express with intense passion their abandoned wishes and those who in a similarly ambivalent fear run from them) not the victims of the same process, two poles of the same deficit – a deficit of the work of remembering, the work

21 Friedrich Nietzsche (1874-1876), *Untimely Meditations*, trans. R. J. Hollingdale, (Cambridge University Press, Cambridge, 1983), pp. 84-168.

22 Friedrich Nietzsche (1887), *On the Genealogy of Morals*, trans. D. Smith. (Oxford: Oxford University Press, 1996), p. 64.

of memory, the work of cultivation and amelioration, and the victims of mechanical repetition, compulsion, suppressed tradition, tradition lacking traditionalism, tradition which became compulsion? Are we then left with no alternative but to choose between compulsive-obsessive disorder and amnesia?

Is it not the reason why, even in the method, historians' work is stigmatized by two contradictory impulses? The first corresponds to the fragmentary historiography inspired by Walter Benjamin in which the work of the historian is a creative act of remembering, reanimating, or renewed reconnection of a whole broken into pieces, a mental effort which in the process of mending the broken mosaic releases the unfulfilled potential of the future. And the second impulse is inspired by the *Ursprungsphilosophie*, which assumes memory to be a mimetic recollection of the lost, mythical and true origins of phenomena, contained in the fundamentally human experiences. Is then the sole alternative the alternative which separates the story of the fall (*Verfallsgeschichte*) and the genesis (*Ursprungsgeschichte*), which – it is not impossible – are one and the same story seen from different perspectives?

What then should be the goal of the working-through of memory? Should its goal be to construct a monument which would replace and conclude the work of our memories, which in a way should remember for us? Should then the goal of memory be to build, for instance, the monument of the Warsaw Uprising? I doubt it. In our time the history of monuments is a history of machines, which only allows events to happen again usually in the form of pastiche and farce. The weakness of monuments lies above all in their lack of relation to the place in which they are erected; they are merely public icons, traces of memory dissociated from the community frameworks; they are symptoms. Monuments follow the rules of their genre; they do not attempt to convey the truth. Unlike natural ruins, castles or coutry houses, they say nothing about the place in which they stand, manifesting nothing more than strangeness, strangeness of the images, which – to use Libera's expression once more – we can watch in a static form, "as if embedded in Plexiglas".

Should then the goal of the working-through of memory be building "agonistic representations", which according to Walter Benjamin helped the defeated resurface and question the validity of the victors' history? Is it necessary to establish agonistic public space to transmit the competing collective memories, through divisions, in places where the traces of the past have been preserved – the traces of victories, defeats, crimes? Finally, is Libera and Foks's exhibition, entitled *What is the messenger doing?,* or Libera's work entitled *Lego: Concentration Camp,* not such an attempt to build agonistic memory, which is above all internally agonistic, that is, internally divided?

We do not have the answers to all these questions; we do not know who the messenger is, although we probably already know *what she is doing.* Should we fear her work? Is it possible that it results in preserving our images in Plexiglas, just like the bodies of prehistoric insects embedded in amber, in a fossilized mass? Perhaps we are fascinated by amber chambers. Perhaps Plexiglas suffices.

III. Between Kinship and Alienation: Three Fantastic Tales on Man in Nature

Animals are good to think with...

Claude Lévi-Strauss[1]

We think and write for animals themselves. We become animal so that the animal also becomes something else. The agony of a rat or the slaughter of a calf remains present in thought not through pity but as the zone of exchange between man and animal in which something of one passes into the other.

Gilles Deleuze, Felix Guattari[2]

It is all too evident that in the course of the last two centuries these traditional forms of treatment of the animal have been turned upside down by the joint developments of zoological, ethological, biological, and genetic forms of knowledge and the always inseparable techniques of intervention with respect to their object, the transformation of the actual object, its milieu, its world, namely, the living animal.

Jacques Derrida[3]

1. Encounters

I never wanted to become an academic, I have always wanted to be Dr. Dolittle, but life calls for compromises [...] Nevertheless, I managed to enter into some kind of conversation with animals in my life.

Jerzy Axer[4]

Encounters with animals are a part of man's history and archaeology. Yet, the history of these difficult relations remains untold. So far, men have shied away from revealing it for the fear that it might seriously undermine their unique status in the realm of living beings. To this day, that is more than 150 years since the

1 Claude Lévi-Strauss (1962), *Totemism*, trans. R. Needham, (Boston: Beacon Press, 1963).

2 Gilles Deleuze, Felix Guattari, *What Is Philosophy?*, trans. H. Tomlinson, G. Burchell, (Columbia University Press, 1994). p. 109.

3 Jacques Derrida, *The Animal That Therefore I Am (More to Follow)*, trans. David Wills, "Critical Inquiry" 28 (2002). p. 394.

4 *I was accepted by a troop of blue monkeys. On amorous baboon in Łódź, friendly blue monkeys in Kenya, and on days off for animals in Moscow Zoo*, Katarzyna Łukaszewska interviews prof. Jerzy Axer, "Uniwersytet Warszawski", June 2009, no 3 (42). pp. 34-35.

publication of Charles Darwin's famous *On the Origin of Species by Means of Natural Selection, or the Preservation of Favoured Races in the Struggle for Life,* our narcissistic nature calls for special treatment and protection of the exceptional beauty of mankind. We still favour a distinction separating man from all other living beings otherwise classified as material beings. This claim was henceforth justified by theology and further by the emerging faculties jointly referred to as the humanities. Theology granted men the status of the children of God, and the humanities exposed the beauty of language, culture, ethics, technology, and so on, which are all irreducible to a single instrument (organ or organism) known in the living world. Both beliefs, in our unique and inherent status and in our unique instrumentation, imply the need to employ special procedures in order to explain human behaviour. This approach was elaborated in the 19th century and came to be recognized as *Geisteswissenschaften.*

It is not my intention to reconstruct the history of our encounters nor to follow the ways man has undertaken to recover the sense of belonging to the animal world. I am also far from advocating the final naturalization of the social sciences. Our propensity for the naturalization of cultural and mental facts is probably equivalent to the propensity for the culturalization of nature. Lévi-Strauss lectured that totemism is a special case of the general problem of classification and an example of a recognized process of role attribution which benefits a given category in order to develop social classification. Totemism is a form of classification establishing a formal logical equivalence between the community of wildlife species and the world of social groups.[5] A classification system, which allows a relationship with some animal species to be established, is thus a system where nature is anthropomorphic and is perfectly complemented by another classification system which prescribes the division of body and mental functions according to natural facts, and therefore one that naturalizes culture. This observation brings me to my main thesis, namely, that the naturalization of culture and the anthropomorphisation of nature are just two poles of one and the same process.

Let me leave out a detailed reconstruction of terms and conditions of both of these approaches; I will instead focus on the most distinctive, in my opinion, turns in the plot, with reference to literature rather than science. I would like to start with a closer look at the portrayal of the animal as seen by Alice in Lewis Carroll's stories; we will then deal with the stories spun by Lemuel Gulliver in Jonathan Swift's novels, and A *Fantastic Zoology* by Jorge Luis Borges. The selection, although arbitrary, is not coincidental. In a nutshell, my basic intuition concerning

5 Claude Lévi-Strauss (1962), *The Savage Mind*, trans. G. Weidenfeld, Nicolson Ltd, Oxford: Oxford University Press, 1996.

each of these literary works is that the experience of nature gained by Alice on the other side of the mirror is infantile, characteristic of pre-Enlightenment experience of an animal, the experience gained by Lemuel Gulliver is the experience of an enlightened man, reared and educated by readings of Hobbes, Descartes, and Newton, and the experience of nature in Borges is nature fully absorbed by culture, nature present only in culture, which is now becoming the only experience of nature available to us who live in the age of late modernity.

The narrative of Lewis Carroll's famous *Through the Looking-Glass, and What Alice Found There* provides ground for a confrontation with the childhood experience of animality. In conclusion of the third chapter of *Traumdeutung,* Freud is forced to confess: *Wovon die Tiere träumen, weiss Ich nich.* Indeed, Freud does not seem to know much about it, and he is even not trying to learn, as to him of a much greater importance are the dreams of humans, and specifically how humans dream of animals, or how their dreams focus on the figure of an animal and how they are later cast as animal characters.[6] Let me treat the narrative of *Through the Looking-Glass* as a dream in which children's friendship with the animal world is fully disclosed. Disclosed here are also all the fears and hopes for this world. To a child, an animal is a fascinating creature, undefeated, supernatural, uncontrollable, and as such it is a model being a child may dream of becoming. For Alice, to follow the rabbit is, above all, to think like a rabbit, and thus become a rabbit.

The history of our encounters with animals entered a new phase in 1726 with the publication of *Travels into Several Remote Nations of the World in Four Parts by Lemuel Gulliver.* The book written by Jonathan Swift heralds a new type of men-to-nature relations. *Travels into Several Remote Nations of the World in Four Parts* can be read as both a fantasy novel and an 18th century satire on English society, but above all it is also a song of the Enlightenment, the age when nature was already approached with ambivalence. Kinship between man and nature had been already forgotten and nature became the object of conquest and conflicting emotions. An exalted human nature did not allow man to recognize the relationship with the fallen nature, governed by the properties of matter or gravitational pull. On the other hand, this nature seemed to be the only hope, the only object of adoration, the only space in which man could exist beyond the limits of the categorical imperative and beyond the state, a man that

6 "What animals dream of I do not know. A proverb for which I am indebted to one of my pupils professes to tell us, for it asks the question: 'What does the goose dream of?' and answers: 'Of maize'. The whole theory that the dream is the fulfillment of a wish is contained in these two sentences" (Sigmund Freud (1900), *The Interpretation of Dreams*, [in:] *The Standard Edition of the Complete Psychological Works of Sigmund Freud*, Volume IV, ed. James Strachey, (London: Hogarth Press, 1957), p. 45).

could exist more as a natural being, and less as a political one. Nature, a common theme for writers of Swift's sort had therefore neared a utopia.

Finally, we will address *Fantastic Zoology* by Jorge Luis Borges. in order to see the relation of the modern (postmodern) man to nature. Borges, a man of the library and a being separated from physical reality by language, can only dream about nature, thus providing a case of a man infinitely remote from nature, infinitely discouraged by nature, and infinitely challenging nature. Borges cannot acknowledge the Darwinian vision of nature in which living beings compete with each other for finite resources and use innovation to fight each other with new survival (adaptation) tools in order to enable a better (more efficient) operation in the world, that is, self-replicating their character. The vision of nature as a spectacle in which all species of living and the dead remain in the fight of all against all, Borges cannot accept either. The vision of a world in which the only stake in the game of reproduction and survival is to leave behind as many offspring (copies) as possible is for Borges full of despair and truly sad, and a reason why he finds interest in extinct species. In a sense, Borges is dealing with monoindividual species which are unable to self-replicate. This brings us to the true singularity of man.

For Borges. unacceptable is a vision where all beings live in harmony and are programmed by a divine preestablished order. For Borges, nature has nothing of the utopian, and it is certainly not a place where a man could seek refuge. So what is the nature Borges is dreaming of? It bears similarity to the way Greeks saw it, which is a metaphor of human fate and burial of human desires. The list of fantastic creatures assembled by Borges in his *Book of Imaginary Beings*, that is, Behemoth, Elves, Phoenix, Unicorn, Minotaur, Nymphs, Eater of Shadows, The Grey Ones, The Wooden Man, Hare Moon, Animal Dreamlife by Poe, and so on and so foth, is a list of creatures unable to replicate: they are creations of human imagination, or, if you like, hallucinations. They tell us something about human imagination and little about the world in which the imagination is supposed to dwell. Borges attracts postmodern man to the realm of fantasy and opens up the gates to the pre-Oedipal phase in experiencing world. The Oedipal phase begins in ancient Rome.

Cicero attributed the following to Scipio:

> And so the state *[res publica]* – the African went on – this is for the people *[res populi]*. However, as to the people, it is certainly not every crowd of people gathered in any form. Nevertheless, the big crowd, united by the recognition of the same rights and the benefit resulting from the common existence.[7]

---

7 Mark Tullius Cicero, *De Res Publica* (*On the Republic*), [in:] *The Political Works of Marcus Tullius Cicero: Comprising his Treatise on the Commonwealth; and his Treatise on the Laws*, trans. F. Barham, (London: Edmund Spettigue, 1941), p. 25.

This presumption is the subject of St. Augustine's critique in *De civitate Dei*, where St. Augustine claims that the Roman republic was never *res populi* due to the lack of true justice. St. Augustine writes:

> This, then, is the place where I should fulfil the promise gave in the second book of this work, and explain, as briefly and clearly as possible, that if we are to accept the definitions laid down by Scipio in Cicero's *De Republica*, there never was a Roman republic; for he briefly defines a republic as the good of the people. Moreover, if this definition were true, there never was a Roman republic, for the people's good was never attained among the Romans. For the people, according to his definition, is an assemblage associated by a common acknowledgment of right and by a community of interests. And what he means by a common acknowledgment of right he explains at large, showing that a republic cannot be administered without justice.[8]

This issue – whether there was the Roman republic or any good of the people, is a paraphrase of a principal problem throughout modern political philosophy: How can a man liberate himself from nature? Hobbes, Rousseau, Kant, Hegel, Schmitt, Freud, and Strauss either demonize the state of nature to encourage mankind to submit to the will of the law and state violence, or they demonize the world of culture in order to indicate a new object of human sighs and dreams – the virgin nature (natural law). The authors mentioned above, Lewis Carroll, Jonathan Swift, and Jorge Luis Borges. – share with us the uncertainty related to the place of man between nature and culture. If there were a Roman republic, if the people's good was attained, perhaps there would be no place for the uncertainty. Politics exists because there was never the Roman republic and people's good was never realized.

I am wondering if any of the three visions of man in nature will appeal to the sensitivity of Jerzy Axer. Will he accept the thesis that the Roman republic did not exist, and people's good has never become reality? Is he able to accept the thesis that the object of his dreams – university understood not as a crowd of people gathered in any manner but as the assemblage of men associated by a common acknowledgment of right and by a community of interests of people – has never been realized and may never be? Is he, an expert on Cicero, more willing to approve of naturalization of man or would he rather opt for the cultivation of a disposition to culturalize monkeys? In Africa, among fellow blue monkeys, he may be seeking traces of man in monkey, but in Europe he is bewildering fellow men with his famed roaring ringtone. Well then, anthropomorphisation or naturalisation, what is his preferred method? When observing blue monkeys, is he thinking more about our animal past or our human future? What does he think of the emergence

8 St. Augustine, *City of God*, trans. H. Bettenson, (London: Penguin Classics, 2003), p. 234.

of speech? Does he see in it a sign of progress on the evolutionary path, or a semantic and aesthetic dead end?

Having the advantage of observing his behaviour in the academia, shamefully not in Africa, I noticed both tendencies, similarly developed and strong: the tendency to naturalize culture and the tendency to culturalize nature. However, a man versed in and holding ancient Roman tradition in high esteem should be prone to think of culture as a fruit of war and domination. In this tradition, culturalization is always one step behind conquest, and the work of culture only supplements the work of nature. On the other hand, human language, and especially its most outstanding achievements such as *style and composition of speech* by Cicero, expressed for example in his work *De oratore*, signal a deep cut throughout the animated world separating sound from speech-making word, the epitome of human genius. The little that I know about his impenetrable human nature gives me the sense that Jerzy Axer is open to accept the views on human advancement through language as expressed by Wilhelm von Humboldt, who used to loftily refer to language as "mental exhalation of a nationally individual life", and saw in it a tool "deeply entangled in the spiritual evolution of mankind".

In section 5 of his famous work *On Language, On the Diversity of Human Language Construction and its Influence on the Mental Development of the Human Species*, Humboldt outlines human development which contains the ground of progress of each generation at any time. Here we find not only this but also interesting remarks on blue monkeys and all other species combined, plus a fine description of our jubilee himself. First, examining human nature against that of the whole species, Humboldt reestablishes the criterion of division of the world into that of men and that of all other species. What makes man different from nature are the directions man follows. While all species succumb to self-cultivation, man's life is naturally conditioned by another direction, which Humboldt refers to as shaping of the world. By means of the opposition between the two criss-crossing and closely-linked tendencies, man forms yet another direction "on which the mightiest and holiest depend". It is thanks to this inner determination that language exerts a special influence. It takes a different form in a people that gladly pursues the solitary paths of withdrawn contemplation, and in nations which chiefly have the need of the mediating understanding for external concerns. For language must first be introduced, by a still obscure and undeveloped feeling, into the spheres upon which it is to pour forth its light. How this broken-off existence of the individual is united with the advancing development of the species, into a region perhaps unknown to us, remains an impenetrable mystery. But the operation of the sense of this impenetrability is pre-eminently an important factor in the inner cultivation of the individual, in that "it awakens the reverential awe towards a thing unknown, which still remains behind after everything knowable has vanished". In the following section Humboldt inspects the combined output of individuals and nation in reference to language. He believes that language is the work of nations, but the terms of the language are still self-creations of individuals. Language can be therefore considered as a world-view that rests upon the collective power of man. "Nothing can be excluded from it, since it embraces everything" – he remarks thus substantiating his vision of a totality of all sounds allowing for its free development by individuals. Totality of language constitutes "the body of its products" which is "a relatively dead mass" comparable to "an inexhaustible storehouse in which the mind can always discover something new". Unable to define the origins of speech contained within sounds, Humboldt only describes it as a "sound-form and the use made of it to designate objects and connect thoughts".[9] To sum this up, language gives us the opportunity to escape nature, but it also allows us to penetrate and master nature with a designed system of names and nomenclature, which designate and differentiate things.

Let me now return to the three types of relations of men to animals and the three stories by Lewis Carroll, Jonathan Swift, and Jorge Luis Borges. We will follow Alice on her way down to the rabbit hole, Gulliver on his journey across the ocean, and Borges in his search for the dragons at the frontiers of human imagination. I am hoping to take this opportunity to expand one of the issues present in Humboldt and recently capturing my attention, namely that of the limits of language against human freedom to exert special influence through language. Our point of departure is on the one hand the recognition of human potential to go beyond language and reach spaces otherwise unavailable to one's experience and on the other the constraints of the freedom to express one's thoughts in language. We still know little of – should we say "wild" – imagination of animals and still not much of animals' dreams, not to mention that the humanity as we know it in the Western world has never developed interest in dreaming, unless one was forced to make a confession to a shrink or when one's imagination got hooked to the possibility of "expanding awareness" through practicing traditional Mesoamerican shamanism with Don Juan or is dedicated to lucid dreaming in the hope for the experience of flying in the skies. Those wishing to satisfy their hidden desires but need to keep money tight and should be warned that dreams are more often serving another function, that of informing the conscious mind of what there is in the cellar. We may one day

9 Wilhelm von Humboldt (1836), *On Language. On the Diversity of Human Language Construction and its Influence on the Mental Development of the Human Species*, trans. P. Heath. (Cambridge: Cambridge University Press, 1999), p. 324.

denounce the figure of the Roman republic on the grounds that it never existed, but there will always be mighty visionaries dreaming out the future shape of the world and striving to turn their dreams into reality. I believe such is the case of Jerzy Axer.

2. Being accepted by a troop of blue monkeys

I think that a zoo can be seen as a theater, where the director and the producer is the city hosting the zoo.

Jerzy Axer[10]

Alice is our first medium to the animal kingdom. Since she finds cultural activities boring and seeks refuge in nature, an encounter with animals is only a matter of time. One day, sitting on the riverbank with her sister (thus involved in kinship) she notices a clothed White Rabbit carrying a pocket watch. This is her first encounter with the animals. As we shall soon learn, the seemingly anthropomorphic creature is in fact a wizard. Contrary to reason, Alice is unafraid of it and out of curiosity she follows the rabbit down the rabbit hole. There she falls a long way past cupboards and book-shelves full of strange objects. After a safe landing she finds herself in a long hall where on a glass table she finds a golden key. She picks it up and starts looking for doors it would fit in. She then finds a little door and looks through the keyhole to discover a beautiful garden behind.

The garden is obviously nature within culture, the essence of what man makes of nature – to shape it the way he likes. Another symbolic thing is the watch carried by White Rabbit which hails the beginning of problems with timing. For Alice, time is from now on going to come out of the framework and will have only accelerated, or slowed down its pace. From now on nothing will take place on time. Time in nature and time in culture are two completely different things. The former is that of growing and dying while the latter is the time of fun and work, of intimate life at home and public life at school or workplace. Any attempt to correlate these two will lead to total desynchronisation.

It is time, or rather desynchronized time, which entraps our bodies. After experiencing turbulences in her time travel when her body first grows nine feet high and then is only ten inches high, sizes so inadequate to the environment she is in, there follows a series of encounters with animals. On her way she

10 *I was accepted by a troop of blue monkeys.* Katarzyna Łukaszewska interviews prof. Jerzy Axer.

confronts a mouse, a pigeon, a parrot, a duck, an eagle, a lizard, a caterpillar, a dormouse, and a turtle. Of course, these creatures are not, strictly speaking, animals, but creations of culture embodied in living beings. In nature, these animals would above all struggle to survive, but instead, they are all animated by humans and dependent on humans, who only pretend to be nature in order to express what in a standardized social life is impossible to express. Alice meets, therefore, people who, just like during Carnival in Brazil, are dressed up as creations of nature. However, they did not hide their true human character, but instead fully exposed their most secret characteristics and passions, finally saying something very true about themselves.

Nature seen through the eyes of Alice exists only as language, language which informs us of culture, which only pretends to be nature. We should be warned then that all culture does in this respect must be awry, vague, or utterly false. Regardless of how eccentric it sounds, it is the nature that allows Alice expand her awareness and consciousness, and approach a new kind of language which reveals more than it conceals. The situation Alice is in is not that of Cartesian subject, which could be presented as follows: [[Entity/Language] Nature], but rather: [Entity [Language/Nature]]. Language, at least the language of what is not concealed in Alice, is on the side of nature, not culture. This is the kind of language envisaged by Hans-Georg Gadamer, who provided comment on the work of already quoted Wilhelm von Humboldt:

> Not only is the world world only insofar as it comes into language, but language, too, has its real being only in the fact that world presents in it. Thus, that language is originally human means at the same time that man's being-in-the-world is primordially linguistic. We will have to investigate the relation between language and world in order to attain the horizon adequate to the fact that hermeneutic experience is verbal in nature.[11]

We will have to investigate the relation between language and the world to find proper language and proper world to describe the experience (occurrences) of animality in language, and language in the animal world.

If language in Alice's world belongs to the world as much as the world belongs to language, and if the world is world only when it presents itself in language, and language is language only when it presents the world, then, it is hardly surprising that the names of animals in this world/language reveal only the real names of people who are not linguistic conventions, but the signatures that are an inherent part of the object, which is not only named but at the same time described. *The Mock Turtle* is obviously not a turtle, but a person who

11 Hans-Georg Gadamer (1960), *Truth and Method,* trans. J. Weinsheimer and D. G. Marshall, (New York: Continuum, 1998).

moves at the speed of a turtle and is as calm as a turtle. The same is true of other animals/people. Alice, like a contemporary evolutionary geneticist, is convinced that natural phenomena, in particular biological phenomena, are in fact textual. Thus she discovers the parts of the text of Nature.

Of course, treating the perceived sensory properties of the animal and vegetal world as excerpts of the text and discovering therein "inscriptions", or "signatures" (signs), Alice makes incorrect diagnoses (as false as those made by "the savage mind" and "totemic thought"), but since she is not equipped with improved methods permitting her to locate a meaningful element where it is, that is at a "micro" level, she still recognizes it, but so to speak – as if through a fog. It would be only a little exaggeration to say, that in order to develop the information theory man needed the discovery Alice had made, namely that the world of information is only a fragment of the natural world. When the validity of the transition from the laws of nature to the laws of information was confirmed, it implied also the validity of the transition in the opposite direction, that which allows people to come closer to the laws of nature by means of information. This is the way Alice has chosen when she entered the rabbit hole, and like a detective started searching for proper inscriptions instead of nature or human culture, which once refused us access.

3. Zoo as an asylum

To me, zoo is a place of asylum.

Jerzy Axer[12]

The Adventures of Lemuel Gulliver differ much from those of Alice. First, they come from two different periods in history, and second, their protagonists are of different ages. The adventures of Alice take place "before time", and Gulliver's are set "in time". Borges, as we shall soon see, comes"after time".

The subject of temporality of the experiencing being calls for a reference to Martin Heidegger and his considerations on time and language. In *Being and Time* Heidegger began with positioning language in the analytics of *Dasein*, but in *On the Way To Language* he came to positioning *Dasein* in language and saw in it the relation of all relations: "[l]anguage is, as world-moving Saying, the relation of all relations".[13] Despite the fact that in *Being and Time* we read:

12 *I was accepted by a troop of blue monkeys*. Katarzyna Łukaszewska interviews prof. Jerzy Axer.

13 Martin Heidegger (1959), *On the Way To Language*, trans. P. D. Hertz, (New York: Harper and Row, 1971), p. 43.

> [d]iscourse is the Articulation of intelligibility. Therefore, it underlines both interpretation and assertion. That which can be Articulated in interpretation, and thus even more primordially in discourse, is what we have called 'meaning'.[14]

Sometimes, however, we should allow discourse to be the articulation of the unintelligibility of being, and in particular of its position in discourse not yet recognized as discourse. Such is the case of Gulliver.

Gulliver is born the third of five sons of a middle-income property owner in Nottingham. He is therefore, like Alice, entangled in kinship. Unlike Alice, who competes only with her younger sister, Gulliver has to challenge two older brothers. The course of his early life is characteristic of that of a young middle-class man living in 18th century England. His profession is determined by his father, and when educated, he is commanded to be a surgeon on a ship named *Swallow*, while upon his return to his motherland he is advised to "alter his condition" and marry. He then accepts the position of a surgeon on *Antelope* and again makes several voyages on different ships, all bearing the names of animals. However, these are not the wondrous names of Alice's Wonderland. The names of ships he embarks on are dead, for in his world language may come alive only if it is foreign enough, the Other.

At this point, we should be able to put forward a fundamental question concerning Gulliver's travels, namely, what makes Gulliver a traveler at all? Why does he travel to distant lands and risk his life instead of staying home with his wife and practicing his profession? The only answer plausible to me is that through travels Gulliver seeks refugee from the curse of programmed time. To escape the bonds of time he simply needs to throw himself out of the context. So far, the course of his life was either decided for him or advised to him, and he simply obeyed and followed. In a sense, upon reaching maturity, Gulliver had reached the limit of his local existence. Everything concerning his social self had at this stage already been set in motion, and things like coincidence, adventure, event and occurrence had been eliminated from his life and language. What was left to him was only boring repetition. This is precisely the situation of a subject of the Enlightenment, conforming to the drama of causality and predictability. Gulliver is thus longing for otherness, but does he really find it? As I see it, it is Gulliver's personal drama that no matter where he reaches, everywhere he takes the breath of England.

His first adventure kicks off in Bristol, in May 1699 on the Antelope heading for the South Sea. The voyage is very prosperous until it ends during the passage to East India. The Antelope goes down regardless of its crew's

14 Martin Heidegger (1927), *Being and Time,* trans. J. Stambaugh, (Albany: State University of New York Press, 1996), p. 54.

labour. Only Gulliver and six other companions make it to the lifeboat to row for life. However, the waves have no mercy. It takes half an hour for the men to give up, and there comes the final flurry from the north. The boat is overturned and Gulliver is the only survivor. He gets to the shore, drinks half a bottle of brandy, falls asleep. Upon waking, he finds his arms, legs, and even hair strongly fastened to the ground. He then feels several slender ligatures across his body and a general rumour. Then on his chest he observes several tiny men with bows who give him food and drink with a specially constructed wooden scaffold. He soon falls asleep again and upon waking finds himself chained in a cell. That same day, he is greeted by the court and the emperor of Lilliput, who mercifully chooses to keep the giant alive, and commissions his men to ensure his comfort during stay.

Over time, thanks to his mild disposition, the giant gains favour of the majesty. The locals get used to him and start calling him Man-Mountain. Gulliver starts taking lessons in Lilliputian and studies the strange customs of the locals, their language and culture. He soon obtains permission to tour the country and visits the capital of the country – Mildendo. When he requests his freedom, the emperor decrees a mandate imposing on Gulliver an alliance against their enemies on the island of Blefuscu, and an obligation to do utmost to destroy their fleet, only now preparing to make a descent. Gulliver learns about political divisions among Lilliputians and recognizes two opposing political camps – Tramecksan and Slamecksan. He then decides to prevent the invasion alone, by an extraordinary stratagem. It takes him half an hour to get to the enemy's harbour where he hooks a cable to each ship and undisturbed swims back to Lilliput with the whole bunch of cables and ships. There, upon the spot, he is made a Nardac, that is, he is granted the highest title of honour.

The emperor is very pleased with the victory but commands Gulliver to go back and take the rest of the enemy's ships into his ports, destroy the enemy's capital and kingdom (thus making him the only emperor) and enslave its people to further expand his command. Gulliver refuses, and provides arguments drawn from the topics of policy and justice, which seem reasonable to the wisest part of the ministry. When Gulliver's case is still pending, there is a fire in the imperial palace, and as there is no water to distinguish it, he bravely uses his own urine and once again saves the empire. The way the fire is put out is not so acclaimed by the emperor, who soon reveals the severe punishment he is hoping to administer to Gulliver for his previous disgraceful disobedience: the majesty wishes to put out his eyes. Informed of these plans, Gulliver decides to not to wait any longer for the enforcement of this sentence, and flees to Blefusku where he is received with honors by a local monarch. By accident, he finds a broken boat, and repairs it with the help of the king's subordinates and leaves the island on the 24th of September

1701, provided with water and food supplies. After several days, he notices an English ship which brings him immediate rescue. Since his stories seem too fantastic to the crew, he presents miniature animals he has taken with him – sheep and cattle. Gulliver returns to his homeland in April 1702. After two months, he undertakes another voyage and embarks on a trade ship named Adventure.

Now that we know the story, it is time to clarify its meaning. Gulliver is a being who nurtures the conviction that a man is a being who at every moment of his existence feels in danger of dehumanization and is afraid to lose his convenient status of something more than just a living being. Gulliver lives in fear that without the state which grants to a man unique status of a citizen, a man lives only a bare life, and thus he is a beast. Alice experiences humanization of nature, and Gulliver experiences naturalization of man. Their experiences are symmetrical and complementary. In all his travels, Gulliver experiences the transition into the state of nature, and therein becomes a bare life and a source of ambivalent emotions. As a bare life, he can be both a hero and a monster. In both cases, he is a being barred from language and becomes an outlaw.

Employing the phrasebook of Giorgio Agamben, Lemuel Gulliver is a refugee. He is then a hero of the fifth chapter of Hannah Arendt's famous book *Imperialism* dedicated to this issue, bearing the ominous title *Twilight of the Nation State and the End of Human Rights.* In her narrative on the roots of anti-Semitism Arendt relates the fate of human rights with the fate of the modern nation-state in such a way that the twilight of the latter necessarily implies the former obsolete.

> The conception of human rights – by Arendt – based upon the assumed existence of a human being as such, broke down at the very moment when those who professed to believe in it were for the first time confronted with people who had indeed lost all other qualities and specific relationships – except that they were human.[15]

In the nation-state, the so-called sacred and inalienable rights of man prove to be completely devoid of protection when it becomes impossible to determine their rights as a citizen of the state.

What Gulliver experiences is that life exposed to death is the primary element of political life, not ordinary natural life. Bare life is neither *bios* nor *dzoē* as the two belong to an indistinguishable sphere where they overlap and exclude another, and both are mutually constitutive. The sovereign is the one to whom all are potentially *homines sacri* and *homo sacer* is the one to whom all are potentially sovereigns. Bare life is thus the most primitive life form to enter political life and the category of *homo sacer* specifies the type of primary

15 Hannah Arendt (1951), *The Origins of Totalitarianism*, (New York: Schocken, 2004), p. 299.

political relations. Life is bare only when it is captured in a sovereign exception, just as Gulliver's bare life is captured by Liliputians. It is an important observation that back home Gulliver is a doctor. Back home he is a sovereign, that is a subject enjoying full life. However, when overseas, his experience is limited to that of a subject to sovereign power, and thus is more corporal.[16]

Here we observe a parallel between Hobbes and Johnathan Swift. Hobbes' state of nature does not necessarily precede the establishment of the state, but it functions just as a state of exception – the internal principle of the State. State of nature is not a state of war of all against all, but a state where each and everyone constitutes bare life to another. The state envisaged by Hobbes, that of a man-wolf, is a state where man is indistinguishable from man-wolf – and thus is contained within "the sphere of werewolf"; and this is where Gulliver belongs outside England. Werewolf is neither natural life nor social life, but bare life. *Homo homini lupus* operates as a political structure of a simultaneous inclusion and exclusion of peace guarded by police (*homo homini deus).* The Establishment of the State is therefore not a single event that takes place once and for good, but it happens all the time through sovereign decision-making and takes form of establishing an exception. This relates directly to life, but not to the free will of citizens. In Gulliver's experience, life becomes a political fact; it is a sphere where transitions between man and animal and nature and culture take place. Thus, the relationship of exclusion unites life and sovereign power, and the basis for political equality is the possibility of being killed.

4. Baboon interested in girls

> *I have very intense memory of a zoo caretaker approaching on a bike and shouting at a baboon: "Again, again, again!". The baboon had jumped out of the playground and was chasing my mum down the alley. Back then I didn't yet understand it, but over time I realized that the baboon was simply interested in girls and the caretaker often had to catch him.*
>
> Jerzy Axer[17]

In the preface to his *Fantastic Zoology* Borges.. remarks:

> The title of this book would justify the inclusion of Prince Hamlet, of the point, of the line, of the surface, of n-dimensional hyperplanes and hypervolumes, of all generic terms, and perhaps of each one of us and of the godhead. In brief, the sum of

---

16 Giorgio Agamben, *Homo Sacer: Sovereign Power and Bare Life*, trans. D. Heller-Roazen, (Stanford University Press, Stanford, 1998).

17 *I was accepted by a troop of blue monkeys*. Katarzyna Łukaszewska interviews prof. Jerzy Axer.

> all things – the universe: We have limited ourselves, however, to what is immediately suggested by the words imaginary beings; we have compiled a handbook of the strange creatures conceived through time and space by the human imagination.[18]

For Borges, zoology, therefore, is the theory of "imaginary beings". Despite this diversity that allows the convention selected by Borges, his imagination is essentially inhabited by a single creature, a creature igniting his imagination as no other, a creature essentially trapped within this imagination, part man and part bull, usually with head of a bull on the body of a man, the one and only, legendary Minotaur *(Μινώταυρος)*.

Let me briefly recall that Minotaur was the offspring of the coupling between Pasiphaë, wife of King Minos of Crete, and the Cretan Bull with whom she fell madly in love out of punishment administered to her husband by Poseidon after he sent to Minos a snow-white bull and was expecting to have it returned as sacrifice. Minotaur is, therefore, the fruit of broken promises, wrongly recognized desires and excessive greed. Minos closed Minotaur in a labyrinth designed by Daedalus and located just below the palace in Konossos. When Minos defeated his main enemy – the Athenians, he demanded that every nine years they send seven unwed girls and seven youths as sacrifice to Minotaur. Minotaur devoured only two "supplies" of young flesh since in the third there came Theseus, the assassin. This courageous young man won the heart of Minos's young daughter Ariadne, who presented him with a ball of thread to ensure he can get back to her if successful.

In this story we have a selection of characters – Daedalus, Theseus, Ariadne. We also have the most vivid symbols of kinship and symbols of heroic attempts to break the bonds of nature – a labyrinth, half-animal/half-man, bestiality. Interesting, however, is the relationship in which our heroes get involved when they oppose each other. Since language is, "as world-moving Saying, the relation of all relations", by discovering relations between those heroes we also discover their language. In this language Daedalus is not only someone who helps Pasiphae enter into sodomy with the bull (and in this sense, the mental father of Minotaur), but also an avowed antagonist of Theseus. Daedalus opposes Theseus by designing a habitat for the fruit of human kinship with nature, that is, Minotaur. Daedalus, therefore, is someone who wants to preserve the human relationship with nature; Theseus, on the contrary, wants to sever and frustrate this kinship. Just as Oedipus liberates Thebes from the curse of Sphinx, Theseus liberates Athens from the obligation to provide offering to Minotaur, as

18 Jorge Luis Borges, *Fantastic Zoology. Book of Imaginary Beings,* trans. A. Hurley, (New York: Zone, 1989), p. 5.

imposed by Minos. Tauromachy destroys the evidence of man's sexual crimes and liberates society from the obsession of sex. It makes obsolete the circular process of restoring its consistency by violence and reconciliation.

The fantastic creatures listed and catalogued by Borges – Behemoth, Elves, Phoenix, Unicorn, Nymphs, Eater of Shadows, The Grey Ones, The Wooden Man, Hare Moon, Animal Dream life by Poe, and others, are modern incarnations of Minotaur. The thing is that not only the creatures Borges wants to talk about are imagined, but also those who brought those beings to life are inventions on their own. Borges tells us: as far as a man makes up and invents, he is himself made up and invented, and thus different from what is natural. To Borges, the Roman republic existed and the good of the nation was realized, but only as a community of imaginative beings involved in imagining.

In a beautiful but now rarely read text *From Fairy Tales to Science Fiction* Roger Caillois says that we should make a clear distinction between fairy tales and fiction. For in fairy tales enchantment is taken for granted and magic is the rule, and therefore, there is no disruption between this world and the real one, whereas in the fantastic, the stability of the world is disrupted, and its seemingly strict and immutable laws are put to a halt for the supernatural and transgressive elements to take effect. Fantasy "manifests a scandal, a fissure, an unexpected, almost unbearable, encroachment upon the real world".[19] Caillois's basic intuition is simple: a fairy tale takes place in the world where spells are natural and magic is the rule. A supernatural element is natural in fairy tales, since it is inherent to the climate of their reality. In fiction (fantastic zoology), the exception becomes a dangerous intervention, undermining the stability of the world, and thus it is an impossible curiosity entering the world of necessity. Exception (a miracle/accident/emergent incident) is then a state of exception in imagination. An imagined creature constitutes bare life of imagination, a being captured in sovereign exception of fantastic life.

The work of Borges appears after man renounced his kinship with nature, and restricted his imagination. This world knows that "there was never the Roman republic", and even more: that the Roman republic existed only as a postulate of imagination. It is not only that we do not recognize the reality of Minotaur, Behemoth, Elves, Phoenix, Unicorn, Nymphs, The Wooden Man, the point being that if we saw them in reality it would be a rape of our imagination so violent (so sovereign) that we would have to react to with a phobia. Here we have sovereign existence, which is reborn only in itself and beyond this existence. We are so enchanted with the spell of knowledge that the magic of imagination triggers in us only the fear of magic as such.

---

19 Roger Caillois, *Anthologie du Fantastique*, Tome I, (Paris: Gallimard, 1966).

5. Caretaker at a zoo

Since childhood I was interested in animals, I even wanted to become a caretaker at a zoo.

Jerzy Axer[20]

Is it possible to talk about communication between man and animal differently than Lewis Carroll, Jonathan Swift, Jorge Luis Borges? Are we able to see something other in an animal than a metaphor for human life or human characters? Are we able to see animal life for anything different than a flying carpet that will allow us to rise into the sky and find a world different from that in which bare life is caught in the logic of exception, and, finally, in which there is no animal known to Darwin, but a space colonized by fantastic creatures which nature never gave the chance to exist? And finally, is Jerzy Axer ready to look at the natural world from one of the three perspectives (monoculars) outlined (designed) herein, or rather reject all the three as alien to him?

I presume that Jerzy Axer would not mind repeating after Humboldt that even if man may go beyond language, and even if he is more than the language he mastered and what he can express in it, he must still capture in a word the elusive spirit, and he still must make use of words as a base if he wants to keep reaching beyond it further. I should also think he would eagerly acclaim the view of Cicero that "people are by no means any crowd of people gathered by any means, but their great crowd, united by the recognition of the same rights and the benefit resulting from the common existence". But looking at the blue monkeys in the African jungle would he not have to make the same confession as St. Augustine, who first observed that "there was never the Roman republic"? And when listening to the birds singing, would he not have to take the risk and agree for the time being with Heidegger's assertion that "language is the ratio of all ratios, the relationship of all relationships"? And if that were so, would he not attest our doubts as to where in a man nature is, and also, where the proper place for a man in nature is? Surely one day we will have to trace the relationship of language and the world to find a suitable and appropriate language to describe a world of experience (events) of animality in the language and the language in the animal world. We surely do not know much of what animals dream of, but we do know of what men dream. They dream that they are not animals, that they can go beyond language, and that there was the Roman republic.

20 *I was accepted by a troop of blue monkeys*. Katarzyna Łukaszewska interviews prof. Jerzy Axer.

IV. Either Thinking or Art

Painting is philosophy.

Leonardo da Vinci[1]

For me, art is no excuse for reality. It is another reality, which is not secondary, compared to 'real' reality. For me, an artist is not somebody who cleans the mirror in order to achieve a bright reflection of what we can see in the mirror. To be more precise: by separating art from so-called reality, I am not trying to say that artists are not at all involved in or responsible for what is happening around them. On the contrary, we all are. We are involved in, and share the responsibility for the world. As human beings, on the same level as others.

Jarosław Kozłowski[2]

How is the pleasure-ego constituted? The subject, just like the external world, is split into pleasurable and unpleasurable parts. Starting from this situation, a new arrangement is made wherein the subject coincides with all that is pleasurable and the world with all that is unpleasurable. This new distribution is achieved by means of an introjection of the portion of the objects in the external world which are sources of pleasure and a projection outwards of whatever is a cause of unpleasure within. The subject's new position allows him to be defined as a 'purified pleasure-ego', all unpleasure now being located outside him.

Jean Laplanche, Jean-Bertrand Pontalis[3]

1. Coming to know each other

Jarosław Kozłowski's work could have remained silent and inaccessible or even alien to me forever. Jarosław Kozłowski himself could have remained for me but another enigmatic figure looming in the catalogue of contemporary aesthetic transgressions. I could have had nothing to say about Jarosław Kozłowski, could have not even sensed his presence and could have not included him in the ontology of my social world. This unawareness and oversight would obviously impoverish me and stand as proof of my general ignorance. Surely Kozłowski

1 Leonardo Da Vinci (1270) *Treatise on Painting*, trans. and ed. A. P. McMahon, (Princeton, New York: Princeton University Press, 1956).

2 Jarosław Kozłowski, Audun Eckhoff, *A Conversation*, Terskel (Threshold: Museet for Samtidskunst, Oslo, no. 15, 1995), p. 46.

3 Jean Laplanche, Jean-Bertrand Pontalis, *The Language of Psychoanalysis*, trans. D. Nicholson-Smith, with an introd. by Daniel Lagache, (London: Hogarth Press, 1973), p. 320.

fares better without me than I do without him. And I mention my own awareness of the exceptional phenomenon whose name is 'Jarosław Kozłowski' only because it seems a plain miracle to me.

When Kozłowski spoke to me for the first time, it was in a critical, even aggressive voice. I was chairing a faculty meeting at the Department of Pedagogy and Fine Arts (at Adam Mickiewicz University in Poznań) and I presented the results of a questionnaire assessing the research activity of the Department members, when a new person, as yet unknown to me, addressed me in approximately the following words: 'I saw these questionnaires of yours and I have to say that they have nothing to do with art and are entirely useless as far as art is concerned'. His tone of voice showed dislike or even disgust with my attempt to reduce art to a catalogue registering artistic effectiveness and statistically calculated quality. This was the voice of Jarosław Kozłowski. What I mean to say is that I intruded upon his world as a distasteful bureaucrat who attempts to regulate the life of the department, while he barged into mine as a careless and incompetent anarchist attempting to provoke a rebellion against the authorities among the already generally insubordinate employees of the Department of Pedagogy and Fine Arts, and to supply them with more reasons for indolence. Needles to say, this event did not inspire us with sympathy for each other; in fact, it created a distance between us. A long year had to pass before the report from the Ministry of Science bestowed a first class status upon the Department, an event rightly considered by everybody a miracle, even if one achieved by my prayers. In the following meeting of the Department, a substantially more upbeat one for me, Kozłowski was the only employee who publicly recognized that the positive evaluation of the Department was the result of my strategy. From then on, my relations with Kozłowski took a turn for the better. The above described criticism, however, preceded, and necessarily so, our coming to know and, consequently, understand each other.

I am telling of my first meeting with the "Kozłowski phenomenon" in such detail in order to recognize the absurdity and fortuitousness of these beginnings, and to acknowledge that they were related to violence and mutual criticism, or at least to suspiciousness and distrust. Sometimes I think that the existence of such institutions as the Department of Pedagogy and Fine Arts can be justified only by the fact that they bring together people who otherwise would never have met. I also reminisce at such length to feel again how strange and disturbing was the accident which brought us together at that particular time and which, as I will try to show, became a pure necessity. For this case shows that there is no genuine knowing which is not preceded by aggressive and total criticism, a criticism so painful that it undermines what we take for granted about the world which we happen to inhabit, undermines what we take for granted about our experience of that world and, consequently, undermines the shape of the things we perceive here and now.

It is important to point out that I had encountered the phenomenon under the name "Jarosław Kozłowski" before I ever came to see his work. This circumstance not only deforms my knowing and understanding, but also and above all entirely preforms it or even makes it possible. Undoubtedly, knowing the personality of an author does not help in understanding his work and an artist's biography is not a good key to his art. And yet when the artist's biography or our relation to him reveals phenomena, objects or ideas which we also find in his work, then both the person and the work acquire the power to speak to us in a new, stronger voice, the power to illuminate a way which a moment ago seemed an unbeaten track.

2. Pleasure

I will therefore follow the clue determined by accident. My next important experience with Kozłowski was of a culinary nature: I discovered he does not eat meat. The importance of this discovery lay not only in the fact that the artist adopted some ethical principle, but in my realization that his attitude to the world is not mindless and conventional. I also found out that Kozłowski controls the pleasure he experiences, that he aims at creating a system of control over what Jacques Lacan calls *jouissance*. This control over pleasure is not merely negative, repressive: it also has a positive, productive dimension. One needs only witness Kozłowski smoking his cigars and the pleasure he derives thereof. He enjoys his cigars, risking ostracism and even conflict with the law. In fact one of the professors, hardly known for refraining from pleasures himself, encouraged me to do something with this guy (Kozłowski) who does not understand what is meant by public space because it should not be contaminated by his whims. We should seriously attend to the hypothesis that the patterns formed by the smoke of Kozłowski's cigars may in fact be a result of some hidden performance, a secret activity that he watches over with no less attentiveness than his official installations.

Kozłowski often says he is suspicious of the category of pleasure. For example, in conversation with Andrzej Szczepaniak in May 2006 he recalls:

> I have refrained from painting for many years because it seemed to satisfy me a little bit too easily, and I seemed to derive too much pleasure from using the painter's instruments. That was dangerous to the degree that it threatened the loss of critical distance towards what I was doing.[4]

4 Jarosław Kozłowski, *In conversation with Andrzej Szczepaniak*, [in:] Jarosław Kozłowski, *Zasłony/Curtains*, exh. cat. Cracow: Galeria Starmach, 2006, p. 32.

He makes a similar and even more emphatic comment in the now famous interview with Jerzy Ludwiński from 1994:

> As a student, I painted a lot and with great zest. I liked the smell of paints, turpentine, I was praised as a promising 'oil painter'. Finally I felt that painting began to resemble eating cream cakes, that I was losing distance towards myself and what I was doing. So I stopped painting [...]. Somewhat similar motivations later made me abandon my linguistic explorations. I noticed I was feeling more and more comfortable with them. I enjoyed arranging various conceptual configurations, combinations of more and more ingenious games and logical paradoxes. And again I felt the necessity to abandon that [...]. Abandonments are important.[5]

Kozłowski felt a pleasure in painting, so strong that it proved dangerous. It made him give up a painter's career. What does pleasure mean to him then? In the simplest terms, pleasure has the important function of signaling, of informing us that what we do no longer resists ourselves and that it requires no effort, no investment of intellect and energy, that the activity we are engaged in has become routine and threatens to become mere mechanical repetition. Here is what pleasure means: it is an effect of a fully formed dynamic of movement installed in us so strongly that it no longer requires conscious control and adjustment. Pleasure thus signals to us growing conformity and should therefore constitute a warning that we should change something in our lives if we do not want to succumb to routine, vanity, narcissism or some other abomination.

Reducing pleasure to the function of signal and information does not, however, exhaust the pleasure principle. Thus I pose the question again: What does pleasure mean to Kozłowski and what activity is it related to? Does his work operate beyond the pleasure principle or conversely, does it remain in total, one could say organic, agreement with that very principle? To put it briefly, for Kozłowski pleasure is related to thinking, but not just any kind of thinking. In 1995, in conversation with Audun Eckhoff, Kozłowski spoke extensively on the topic of thinking, directly linking the act of thinking to art:

> Transformation is a very essential idea for art in general. Whether we paint or draw, or whichever tools we use. I think this concept is very basic. But the process is somehow analogical to the concept of thinking, which in my instance is triggered by simple curiosity. I am curious to draw a line or to build some structure which doesn't exist. In the process of making or transformation, the art work is imbued with a new existence, another life. But the beginning is always curiosity. I like questions very much. And for me, this is more about asking questions than giving answers. It parallels the division between the artist as investigator, someone who is

5 Jarosław Kozłowski, Jerzy Ludwiński, *Conversation*, [in:] Jarosław Kozłowski, *Rzeczy i przestrzenie/Things and Spaces*, exh. cat. Łódź: Muzeum Sztuki, 1994, p. 94.

searching for some new sense or new ideas, and the artist who already knows and is telling the truth.[6]

This premise allows Kozłowski to explain why it is so difficult for him to enclose a thought in a single work of art, one installation or one painting, why his works engender a series, continuities, histories which mutually position each other, commenting, undermining and renegotiating meanings. This act of renegotiation, the conversation between works created by the artist: that is what thought is. Thinking must be intertwined with seriality, with the process of evolution, with transformation and with something which materializes in the openness and incessantness of supplementation and commentary. Hence my strong thesis: that the proper topic of Kozłowski's work is the very act of thinking and his installations, paintings, drawings and performances are merely transitional points of this process, this action, this dynamic; his works of art are merely a temporary dwelling in objects, ideas, events or acts, which have been accidentally chosen by thought as a site for habitation.

Pleasure is then the reason why Kozłowski abandons painting and continues his work in another field, in another place, with the use of a different tool. His art is the effect of such dislocations of the pleasure principle. It does not come into being beyond the pleasure principle. His asceticism, rationality, self-control, minimalism, orderliness, restraint, that is, all these Apollonian virtues which are commonly attributed to Kozłowski's work, are by no means synonymous with some deeper work of eradication, repression or denial of pleasure conceived of as the forbidden fruit. They are at most a symptom of sublimation, of a transfer of pleasure from the narrowly defined sphere of events and physical actions to the sphere of symbolic events and activity. Abandonments are important, even crucial because only they allow him to continue the process of thinking. Let us pause, however, and ask: thinking about what and with what?

The later part of the question is perhaps easier to answer. Remaining faithful to the pleasure principle, we can say without much ado that there is no object or medium Kozłowski could not think with. To begin with, he thinks with his body. He thinks with his body when he engages in the so-called drawing actions, something he has been doing since the seventies. In those usually short performances, the artist comments on the history of art or an arbitrarily chosen episode of it, as in *The Cavalryman and the Girl, Leda with the Swan* (1978) or in Mona Lisa in the *Fourth Dimension* (1979). These are now past, however; abandonments are important, after all, and never accidental. Continuations are equally important, and never fully calculable. Beginning with 1988, all the successive actions are given a common title, *Continuum*, and assigned

6 Jarosław Kozłowski, Audun Eckhoff, *A Conversation*, p. 47.

consecutive numbers. In *Continuum I*, an alarm clock appears for the first time, measuring the time it takes for a blackboard to dry when wiped thoroughly after its surface was covered with chalk drawings. A collection of 27 defunct alarm clocks (smashed with the artist's hand) is the trace of the *Continuum* series created thus far. Each event has the same script but differs in time, location and the condition the artist is in (his age). Because *Continuum* requires physical effort and the artist's energy resources change with age, the act itself is always unique and unrepeatable despite its repetitive character. There is no doubt that the *Continuum* series constitutes for the author the act of thinking in its pure form, in the form of his body, which repeats the narration and plot designed by the painter and, more recently, the narration (the way of the cross) and the plot of Kozłowski's life. *Continuum* is thus a twofold self-meditation: attending to the history of the discipline he represents the artist attends to himself and comments on himself, he attends to his own finiteness and countability.

I do not know what amount of pleasure is secreted in Kozłowski during the successive drawing actions. I also do not know whether the activated quanta of pleasure, which are indistinguishable from thinking itself, are for him useful indicators, informing him about the necessity of abandonment or continuation. I do know, however, that the artist's body is not his only thinking tool. He thinks equally easily with objects, places, or even with whole structures, such as time and space. I have no doubt whatsoever that such works as *Sharp Objects* or *Soft Protections* are an attempt to think with objects; works such as *Sleeping Room. Nomadic Version* and *Gravity Room* are attempts to think with places; and finally works such as *Swedish Bathhouse. Australian Version*, *United World. Utopian Version*, or *Time Vacuum* are attempts to think with whole spaces. I repeat the question then: What is thinking for Kozłowski and why is he so omnipresent? How is it possible for his art to think with practically anything so that, to paraphrase the artist, the boundary between object and concept becomes uncertain?

Well, the answer is apparent already. Kozłowski says that the classical error made in our understanding of thinking is to reserve this process for a narrowly defined internal activity of our brain, when in fact thinking may be and is public in character and takes place not within some internal space, but within the space of the world itself. It is an error also to restrict the process of thinking to purely human activity bounded by our convictions and to believe that thinking is anthropological in character and remains the eccentric attribute solely of humans. Were it so, we would be infinitely lonely and infinitely impotent in our cognitive activities. But it is not so. One thinks with objects, events and even structures, provided that we snatch them out of the torpor of banality and triviality, that we allow objects to speak and release meanings concealed by our pragmatism. Thinking is a power which allows objects, ideas and words to speak for themselves, which means, *inter alia*, that thinking is more on the side of the object that on the side of the subject, were we to uphold that distinction.

Let us correct and sharpen up the main thesis: it is not so much that Kozłowski thinks with everything that surrounds him, but that through his activity he creates the conditions under which things/concepts/words/bodies can think for themselves, that is, can become thinking beings.

> Somewhere in the Universe
> Someone is thinking and thinking[7]

In reality, somewhere in the cosmos there are beings who renew the act of thinking. This act of thinking does not result, however, in their isolation from the world of external, indifferent, thoughtless, inanimate nature, but allows them to blend into the landscape of the world.

3. Drawing

The difficult art of drawing does not exhaust itself in the systematic covering of a blackboard with chalk, the thorough erasure of the chalk marks with a sponge and the waiting for the signs of erasure to dry. Even if this act is systematically repeated and its duration is measured with an alarm clock which is subsequently destroyed. The activity of thinking is not exhausted in thinking with the body, through the body and in the body. In conversation with Jaromir Jedlinski, Jarosław Kozłowski observes:

> Drawing is akin to thinking. Drawing is the most direct recording of ideas and emotions, a recording which is, at the same time, the most analytical and free of the rituals of the craft. It is amazing that for so long it has been considered a secondary form of expression serving – as sketch or note – as aid in the composition of the image in painting, sculpture or graphic plate [...]. For me, at the turn of the seventies, it became the basic tool for uncovering the secrets of the language of art and for shaping artistic awareness.[8]

Drawing is the thinking of the hand and eye; it is the thinking of the very surface of things.

When I first read the conversation cited above, I was struck by how closely Kozłowski's comments on drawing as a form of thinking, an exercise in thinking, correspond to certain intuitions on painting I had encountered earlier in

---

7 Jarosław Kozłowski, *Grey Thoughts*, (London: Matt's Gallery, 1990).

8 Jarosław Kozłowski, *In conversation with Jaromir Jedliński*, [in:] Jarosław Kozłowski, *Hot News*, exh. cat. Poznań: Galeria Muzalewska, 2002, p. 33.

the work of Claude Lévi-Strauss.[9] Lévi-Strauss's essay is one long meditation on a sentence from Vasari, who defined painting as "intellectual cognition". According to Lévi-Strauss, the first task of art is to select and organize the flow of information sent to our eye by the external world. Art models thinking. By ignoring some pieces of information, reinforcing or reducing others, shaping those he or she has chosen, the drawing artist lends a coherence, which becomes the marker of his style, to this multiplicity, this excess of information, flowing from the world and flooding our senses.

Lévi-Strauss asks: Does a photographic or film camera behave in the same way? And answers: to agree to equate the work of the eye with the work of the lens would be to fail to recognize that the physical and mechanical demands of the machine, the chemical properties of the light-sensitive surface, the possibilities the cameraman has in the choice of subject, angle and lighting give him a very limited freedom in comparison to the practically boundless freedom of the eye, the hand and thought. Further, Lévi-Strauss comments on the paradox in the history of contemporary drawing: the importance of the subject wanes progressively for the sake of what is euphemistically called the work of the artist (or drawing technique) while it is only when we insist on treating drawing as a means of cognition that the mastery of a craft inherited from the old masters becomes meaningful again, and again becomes a sovereign topic of research and reflection.

This very paradox is addressed by Kozłowski in the works addressing the subject of seeing. The drama is played out between the subject and object of seeing. And I use both categories (subject/object) more as a result of a lexical powerlessness and inertia than intentionally. Such works by Kozłowski as *Eyewitness*, *Double Exposure*, *Double Image*, *Sleep Well*, *Single Lighting* are not merely examples of a critique of cognition, which simultaneously take on the complex problem of the ethics of seeing, but above all they are drawings understood as "intellectual cognition". Drawing is "the basic tool for uncovering the secrets of the language of art". If it is so, drawing becomes an a priori condition of art (a proto-art or a meta-art), rather than art understood in the conventional and banal way. Kozłowski does not merely ask the question as to what we see and who has the right to see, but asks much more than that: How does what we see transform into the seer?

Drawing is not merely a collection of lines left by the movement of the painter's hand on paper and cannot be reduced to the thickness of the lines organizing the finite, enclosed space. Drawing is omnipresent; we can find it on

9 Claude Lévi-Strauss, *A un jeune peintre*, [in:] Claude Lévi-Strauss, *Le Regard éloigné*, (Paris: Plon, 1983).

maps of cities, in layers of ploughed earth, in the lines of the landscape, in the lines of one's palm, in star constellations, in mountain ranges, in lines demarcating the political map of the world, in outlines of clouds, in the constellations of our words, in the holograms of our brains, and in cigar smoke. Kozłowski's early works, *Metaphysics*, *Physics*, and *-ics*, refer to drawing conceived in this manner (as geometry).

Metaphysics (1972) embraces relations defined by the code of colloquial language, between concepts and objects visible on the black and white photograph projected on the wall of the gallery. Those objects are marked by numbers drawn on the wall and constitute parts of a typical home interior. Kozłowski is asking about the relationship between a sign and its referent, about the principle which allows us to separate objects from what surrounds them, to mark boundaries between objects. He is asking about the boundary of an object, its drawing, its map. Obviously the determination of the unambiguous relation between the concept and its referent poses difficulties, because the concept does not determine the exact temporal and spatial boundaries of the object. In trying to define a general model of the object which constitutes the referent of a given term, a model which would allow for a precise determination of its boundaries, Kozłowski refers to the system of point-free geometry conceived of by Stanisław Leśniewski, a figure known also for his philosophical reflections. In point-free geometry, all space is understood as a great solid which freely subdivides into other solids,. In classical geometry, those masses are considered to be collections of points; here they are the primary objects. Conceived as a solid, the object becomes – in the light of this theory – a concrete body, and at the same time a substratum of future divisions. Kozłowski's task in this work is not only an exercise in logic and set theory, nor is it a mere rehearsal of things long known to philosophers. It is rather an attempt to reach the numerical code which positions and determines our understanding of things, which determines our most elementary orientation in the world and ability to recognize an object at all.

Physics (1973) describes the logical scaffolding of the situation presented in the photograph in *Metaphysics*. It is made up of seventy-four panels with compound sentences based on patterns of tautology. The simple sentences which constitute the compound sentences describe the interior represented in the photograph used in *Metaphysics*. Since *Physics* pertains, however, only to the formal relations between sentences and not to the relation of these sentences to reality, the photograph from *Metaphysics* it uses is out of focus.

While *Metaphysics* and *Physics* described relations, semantic and syntactic respectively, whose character was determined by necessity, *-ics* (1974) concerns only the sphere of possibility. In this case, it is the viewer's task to interpret numbers placed on the wall in an order identical to that in *Metaphysics* by identifying them with adjectives read aloud (from tapes) in alphabetical order. Adjectives are elements of language which do not denote objects (although they connote qualities); detached from objects, they map out the structure of potential reality. And again: the point is not to perform a simple language exercise, but to make the viewer aware of how complex the system of coding used by his brain is. Recoding the language of objects as the language of images is recognizable to our brains; recoding the language of images as the language of logical formulas is conceivable, but the reversal of this translation goes beyond the cognitive capacities of our thinking organs.

Object Drawings (1980) are a type of modification of the model of relations presented in *Metaphysics*, the relations between the names used in colloquial language and objects. The drawings of *Object Drawings* are made on sheets of paper: graphite prints of the surfaces of the exhibited pieces of furniture are placed on top of those pieces. The names of objects are replaced in this work by their indexes, an almost mechanical reproduction of their shapes. They remain readable also as *Post-Object Drawings* (Galerie Vor Ort, Hamburg, 1980) shown, similarly to the numbers in *-ics*, separately from the objects they denote. In these works, drawing is used as something concrete, as a code which became the object itself. Let us repeat: drawing is the thinking of the hand and eye, the thinking of the very surface of things, a guessing at the very signature of the object.

> Somewhere in the Universe
> Someone is thinking straight
> His thoughts are very grey
> But sometimes grey means red[10]

In reality, there are beings somewhere in the cosmos who are trying to think without mediation, but their thought is not aligned with the object of thinking and the surface of things cannot be translated into the content of their thought.

4. The lost dignity of objects

One day after a faculty meeting Kozłowski approached me and told me that I had a very elegant watch. I was doubly surprised. First, because he had astonished me with his perceptiveness and ability to register a fact which my eye could not register. Second, I was surprised that he paid any attention to such a detail as a watch. Only recently, after I acquired a certain familiarity with his

10 Jarosław Kozłowski, *Grey Thoughts*.

work and saw the role played in it by watches and various other objects of everyday use, did I realize how many meanings and how much, I dare say, tenderness were hidden in this little remark about my watch. There is no motif Kozłowski emphasizes more that his ostentatious aversion, if not hatred, towards the demand for functionality. But this aversion may be easily misinterpreted as plain dislike of the administrative-economic paradigm characteristic of our social world. I believe that Kozłowski is not aiming at a critique of the postpolitical world of liberal and global exchange, but rather he desires to reach and recover the lost dignity of the object, where "dignity" means "the proper meaning of". Let us add that the same gesture of liberation pertains also to words and concepts. Only words and concepts are not being liberated from the demand for pragmatically limited functionality, but from the demands of semantic pragmatism, from the subjugation to the conventionality of humanly assigned meanings, that is, they are liberated from the oppression of signification. Thus, with Kozłowski the movement of the liberation of objects and the movement of the liberation of concepts go in opposite directions.

In conversation with Jerzy Ludwiński, the artist presents his concept of the three rings:

> The objects in the third ring thus often look 'the same' but their new status and the different internal relations between them make them no longer be what they are in the reality ring, and they have even less in common with their 'representations' or 'transformations' in the art ring. They acquire a new identity and with it they recover their lost dignity.[11]

It is from this – ethical rather than purely conceptual – point of view that I want to read Kozłowski's opinion expressed earlier in the same text that "[f]rom [his] current perspective [he] would not make a too clear-cut distinction between object and idea", and that objects undergo continual dislocations, displacements and reconfigurations in relation to each other, or furthermore, that "objects may be good carriers of ideas, ideas are often reified".[12]

How does Kozłowski recover the original dignity of objects? And are not his goals in this project too farfetched, too revolutionary and utopian? Is the project feasible? Is it that after the epoch of freeing people from the prison of tradition and superstition, of recognising successive minority groups, and of animal liberation, the time has come to liberate objects? And does Kozłowski turn out to be the prophet of this liberation, donning the mask of the messiah of all that which had been reduced to the function of a servile object? In the light of what was said here, the recovery of the original dignity of objects would mean above

11 Jarosław Kozłowski, Jerzy Ludwiński, *Conversation*, p. 102.

12 *Ibid.*, p. 94.

all making them objects of thought, releasing in them the power to announce their proper meaning, their name. But how is that to be achieved? How are we to initiate a revolution, not among the human masses this time, but among the masses of objects enslaved by the dogma of functionality?

Importantly, Kozłowski's work makes use of ready objects, mostly things of everyday use. Such objects were part of his art right from the beginning, but they were usually interwoven in multilayered utterances in which the artist also used other media, such as drawing, photography, sound and color. In arranged artistic situations, those objects usually performed their functions actively: fans caused the air to circulate, lamps gave light, metronomes and clocks measured time, the table held plates, and a key opened the door. Kozłowski soon realized that as a result his intention was not sufficiently and fully radical, and that he still was situating himself on the side of the aggressor, the one who harnesses and subjugates, on the side of the master.

Fundamental change came perhaps with the work called *Sharp Objects* (1992). In essence, Kozłowski refused to sacrifice anything anymore to situationally conceived functionality; he was not satisfied with local, partial revolution anymore and demanded total liberation. This liberation, however, turned out a surprise. The artist does not help the chair to achieve new status by liberating it from its oppressive condition of a machine for sitting, nor does he liberate the clock by lifting off its stigma of a machine for measuring time. He performs an act which is much more violent; in a way he wounds objects, decomposes and cuts them, crops and sews them up, arranges and glues them together again. Thus, he inflicts pain on objects, even destroys and tortures them. A legitimate question arises as to whether it suffices to join the chair to the cabinet with bandage and band aid, or like a farmer to plant scythes in our chairs and tables, or to allow heaps of our daily newspaper to glue the sawed off leg of a table to the floor to become the liberator of the martyred still life of the objects of this world and earn the title of the messiah of dead matter. Does it suffice to pin books to the shelves, imprisoning them in one's catalogue logic, to make us aware, the way Kozłowski's Library does, that libraries are prisons and books conceived as receptacles for information have become unable to speak and say more through their silence, their imprisonment, than through their flowery text wrought in ink?

One needs to point out also that in Kozłowski's work liberation is related to the opposite gesture, namely, the objectification of ideas. Ideas are not thought when, as is generally believed, something is conceptualized, but when they are reified. A perfect example of this may be found in the work from 1977 called *Exercise in Semiotics*. It consisted of a sequence of 49 mass-produced postcards with reproductions of roses of various brands and colors. Each pair of identical photographs was marked with the same commentary doubled by its opposite. If the caption under one photograph read, 'this pretty red rose is a red rose', under the next, identical photograph, the caption said, 'this pretty red rose is not a red rose'. The real color of the roses was irrelevant. The artist intended for the term "the rose" to mean THE ROSE. Such miracles had been possible only in the Cana of Galilee and, maybe, also in Hegel's philosophy. Kozłowski seems to be saying that now they are to be common experience. Democracy means also, or above all, the democracy of cognition.

The question therefore is the following: Why, despite Kozłowski's rough treatment of his objects, when he paints furniture with black paint and pierces tables with sharp scythes, when looking at those objects do we not see them as victims; rather, wounded (liberated) they seem to become counter-objects, actively struggling for their identity and sovereignty? Analogously: How does it happen that concepts treated by Kozłowski with logical neutrality and mathematical precision are in the end granted by him a subjectivity and a vitality, which makes them causal agents capable of influencing the world of objects? The answer is that through the manipulations of the artist these objects and ideas reveal their active, thinking nature. There is nothing which disturbs him more than the passive nature of objects. Thinking is always active and activity is never peaceful. The armchair will not allow anyone reclining in it to feel at ease, the television will resist transmitting information, the typewriter will rebel against writing. Yet an attentive viewer will be able to register in each object a tiny fragment of their original surface, which has not been painted over. This trace of previous status constitutes a stigma of their former, slave nature. It is a souvenir of human domination, of the epoch of enslavement, a warning against what we (things) will become if we stop thinking.

Kozłowski was equally ruthless with the objects from the series *Soft Protections* (1994-95). Furniture, carpets, and other smaller things such as radios, lamps, clocks, mirrors, ashtrays, and so on, were glued together out of two parts of separate objects of the same type. This time the artist played the doctor and he dressed the cuts with bandages and band aid. Here objects enter illegal unions, and merge into larger entities, losing the identity bestowed upon them by socially sanctioned codes. But, can this be read as an expression of authentic care, as if Kozłowski was dealing with a being capable of experiencing pain? Do we have the right or even a duty not to feel at home, as if we were not in our own room (in its Danish, Swiss or Polish version), but in a hospital room where the wounded are being treated after a dramatic battle? Or maybe we are watching a spectacle of objects created as a result of an illegal, extraspecies or interspecies copulation? Maybe we are witnessing a recording not so much of the consequences of the violation of the incest taboo, as of the transgression of the boundary of a species?

In one of the versions of this installation, the furniture and objects constituting the typical furnishings of the rooms named in the titles were stacked one on top of the other, with those bearing the burden of the rest placed on wheels. What did this mean? Moving to a different house, existential instability, an interval in the order of things? Did the magazines, those prosthetics of the interspecies, supporting the legs of the furniture and lining the paintings constitute a guarantee against the loss of meaning of the objects? Or did the hierarchical construction signify exploitation and a pecking order which exist even in the world of objects, some carrying the burden of others, so that even here equality is impossible? Perhaps Kozłowski does not want to liberate things at all, but is simply angry with them and like an evil demiurge vents his fury on the objects of initial adoration which have disappointed his divine expectations with their passive nature?

> Somewhere in the Universe
> Someone is thinking awry
> His thoughts are very grey
> But sometimes grey means brown[11]

In reality, sometimes some beings in the cosmos think something out of kilter and out of line, and then contradictions appear which are the reversal of tautology.

5. Time and space

Whenever I meet Kozłowski he asks me about the time and generally seems to be an organism lost in time. But he has never asked me about a place or the way to get to a place. He is not lost in space. It seems that, in the case of Kozłowski, the deficit of temporal orientation was transformed into an abundance and brilliance of spatial orientation. The artist's obsession with time is present both in his utterances and in specific actions. Let us try to translate this thought into the language of his work.

Time has entered space no less violently than space had entered time, as we can see in the episodic and accidental quality of the relation between objects in the 1997 work *Temporary Objects*. The idea seemed simple: the artist borrowed objects from various people's homes, which then were used as the material to build temporary formal arrangements in the National Museum in Poznań. For the duration of the exhibition, the objects were given the status of art, a status which was only temporary as they later returned to their homes to continue performing their utilitarian functions. The unstable relation between thing and idea, the object of contemplation and the functional object finds its analogy in the unstable and uncertain relation between time and space. The clock is the best example.

The clock is a paradoxical tool. It serves to measure time, but it measures time with its arms travelling in space. This travel, as we know, is illusory, because the hands travel around their own axis. The clock imitates the revolutions of the earth around its own axis and its arms persist in a circular, eternally repeatable journey. For Kozłowski, it is a paradox that movement in space can measure time. This paradox is best illustrated by his 1999 work, *Time Vacuum*. It consists of 24 clocks placed on the outside walls of twelve ends of 19th century, historic buildings. These buildings have been moved from the centre of the old town to the History Museum in Reykjavik (The Arbaer Museum), where one can learn about old ways of life. Each clock shows a different time. The hands of twelve of these clocks move in the right direction, "clockwise", and twelve move in the opposite direction, "anti-clockwise", constructing an amazing relationship between space and time, a type of spatio-temporal corrugation. *Gravity Room* is based on a similar principle. In it Kozłowski subjects to revision one of the basic laws of physics, the law of gravity. The simple procedure of placing a plain home interior upside down, fixing on the ceiling and walls of what usually sits on the floor – tables, sofas, cabinets and cases – denies the existence of gravity. There is more at stake here, however, than a simple gesture of deconstruction or reversal; the point is to undermine our most elementary spatial intuitions of "up" and "down". Assuming that Kozłowski has outgrown the phase of childhood negativity, the question arises: why do such things, why the perversity?

Let us ponder the significance of the Reykjavik event. First, an operation in space is performed: houses are moved from one place to another, or, rather, a group of houses is uprooted and turned into a heritage park. This operation is, however, also taking place in time, because it is performed on historical buildings which are moved from a living space to a space of contemplation. They are, to put it bluntly, torn out of their proper space and time, and lodged in spacelessness and timelessness, in a vacuum. Kozłowski's operation, consisting of placing the 24 clocks only puts a stamp on an operation that has already been completed, merely describing it and giving it a signature. In a vacuum, clocks lose their spatial orientation and begin to work counter clockwise. It would be an error to claim the clocks are out of order, they were in fact ordered by the operation described above. They behave the way we would behave in an undefined, unstructured, undetermined reality. What I called thinking with structures finds a perfect demonstration here. Kozłowski is no longer satisfied with liberating objects or spaces; his revolutionary appetites have grown substantially, he demands something more profound: a liberation of the formal conditions of thinking or, as Kant would say, of the a priori conditions of space and time. And what happens after this structural liberation?

Let us look at the example of *Three Thirty and Fifty One*, a book published in 1989 by Kunsthallen Brandts Klćdefabrik in Odense. The departure point is constituted here by photographs of watches taken at various times. The watches change and, judging from the shape of the hand, the hair and clothing, so do their wearers. The time shown by the first watch is 3:30:51 and such is the title of the photograph and the whole book. This dial and the time shown by its hands opens a series (in time) in which color becomes an important element. There is the 12:09 of white, 03:30 of black, 11:15 of blue, 06:45 of yellow, 11:14 of red and finally 28 seconds of orange (a photograph of two hands in gloves and two watches showing 01:10 and 08:52 respectively); at the end, the time 3:30:51 is shown again, this time digitally.

What is happening here? What does this series signify? What effect is created by this strange, disturbing contamination of time, space and color? I believe that what is at stake here is more than just a discovery of a private, subjective dimension of time. The point is not merely that there are many kinds of time, that time is immanently connected to place and that "there are no two points on Earth which at the same moment of astronomical time would remain in an identical relation to the Sun".[13] The point is not a simple spatio-temporal relativity. True, Kozłowski's speculations are not unlike the anguish of young Hans Castorp in Thomas Mann's *The Magic Mountain* (*Der Zauberberg* (1924)). The later was tortured with questions such as: Does time in the sanatorium hidden away in the mountains run differently from the time of healthy people living in their towns? Is the biological time of the body cells of a certain Russian woman with a French name, Klaudia Chauchat, which Castorp has come to desire, comparable to the time of his own mortal body? It seems, however, that Kozłowski's speculations are not exhausted in the psychology of the experience of time, nor in the personal phenomenology of time awareness. The artist is not merely after experiments and questions like: Does time in a closed, dark room run more slowly (or more quickly) to the prisoner than time in a bright, open space? He aims to say more: not only that space participates in time, not only that space is time, but also that all elements situated in space become time. He is not after the time of a certain color, but after the color of time. The color of the dial is not irrelevant to time

13 Jarosław Kozłowski, *Czas aktualny sztuki i cywilizacji pośpiechu. Czy istnieje więź bezkolizyjna?* [*The current time of art and the civilization of rush. Is there a safe connection?*], [in:] SytuARTacje. Jankowice 2-11 luty 1978 Poznań: Oficyna, 1978.

itself, is not, as it would seem, an accidental, neutral parameter, but essentially modifies time. The subject proper to the fine arts is, then, not space, but time. Drawing organizes time.

Time and space regulate not only the world's cosmology; the map of the world is not limited to a geographical map, but is supplemented by a political map. In the works in the *United World* series, miniature flags with the colors of different countries perform the function of guarding and fixing meanings resulting from the juxtaposition of objects. The position of the flags – horizontal or perpendicular – suggests a specific type of construction of meaning. In *Totalitarian Version* (The Brno House of Arts, 2000), the placement of the objects is defined by the principle of accumulation. House objects are piled up like a rotunda and separated from the rest of space by a polygon of steel grating. The flags shooting straight up, placed on the top edge of the grating, make us associate the construction with the order of some unidentified sublime ideology. The distribution of objects in *Democratic Version* (BWA, Zielona Góra, 2001) is defined by the principle of dispersal. The monolith of the cylindrical construction is replaced here by an irregularly shaped aggregate of objects of everyday use, branching out horizontally in many directions and covered with transparent foil. The flags point in many directions, suggesting the principle of plurality which is the key to the democratic order. Kozłowski's thought moves in a similar direction to that of Hannah Arendt's, who in *The Origins of Totalitarianism* compares constitutional governments to a space in which law is like a hedge between buildings, facilitating orientation in pace. Tyranny is like the desert; we move in an unknown, open, flat and uniform space and the will of the tyrant falls on us like the sandstorm on a nomad. Totalitarianism has no spatial topology: it is like an iron ring bracing the thinking substance until everything within it becomes uniform. Perhaps, however, Kozłowski is closer in his thinking to Thomas Hobbes or Jonathan Swift, for whom freedom in all regimes, be it democracy, aristocracy or monarchy, is always the same, because it is defined by the space of the state to which we belong.

> Somewhere in the Universe
> Someone is thinking in two
> His thoughts are very grey
> But sometimes grey means blue[14]

In reality, somewhere in the cosmos, someone is thinking for two, and even for three, for five, for the million, billion or even the whole multiplicity and then, behold, grayness becomes the blue of the sky. It becomes the blue of the sky, because the sky is the only grayness there is.

---

14 Jarosław Kozłowski, *Grey Thoughts*, n.pag.

6. Weariness

Jarosław Kozłowski's work could have remained silent and inaccessible or even alien to me forever. I could have never known anything about him. Perhaps I still do not. I know nothing about him, but that he does not eat meat, that he likes to cover blackboards with chalk and has an eye for watches. But he knows something about himself. In the conversation with Jaromir Jedliński, quoted above, the artist says:

> The reason why I come back to watercolor painting today, after a break of several years, is different again. To begin with, I am tired with the inter- and multi-media canon of art so omnipresent today and the pushy journalism and infantile scandals of so-called 'critical art'. Secondly, I am amused by the 'serious' diagnoses of the exhaustion or the end of painting, pronounced stubbornly and with such surprising satisfaction. Against these popular opinions I believe that no language of art expires [...].[15]

In a conversation with Andrzej Szczepaniak in May 2006 he adds:

> In my opinion, every work of art should be critical, whether it's Polish or not and whether it's called 'critical art' or not. This applies equally to what's outside and what's intrinsic, because otherwise it sinks into self-satisfaction and academicism.[16]

Kozłowski often emphasizes that he does not feel an artist and certainly does not feel a born artist. The only thing he is for sure is a human being. This is an important declaration which distances him from contemporary antihumanism: there are thinkers who use every opportunity to emphasize their inhuman character. Today, being human has become an embarrassing privilege.

In a conversation with Audun Eckhoff in 1995, Kozłowski confesses:

> I chose to work and act in the field of art, and it was a very conscious decision. I was not born an artist. If one wants to become a shaman, one has to believe in his or her peculiar 'mission' and one's privilege of, for example, knowing better than others. For me, it is too pretentious and rather too megalomaniac. And I have always been skeptical, as much towards all the truths which were given to me, as towards myself. So in order to work in the field of art, creating my ideas in the language of art, I had to face the question of what the phenomenon of art actually is. I believe it is simply a matter of a curiosity in the language you use and the whole structure you are working in, including its borderlines. When I began to question different aspects of art — to use the fashionable term: to deconstruct its mythologies — there was a very important need for me to know more about what I myself am doing. What is real in what I do, and what is fiction? What do I do in accordance with assumed standards, and what is my personal and honest contribution?[17]

---

15 Jarosław Kozłowski, *In conversation with Jaromir Jedliński*, p. 35.

16 Jarosław Kozłowski, *In conversation with Andrzej Szczepaniak*, p. 20.

17 Jarosław Kozłowski, Eckhoff, *A Conversation*, p. 45.

Further on, the artist deconstructs the myth of freedom in art, of the free act of creation, of the sovereignty and divine autonomy of the artist. He demonstrates how much the language of art is embroiled with the language of politics, business and even military defence.

Kozłowski's art is doubtlessly critical art, but it has nothing to do with so-called Polish critical art. He is light years away from Zbigniew Libera, Artur Żmijewski or Katarzyna Kozyra, who are concerned mostly with the passivity of the population, with the creation of a silent majority and with the dead masses of consumerism. The critical aspect of their works is mostly social and political; it is to activate passive citizens. Kozłowski activates an entirely different critical sense which has to do primarily with the analysis of the possibilities and impossibilities of the very conditions of the existence of the world and its objects. The artist does not take the side of Karl Marx, Michel Foucault and Giorgio Agamben, but, rather, of Immanuel Kant, Edmund Husserl and Ludwig Wittgenstein. The criticism of the Polish critical school is for him not critical enough. Today, however, Kozłowski is weary of his own excess of criticism. Perhaps he is also weary of what he discovered in his critical analysis.

One of the signs of his weariness is the piece *Rhetorical Figures* presented in the Oko/Ucho Gallery in Poznań and in the Warsaw Gallery Le Guern, where Kozłowski showed the third version of this work. In the former, he was interested in the rhetoric of the image/object; in the later, completed for the Art, Life and Confusion exhibition in Belgrade (2006), he pointed to the rhetorical overuse of slogans, both in everyday language and in more official utterances. LED displays with the short text "No news from..." were installed at different locations in the city – in the gallery, in the museum, in the street – and announced the lack of news from 23 places situated at different geographical and political locations. In his latest project, the artist returns to the rhetoric of art itself, to artistic ostentatiousness and the meagerness of the artistic message. The gigantic construction of cardboard boxes covered with mortar acquires meaning in juxtaposition with the brief message: "No news".

I am looking at the catalogue of *Rhetorical Figures* published by the Oko/Ucho Gallery. In this collection of black images, again, each image bears the title "No News From..." followed by the name of the place: Berlin, Brussels, London, Madrid, Moscow, Oslo, Paris, Rome, Warsaw, New York, Peking, New Delhi, Tokyo, Cairo, Tel Aviv, Johannesburg, Nairobi, São Paulo, Sidney. This resembles the late poetics of Samuel Beckett, for example the short stage work *Breath*. The play lasts no longer than thirty seconds and consists only of the sound of inhaling and exhaling and a short exclamation at the beginning and at the end. The lack of news is not synonymous with good news in Kozłowski's work; rather, it is synonymous with black news, the worst news, the news of catastrophe. But because this black news comes from all corners of the world, it becomes monotonous; it inspires not so much shock as weariness: weariness with catastrophes.

The question is, then: Does all the critical analysis undertaken by Kozłowski in his highly creative life have to come down to the statement: "No news from anywhere. No news from Kozłowski"? Kozłowski's oeuvre does say something important about the consequences of inverting the world with thought. His whole oeuvre is thought, thought released from the pleasure principle. To say "released from the pleasure principle", however, does not mean a departure from and acting beyond the pleasure principle, but an attempt to connect thinking to this principle at its source and to make thinking the only pleasure. Is Kozłowski's inverted world inhabitable? Is Kozłowski's a world which may not only be thought, but also lived in, settled? Is life possible here – life perceived as a process of exchange of information and energy with the environment, life perceived as a one-directional process of the dissipation of energy and matter or, finally, life perceived as a multiplication of life, a replication – if in his world even the kitchen is nomadic and the living room is moving on wheels in an unknown direction? How much would we have to change, how lonely and homeless must we become to release within ourselves a disposition to settle in those rooms? Are we like that already? Is the price to pay for the liberation of objects my own death on the scythe which suddenly grew out of my armchair?

Perhaps today we need to imagine Kozłowski strolling in a united world, where European standards have been adopted, in search of his personal file. He is infinitely sad. Personal files are held in temporal spaces connected with soft protections. His file can be found in the Negative Room in which orientation vanishes. He has 20 minutes to find his file, he checks his watch, only to see that its hands are moving backwards. His only hope are mathematics and geometry; he knows objects have been given numerical reference. He once knew them. The problem is that when he is looking at the numbers only, he cannot connect them with objects. With the process of thinking, the number of unknowns grows instead of decreasing. The artist abandons the hope to find his file and instead begins exercises in ethics; those, however, plunge him into an uncertainty whether what he sees is vertical or horizontal. He does not know and there is no way he could find out. Reason is of no use in this matter. He despairs. Ethics was his last hope.

Kozłowski is searching for a way out of the world and finds it in the sphere of imagination. He leaves the prison of personal files in Reykjavik. Instead of going into a historical building with two clocks over the entry, he goes into an Australian version of a Swedish bathhouse. A surprise awaits him there. Red light strikes his eyes and a stern voice says: "sleep well". Still, he goes inside.

From the maddening play of projectors a pair of eyes emerges. He realizes these are his own eyes. But they are not symmetrical; they are the positive and negative of an eye reflected in mirrors to the accompaniment of music or, rather, a cascade of ticking clocks and metronomes, which mutually invalidate one another.

There is no quartz clock. Kozłowski is watching Kozłowski. Kozłowski becomes Kozłowski's eyewitness. Kozłowski sees Kozłowski's brain. Kozłowski's brain had already tried to think straight, in reversals, in doubles, strangely, narrowly, clearly, excessively, directly, with bravado. His thoughts had been: red (straight), brown (oval), blue (double), orange (storied), yellow (thoughtful), green (square), golden (round). Currently they are grey (invisible). Kozłowski's eye is watching as his hand draws nervously on the board, lines becoming thicker and thicker, only to be erased with a wet sponge. Kozłowski is out of breath. Kozłowski's hand smashes the first/last alarm clock against the wall. "No news from Kozłowski".

Somewhere in the Universe
Someone is thinking away
His thoughts are very grey
But sometimes grey means grey[18]

18 Jarosław Kozłowski, *Grey Thoughts*, n.pag.

V. The Art of Creating Concepts

In thinking we do not produce thoughts, we grasp (fassen) them. For what I have called thoughts stand in the closest connection with truth.

Gottlob Frege[1]

Hence the notion of the concept cannot be explicated without at the same time sketching the background against which it is set; and the "correctness" of the particular notion of concept cannot be evaluated without at the same time evaluating the world view in which it plays a role.

Ray Jackendoff[2]

1. The sources

There is strong evidence that any time Robert Piłat publishes a book it is destined to be a publishing event that no passionate or meditative reader can give it a miss. The 1993 book *Does Consciousness Exist?* was carried on phenomenological and psychological investigations and it was only in his next work published in 1999, *Mind as a World Model,* where Piłat reformulated his interests and redirected his writing passion into cognitive science, even though phenomenology remained an important partner of discussion and a source of numerous inspirations. The book revealed in full Piłat's writing talent, in particular his skill of contrargumentation; every thesis in the book meets its antithesis. Reading *Mind as a World Model* is like sitting on a legal trial or watching a court drama where after defining the article of controversy, the floor is given to the parties to engage in a heated dispute before the final judgement is heard out loud. I must confess that it was a very important book to me and that it put in order many of the not so clear disputes in contemporary cognitive sciences.[3]

---

1 Gottlob Frege (1918). *The Thought: A Logical Investigation.* trans. P. T. Geach and R. H. Stoothoff, "Beiträge zur Philosophie des deutschen Idealismus", 1, pp. 58-77.

2 Ray Jackendoff, *Languages of the Mind. Essays on Mental Representation.* (London: The MIT Press, 1992), p. 21.

3 Robert Piłat, *Czy istnieje świadomość [Does Consciousness Exist?]*, Warszawa: IFiS PAN 1993; Robert Piłat, *Umysł jako osobisty model świata [Mind as a World Model]*, Warszawa: IFiS PAN 1999; Robert Piłat, *Doświadczenie i pojęcie [Experiencing and Concepts]*, Warszawa: IFiS PAN, 2006.

The following Piłat book, *Experiencing and Concepts,* was not accidentally subtitled *The studies in phenomenology and philosophy of mind*, as it heralded the change of scientific outlook and anticipated the great coming of the epic on concepts – the book under discussion, *On the Nature of Concepts.* It was published in 2007 by the Institute of Philosophy and Sociology of Polish Academy of Sciences, and its title could not be more daring and adequate. Already in the previous book on the existence of consciousness there were traces of the new book's core idea, namely that of mind as a world model. In the last chapters of that book Piłat only reveals his key concept – his personal world model – to be later meticulously developed in the next stage of his work. Similarly, *Existence and Concept* gave a foretaste of the author's strong dissatisfaction with the theory of conceptual representation and, with it, the state of contemporary cognitive sciences. When read from a certain angle, *On the Nature of Concepts* is an indirect critique of cognitive reason. It is an expression of the author's discontent with grounding cognitive theories in philosophy and, in general, with the weakness of contemporary cognitive sciences. To deepen the philosophical grounding and to better explain specific problems of cognitive sciences, Piłat builds numerous references to Kant, Husserl, Hegel, Frege, Jaspers and even to Heidegger. On the other hand, though, the book begins with a reconstruction of Quine's views on the irrelevance of concepts for scientific knowledge, and Putnam's on meaning as the contingent use of expressions – but not as a complete set of features necessary to specify the reference object. This multitude of literary traits makes the book exceptionally opulent, but it also makes readers ask what connects such a varied and not necessarily coherent polyphony of inspirations.

2. The intention

What I find disturbing and discouraging in the book is the scope of research interests and the daring way in which theses are formulated. This is both its advantage and its disadvantage. Piłat attempts to provide a complete book on concepts, but this makes him inspect concepts at all possible levels. Hence, we have an extensive part devoted to the empirical base of concepts (conceptual content of the experience), but also on the normative nature of concepts, categorisation, categorical mistakes, the relation between concepts and language, learning concepts, transforming concepts and the use of concepts, and finally on meaning and cognition (in the context of truth, reasoning, thinking, and formulating theories). The extensive work and the need to write a complete study (almost encyclopaedic) on the nature of concepts explains why the chapters of the book are uneven. To make things more complicated, Piłat employs multiple methods to justify the judgements cast. After the brave and absorbing chapters on the conceptual content of experience and the empirical nature of concepts (conceptuality of existence), the final chapters sound a little unconvincing and biased. Piłat is well aware of that fact and approaching the end od the book he says, melancholically: "[...] my argumentation is not a uniform line of reasoning, but searching for the evidence, going into many directions and researching philosophy too".[4] However, this distracted detective-like approach is accompanied by clear and focused metaphysics.

The extensiveness of Robert Piłat's book is matched by its full philosophical intensity. It is not his intention to provide an encyclopaedic knowledge on concepts, as he is aiming higher. The book's concern, in fact, is seeking to formulate a certain radical philosophical thesis (ontological), and to decide upon the existence or nonexistence of philosophy itself. Even though, as we read in the introduction, Piłat declares that he is not after synthesising knowledge on concepts but only showing "why such synthesis is not possible"[5] and only working out "a sufficiently precise notion of concept", it seems to me that the awareness of the impossibility of creating the unitary theory of concepts came to Piłat only at the very end of writing, and the declaration is a statement of the failure rather than success of the project.

Piłat is not content with the knowledge of how concepts function in mind, culture, language, and so on. Instead, he attempts to answer a challenging and everlasting philosophical question about the nature of things: "What are concepts as such?" It seems that an answer to that question is vital to Piłat not only for cognitive reasons. Piłat considers concepts to be the actual domain of philosophical work, and a philosophical project without concepts or deprived of conceptual truths to be a broken and diminished one. He says:

> To abandon explanations of the principles of the conceptual universe – the general theory of concepts – is to abandon crucial aspirations of human mind. Those aspirations always enlivened philosophy and this is why the history of the general theory of concepts parallels the history of philosophy itself.[6]

Those are indeed the aspirations of Robert Piłat's book on the nature of concepts. He seeks to restore a particular philosophical hope which was gradually abandoned in the course of the 20th century. We are speaking here of the philosophy inspired by Nietzsche, Heidegger and Derrida – philosophy free

---

4 Robert Piłat, *O istocie pojęć [On the Nature of Concepts]*, (Warszawa: IFiS PAN 2007), p. 303.

5 *Ibid.*, p. 9.

6 *Ibid.*, p. 29.

from the need of justifying claims by references to or a construction of universalistic dictionaries. And there is also the philosophy inspired by Darwin, Dawkins and Dennett – attempting to naturalise epistemological problems and to approach them in accordance with the project of reverse engineering.

Piłat makes his point crystal clear at the very beginning of the epic. He says: "I defend the thesis that concepts are ideal objects related to the modal properties of the world. I distinguish those concepts from conceptual representations researched by cognitive psychology and semantics".[7] This thesis repeats itself as mantra. The trouble is that when Piłat undertakes analytical work he refers to only two sources of inspiration: the semantic theory of Renate Bartsch, intending to provide the extensional conditions of creating and understanding concepts, and the theory of conceptual spaces of Peter Gärdenfors, intending to understand how conceptual representations appear and how they relate to other representations and the operations performed on them. For Bartsch, representations are functions, abstract objects; and to Gärdenfors representations are processes in the real nervous systems. *Prima facie* it is not clear what the relations between the three elements are: Piłat's strong thesis of conceptual realism (ontological thesis); Bartsch's thesis that conceptual content is not dependant on the properties of mental representation, but the qualities of formal construction modelling the use of expressions in various situations (semantic thesis); and Gärdenfors's thesis in which concepts refer to regions in conceptual spaces that possess no integrated coordinates, meaning that in the actual experience they do not come along together (cognitive thesis). Neither Bartsch nor Gärdenfors need to support their claims in conceptual semantics (Bartsch) and conceptual geometry (Gärdenfors) with the strong thesis of conceptual realism. In other words, if we are to assess the value of Robert Piłat's proposal, it is absolutely necessary to learn the line of reasoning which supports his claim that approaching concepts as abstract objects can help explain something that the semantic or cognitive theory cannot do.

Piłat asserts that he is not after a synthesis but understanding differences between paradigms, because "right here is the knowledge that can enrich the philosophy of mind, not in potential syntheses".[8] Even so, it is clear that this single articulation alone does not meet expectations. We soon learn that apart from the cognitive and semantic theory of concepts, this book has one more "protagonist", "namely concepts on their own, which cannot be reduced to the cognitive form of their representation in mind nor to semantic structure of sets".[9]

7 *Ibid.*, p. 10.
8 *Ibid.*, p. 45.
9 *Ibid.*, p. 50.

Let me confess that to me this third "hero" is mostly a declarative figure, and the major problem that Piłat brings on himself is the inability to clearly demonstrate the gains to the two other theories were such a postulate accepted.

If that was not enough, the assumption of strong conceptual realism may bring more problems than gains. If we accepted Piłat's thesis that concepts are abstract objects, then we should also assume that concepts are not (1) equivalent to intentional states of mind, and (2) parts of a language or any other symbolic system. If that was true, then speaking of a relation of concepts to the world we would be in fact speaking of a relation of objects to other objects, not of cognitive representations to the world. In place of a reference, which belongs to the representational dictionary, we would rather choose a completely different ontological relation. Piłat approaches this relation in the second volume of Hegel's *Science of Logic*, but does not include it in further analysis.

3. Modality

The key concept for Piłat is possibility. He says: "concepts are possible, abstract individuals, to which our mind and sensuality remain in a relation of partial exemplification",[10] and "[n]ecessity is not a feature analytically derived from causality. Causality is more of a cross-section within the scope of possibility".[11] Piłat also says:

> [t]he conceptual universe is not simply a set of concepts ascribed to individuals or a group, but a field of dynamic conceptual transformations. Only in such a shape may the conceptual universe organize whatever is possible. Whatever is possible is incidental – and incidentality, by nature, excludes static representation.[12]

Finally Piłat comes to conclusions: "the relevance of our conceptual systems ensues from the fact that it brings order to the sphere of possibility",[13] and: "it is not reality put in relation to the possibility – as its own production – but the other way round: the possibility emerges from the real. Reasoning is a transgression beyond the real to what is possible".[14] Well, the question is: Can we, from that set of claims, construe a coherent proposal of approaching modal terms? Can we comprehend what Piłat thinks of two difficult relations – possibility/necessity and necessity/causality? And what meaning of possibility is he referring to?

10 *Ibid.*, p. 56.
11 *Ibid.*, p. 59.
12 *Ibid.*, p. 34.
13 *Ibid.*, p. 24.
14 *Ibid.*, p. 308.

Asking about the category of possibility we could be – for example – thinking of at least three mutually nonreducible propositions: (1) logical and/or conceptual possibility (when we ask if something can exist in a given world set by the principles of logic); (2) metaphysical possibility (when we ask if something can exist in a given possible metaphysical world set by prerequisite propositions *a posteriori*); (3) nomological possibility (when we ask if something can exist in a given possible world set by the laws of physics/chemistry/biology in the existing world). Those three ways of apprehending possibility/necessity are still not comprehensive enough to denote all variants. We heard of other possibilities:[15] logical (related to the given set of laws of a given system of logic – perhaps not the classical: what is logically impossible in classical logic may be possible thanks to the laws of paraconsistent logic authorising contradiction), metaphysical (related to the set of synthetical statements *a priori* – like in Kripke's sense: identicalness *a posteriori* like "Water is H_2O"), ontological (defined by the relations between the objects), empirical (related to the conditions of a given temporal system), physical (related to the set of physical laws valid in the present world), conceptual (related to the conceptual abilities of a given subject), linguistic (related to the generative power of a given language). And still, these are not all the possible meanings. We have left out the category of Aristotelian potential (potentiality, power) and the Hegelian category of becoming, which – as we shall soon see – is most attractive to Piłat.

Piłat provides no such distinctions and therefore – in various contexts – he uses "possibility" with different meanings. I suspect that behind Piłat's way of thinking about the category of possibility lies the Kantian objection, that of nondetermining the category of determination. According to Piłat, in the modal organisation of the events and processes (causal chains) there is a function which selects the chain of determination from all possible causal chains. The explanation of events is nothing else but the modelling of this function. The choice of modelling structure from the pool of possibilities is a subject's reflexive way of relating to reality and cannot be described in terms of physical interactions between the organism and the environment. This is all fine, but then we should expect Piłat to elaborate some kind of a modal logic or at least use an already existing model. What surprised me most was that despite continuous references to modal concepts, there is only one – if I am not mistaken –

15 See: Witold Marciszewski, *Logika modalna* [*Modal Logics*] [in:] *Mała encyklopedia logiki*. (Wrocław: Ossolineum, 1988). Robert Poczobut, *Superweniencja. Zarys problematyki* [*Supervenience. The Outline of Problems*]. "Filozofia Nauki". 8(30), 2000, pp. 25-44. Witold Marciszewski, *Podstawy logicznej teorii przekonań [The Fundation of Logical Theory of Belief]*, (Warszawa PWN, 1972).

reference to the already elaborated methods of modal logic. In the case of the category of possibility/necessity, Piłat relies solely on his own semantic intuition.

Let us take a closer look at that modal intuition. It seems to me that, again, it is inspired by phenomenology. For Husserl, the constitution is a separation from within the scope of what is possible. But since the scope of possibility is theoretically infinite and since it contains negative possibilities too, it yields serious problems that are hoped to be solved with the help of the conceptual content. If there exist a multiplicity of relations connecting a cognitive organism to a set of objects, then only the contextual content may have a referential function in relation to the scope of possibility. I must assume, then, that Piłat follows Husserl's intuitions in that the intentional subject manifests itself in experience as invariant, focussing on itself even the simplest conscious perception. For the time being I will pass over two important problems – (1) how to interpret the contextual content which focuses the perception on the invariant and (2) does focusing on the invariant in the experience have a purely intuitive and nonsensual component, or maybe it is managed by a physical mechanism? Instead, I will focus solely on the work of modal concepts.

Jaakko Hintikka used to say, in his own words "without beating about the bush", that a concept is intentional if and only if it takes into account many possible states of things or courses of events (in his interpretation – possible worlds). To Hintikka, this means that the semantics of possible worlds is the logic of intentionality, and the intentional is what requires a reference to the semantics of possible worlds.[16] A reference to Hintikka is thus justified insofar as he considers speaking of possible worlds to be idle talk, as long as the consequences for possible experience are not defined, which in turn implies that a possible world is defined by the related entirety of the experience. The trouble is that after this assertion Hintikka gets down to building modal logic and the ontology of possible worlds, unlike Piłat. References to Renate Bartsch and Peter Gärdenfors, and then to the effects of metaphorisation (Lakoff, Fauconnier, and Langacker) appear insufficient and only paraphrase the problem without outlining the solution. This arbitrariness and the unclear way of dealing with the dangerous category of possibility have far reaching implications.

16 Jaakko Hintikka, *The Intentions of Intentionality and Other New Models for Modalities*. (Dordrecht: Reidel, 1975), p. 34.

4. What is a concept that a person may not grasp?

The title of this chapter is of course a paraphrase of a title of a well known essay by Ray Jackendoff on concepts and conceptual semantics.[17] To Jackendoff, there are reasons to speak of "E-concepts" and "I-concepts". "E-concept" is something given in the external world, for example, the concept of a natural number or a cardinal number, which conceptual realists approach as if it existed independently of whoever knew it or comprehended it. "I-concept", on the other hand, is a unit in one's head that can be passed to other persons only through language or some other channel of communication. To the degree that generative grammar allows us to better understand the human ability to use language, the choice of "I-language" as a subject of study (Noam Chomsky's choice) is entirely justified. Similarly, to the degree that conceptual semantics allows us to better understand the human ability to use concepts, the choice of "I-concept" (Jackendoff's choice) as a subject of study is fully justified too.

The problem is that even though Piłat implicitly refers to the above distinction, he does so without showing interest in a better understanding of the human ability to use concepts, and instead focuses on concepts alone and their ambiguous ontological status. Hence, the emphasis in Piłat's book falls on "E-concepts". This forces Piłat to attempt to answer a challenging question: How are humans able to reach and to grasp concepts? If humans are not so much into generating concepts – since they can only generate and learn conceptual representations, not concepts on their own – then how can we explain the phenomenon of the productivity of concepts? Here Piłat's answer is similar to the one given once by another giant of conceptual realism, Roger Penrose,[18]

---

17 Ray Jackendoff, *Languages of the Mind. Essays on Mental Representation.* (London: The MIT Press, 1992).

18 Penrose – who, like Piłat, was inspired by the findings of Kurt Gödel – claims that no nontrivial mathematical theorem can be proved solely in a formal way – that is, using axioms and tautological rules of reasoning. Definitions and mathematical operations are performative, that is to say they create new mathematical states of things which, as a result, make the nontrivial mathematical theorems equal to synthetic statements – but not to purely analytical statements. Thus, these definitions and operations are authentic findings and not just simple consequences of the axioms. This fact makes mathematics similar to the empirical sciences, disciplines authentically experiencing the world. Mathematics is not more deductive than other theories in empirical disciplines (Robert Penrose, *The Emperor's New Mind: Concerning Computers, Minds, and The Laws of Physics.* (Oxford: Oxford University Press 1989). Robert Piłat once pronounced that the weakness of Penrose's proposal results from the lack of philosophical awareness, and even lack of philosophy itself, in the work of the author. This may be true – a deepened philosophical consciousness could have warned Penrose not to pronounce many hasty

whom Piłat appears to dislike. Reflexive (conceptual) intuition is this cognitive power which can explain how the unlimited number of varied syntactic structures corresponds with the unlimited number of varied concepts. All concepts share some of the features which Kurt Gödel ascribed to mathematical concepts: "as constructions of intentional objects, they come ahead of any representation of these concepts".[19] According to Piłat, we can formulate abstract intuitions, and in order to name them and then to determine if they are true we reach for the arithmetics allowing such determination to be made. "The ability to formulate abstract intuitions is what distinguishes the human mind from machines".[20] This, however, may bring other controversies and doubts. Is the category of reflexive intuition to be trusted so much? Can the dark be explained with the darker? A reflexive intuition is defined by references to the category of possibility, but the category of possibility can only be defined in the act of conceptual intuition.

Piłat's reasoning is as follows. The shape of a given concept is at the same time a disposition to a certain type of mental activity and actions. If so, the disposition must take the form of an acceptance of a certain possibility – namely, the possibility of acquiring some other concept. Piłat says:

> If we speak of a possibility of a concept, it cannot belong to the same level of conceptual representation as a concept already acquired. Again, we see the necessity to distinguish between concepts effectively present in the cognitive system – that is conceptual representations – and concepts as such, that make up the layer of abstract objects which are built on top of conceptual representations. The possibility of acquiring a concept is simultaneously the actual acceptance of a given possibility, or more precisely, a disposition to accept a given possibility or a certain modal judgement.[21]

It appears that in this line of reasoning the ontological order is continuously confused with epistemic order. Cognitive representations, which belong to the epistemic order, are concepts effectively present in the cognitive system. But, there are also concepts as such, which constitute the ontological order. Conceptual intuition is the acceptance of a certain possibility, but there is also a category of "possibility of concept" – right at the borderland of ontology and

---

statements, such as the one suggesting human consciousness is a result of quantum gravity effects in microtubules – but it makes us ask whether a deepened philosophical consciousness in Robert Piłat's book is not a cause of his excessive trust in the instructive power of philosophy, able to illuminate the "darkness of existence" and to exhibit the whole as a "pool of possibility of events".

19 Robert Piłat, *O istocie pojęć [On the Nature of Concepts]*, p. 115.

20 *Ibid.*, p. 113.

21 *Ibid.*, p. 165.

epistemology. Since concepts are abstract objects, "possibility of concept" is the ontological possibility of the existence of a certain object, but if concepts are conceptual representations, then "possibility of concept" results from the correction of our knowledge.

To better understand the complex relations between what is epistemic and ontological, let us again return to Saul Kripke. Kripke notices that the statement: "The evening star is the morning star" is *a posteriori* – its validity was established through astronomical observation. However – Kripke claims – this statement is also necessary. "The morning star" and "the evening star" are proper names, and as such, in all possible worlds, they refer to the same object of the real world – Venus. It means that the statement "the evening star is the morning star" is true in all possible worlds, and thus, it is necessary.[22]

However, is it not that this statement, like all statements based on observation, is uncertain? Does it not imply that this particular statement could possibly be false? The possibility we are referring to here is epistemological. If we consider all we know, it is possible that one day we might discover that our observations were inaccurate. The statement "the evening star is the morning star" is equipped with a particular quality which makes it valid in all possible worlds: if it is already true, then it is true in all possible worlds. In this sense, this statement is necessary. This is what Kripke describes as metaphysical necessity.

The statement "the evening star is the morning star" is thus a statement metaphysically necessary. Of course, other statements of the same kind are also metaphysically necessary, for example, "monkeys are animals", "the heat is a movement of molecules", "the light is a stream of photons", and so on and so forth. All these statements refer to the nature of certain objects – a monkey, heat, light, and so on. Let us consider the statement "the heat is a movement of molecules". It is *a posteriori* – many years of thorough research and experimenting were needed to find out that heat is the movement of molecules. As any *a posteriori* statement, it is uncertain, that is, it is possible that one day it will come out that in spite of our efforts we were mistaken and that heat is not at all the movement of molecules. This possibility is epistemological; it describes the cognitive situation we are currently in. It is an expression of the uncertainty related to all empirical knowledge. However, it does not undermine the metaphysical necessity of this statement.

Let us assume, for the time being, that we are not mistaken and heat is indeed the movement of molecules. In this case, this sentence is not only true but also necessary. "Heat" from some other world, "heat" found in a distant

22 Saul Kripke, *Naming and Necessity*, (Cambridge: Harvard University Press, 1980).

region of the universe, would be considered heat (as described in our language) only if it is the movement of molecules. A phenomenon similar to heat in all respects (that is affecting our senses identically), but not the movement of molecules, cannot be (and would not be) described as heat. If heat is indeed the movement of molecules, it is necessarily the movement of molecules.

In this example we can clearly see that epistemological possibility is harmonised with metaphysical necessity. The accidentality of our knowledge determines the possibility of correcting our concepts. The validity of our knowledge in all possible worlds decides in favour of its necessity. According to Piłat, concepts as such, unlike conceptual representations, express the possibilities of the world. But what are these possibilities? Well, if the extensions of concepts are sets of possible things and states of things, then the possibilities Piłat is referring to rest in extending concepts and increasing the complexity of their content as new referential objects appear. To me, this process is exclusively epistemological as the concepts get affected by their extensions and their growing complexity. Piłat demonstrates how the contents of certain concepts evolve, as a matter of logical or conceptual – but not metaphysical – possibility. The problem is that according to his main thesis, Piłat should be in fact referring to the idea of metaphysical possibility and questioning whether something can exist in a metaphysically possible world set by necessary *a posteriori* statements.

Instead, Piłat claims that "contingent truths about the world expressed in scientific theories all have at their base certain conceptual truths *a priori*, that is, truths in relations between concepts. The expression of these relations is the possibility of proving identical extensions of two concepts with different connotations".[23] Excellent, but the truths included in relations between concepts still refer to logical or conceptual possibility. To put it bluntly: if concepts are objects but not representations, then Piłat should rather be searching for the evidence for the *a priori* structure of the universe, which for some reason allows for, or excludes, certain states of things, but not for the *a priori* form of knowledge. We should then begin work on ontology similar to that of Wittgenstein in *Tractatus Logico-Philosophicus*, which aims at defining the space of possibility and impossibility for the state of all things. "Each thing is, as it were, in a space of possible states of affairs. This space I can imagine empty, but I cannot imagine the thing without the space".[24] Piłat however, formulates

23 Robert Piłat, *O istocie pojęć [On the Nature of Concepts]*, p. 306-307.

24 Ludwig Wittgenstein (1922), *Tractatus Logico-Philosophicus.* trans. David Pears and Brian McGuinness, (London: Routledge 1961). In Polish literature, a similar project was undertaken by Bogusław Wolniewicz (Bogusław Wolniewicz, *Ontologia sytuacji [The Ontology of Situation]*, (Warszawa PWN, 1985).

epistemological arguments after putting forward ontological theses. It is not a weakness of his book, but proof of how difficult it is to harmonise the successes of cognitive sciences with an interesting philosophical ontology.

Piłat defends his position in yet another way. To him, there exists a conceptual universe preordaining the existence or nonexistence of certain objects. This means that conceptual relations have metaphysical consequences. "While there are concepts referring *a priori* to nonexisting objects, there seem to be no *a priori* conditions of existence of certain objects".[25] If so, the power of concepts would be a negative one – excluding certain states of things. This means that concepts would more likely set the conditions of impossibility of certain objects rather than conditions of their possibility. Here, we discover Hegel again. Piłat quotes Hegel's saying that concepts are the other side of things trying in this way to link the representation of existence and the existence of representation, and to describe the movement of substance. If we were to follow the flow of Piłat's thought, then we would have to accept that his favourite category of possibility is not the conceptual, logical, metaphysical, nor even nomological, but the Hegelian category of possibility – potentiality in movement – which reveals the truth of the concept itself. Piłat, indulging himself with the notion of concept as the other side of existence, forgets about other aspects of Hegel's philosophy. Let me mention only one.

In the last part of *Phenomenology of Spirit* Hegel says:

> The self-knowing Spirit knows not only itself but also the negative of itself, or its limit: to know one's limit is to know how to sacrifice oneself. The sacrifice is the externalisation in which Spirit displays the process of its becoming Spirit in the form of free contingent happening, intuiting its pure Self as Time outside of it, and equally its Being as Space.[26]

This might explain why a concept is something that a person cannot grasp. What cannot be grasped is this constant becoming – the movement consisting in the externalisation and restitution of a concept's existence, which dies away at its limit.

Would Robert Piłat like to attempt to describe this Hegelian odyssey of mutual references to the subsequent sequences of existence in search of the absolute concept? Would he ever wish to undertake this negative work himself, the work of concepts seeking their own content in constant and intensifying acts of annulation? "The True" – Hegel says – "is the whole. But the whole is

25 Robert Piłat, *O istocie pojęć [On the Nature of Concepts]*, p. 288.

26 Georg Wilhelm Friedrich Hegel (1807), *Phenomenology of Spirit,* trans. A. V. Miller. (Oxford: Clarendon Press, 1977), p. 462.

nothing other than the essence consummating itself through its development".[27] I dare to doubt Robert Piłat's Hegelianism; but I would rather let it go here and conclude with a recognition that hereby the metaphysical nature of the analyst wandering upon the land of Cyborgs felt an irresistible desire to experience for a little while the true life of conceptual subjectivity. Someone else reading *On the Nature of Concepts* could however doubt the cognitive orientation of the author, and conclude that his metaphysical nature has prevailed over the dead language of the analyst (engineer), manifesting itself so severely that it may as well attempt to correct the ontological argument for the existence of God.

5. Spider: concepts as monsters

Thus, unexpectedly, the reading of Robert Piłat's *On the Nature of Concepts* brings us closer to the strong intellectual position of Gilles Deleuze and Felix Guattari. For them, philosophy is neither contemplation nor reflection or communication, since no one needs philosophy to see, to consider or to communicate. Public relations specialists have long ago deprived philosophers of communication skills, science has long ago taken away their claims to undertaking reflection, and the visual arts their claims to perception and insight. Philosophy is a disposition (power) to create new concepts, and to sport this disposition is to prove its strength and authenticity.

Thus understood, philosophical achievement makes concepts not so much preexisting entities (the position of conceptual realism), nor words as such (the position of nominalism), nor interwoven clusters of similarities (the position of connectionism), but rather lofty structures if not sheer works of art. Indeed, the art of creating concepts is the most radical of all arts known to a man. Likely, each concept sporting a finite number of features branches out into other concepts – similarly complex, varying in composition and content – founding elements of yet another field. Philosophers do not sap under the surface of reality as moles do, they do not devour all organic waste like whales, and they do not just slip on the surface of things like snakes. Instead, philosophers best resemble spiders since in order to survive they produce webs akin to conceptual networks. The authors of *What Is Philosophy?* rightly conclude that:

> The concept of a bird is found not in its genus or species but in the composition of its postures, colors, and songs: something indiscernible that is not so much synesthetic as syneidetic. A concept is a heterogenesis – that is to say, an ordering of its components by zones of neighborhood. It is ordinal, an intension present in all the features that make it up. The concept is in a state of survey [*survolt*] in relation

27 *Ibid.*, p. 20.

> to its components, endlessly traversing them according to an order without distance. It is immediately co-present to all its components or variations, at no distance from them, passing back and forth through them: it is a refrain, all opus with its number (*chiffre*).[28]

If indeed, as Deleuze and Guattari suggest, "concepts are like multiple waves, rising and falling, but the plane of immanence is the single wave that rolls them up and unrolls them" then maybe it will come easier for us to comprehend why concepts are incomprehensible. It is not so much because these are of an abstract nature, nor because these exist in worlds beyond our bodies, nor because they have a wavelength form (rather than being corpuscular), but because they derive from our own actions, practice of thinking and creating, and as such are inseparably intertwined with this practice. The stronger they do so, the more transparent they seem to us. Each concept is thus a spider web, a liquid undergoing polymerization/coagulation in reaction with the air. „Concepts are really monsters that are reborn from their fragments".[29]

28 Gilles Deleuze, Felix Guattari, *What Is Philosophy?*, trans. H. Tomlinson, G. Burchell, (Columbia University Press, 1994), pp. 20-21.

29 *Ibid.*, p. 155.

VI. The Spectacle of Absolute Power

Whatever this is that I am, it is a little flesh and breath, and the ruling part. Throw away thy books; no longer distract thyself: it is not allowed; but as if thou wast now dying, despise the flesh; it is blood and bones and a network, a contexture of nerves, veins, and arteries. See the breath also, what kind of a thing it is, air, and not always the same, but every moment sent out and again sucked in. The third then is the ruling part: consider thus: Thou art an old man; no longer let this be a slave, no longer be pulled by the strings like a puppet to unsocial movements, no longer either be dissatisfied with thy present lot, or shrink from the future.

Marcus Aurelius[1]

The externality of the spectacle in relation to the active man appears in the fact that his own gestures are no longer his but those of another who represents them to him. This is why the spectator feels at home nowhere, because the spectacle is everywhere.

Guy Debord[2]

1. The spectacle

Ridley Scott's *Gladiator* evokes diverse emotions and arouses conflicting interpretations. This fresco could be seen as a typical Hollywood action movie, comparable to the multiple reincarnations of Bruce Willis's *Die Hard*, or as a symptom of a growing demand in contemporary American society for a new hero to address its hidden desires. Then, *Gladiator* would be a portrayal of a kind of 21st century Achilles who lives fast and claims the eternal fame of a hero, a hero tailored to the times wc live in, cast in a mould of our civilization of war. Or else, it is just a fine martial arts spectacle, a feast to the hungry eyes of spectators. To some, perhaps more naïve ones, it is a good source of historical information.

---

1 Marcus Aurelius. *Meditations*, http://classics.mit.edu//Antoninus/meditations.2.two.html

2 Guy Debord. *Comments on the Society of the Spectacle*, trans. Malcolm Imrie, (London: Verso 1990). Thesis 30, p. 10. *Society of the Spectacle* is an expression first used in 1967 by Guy Debord, in reference to contemporary rather than ancient times. To Debord, the contemporary world seems to have passed a critical point or "focal length": it is a world in reverse. The appearance becomes the reality, and a real user now only consumes illusions. Commodity is in fact a real illusion, and the spectacle is its generalized manifestation.

Let me have a brief look at the plot. The story is set at the end of the 2nd century. The aging Emperor, Marcus Aurelius (Richard Harris) wants general Maximus (Russell Crowe), one of the greatest Roman commanders, to take his place and to be his heir over his own son, Commodus. Caesar's son (Joaquin Phoenix) is made aware of this plan and, to prevent it happening, he chooses to kill his father and sentence Maximus and his family to death. It is worth mentioning right here that Commodus is tormented by an Oedipus complex. His drama is one of an inept and introvert son who is suffering because of the greatness and excessive fame of his father – a wise philosopher and sagacious ruler. The tragedy of Maximus, on the other hand, is one of a sovereign and fully integrated father, fighting his wars in faraway lands, expanding the civilization. Maximus wants to decrease the amount of barbarism at the expense of violence, yet he longs for home, the fields of corn, olive groves, and patches of basil.

It is a sheer miracle that Maximus manages to escape the execution, but the army that hailed Commodus as a legal heir obeys his orders to kill Maximus's family and burn his home. Unaware of this, the general gets captured and is then made to take part in the gladiator games. Nonetheless, our hero makes his way up as a gladiator and gains celebrity status. He finally gets to Rome where the games are organized under the auspices of Commodus, who comments on Maximus: "the general who became a slave. The slave who became a gladiator. The gladiator who defied an emperor. Striking story!". Yearning for justice, and left with nothing but his bravery and lethal dexterity – his bodily skills – Maximus wants to take revenge for the death of his beloved wife and his only son. Burning in the flames of his Oedipus complex, and holding absolute authority, Commodus will do his utmost to annihilate general/gladiator Maximus. This means employing all the dirty tricks possible and the meanness that he cherishes so much. The Roman public is there not only to witness this duel, but to generate collective desires and whims. The stands of the arena are where the opinions are formed, and where notions and judgements are passed: both Commodus and Maximus must take into account the Roman public and its desires and judgements. Caesar must take into account public desires, and the gladiator must play on the emotions of the crowd. Either way, the Roman public is to render its judgement in a trial between a Father who was forced to become a gladiator, and a son who became Caesar thanks to intrigue and the founding murder of his own father.

We are tempted to read *Gladiator* as a typical action movie, probably because of its spectacular quality. If we did so, we would deny its claim to depict the fall of ancient Rome, and we would overlook the insightful analysis of power relations that had led to it. Similarly, thinking of other Ridley Scott films, we are tempted to read *Blade Runner* in a simplistic fashion, as a noir crime story where Harrison Ford is a Chandlerian Philip Marlowe future detective, chasing a group of cyborgs who pretend to be super humans, and accidentally falls for one of them, a robotess. If we followed such a reading, we would miss Scott's concern with the implications of Turing's thesis – regarding the mechanical nature of our thinking and the intellectual organization of machines. In a similar way, we might have remembered something more from *Alien* than a snake-like creature coming out of one of the USCSS Nostromo crew and then hastily changing into a killing machine (Chestburster). We could apply a Freudian analysis here: the snake represents a death drive – Tanathos – a parasite let loose from the inside to later attack its host in revenge for its long suppression.

In other words, it is my intension here to reject the temptation of trivializing the intellectual work of Ridley Scott. I have generous respect for his achievement and I intend to read *Gladiator* as a spectacle of power and its hidden mechanics, looking for aspects of both power and powerlessness. The spectacle I am about to inspect is about masses and multitude, not individual life stories. This drama is about watchful human hordes deciding upon life and death, rather than individuals who are so mean that they make Lady Macbeth seem pure good, or rather than those who are so daring that in comparison Achilles' bravery seems no better than castration anxiety. This spectacle is about the role of the multitude, a mediator between a sovereign who wants to see the gladiator's misery, and a gladiator who wants Caesar stripped naked and his empty loftiness revealed to the public.

2. The masses

Hannah Arendt claimed that totalitarian regimes occur wherever the masses have acquired the appetite for political organization. If what Arendt says is true, *Gladiator* demonstrates a totalitarian regime. The Roman public does not dare to create a sovereign political organization, but is bound in a political community upon its aesthetic judgement and pleasure principle: here, the pleasure of watching a cruel spectacle and rendering the final judgement upon competitors. The masses are not bound in a community of interests, for the masses lack class standing. The masses are in a state of rapture, unified in frenzy, rendering judgements upon the object of their ecstasy. Arendt says:

> The term masses applies only where we deal with people who either because of sheer numbers, or indifference, or a combination of both, cannot be integrated into any organization based on common interest, into political parties or municipal governments or professional organizations or trade unions. Potentially, they exist in

> every country and form the majority of those large numbers of neutral, politically indifferent people who never join a party and hardly ever go to the polls.[3]

If masses "potentially exist in every country", then maybe they exist in all times and throughout all historical eras, including ancient times. Ancient masses are exactly what is subjected to rule. The mass is something vague, something which does not exist, or at least whose existence is dependent on being delimited by a particular definition: there is folk/mass/herd calling for a leader, there is folk/mass/child requiring protection of a mighty father, there is folk/ mass/electorate eager to be pleased and activated, and finally – from the sociological perspective – folk/mass/public opinion. So what kind of a mass is the crowd gathered in the Colosseum in the 2nd century after Christ?

Arendt claims that the birth of the totalitarian apparatus laid to rest two misconceptions associated with liberal-democratic regimes. The first illusion was based on a fallible notion that most people actively participate and want to participate in governing, and that most men are affiliated with one or another political party. Totalitarian movements proved that passive and impartial masses may win a majority and that democracy could then be a principle shared by the minority. The second illusion was that politically passive masses can be in fact ignored. Totalitarian regimes have all well demonstrated that masses do not comprise of mute or impartial participants or neutral arbiters, nor that they are a mere background to political life and plankton in a food-chain. Instead, the masses are a decisive catalyst of all relevant political decisions.[4] So it is not only a phenomenon of the times we live in that politicians seek support among the undecided and try to persuade them into voting. Along with institutions and organizations open to public view, democratic governments are supported by silent approval and the acceptance of impartial and mute social strata. As I mentioned above, Arendt claims that both illusions were dispelled by the experience of the 20th century totalitarianisms. These experiences illustrate two discoveries (inventions) of the modern age.

Arendt's perspective is historical, sociological, and her focus is the 20th century. Her concern is clearly not with the ancient multitude. When in *The Human Condition* she actually describes the ancient world, she does so from the aristocratic point of view. Exploitation was not the key aspect of slavery. Aristocrats used slaves to avoid work and have time for spectacles similar to the one portrayed by Ridley Scott. Work, unlike political activism and the struggle for immortality, was a bankrupt activity. According to Arendt, slavery was a

---

3 Hannah Arendt. *The Origins of Totalitarianism*, (New York, Harcourt, 1951).

4 See also: Jacob L. Talmon, *The Origins of Totalitarian Democracy*, (New York: Praeger, 1952).

way of acquiring a cheap labor force and was not meant to yield profits – it was a way of excluding work from the conditions of human life.[5] The work of the Gladiator, himself part of a degraded and inhumane world, is to kill. This job suits Maximus perfectly. He is forged in the heat of battle, talented and skilful. The crowd respect him and grant him celebrity status. He is free to risk his life and take away somebody else's life, as well as their public life. For a gladiator there is no other risk than losing his zoe, his biological life. In no way is he risking his bios, his cultural life, as he is deprived of it. The power of killing belongs to Caesar, but his position is far better: he doesn't have to risk his life.[6]

In my view, Scott's staging dares to address many of the political issues that were so important to Arendt. Scott tells us, I believe, that all modern political discoveries or inventions are an inherent part of politics, they are a part of the politics of spectacle. Arendt was right in saying that there are two basic political illusions. The first is a feature of our times and refers, *grosso modo*, to mightily overrated forms of indoctrination and persuasion. Contemporary leaders who appear on our TV screens believe that the power of propaganda is immense. They share – to use a rather blunt mental abbreviation – the aesthetics of navy blue shirts in public service: at the beginning of 20th century it was the charm of brownshirts that occupied minds of so many.

On the other hand, there is the equally troubling 19th century misconception, based on a notion that the people's voice is the voice of God, while in fact it is only the voice of a mob. Unaware of both illusions, Commodus appears grotesque. When he challenges the masses as a Caesar, not as a sophist or rhetor, he faces a stark choice: either his will or the mob's shall prevail, either he is or he is not Caesar. Commodus has will but not a strong will, he has power but no skills to handle it, he has freedom but he cannot call himself into being. When Commodus fails to assert himself, the mob refuse to obey him and dismiss his doubtful decisions; he behaves a little like Georges

5 Hannah Arendt, *The Human Condition*, (Chicago: University of Chicago Press, 1958).

6 In *Homo sacer* Agamben suggests that Greeks had no single term to express what we mean by the word "life". They used two terms that are semantically and morphologically distinct: *zoe*, which expressed the simple fact of living, common to all living beings (animals, men, or gods), and *bios*, which indicated the form or way of living proper to an individual or a group. In the classical world simple natural life is excluded from the *polis* in the strict sense, and it remains confined – as merely reproductive life – to the sphere of the *oikos*, "home". According to Agamben, the entry of *zoe* into the sphere of the *polis* – the politization of bare life as such – constitutes the decisive event of modernity and signals a radical transformation of the political-philosophical categories of classical thought (Giorgio Agamben, *Homo Sacer: Sovereign Power and Bare Life*, trans. D. Heller-Roazen, (Stanford University Press. Stanford, 1998). pp. 1-5).

Benjamin Clemenceau, the French prime minister much despised by Arendt, who first recognized that "People are the God". What the masses are craving for, Commodus is likely to give. Unfortunately for him, he is a clumsy salesman and an incompetent analyst of the real needs of the Roman public. His ambiguous relation to the masses – which will finally cost him his life – is a mix of charming and despising the crowd, with possibly the worst timing possible. Commodus is charming when he should be spiteful, and spiteful when some charm is most needed.

Arendt claims that 20th century tyrants emerge from the mob and will seek its support. Those tyrants understood well that the mob is not only a waste but also a side effect of bourgeois society. But the tyrants of the 2nd century emerged from the aristocracy – says Ridley Scott – and there could be no better social standing than the one offered to Commodus. Family background means nothing though, as all the virtues of fathers turn against their sons, and the greatness of fathers is in demeaning and undervaluing.

The mob is a collection of people who have fallen out from the classes. It can therefore easily be taken for "the people", as this term comprises all social strata. There is, however, a significant difference between the mob and the people. In a revolutionary struggle, the people are fighting for real representation, and the mob requires only a fantasy, a hyper-father, a super-human, a mega-star, an Übermensch, or a gladiator. The inner desires of a mob are vested in a father figure, and the logic employed is that of resentment. The mob hates "society" for its rejection of the mob. The Senate is similarly rejected – as it does not represent the mob. The only principle the mob complies with is that of leadership. This principle is applied to all levels of the reproduction of power and breaks down into numerous icons of the leader, marking all public spaces and homes, demonstrating His authority, explaining daily events. This is why the masses find their shepherd in Maximus, the icon of a fallen general, instead of Commodus, the icon of unjustly extolled son of Ceasar. There are reasons why the mob in the Colosseum finds Maximus to be a shepherd to follow. The bloodbath presented on the arena is tempting for the hungry eyes of the mob; the spectacle creates an overwhelming illusion of identification with the hero. The mob is possessed by multiplied joint mechanisms of projection and introjection. Thus, it accepts its humble role of bleating sheep and finds in Maximus its hypnotiser and its master, to revere and worship.

The author of *The Human Condition* is right to say that the most striking difference between modern and ancient sophism is that the ancient sophists were satisfied with lofty victories of rhetoric over truth, while the modern ones dare for more, they wish for lasting victories over reality, they long for the victory of their ideology, the victory of systemic fiction, or a totalitarian simulation.[7] Ancient sophists eagerly frustrated and sneered at human thought, the modern ones frustrate human activism and sneer at the human world that has been slowly changing over thousands of years. Commodus might have won had he been able to transform into a 20th century sophist, that is, if he had not only annihilated Maximus and his family, but also made sure that there was absolutely nothing left of him in peoples' memories. In a way he did, he took away from Maximus his glorious death at the battlefield, but he failed to erase him from soldiers' memories. The death that Commodus took away from Maximus thus brings about his own death in the Roman Colosseum. So this is the finale of the plot. Descending from his comfortable throne, Commodus finds himself dead, on the clay, in sand, and covered with dust.

The Colosseum scenes are crucial for the drama's dynamics. Take the first scene, when after some great and uneven fights Maximus wins and is called upon to reveal his name in public. Commodus is taken aback (as for him Maximus has already vanished) and once again sentences Maximus to death. And once again he fails. Such is his absolute authority, people get killed, only this time – a man is going to be killed twice. This does not happen though. What Commodus took away, he naively repairs; Maximus is given a second life. The crowd – amazed with his fighting skills, bravery, and efficiency – forces the Caesar to change his verdict and save the gladiator's life. Commodus cannot tell the mob from the people and he has to obey the crowd's verdict. He loses his name, the name of absolute authority. The absolute monarch is defeated, deposed, his reign lost to history. Maximus is cherished in human memory, no victory could have been bigger.

When asked what his name was, the gladiator answers: "my name is Maximus Decimus Meridius, commander of the Armies of the North, General of the Felix Legions, loyal servant to the true emperor Marcus Aurelius. Father to a murdered son, husband to a murdered wife. And I will have my vengeance in this life or the next". The answer is a challenge directed at the Caesar. Earlier, as we remember – Maximus hears this warning from Juba: "you have a great name. He must kill your name before he kills you". But Juba is wrong. In the end, it is not Maximus's name that is to be killed: rather, it is his name that kills the Caesar.

The second crucial scene is the final one. It is a direct fight between the Caesar and the gladiator. The genius of this scene is not in the fact that Maximus, who has been hurt unsportingly, can still win against arrogant Commodus. The

---

7 Dana Villa, *Politics, Philosophy, Terror: Essays on the Thought of Hannah Arendt.* (Princeton: Princeton University Press, 1999).

genius – and unrealism – of this scene is in the fact that a gladiator can reverse power relations. The one who is the sovereign and the only subject before god is forced to stand up and descend to the ground – and to feel the soil in his mouth. To fight for his authority, he becomes another actor in the spectacle. The one who opposed him and forced him to do that must be a superhuman or at least a nonhuman. This time, the army will not obey. Commodus will receive no more arms, the army will defend its honour, the guards will withdraw their support from the tyrant, they will turn around from this monster. Is it only because it is all a spectacle and the audience is a crowd, a mob or a people? Or maybe because it is a spectacle, and not a well planned show. Was public space in Rome is in a position to help Maximus win? Was it a drama of human life, a drama set in public where battles of priority and for immortality were taking place? Proximo's words, "we mortals are but shadows and dust", are made to resonate in the speech that Maximus gives to his soldiers before battle: "what we do in life echoes in eternity". So now, if we combine the figures of Proximo and Maximus, we come up with: "what we do in life as shadows echoes in dust".

3. The spectacle of torture/a TV spectacle

So why say that the reversal of power relations is both imaginary and unrealistic? In *Discipline and Punish: The Birth of the Prison*, Foucault is contrasting ancient and modern times: the society of spectacle against disciplined society, a society under surveillance. The society of spectacle provides the masses with a limited amount of events, scenes and actions. It is reflected in the architecture of temples, theatres, and circuses. A monarch is clearly visible, but his people are not. Individualization is ascending – the more power or privilege, the more unique and exceptional a person is. It is a part of every ritual, discourse, or spectacle.

Modernity, identified with the panoptic society, provides a few people (in extreme situations one person) with immediate insight into the lives of many and of each individual behaviour. The view of a monarch is thereby exchanged for the view of a single man. This exemplifies descending individualization. As authority becomes more anonymous and as it is increasing in functionality, the people are undergoing even stronger individualization. The basic architectural unit of the modern world is not a theatre or a stadium, but the panopticon – a prison building invented by Jeremy Bentham:[8] a circular structure resembling a

8 Jeremy Bentham, *The Panopticon Writings*, edited and introduced by Miran Bozovic, (London: Verso, 1995).

ring with wide windows opening prison cells on the view from the inside. Foucault – in Arendt's style – writes that:

> In a society, which does without community life and forum, whose constitutive elements are private individuals on one hand side and the state on the second, relations can be regulated by a form that is the exact opposite of the spectacle.[9]

The obsession of being under surveillance and the privilege of observing are the two basic tendencies of modernity that keep overlapping and stay entwined. "Full lighting and the eye of a supervisor capture better than darkness, which ultimately protected. Visibility is a trap".[10] The Panopticon is an optical device; a kind of *camera obscura* where a man is not spied on, nor he is a spy; instead, he is transparent in the building where the task of exercising control is dispersed throughout the whole society. "The Panopticon is a royal menagerie" – says Foucault – "the animal is replaced by man, individual distribution by specific grouping and the king by the machinery of a furtive power".[11]

Interestingly, Paul Veyne's commentary on Michel Foucault's work is exclusively devoted to gladiators and the spectacle they were creating. Veyne wants to understand the uniqueness (rarity) of Foucault's work. He poses an opening question: Why did gladiator games cease to continue, slowly and irregularly, in the 4th century after Christ, exactly when Christian Caesars were in reign? The most obvious answer – that all this was due to the dawn of Christianity – is not one that would satisfy Veyne. The Christians held contempt for gladiator games as much as they did for all spectacles turning people's attention from their natural goal: redemption. Among such delusive spectacles was bawdy theatre that should have been damned. The pleasure of watching a bloodbath is short, it is in fact a purely voyeuristic pleasure. The pleasure of watching verbal obscenities however is prolonged, it encourages the spectators to live bawdily outside the theatre and long after the spectacle finished. Gladiator games disappear, unlike the verbal fencing of the actors. Veyne says:

---

9 Michael Foucault, *Discipline & Punish: The Birth of the Prison*, trans Alan Sheridan, (New York: Vintage Books, 1995), pp. 195-228.

10 *Ibid.*, p. 241.

11 *Ibid.*, p. 244. The division between the amphitheatre and the prison is not a decisive one. There is a second overlapping division between a society of torture and disciplinary society. So, once again and in brief: the society of sovereignty was founded on bloody spectacles, and therefore it is an effect of a social formation where the workforce and human body are not useful and do not have exchange value. A disciplinary society is based on a network of prisons and standardization. It is the effect of industrial social formation, where power is not confirmed through spectacles of blood and violence, but thanks to omnipresent disciplines. These disciplines are in fact techniques to administer punishment and correction – not to the body but to the "non corporal", the soul.

> In ancient times, the gladiators had the ambivalent reputation of today's porn stars. Even if they were not fascinating as stars of the arena, they were at least scary. They volunteered to put their life at stake. They were both victims and the killers, potential suicides and dead corpses. For the same reason, they were seen impure and no better than prostitutes.[12]

Ancient Rome was happy with violence, it was legal, and the state's monopoly on violence did not evoke fears yet, unlike today. Individual institutionalized violence was a treat, comparable to the porn industry's feats today. However, in the 4th century fear took over ill fascination. But before this dramatic shift took place, it was thought by such prominent figures as Cicero and Plinius that gladiator games were the best way to educate the Roman public in soldierly *virtus*. It is therefore general/gladiator Maximus and his deeds that enter the hall of fame as an iconic representation of Roman virtues and the ethics of fortitude. Let us not forget that the Senate backed the preservation of gladiator games in the same fashion as the French Academy shielded orthography. In both cases, the integrity of the community was at stake. According to Veyne, it was exactly when Roman Caesars were no longer bound by the Senate's opinion and when they started administering through officials that they could finally shed all limitations imposed by the herd, and could freely act as fathers. As a result, they became paternalistic, and found themselves comfortable with Christianity and uncomfortable with gladiator combats.

The genius and great fantasy of Scott's spectacle is founded on the individualization of a porn star in ancient Rome, to the extent that it becomes a threat to Commodus. Maximus becomes a defender of the Roman public, and his fights are devoted to the preservation of community, just like the struggle of purist linguists to preserve community by protection of the rules of grammar and vocabulary of a given language. Maximus resembles Emile Zola, admired by Arendt for his courage and the will to oppose the masses. But Maximus is not against the masses; he is to fulfill their strongest desires, he is to satisfy their hunger for a bloodbath, he is to show them a glimpse of the harvest of apocalypse. Maximus's good fortune is that he is a master in the art of killing, and that the masses can entrust him with their fear and love. They can see him as a superhuman, both a ferocious judge and a gracious savior, whose power enslaves their imagination: some with fear and some with hope to be saved and protected.

Ridley Scott's good fortune is that he is able to present this spectacle in the cinema, on the big screen, for an audience which, like in ancient Rome,

---

12 Paul Veyne, *Foucault Revolutionizes History* [in:] A. I. Davidson (ed.) *Foucault and His Interlocutors*. (Chicago: University of Chicago Press), 1997, pp. 146-182.

desperately needs something more than comedy series or other endless shows imitating the banality of life in a mass society. His good fortune is that he is able to provide an accurate diagnosis of contemporary society. Scott is prophetic in saying that the comeback of the masses is a return of the multitude, multiplicity, and the Empire, which is going to be even more limitless than the Roman Empire.

Michael Hardt and Antonio Negri claim – continuing the work of Arendt and Foucault – that contemporary power is a syndrome: a monarchy turning into tyranny (with law as a global force), aristocracy turning into oligarchy (economy meaning financial speculation), and a democracy turning into ochlocracy (power of people meaning the power of quantity, mediocrity, and various superstitions). Contemporary Rome is a trinity of Washington (bomb), New York (money) and Los Angeles (ether). The contemporary masses are the multitude and it is the multitude that called the Empire into being. This multitude shall decide upon its future. We find this passage in *Empire*:

> The multitude is the real productive force of our social world, whereas Empire is a mere apparatus of capture that lives only off the vitality of the multitude – as Marx would say, a vampire regime of accumulated dead labor that survives only by sucking off the blood of the living.[13]

The spectacle is continued upon the masses' request and only the masses are the sphere of animal life. If we assume that Marcus Aurelius is right in his opinion that a man comprises of a body, breath and will, then today the masses are body, the media give ether – and thus give force to the breath (wind) – and finally the will is at the gladiator's service. This means that biological life of the masses –

13 Michael Hardt and Antonio Negri. *Empire*, (Harvard University Press, 2001). Hardt and Negri claim that the concept of the multitude should be contrasted with a series of other concepts that designate plural collectives, such as the crowd, the masses, and the mob. The components of the masses, the mob, and the crowd are not singularities – and this is obvious from the fact that their differences so easily collapse into the indifference of the whole. Moreover, these social subjects are fundamentally passive in the sense that they do not act by themselves but rather must be led. The multitude designates an active social subject, which acts on the basis of what the singularities share in common. The multitude is an internally different, multiple social subject whose constitution and action is based not on identity or unity but on what is common (Michael Hardt and Antonio Negri, *Multitude: War and Democracy in the Age of Empire*, New York: Penguin 2004, p. 100). Hardt and Negri do not provide a technical answer to the question of how it is that the multitude (multiplicity) keeps from degenerating into a mob, or why it is that the multitude sustains all noble features of diversity, while at the same time is spun of dense communicative-corporative networks, which on its own allow for the establishment of community. This is a tough question. Is this cohabitation of idiosyncratic differences and cooperative ties not, in fact, a miracle?

those grand silent populations – became the subject of politics and surveillance. The media generate the activity of the masses, yet they accustom passivity while supporting false or apparent activities, allowing for numb eye movements and occasionally fierce mouse clicks. Thanks to this apparent activity of the masses, the gladiators shine on our screens. They are our stars; pop-stars and porn stars, providing extreme virtual pleasures and cybernetic violence. Real violence and earthly pleasures we forgot. And we will not allow for their return.

4. Tele-vision/absolute authority

Finally, I would like to contrast the narrative of *Gladiator* by Ridley Scott with *Minority Report* directed by Steven Spielberg in 2002, and based on a short 1954 novel by Philip K. Dick. The films share more than just a fantasy plot. To be sure, Scott was there before with *Blade Runner*, and he had taken on the power/spectacle issue. But we might venture to say that, while Scott in *Gladiator* provides an archaeology of techniques of domination and social influence, Spielberg in *Minority Report* projects their bright new future. Let us repeat after Marcus Aurelius the passage referring to human will: "[c]onsider that you are an old man, and do not let this noble part of you languish in slavery any longer. Let it not be overborne with selfish passions; let it not quarrel with fate, or be uneasy at the present, or afraid of the future".[14]

Let us quickly review the plot of *Minority Report*. It is the year 2054. in Washington, the murder rate is nil thanks to the use of an unprecedented tool: three clairvoyants emerged in water, seemingly in a coma, projecting future genocides right onto police TV screens. The creatures are like a Nemesis. More accurately, with bios on our mind, they are representing her punishing hand, infallible, ruthless, and always just. It is the Law made immanent. The visions are transformed into a precise description, and then a police prevention force is directed to the future murder site – all guided by agent John Anderton (Tom Cruise). A turning point is when John Anderton is himself suspected of being guilty of a future crime, as he is supposedly intending to murder a man. The problem is, he does not know much about the victim. The system based on precognition is imperfect, hence the title. There are three judges, and the judgement they render is considered accurate when it is passed by a majority. A dissenting vision, a so-called "minority report" is ignored. However, this report is the only hope of agent Anderton. He must find this report to be proved innocent. But in doing so, he is attempting to validate an alternative reality and

---

14 Marcus Aurelius. *Meditations*, http://www.btinternet.com/~glynhughes/squashed/ marcusa.htm

prove that the system based on precognition of human will is flawed. Unfortunately for him, the report is well hidden by the sovereign. The sovereign does not believe in the power of nature but rests his convictions in the might of a monarch. In defence, Anderton assumes the power of a decision maker, and as such he wants himself to decide the state of exception.

One of the definitive scenes of *Minority Report*, and at the same time one of the most visionary precognitions of Philip K. Dick, is the one in which Anderton's eyes are scanned and his identity detected.[15] This sophisticated technique sparks Orwellian connotations. This is a world where the retina is scanned to check consumer identity. There is e-paper, data is transferred wirelessly: all continuously improved by Xerox PARC staff. It is a world where identity means biometric data. It is a world of *homini sacri* – those doomed people so well portrayed by Giorgio Agamben.

For Agamben, the paradigm of biopolitical power is the camp. A camp is where the exception is a principle, and power is exercised over "bare life". But where is the camp, or more to the point: What is it? Agamben says that a camp is where sovereign power transforms people into the bare life form (*zoe*), and that it is life that can be exterminated without risking homicide, or without the risk of victimising qualified life (*bios*). The Bari stadium became a camp when in 1991 Italian police used it to contain illegal Albanian immigrants. Vélodrom d'Hivre in Paris became a camp when the Vichy government ordered the Jews to gather there before sending them to fascist Germany. But camps are also found at French airports, in *zones d'attentes* where refugees applying for French citizenship are kept. In his conclusions, Agamben is not that far from Foucault when he defines biopolitical power. But while for Foucault biopolitical power is related to exercising control over life, for Agamben it means first creating a special zone surpassing the differentiation between a fact and a norm, or biology and law. This zone is in a camp. Bare life is not just life, it is a blend of life and law, which restrains natural energies by inscribing it into the machinery of power based on the sovereign exception.[16]

---

15 While this particular scene does not appear in Philip K. Dick's short story, the filmmakers could have been influenced by his other works. Dick's oeuvre is replete with images of mass surveillance and elaborate ways employed by the authorities to spy on and detect the identity of the citizens. These include police checkpoints (*Flow My Tears, The Policeman Said* or *Do Androids Dream of Electric Sheep*), surveillance technologies (*The Man Who Japed*), or the use of telepathy to test loyalty or gain secret information (*Ubik*, *The Hood Maker*).

16 We could also compare the plot of Scott's *Gladiator* with Clint Eastwood's *Absolute Power*. As some may remember, veteran burglar Luther Whitney (Clint Eastwood), while on a job in the home of a wealthy Washington politician, is accidentally witness to the

John Anderton finds himself trapped in the bare life zone, where he is being followed by the authorities. Or to be more precise, it is his iris that the authorities must first put to examination. The eye of the Guard must meet with Anderton's eye, and find data in his unique retina. But Anderton knows all that well. The first thing he does on the run therefore is to exchange his eyeballs. This wise move is surely not enough to fool the biopolitical power, and Anderton will be put to yet another test: a water ordeal. He will hide himself from spider-resembling creatures by immersing in ice-cold water to simulate lifelessness. Let us recall the beginning of Gladiator, when Marcus Aurelius asks the fundamental question, "And what is Rome, Maximus?" To which Maximus daringly replies: "I've seen much of the rest of the world. It is brutal and cruel and dark, Rome is the light". The fugitive from the all-seeing and all-scanning absolute power of *Minority Report* could have asked the medical technician exchanging his eyeballs: "And what is freedom?" And the technician would have said: "Freedom is darkness and the gloom of the city". To provide one last glimpse of light before darkness falls let us hear the words of Maximus spoken just before the battle: "at my signal, unleash hell".

---

murder of a woman with whom the President of the United States is involved in a potentially scandalous affair. She is murdered, no less, by one of the President's bodyguards. The murder scene is cleaned up and an official version of the story prepared in which the burglar is cast as the killer. Now, Luther needs to prove himself innocent, and so he challenges the representatives of absolute power of the modern world, a contemporary Empire. The Caesar turned into the president of the United States, and gladiator into Dirty Harry, who in addition to having a miserable salary, employs himself as an "honest thief" in this movie. Both films show some diverse, yet similar traits of a struggle of an individual against omnipotent authority. It is a struggle taking place in two diverse worlds, two empires, and along the lines of two different scenarios. One difference is of our interest here: if Maximus wants to defend Caesar, he must enter public space (the arena) and challenge the highest representative of absolute power before the hungry eyes of the mob. It is a collective and physical spectacle. By contrast, if Luther Whitney wants to prove beyond doubt that the most powerful are guilty, he has to disguise himself,and constantly change his personality to be invisible in the private sphere, hidden from the view of assassinators, agents, and media attention. The crucial scene in *Absolute Power* is the one in which, at the airport, Whitney notices the president speaking on TV and he makes a decision not to flee the country. Whitney now wants to stay in the Empire and do his utmost to reveal the hypocrisy of those in power. Being visible works against the authorities and for the fugitive. Being visible is like being trapped.

VII. *Szymon Wróbel* by Szymon Wróbel

In the course of my education I have received a psychology degree and the diploma in clinical psychology is about the only diploma I can produce on request. I have received my education at a university adhering to a radical positivist methodology. One of the key exams during my studies was the methodology of empirical research and statistics exam. Both subjects were taught by Professor Jerzy Brzezinski, who is still regarded the greatest authority in the field of psychometric testing. Only three or four students out of a hundred would pass the statistics exam at the first attempt. Since I was an avid student and had the advantage of having attended a high school course with an extended mathematics and natural science curriculum I found myself among the lucky few. All in all, my university instilled in me a strong belief that intersubjective truth is the only truth available, and that reasoning is of more value than making the assertions. The university thus did utmost to instill a belief that only a research based on a proven methodology meets the threshold of knowledge aspiring to scientific truth. Before my graduation, however, there occurred an unprecedented twist in the story.

The studies did not furnish me with a good selection of literature to fully occupy my mind and, having much spare time, I was destined to reach yet another threshold of knowledge. What pardons me is that these were the times preceding the fall of communism when no other entertainment except for reading books was available. On a personal note, these were also emotionally hard times to me as I had seen my mother, about the only person with whom I had an emotional relationship, pass away following a long and gruesome illness. Vastly depressed, a constitution that has probably since become part of my daily life, I began reading voraciously and obsessively in the alphabetical order. I could only think of the big names. And so there came the works of Aristotle and Adorno, and as the time went by of Wittgenstein and Žižek.

There was, however, a side effect to this "bibliotherapy". Its damaging effect on the young scientific mind was diagnosed for all to see in my Masters exam. The thesis alone: *Zero point of knowledge* was honored. Yet, some would refer to it as the most "monstrous" thesis in the history of my department. To my supervisor, today one of the most prestigious cognitive psychologists in this country, the student was clearly resistant to the education effort of the Faculty of Social Sciences and doomed to become a philosopher rather than empirical psychologist. I was thus destined to surrender my whole future life to philosophy that, following Socrates, Montaigne, Spinoza, Nietzsche, Derrida and Foucault, is an attempt to reflect upon life and entwine the truth of one's words with the conditions of life and the life of both body and mind. Today, I see that unlike philosophy, psychology would not let me escape my loneliness and overcome my depression. It was the ongoing meditation or the practice of philosophy exercised in company with the works of great minds. This surely had a dissociative effect and intensified my loneliness, but it also relieved me by providing knowledge that my loneliness was preceded by the loneliness of the minds similarly detached from the world. I have never completed any formal education in philosophy though.

I am saying all this to make an essential point. My own experience tells me that even psychological studies, by definition meant to introduce a psychologist to the intimate details of another person's life, are thanks to their methodological advancement predestined to do the opposite and to distance a psychologist and a patient. The truth of science eclipses our own truth. A latent prerequisite in a scientific cognition of the world is to deny the subjective experience. While our self-knowledge is atrophied, our scientific knowledge expands. Of course I respect the university, I respect the methodology, but I am now also convinced that the advantage of the methodology over the reflection is not necessarily a good thing, and, as my experience proves, it may even put a student in a depressive position. To extrapolate, studies often have a secluding effect and detach students from the world. The humanities devoid of double reflection, that is, the reflection on the other entwined with the reflection on oneself, are simply an open invitation to deepen one's depression.

The conclusion of a case study on "Szymon Wróbel" is an ambiguous one and its moral is highly uncertain. I do not agree with positivist beliefs that science brings order to the world and that only the truths assumed objectively present humanity with happiness. However, I also do not ascribe to the relativistic tendency to suggest that the truth is unavailable at all or impossible to be established. If we are unable to objectively determine how many chairs there are in the room, we'd better disperse and seek truth no further, as it is the public money that allows us to produce knowledge. What should I then recommend to all of us and what is my own stance in this conundrum? How do I envisage the humanities developing in the future? Well, unsurprisingly, the humanities will continue to imitate natural science and argue for the objectivity and the method. Even less unsurprisingly, the humanities will wage inconclusive wars to delineate disciplinary boundaries.

I am not saying the effort will be in vain, but that it will be part of the maturing process and it will bear the mark of our times. In my own endeavors I would rather invest my limited time in the humanities which invite us to seek one's own voice, and to entwine the truth discovered in the books with personal experience. Therefore, my way out of this conundrum is to immerse in personal and individual truth, particular and unique truth, and in what some refer to as an idiosyncratic or idiomatic knowledge, as opposed to nomothetic knowledge. I hope one day the humanities will shake off the obsession with objectivity characteristic of the immature disciplines, and allow something more than a correlation of variables, the accumulation of knowledge, and interpretation of other people's texts. Hopefully, one day the humanities will indulge in the luxury of self-understanding, which would be a part of the project pretentiously called the understanding of humanity and which includes understanding the humanities' own strangeness and its lack of deep probing of what we call a man fully integrated with the society.

References

Adorno, W. Theodor (2009). *In Search of Wagner*, trans. R. Livingstone, London: Verso.

Agamben, Giorgio (1998). *Homo Sacer. Sovereign Power and Bare Life* (1995/1998), trans. D. Heller-Roazen, Stanford: Stanford University Press.

Agamben, Giorgio (1999). *Remnants of Auschwitz. The Witness and the Archive*, trans. D. Heller-Roazen, New York: Zone Books.

Althusser, Louis (1971). *Ideology and Ideological State Apparatuses*, trans. Ben Brewster, New York: Monthly Review Press.

Althusser, Louis (1972/1999). *Machiavelli and Us*, trans. G. Elliott, ed. F. Matheron, London: Verso.

Arendt, Hannah (1951/1973). *The Origins of Totalitarianism*, New York: Harcourt Brace Jovanovich.

Arendt, Hannah (1963). *On Revolution*, New York: Viking.

Arendt, Hannah (1978). *The Life of the Mind: Volume II: Willing*, ed. M. McCarthy. New York: Brace Harcourt.

Arendt, Hannah (2005). *The Promise of Politics*, ed. J. Kohn, New York: Schocken.

Aristotle (2006). *Rhetoric. Poetics,* trans. S. H. Butcher, W. Rhys Roberts, New York: Barnes & Noble Classics.

Atwood, Margaret (2002). *Negotiating with the Dead: A Writer on Writing*, Cambridge: Cambridge University Press.

Augustine St. (2003). *City of God,* trans. H. Bettenson, London: Penguin Classics.

Axer, Jerzy (2009). *I was accepted by a troop of blue monkeys. On amorous baboon in Łódź, friendly blue monkeys in Kenya, and on days off for animals in Moscow Zoo, Katarzyna Łukaszewska interviews prof. Jerzy Axer*, "Uniwersytet Warszawski", June, 3 (42), pp. 34-35.

Balibar, Étienne (1994). *Masses, Classes, Ideas: Studies on Politics and Philosophy Before and After Marx*, trans. J. Swenson, New York: Routledge.

Barthes, Roland (1964). *Elements of Semiology*, trans. A. Lavers and C. Smith, New York: Hill & Wang.

Barthes, Roland (1968). *Writing Degree Zero*, trans. A. Lavers, C. Smith, New York: Hill and Wang.

Barthes, Roland (1972). *Mythologies*, trans. Annette Lavers, New York: Hill & Wang.

Barthes, Roland (1982). *Camera Lucida. Reflections on Photography*. trans. Richard Howard, New York: Hill and Wang.

Barthes, Roland (1983). *The Fashion System*, trans. Matthew Ward and Richard Howard, New York: Hill & Wang.

Barthes, Roland (1986). *Science versus Literature*, [in:] "Times Literary Supplement", September 28, 1967. Reprinted as *"From Science to Literature*, [in:] Roland Barthes: *The Rustle of Language*. trans. Richard Howard. Oxford: Basil Blackwell.

Barthes, Roland (1994). *Roland Barthes by Roland Barthes*, trans. Richard Howard, Berkeley: University of California Press.

Barthes, Roland (2002). *A Lover's Discourse: Fragments*, trans. Richard Howard, London: Vintage Books.

Bauman, Zygmunt (1995). *Postmodern Ethics, Life in Fragments. Essays in Postmodern Morality*, Oxford: Blackwell.

Bauman, Zygmunt (2000). *Liquid Modernity*, Cambridge: Polity Press.

Bauman, Zygmunt (2003). *Handlarze strachu* [*Merchants of fear*], "Krytyka Polityczna", 4, pp. 15-22.

Bauman, Zygmunt (2004). *Europe: An Unfinished Adventure*, London: Polity Press.

Beck, Ulrich (1994). *The Reinvention of Politics*, [in:] Ulrich Beck, Anthony Giddens, Scott Lash, *Reflexive Modernization: Politics, Tradition and Aesthetics in the Modern Social Order*, Cambridge: Polity Press.

Beck, Ulrich (1986). *Risikogesellschaft: auf dem Weg in eine andere Moderne*, Frankfurt/M: Suhrkamp.

Beck, Ulrich, Giddens, Anthony, Lash, Scott (1994). *Reflexive Modernization: Politics, Tradition and Aesthetics in the Modern Social Order*, Cambridge: Polity Press.

Beck, Urlich, Grande, Edgar (2007). *Cosmopolitan Europe*, Cambridge: Polity.

Beckett, Samuel (1974). *First Love and Other Shorts*, New York: Grove Press.

Benhabib, Seyla (1996). *From Identity Politics to Social Feminism: A Plea for the Nineties*, [in:] Seyla Benhabib (ed.), *Democracy and Difference: Contesting the Boundaries of the Political*, Princeton: Princeton University Press.

Benjamin, Walter (1977). *A Short History of Photography*, trans. Phil Patton, Artforum 15, 6 [February 1977].

Benjamin, Walter (2002). *The Arcades Project*, trans. H. Eiland and K. McLaughlin, ed. R. Tiedemann, New York: Belknap Press.

Benner, Erica (2009). *Machiavelli's Ethics*, Princeton: Princeton University Press.

Bentham, Jeremy (1995). *The Panopticon Writings*, ed. M. Bozovic, London: Verso.

Bergson, Henri (1896/1990). *Matter and Memory*, trans. N. M. Paul, W. S. Palmer, New York: Zone Books.

Berlin, Isaiah (1980). *The Originality of Machiavelli*, [in:] Isaiah Berlin, *Against the Current: Essays in the History of Ideas*, ed. H. Hardy, London: Hogarth Press.

Betz, Hans-Georg (1994). *Radical Right-Wing Populism in Western Europe*, Basingstoke: Macmillan.

Bickford, Susan (1997). *Anti-anti-identity politics: feminism, democracy, and the complexities of citizenship*, "Hypatia", 12, p. 4.

Biedenkopf, Kurt, Geremek, Bronisław, Michalski, Krzysztof, Rocard, Michel, (2004). *What holds Europe together?*, Fall, "Newsletter" IWM Wien, nr 4.

Bielik-Robson, Agata (2010). *Polski Triumf Tanatosa* [*Polish Triumph of Thanatos*], [in:] *Żałoba* [*Mourning*], Warszawa: Wydawnictwo Krytyki Politycznej.

Bloom, Harold (1973). *The Anxiety of Influence: A Theory of Poetry*, London: Oxford University Press.

Bloom, Harold (1975). *A Map of Misreading*, New York: Oxford University Press.

Borejsza, Jerzy, Ziemer, Klaus (eds.) (2006). *Totalitarian and Authoritarian Regimes in Europe. Legacies and Lessons from the Twentieth Century*, Bergham Books.

Borges, Jorge Luis (1944/2000). *Funes the Memorious,* [in:] Jorge Luis Borges, *Labyrinths*, trans. J. E. Irby, London: Penguin Classics.

Borges, Jorge Luis (1989). *Fantastic Zoology. Book of Imaginary Beings,* trans. A. Hurley, New York: Zone.

Bradley, Patrick J. (2010). *Irony and the Narrator in Xenophon's Anabasis*, [in:] Vivienne J. Gray (ed.), *Xenophon*, Oxford: Oxford University Press.

Butler, Judith (1990). *Gender Trouble: Feminism and the Subversion of Identity*, New York: Routledge.

Butler, Judith (2000). *Antigone's Claim*, New York: Columbia University Press.

Caillois, Roger (1966). *Anthologie du Fantastique*, Tome I, Paris: Gallimard.

Canovan, Margaret (1981). *Populism*, New York: Harcourt Brace Jovanovich.

Castells, Manuel (1996). *The Rise of the Network Society.The Information Age: Economy, Society and Culture Vol. I*, Cambridge: Blackwell.

Chomsky, Noam (1968). *Language and Mind,* New York: Harcourt Brace Jovanovich.

Cicero, Mark Tullius (1941). *De Res Publica (On the Republic),* trans. F. Barham, [in:] *The Political Works of Marcus Tullius Cicero: Comprising His Treatise on the Commonwealth; and His Treatise on the Laws*, London: Edmund Spettigue.

Copjec, Joan (2002). *Imagine There's No Woman: Ethics and Sublimation,* Cambridge: MIT Press.

Critchley, Simon (1992). *The Ethics of Deconstruction: Derrida and Lévinas*, Oxford: Blackwell.

Culler, Jonathan (1982). *On Deconstruction: Theory and Criticism after Structuralism*, Ithaca: Cornell University Press.

Dalton, Russell J. (1996). *Citizen Politics: Public Opinion and Political Parties in Advanced Industrial Democracies*, Chatham: Chatham House.

Davis, Colin (2007). *Haunted Subjects. Deconstruction, Psychoanalysis and the Return of the Dead*, Basingstoke: Palgrave Macmillan.

Debord, Guy (1990). *Comments on the Society of the Spectacle*, trans. M. Imrie, London: Verso.

Deleuze, Gilles (1962/1983). *Nietzsche & Philosophy,* trans. H. Tomlinson, New York: Columbia University Press.

Deleuze, Gilles (1977). *Intellectuals and Power: A Conversation Between Michel Foucault and Gilles Deleuze*, [in:] *Language, Counter-Memory, Practice: Selected Essays and Interviews by Michel Foucault*, ed. D. Bouchard, Ithaca: Cornell University Press, pp. 205-217.

Deleuze, Gilles, Guattari, Félix (1994). *What Is Philosophy?*, trans. H. Tomlinson, G. Burchell, New York: Columbia University Press.

Derrida, Jacques (1967/1976). *Of Grammatology*, trans. G. Chakravorty Spivak, Baltimore: Johns Hopkins University Press.

Derrida, Jacques (1967/1978). *Cogito and the History of Madness*, trans. A. Bass, [in:] Jacques Derrida, *Writing and Difference.* London: Routledge, pp. 31-63.

Derrida, Jacques (1982). *Margins of Philosophy*, trans. A. Bass, Chicago: The University of Chicago Press.

Derrida, Jacques (1983). *The Time of a Thesis: Punctuations*, trans. K. McLaughlin, [in:] Alan Montefiore (ed.), *Philosophy in France Today*, Cambridge: Cambridge University Press.

Derrida, Jacques (1986). *There Is No "One" Narcissism (Autobiophotographies).* An interview broadcast in the program prepared by Didier Cahen over France-Culture, *Le bon plaisir de Jacques Derrida*, March 22, 1986, published under the title *Entretien avec Jacques Derrida* in "Digraphe" 42, December 1987; http: //www.hydra.umn.edu/ Derrida/narc.html (Date of access: February 19, 2006).

Derrida, Jacques (1987). *Psyché: Inventions de l'Autre*, Paris: Galilée.

Derrida, Jacques (1988). *Letter to A Japanese Friend*, [in:] David Wood, Robert Bernasconi (eds.), *Derrida and Difference*, Evanston, IL: Northwestern University Press.

Derrida, Jacques (1989). *Of Spirit: Heidegger and the Question*, trans. G. Bennington and R. Bowlby, Chicago: University of Chicago Press.

Derrida, Jacques (1992). *Mochlos: Or, the Conflict of the Faculties*, [in:] Richard Rand (ed.), *Logomachia: The Conflict of the Faculties*, Lincoln, NE: University of Nebraska Press.

Derrida, Jacques (1992). *The Other Heading*, trans. P.-A. Brault and M. Naas, Bloomington: Indiana University Press.

Derrida, Jacques (1994). *"To Do Justice to Freud": The History of Madness in the Age of Psychoanalysis*, trans. A. Pascale Brault, M. Naas, "Critical Inquiry", 20 (2), pp. 227-266.

Derrida, Jacques (1994/1997). *Politics of Friendship*, trans. G. Collins, New York: Verso.

Derrida, Jacques (1997). *Of the humanities and the philosophical discipline. the right to philosophy from the cosmopolitical point of view (the example of an international institution),* "Surfaces", IV, Folio 1, Montréal Vendome: Editions UNESCO Verdier PUF.

Derrida, Jacques (2002). *The animal that therefore i am (more to follow)*, trans. David Wills, "Critical Inquiry", 28, pp. 369-418.

Derrida, Jacques, Habermas, Jürgen (2006). *February 15, Or What Binds Europeans Together: A Plea for a Common Foreign Policy, Beginning in the Core of Europe,* [in:] *The Derrida-Habermas Reader,* ed. L. Thomassen, Chicago: The University of Chicago Press.

Dillery, John (1995). *Xenophon and the History of His Times*. London, New York: Routledge.

Dufresne, Todd (2000). *Tales from the Freudian Crypt: The Death Drive in Text and Context*, Stanford: Stanford University Press.

Dworkin, Ronald (2000). *Sovereign Virtue: The Theory and Practice of Equality,* Harvard: Harvard University Press.

Dzwończyk, Joanna (2000). *Populistyczne Koncepcje w Społeczeństwie Postsocjalistycznym na Przykładzie Polski* [*Populist Concepts in a Post-Socialist Society as Exemplified by Poland*], Toruń: Wydawnictwo Adam Marszałek.

Erikson, H. Erik (1950). *Childhood and Society*, New York: Norton.

Erikson, H. Erik (1968). *Identity: Youth and Crisis*, New York: Norton.

Foks Darek, Libera Zbigniew (2006). *Pinup girls: Darek Foks and Zbigniew Libera in conversation with Dorota Jarecka and Justyna Sobolewska*, "Wysokie Obcasy", 4 February, no. 5 (355).

Foks, Darek, Libera, Zbigniew (2005). *Co Robi Łączniczka?* [*What Is the Messenger Doing?*], Katowice: Ars Cameralis Silesiae Supreriosis.

Foucault, Michel (1961/1965). *Madness and Civilization: A History of Insanity in the Age of Reason*, trans. R. Howard, New York: Random House.

Foucault, Michel (1963/1977). *Préface à la transgression hommage à Georges Bataille, A Preface to Transgression*, trans. D. F. Bouchard and S. Simon, [in:] *Language, Counter-Memory, Practice: Selected Essays and Interviews by Michel Foucault*, ed. D. Bouchard, Ithaca: Cornell University Press.

Foucault, Michel (1963/1997). *The Birth of the Clinic: An Archaeology of Medical Perception,* trans. A. M. Sheridan Smith, London: Routledge.

Foucault, Michel (1966/1992). *The Order of Things. An Archaeology of the Human Sciences,* London: Vintage.

Foucault, Michael (1975/1995). *Discipline & Punish: The Birth of the Prison,* trans. A. Sheridan, New York: Vintage Books.

Foucault, Michel (1976/1998). *The History of Sexuality Vol. 1: The Will to Knowledge*, trans. R. Hurley, London: Penguin.

Foucault, Michel (1984). *Polemics, Politics, and Problemizations: An Interview,* [in:] *The Foucault Reader,* ed. P. Rabinow, New York: Pantheon Books.

Foucault, Michel (1984). *What Is an Author?*, trans. P. Rabinow, [in:] *The Foucault Reader,* ed. P. Rabinow, New York: Pantheon Books, pp.226-230.

Foucault, Michel (1984). *What is Enlightenment?,* trans. C. Porter, [in:] *The Foucault Reader,* ed. P. Rabinow, New York: Pantheon Books.

Foucault, Michel (1984/1990). *The Uses of Pleasure*, *and Care of the Self*, trans. R. Hurley, [in:] *History of Sexuality*, 3 Volumes, New York: Vintage Books.

Foucault, Michel (1990). *Nietzsche, Freud, Marx,* trans. A. D. Schrift, [in:] Gayle L. Ormiston, Alan D. Schrift (eds.), *Transforming the Hermeneutic Context From Nietzsche to Nancy*Albany: State University of New York Press.

Foucault, Michel (1990). *The Use of Pleasure. Volume II of The History of Sexuality*, trans. R. Hurley, New York: Vintage Books.

Foucault, Michel (1994). *The Art of Telling the Truth*, [in:] Michael Kelly (ed.), *Critique and Power: Recasting the Foucault/Habermas Debate*, Cambridge, MA: MIT Press.

Foucault, Michel (1997). *Madness, the Absence of Work (d'œuvre)*, [in:] A. I. Davidson (ed.), *Foucault and his Interlocutors*, London: Chicago University Press.

Foucault, Michel (2003). *Society Must Be Defended. Lectures at the Collège de France, 1975-76*, trans. D. Macey, London: Macmillan.

Fraser, Nancy (2000). *Rethinking recognition*, "New Left Review", May-June, 3.

Frege, Gottlob (1918). *The Thought: A Logical Investigation,* trans. P. T. Geach, R. H. Stoothoff, „Beiträge zur Philosophie des deutschen Idealismus", 1, pp. 58-77.

Freud, Sigmund (1900/1957). *The Interpretation of Dreams*, [in:] *The Standard Edition of the Complete Psychological Works of Sigmund Freud, Volume IV*, ed. J. Strachey, London: Hogarth Press.

Freud, Sigmund (1905). *Jokes and their Relation to the Unconscious* [in:] *The Standard Edition of the Complete Works of Sigmund Freud*, Volume XIII., ed. by James Strachey et al. The Hogart Press and the Institute of Psychoanalysis, London: Hogarth Press, 1953-74.

Freud, Sigmund (1910/1957). *Leonardo da Vinci. A Psychosexual Study of an Infantile Reminiscence*, trans. A. Brill, [in:] *The Standard Edition of the Complete Psychological Works of Sigmund Freud, Volume XI*, ed. J. Strachey, London: Hogarth Press.

Freud, Sigmund (1914-1916). *On Narcissism*, [in:] The Standard Edition of the Complete Psychological Works of Sigmund Freud, Volume XIV (1914-1916): *On the History of the Psycho-Analytic Movement, Papers on Metapsychology and Other Works*.

Freud, Sigmund (1915/1974). *Instincts and their Vicissitudes*, [in:] *The Standard Edition of the Complete Psychological Works of Sigmund Freud, Volume XIV*, ed. and trans. J. Strachey, London: Hogarth, pp. 109-140.

Freud, Sigmund (1917). *Mourning and Melancholia*, [in:] *The Standard Edition of the Complete Psychological Works of Sigmund Freud, Volume XIV (1914-1916): On the History of the Psycho-Analytic Movement, Papers on Metapsychology and Other Works*, ed. and trans. J. Strachey, London: Hogarth, pp. 237-258.

Freud, Sigmund (1920/1968). *Beyond the Pleasure Principle*, [in:] *The Standard Edition of the Complete Psychological Works of Sigmund Freud, Volume XVIII (1920-1922)*, ed. and trans. J. Strachey, London: Hogarth.

Freud, Sigmund (1922/1957). *Group Psychology and the Analysis of the Ego*, [in:] *The Standard Edition of the Complete Psychological Works of Sigmund Freud, Volume XVIII*, ed. James Strachey, London: Hogarth Press.

Freud, Sigmund (1927/1968). *The Future of an Illusion*, trans. J. Strachey, [in:] T*he Standard Edition of the Complete Psychological Works of Sigmund Freud, Volume XXI*, ed. and trans. J. Strachey, London: Hogarth,.

Freud, Sigmund (1930/1968). *Civilization and Its Discontents*, [in:] *The Standard Edition of the Complete Psychological Works of Sigmund Freud, Volume XXI*, ed. and trans. J. Strachey, London: Hogarth,.

Freud, Sigmund (1932/1974). *New Introductory Lectures on Psycho-Analysis*, [in:] *The Standard Edition of the Complete Psychological Works, Volume XXII (1953-74)*, ed. and trans. J. Strachey, London: Hogarth,.

Freud, Sigmund (1938/1960). *Abriß der Psychoanalyse*, Frankfurt/M: Fischer Taschenbuch Verlag.

Freud, Sigmund (1939/1957). *Moses and Monotheism*, [in:] *The Standard Edition of the Complete Psychological Works of Sigmund Freud*, Volume XXIII, ed. and trans. J. Strachey, London: Hogarth.

Freud, Sigmund (1985). *Delusions and Dreams in Jensen's Gradiva'*, and *The Uncanny*, [in:] *Art and Literature, Vol. 14*, The Pelican Freud Library, Harmondsworth: Penguin.

Friedrich, Carl J. (1953). *The Unique Character of Totalitarian Society*, [in:] *Totalitarianism, Proceedings of a Conference held at the American Academy of Art and Sciences*. Cambridge: Harvard University Press.

Friedrich, Carl J., Brzezinski, Jerzy (1966). *Totalitarian Dictatorship and Autocracy*, Cambridge: Harvard University Press.

Fukuyama, Francis (1992) *The End of History and the Last Man*, London: Penguin Books.

Gadamer, Hans-Georg (1960/1998). *Truth and Method,* trans. J. Weinsheimer, D. G. Marshall, New York: Continuum.

Gasché, Rodolphe (1986). *The Tain of the Mirror: Derrida and the Philosophy of Reflection,* Cambridge: Harvard University Press.

Gasché, Rodolphe (2009). *Europe, Or the Infinite Task: A Study of a Philosophical Concept,* Stanford: Stanford University Press.

Gellner, Ernest (1983). *Nations and Nationalism,* New York: Cornell University Press.

Giddens, Anthony (1991). *Modernity and Self-Identity. Self and Society in the Late Modern Age*, Cambridge: Polity Press.

Giddens, Anthony (1994). *Living in a Post-traditional Society*, [in:] Ulrich Beck, Anthony Giddens, Scott Lash (eds.), *Reflexive Modernization: Politics, Tradition and Aesthetics in The Modern Social Order*, Cambridge: Polity.

Gilligan, Carol (1993). *In A Different Voice: Psychological Theory and Women's Development, Harvard:* Harvard University Press.

Girard, René (1972). *La Violence et le Sacré*, Paris: Grasset.

Gramsci, Antonio (1968). *The Modern Prince*, trans. Louis Marks, [in:] Antonio Gramsci, *The Modern Prince and Other Writings,* New York: International Publishers.

Habermas, Jürgen (1968). *Erkenntnis und Interesse.* Frankfurt am Main: Suhrkamp.

Habermas, Jürgen (1985/1995). *The Philosophical Discourse of Modernity. Twelve Lectures,* trans. F. Lawrence, Cambridge: The MIT Press.

Habermas, Jürgen (1994). *Three Normative Models of Democracy,* "Constellations", Volume 1 (1).

Hadot, Pierre (1995). *Philosophy as a Way of Life*, trans. M. Chase, Oxford: Blackwell's.

Halbwachs, Maurice (1925/1992). *On Collective Memory*, trans. L. A. Coser, Chicago: The University of Chicago Press.

Hardt, Michael, Negri, Antonio (2004), *Multitude: War and Democracy in the Age of Empire*, New York: Penguin.

Hegel, Georg Wilhelm Friedrich (1807/1977). *Phenomenology of Spirit,* trans. A. V. Miller, Oxford: Clarendon Press.

Hegel, Georg, Wilhelm, Friedrich (1807/1985). *Phänomenologie des Geistes. Werke* 3, Frankfurt: Suhrkamp Verlag.

Heidegger, Martin (1929). *Kant und das Problem der Metaphysik*, Bonn: Friedrich Cohen.

Heidegger, Martin (1927/1996). *Being and Time,* trans. J. Stambaugh, Albany: State University of New York Press.

Heidegger, Martin (1959/1971). *On the Way to Language*, trans. P. D. Hertz, New York: Harper and Row.

Herbert, Zbigniew (2007). *Mr. Cogito and the Imagination*, trans. J. Carpenter, B. Carpenter, [in:] Zbigniew Herbert, *The Collected Poems: 1956-1998,* trans. C. Miłosz, P. D. Scott, A. Valles, ed. A. Valles, The Ecco Press.

Higgins, William Edward (1977). *Xenophon the Athenian: The Problem of the Individual and the Society of the "Polis"*, Albany: State University of New York Press.

Hintikka, Jaakko (1975). *The Intentions of Intentionality and Other New Models for Modalities*, Dordrecht: Reidel.

Hobbes, Thomas (1651/2010). *Leviathan or The Matter, Forme and Power of a Common Wealth Ecclesiasticall and Civil*, ed. Ian Shapiro, New Haven: Yale University Press.

Honneth, Axel (1995). *The Fragmented World of the Social, Essays in Social and Political Philosophy*, ed. Charles, W. Wright, New York: State University of New York Press.

Honneth, Axel (1995). *The Struggle for Recognition. The Moral Grammar of Social Conflicts*, trans. J. Anderson, Cambridge: Polity Press.

Horkheimer, Max, Adorno, Theodor W. (2002). *Dialectic of Enlightment. Philosophical Fragments,* trans. E. Jephcott, California: Stanford University Press.
Houellebecq, Michel (2012). *The Map and the Territory*, trans. Gavin Bowd, New York: Vintage.
Humboldt, Wilhelm von (1836/1999). *On Language. On the Diversity of Human Language Construction and its Influence on the Mental Development of the Human Species*, trans. P. Heath, Cambridge: Cambridge University Press.
Hutchinson, Godfrey (2000). *Xenophon and the Art of Command*, London: Greenhill Books.
Hutton, Patrick H. (1988). *Foucault, Freud, and The Technologies of the Self,* [in:] Luther Martin, Huck Gutman, Patrick H. Hutton (eds.), *Technologies of the Self*, Massachusetts: University of Massachusetts Press.
Ionescu Ghi, Gellner Ernest (1969). *Populism. Its Meanings and National Characteristics*, London: Weidenfeld and Nicolson.
Irigaray, Luce (1985). *The Eternal Irony of the Community*, [in:] *Speculum of the Other Woman*, trans. G. Gill, Ithaca: Cornell University Press.
Jackendoff, Ray (1992). *Languages of the Mind. Essays on Mental Representation,* London: The MIT Press.
Jacob, François (1970/1993). *The Logic Of Life. A History of Heredity*, trans. B. E. Spillmann, New York: A Division of Random House.
Janion, Maria (2007). *Gorączka Romantyczna* [*Romantic Fever*], Warszawa: PIW.
Johnson, Barbara (1980). *The Critical Difference: Essays in the Contemporary Rhetoric of Reading,* Baltimore: Johns Hopkins University Press.
Kaczyński, Jarosław (2006). *Interview with Kublik and Olejnik, We mnie jest czyste dobro* [*There is pure good in me*], "Gazeta Wyborcza", 3 February.
Kant, Immanuel (1781/1977). *Kritik der Reinen Vernunft*, [in:] Immanuel Kant, *Werke in Zwölf Bänden*. Band 3, Frankfurt am Main: Suhrkamp Verlag.
Kant, Immanuel (1784/1996). *An Answer to the Question: What is Enlightenment?,* [in:] *What is Enlightenment? Eighteenth-Century Answers and Twentieth-Century Questions,* ed. J. Schmidt, Berkeley: University of California Press.
Kant, Immanuel (1793/1977)). *Die Religion Innerhalb der Grenzen der Bloßen Vernunft.* [in:] Immanuel Kant, *Werke in Zwölf Bänden*. Band 8, Frankfurt am Main: Suhrkamp Verlag.
Kazin, Michael (1995). *The Populist Persuasion: An American History*, New York: Basic Books.
Kołakowski, Leszek (2003). *Can Europe happen?*, "New Criterion", May, 21, 9, pp. 17-21.
Kordela, Kiarina (2007). *Surplus, Spinoza, Lacan*, Albany: State University of New York Press.
Kozłowski, Jarosław, Audun, Eckhoff (1995). *A Conversation*, "Terskel/Threshold: Museet for Samtidskunst", 15.
Kozłowski, Jarosław (1990). *Grey Thoughts*, London: Matt's Gallery.
Kozłowski, Jarosław (2002). *In conversation with Jaromir Jedliński*, [in:] Jarosław Kozłowski, *Hot News*, exhibition catalogue, Poznań: Galeria Muzalewska.
Kozłowski, Jarosław (2006). *In conversation with Andrzej Szczepaniak*, [in:] Jarosław Kozłowski, *Zasłony/Curtains*, exhibition catalogue, Cracow: Galeria Starmach.
Krasnodębski, Zdzisław (2005). *Demokracja Peryferii* [*The democracy of the Outskirts*], Gdańsk: Słowo/Obraz Terytoria.

Kripke, Saul A. (1980). *Naming and Necessity*, Cambridge: Harvard University Press.
Kristeva, Julia (1987). *Tales of Love*, trans. L. Roudiez, New York: Columbia University Press.
Kristeva, Julia (1999). *Psychoanalysis and Freedom*, trans. C. Levin, "Canadian Journal of Psychoanalysis", 7, 1.
Kuhn, Thomas Samuel (1962). *The Structure of Scientific Revolutions*, Chicago: University of Chicago Press.
Lacan, Jacques (1999). *Le Séminaire, Livre* XX: *Encore*, ed. J.-A. Miller, Paris: Éditions du Seuil.
Lacan, Jacques (1966). *Propos sur la Causalité Psychique*, [in:] Jacques Lacan, *Écrits*, Paris: Seuil.
Lacan, Jacques (1978). *The Seminar of Jacques Lacan, Book 11: The Four Fundamental Concepts of Psycho-Analysis*, trans. D. Porter, ed. J.-A. Miller, New York: Norton.
Lacan, Jacques (1988). *The Seminar of Jacques Lacan 1954-1955, Book II, The Ego in Freud's Theory and in the Technique of Psychoanalysis*, trans. S. Tomaselli, ed. J.-A. Miller, New York: W. W. Norton & Co.
Lacan, Jacques (1992). *The Seminar of Jacques Lacan, Book VII: The Ethics of Psychoanalysis*, 1959-60, trans. D. Porter, ed. J.-A. Miller, New York: Norton.
Lacan, Jacques (1998). *The Seminar of Jacques Lacan, Book XX: On Feminine Sexuality: The Limits of Love and Knowledge, Encore 1972-1973*, trans. B. Fink, ed. J.-A. Miller, New York: Norton.
Lacan, Jacques (2001). *Le Séminaire de Jacques Lacan, Livre VIII: Le transfert*, 1960-1961, ed. Jacques-Alain Miller, Paris: Éditions du Seuil.
Lacan, Jacques (2006). *The Seminar of Jacques Lacan. Book XVII, The Other Side of Psychoanalysis*. trans. R. Grigg, ed. J.-A. Miller, W. W. Norton & Co., New York.
Laclau, Ernesto (1996). *Why do Empty Signifiers Matter to Politics?* [in:] Ernesto Laclau, *Emancipation(s)*, London: Verso. pp. 36-46.
Laclau, Ernesto (2005). *On Populist Reason*, London: Verso.
Laclau, Ernesto, Mouffe, Chantal (1985). *Hegemony and Socialist Strategy: Toward a Radical Democratic Politics*. 2nd Edition, London: Verso.
Lahtinen, Mikko (2009). *Politics and Philosophy. Niccolò Machiavelli and Louis Althusser's Aleatory Materialism*, Leiden: Brill.
Lakoff, George (1996). *Moral Politics*, Chicago: University of Chicago Press.
Laplanche, Jean, Pontalis, Jean-Bertrand (1967). *Vocabulaire de Psychanalyse*, Paris: PUF.
Laplanche, Jean, Pontalis, Jean-Bertrand, (1973). *The Language of Psychoanalysis*, trans. D. Nicholson-Smith, London: Hogarth Press.
Laqueur, Walter (2005). *Europa im 21. Jahrhundert*, „Merkur", 59, pp. 653-666.
Latour, Bruno (2004). *Politics of Nature: How to Bring the Sciences Into Democracy*, trans. C. Porter, Cambridge: Harvard University Press.
Le Bon, Gustave (1896/1977). *The Crowd: A Study of the Popular Mind*, New York: Macmillan & Co.
Lefort, Claude (1986). *Le travail de l'oeuvre, Machiavel*, Paris: Gallimard.
Lefort, Claude (1986). *The Political Forms of Modern Society: Bureaucracy, Democracy, Totalitarianism*, Cambridge: MIT Press.
Lefort, Claude (1989). *Democracy and Political Theory*, Cambridge: MIT Press.

Lefort, Claude (2000). *Writing: The Political Test*, Duke University Press.

Lefort, Claude (2007). *Complications: Communism and the Dilemmas of Democracy*, New York: Columbia University Press.

Leonardo, Da Vinci (1270/1956). *Treatise on Painting*, trans. and ed. A. P. McMahon, Princeton: Princeton University Press.

Lévinas, Emmanuel (2001). *Is it Righteous to Be?*, ed. J. Robbins, Stanford: Stanford University Press.

Lévi-Strauss, Claude (1962/1963). *Totemism*, trans. R. Needham, Boston: Beacon Press.

Lévi-Strauss, Claude (1955/1973). *Tristes Tropique*, trans. J. Weightman, D. Weightman, London: Cape.

Lévi-Strauss, Claude (1962/1996). *The Savage Mind*, trans. G. Weidenfeld, Oxford: Oxford University Press.

Lévi-Strauss, Claude (1983). *A un Jeune Peintre*, [in:] Claude Lévi-Strauss, *Le Regard Eloigné*, Paris: Plon.

Lilla, Mark (2001). *The Reckless Mind*, New York: New York Review of Books.

Lyotard, Jean-François (1984). *The Postmodern Condition. A Report on Knowledge*, Manchester: Manchester University Press.

Machiavelli, Niccolò (1513/1985). *The Prince*, trans. H. Mansfield, Chicago: University of Chicago Press.

Machiavelli, Niccolò (1517/2003). *Discourses on Livy*, trans. J. Leslie, S. J. Walker, rev. Brian Richardson, London: Penguin Books.

Machiavelli, Niccolò (1525/1988). *Florentine Histories*, trans. L. F. Banfield, Harvey Mansfield, New York: Princeton University Press.

Machiavelli, Niccolò (1520/2001). *The Art of War*, trans. E. Farnesworth. Princeton: Da Capo Press Edition.

Mara, Gerald M. (2008). *The Civic Conversations of Thucydides and Plato: Classical Political Philosophy and the Limits of Democracy*, Albany: State University of New York Press.

Marciszewski, Witold (1972). *Podstawy Logicznej Teorii Przekonań [The Fundation Of Logical Theory Of Belief]*, Warszawa: PWN.

Marciszewski, Witold (1988). *Logika Modalna* [*Modal Logics*], [in:] *Mała Encyklopedia Logiki* [*A Concise Encyclopedia of Logic*], Wrocław: Ossolineum.

Marcuse, Herbert (1966). *Eros and Civilization. A Philosophical Inquiry into Freud*, trans. A. Blunden, Boston: Beacon Press.

Marczewska-Rytko, Maria (2006). *Populizm na Przełomie XX I XXI Wieku. Panaceum czy Pułapka dla Współczesnych Społeczeństw?* [*Populism at the Turn of the 20th-21st Centuries: Remedy or Trap for Contemporary Societies?*], Toruń: Wydawnictwo Adam Marszałek.

Markowski, Radosław (ed.) (2004). *Populizm a Demokracja* [*Populism and Democracy*], Warszawa: Instytut Studiów Politycznych PAN.

Marx, Karl, Engels, Friedrich (1848/1962). *The Communist Manifesto, Selected Works, 2 vols*, Moscow: Foreign Languages Publishing House.

Mazzoleni, Gianpietro et al. (eds.) (2003). *The Media and Neo-Populism: A Contemporary Comparative Analysis*, Westport, VA: Praeger.

Mead, George Herbert (1934/1965). *Mind, Self, Society*, Chicago: University of Chicago.

Mény, Yves, Surel, Yves (eds.) (2002). *Democracies and the Populist Challenge*, Basingstoke: Palgrave.

Mickiewicz, Adam (1899). *Wybór Listów* [*Selected Letters*], ed. J. Kallenbach, Kraków: Spółka Wydawnicza Polska.

Miller, Jaques-Alain (2003). *Lacan et la Politique. Entretien avec Jaques-Alain Miller Propos Recueillis par Jean-Pierre Clero et Lynda Lotte*, [in:] "Cités. Philosophie, Politique, Histoire", T 16.

Millett, Kate (1969). *Sexual Politics*, New York: Doubleday and Company.

Mouffe, Chantal (1993). *The Return of the Political*, New York: Verso.

Mouffe, Chantal (2005). *On the Political*. Abingdon: Routledge.

Mudde, Cas (2000). *The Ideology of the Extreme Right*, Manchester: Manchester University Press.

Mudde, Cas (2007). *Populist Radical Right Parties in Europe*, Cambridge: Cambridge University Press.

Nadon, Christopher (2001). *Xenophon's Prince: Republic and Empire in the "Cyropaedia"*. Berkeley: University of California Press.

Negri, Antonio (1999). *Insurgencies. Constituent Power and the Modern State*, trans. M. Eoscagli, Minneapolis: University of Minnesota Press.

Nehamas, Alexander (1998). *The Art Of Living. Socratic Reflections from Plato to Foucault*, Berkeley: University of California Press.

Nietzsche, Friedrich (1872/1967). *The Birth of Tragedy*, trans. W. Kaufmann, [in:] *The Birth of Tragedy and The Case of Wagner*, New York: Random House.

Nietzsche, Friedrich (1873/1989). *On Truth and Lying in an Extra-Moral Sense*, trans. S. L. Gilman, [in:] *Friedrich Nietzsche on Rhetoric and Language*, Oxford: Oxford University Press.

Nietzsche, Friedrich (1876/1983). *Untimely Meditations*, trans. R. J. Hollingdale, Cambridge: Cambridge University Press.

Nietzsche, Friedrich (1887/1996). *On the Genealogy of Morals*, trans. D. Smith, Oxford: Oxford University Press.

Nietzsche, Friedrich (1886/1966). *Beyond Good and Evil*, trans. W. Kaufmann, New York: Vintage Books.

Nietzsche, Friedrich (1973). *Nietzsche Werke: Kritische Gesamtausgabe, Vol 25*, ed. Colli and Montinari, Berlin: Walter de Gruyter.

Norris, Christopher (1982). *Deconstruction, Theory and Practice*, New York: Methuen.

Palikot, Janusz (2011). *Tajemnice Platformy, Rządu i Parlamentu* [*Secrets of the Platform, the Government and Parlament*], Warszawa: Wydawnictwo Czerwone i Czarne.

Panizza, Francisco (ed.) (2005). *Populism and the Mirror of Democracy*, London: Verso.

Patterson, Orlando (1982). *Slavery and Social Death*, Cambridge: Harvard University Press.

Penrose, Robert, (1989). *The Emperor's New Mind: Concerning Computers, Minds, and The Laws of Physics*, Oxford: Oxford University Press.

Piłat, Robert (2006). *Doświadczenie i Pojęcie* [*Experiencing and Concepts*], Warszawa: IFiS PAN.

Piłat, Robert (2007). *O Istocie Pojęć* [*On the Nature of Concepts*], Warszawa: IFiS PAN.

Piłat, Robert (1993). *Czy Istnieje Świadomość* [*Does Consciousness Exist?*], Warszawa: IFiS PAN.

Piłat, Robert (1999). *Umysł Jako Osobisty Model Świata* [*Mind as a World Model*], Warszawa: IFiS PAN.

Pinker, Steven (2002). *The Blank Slate: The Denial of Human Nature and Modern Intellectual Life*, New York: Viking Penguin Press.

Pitkin, Hanna Fenichel (1984). *Fortune Is a Woman: Gender and Politics in the Thought of Niccolo Machiavelli*, Los Angeles: University of California Press.

Plato (1997). *The Symposium*, trans. Alexander Nehamas and Paul Woodruff, from *Plato: Complete Works*, ed. by John M. Cooper, *Cambridge*: Hackett Publishing Company, pp. 457-506.

Plato (2001). *Alcibiades*, Nicholas Denyer (ed.), Cambridge: Cambridge University Press.

Plutarch (1916). *The Life of Alcibiades*, [in:] Plutarch, *The Parallel Lives*, trans. B. Perrin, Harvard: Loeb Classical Library Edition.

Pocock, John Greville Agard (1975). *The Machiavellian Moment: Florentine Political Thought and the Atlantic Republican Tradition,* Princeton: Princeton University Press.

Poczobut, Robert (2000). *Superweniencja. Zarys Problematyki* [*Supervenience. The Outline of Problems*], "Filozofia Nauki", 8, 30, pp. 25-44.

Proust, Marcel (1971). *On Reading*, trans. Jean Autret and William Burford, New York.

Rahe, Paul A. (ed) (2006). *Machiavelli's Liberal Republican Legacy*, Cambridge: Cambridge University Press.

Rancière, Jacques (2007). *Hatred of Democracy*, trans. S. Concoran, London: Verso.

Ricoeur, Paul (1965/1970). *Freud and Philosophy: An Essay on Interpretation*, trans. D. Savage, New Haven: Yale University Press.

Ricoeur, Paul (2000/2004). *Memory, History, Forgetting*, trans. K. Blarney and D. Pellauer, Chicago: The University of Chicago.

Rifkin, Jeremy (2004). *The European Dream: How Europe's Vision of the Future Is Quietly Eclipsing the American Dream,* New York: Penguin.

de Romilly, Jacqueline (1956). *Histoire et raison chez Thucydide*, Belles Lettres, Paris.

Ronell, Avital (2004). *Crack Wars: Literature, Addiction, Mania*, Urbana: University of Illinois Press.

Rorty, Richard (1982). *Philosophy as a Kind of Writing*, [in:] *Consequences of Pragmatism. (Essays 1872-1980)* Minneapolis: University of Minnesota Press.

Rorty, Richard (1989). *Contingency, Irony, and Solidarity*, Cambridge: Cambridge University Press.

Rorty, Richard (1991). *Moral Identity and Private Autonomy: The Case of Foucault,* [in:] Richard Rorty, *Essays on Heidegger and Others. Philosophical Papers, Volume 2,* Cambridge: Cambridge University Press.

Rorty, Richard (2000). *Education as Socialization and as Individuation*, [in:] Richard Rorty, *Philosophy and Social Hope*, New York: Penguin.

Rosen, Stanley (1987). *Hermeneutics as Politics,* New York: Oxford University Press.

Sandilands, Catriona (1995). *From Natural Identity to Radical Democracy*, "Environmental Ethics", 17.

Schmitt, Carl (1927/2007). *The Concept of the Political*, trans. G. Schwab, Chicago: University of Chicago Press.

Schmitt, Carl (1938/1996). *The Leviathan in the State Theory of Thomas Hobbes: Meaning and Failure of a Political Symbol*, trans. G. D. Schwab, E. Hilfstein, London: Greenwood Press.

Scruton, Roger (1986). *Authority and Allegiance*, [in:] J. Donald and S. Hall (eds.), *Politics and Ideology*, Cambridge: Open University Press.

Skinner, Quentin (1978). *The Foundations of Modern Political Thought, Volume I: the Renaissance*, Cambridge: Cambridge University Press.

Skinner, Quentin (1979). *Machiavelli*, Oxford: Oxford University Press.

Sloterdijk Peter (1983), *Critique of Cynical Reason*, trans. Michael Eldred, Minneapolis: University of Minnesota Press, 1988.

Sloterdijk, Peter (2010). *Rage and Time*, trans. M. Wenning, New York: Columbia University Press.

Śpiewak, Paweł (2005). *Pamięć po Komunizmie* [*The Memory of Communism*], Gdańsk: Słowo/Obraz Terytoria.

Spinoza, Benedict de (1670/1951). *A Theologico-Political Treatise/A Political Treatise*, trans. R. H. M. Elwes, New York: Dover Publications.

Stavrakakis, Yannis (2005). *Religion and Populism in Contemporary Greece*, [in:] F. Panizza (ed.), *Populism and the Mirror of Democracy*, London: Verso.

Strauss, Leo (1952). *Persecution and the Art of Writing*, Chicago: University of Chicago Press.

Strauss, Leo (1958). *Thoughts on Machiavelli*, Glencoe: The Free Press.

Strauss, Leo (1964). *The City and Man*, Chicago/London: The University of Chicago Press.

Strauss, Leo (1972). *Xenophon's Socrates*, Ithaca: Cornell University Press.

Strauss, Leo (1987). *Plato*, [in:] Joseph Cropsey, Leo Strauss, *History of Political Philosophy*, Chicago/London: The University of Chicago Press, third edition.

Strauss, Leo (2000). *On Tyranny: Including the Strauss-Kojève Correspondence*, Victor Gourevitch and Michael S. Roth (eds.), Chicago: University of Chicago Press.

Swartz, M., Blazer, D., George, L., Winfield, I. (1990). *Estimating the Prevalence of Borderline Personality Disorder in the Community*, "Journal of Personality Disorders", 4, 3.

Szacki, Jerzy (2004). *Pytania o Populizm* [*Questions About Populism*], "Krytyka Polityczna", 4, pp. 28-35.

Taggart, Paul (1996). *The New Populism and the New Politics. New Protest Parties in Sweden in a Comparative Perspective*, Basingstoke: Macmillan.

Taine, Hippolyte (1878). *The French Revolution*, trans. J. Durand, London: Daldy, Isbister & Co.

Talmon, Jacob L. (1952). *The Origins of Totalitarian Democracy*, New York: Praeger.

Taylor, Charles (1992). *Multiculturalism and "The Politics of Recognition"*, ed. A. Gutmann, Princeton: Princeton University Press.

Thucydides (2009). *The Peloponnesian War*, trans. M. Hammond Oxford/New York: Oxford University Press.

Todorov, Tzvetan (1997). *Facing the Extreme: Moral Life In the Concentration Camps*, New York: Owl Books.

Torfing, Jacob (2004). *Discourse Theory: Achievements, Arguments and Challenges* [in:] D. Howarth, J. Torfing, *Discourse Theory in European Politics: Identity, Policy and Governance*, Basingstoke: Palgrave.

Torfing, Jacob (2004). *New Theories of Discourse: Laclau, Mouffe and Žižek*, Oxford: Blackwell.

Veyne, Paul (1997). *Foucault Revolutionizes History* [in:] A. I. Davidson (ed.), *Foucault and His Interlocutors*, Chicago: University of Chicago Press.

Villa, Dana (1999). *Politics, Philosophy, Terror: Essays on the Thought of Hannah Arendt*, Princeton: Princeton University Press.

Wagner, Richard (1874/1977). *The Ring of the Nibelung*, New York: Norton.

Weber, Max (1950). *The Protestant ethic and the spirit of capitalism*, trans. Talcott Parsons, New York: Charles Scribner's Sons.

Winch, Peter (1972). *Ethics and Action,* London: Routledge.

Winnicott, Donald Woods (1964). *The Child, the Family, and the Outside World*, London: Penguin Books.

Wittgenstein, Ludwig (1921/1961). *Tractatus Logico-Philosophicus,* trans. D. Pears, B. McGuinness, London: Routledge.

Wittgenstein, Ludwig (1953/1958). *Philosophical Investigations,* trans. G. E. M. Anscombe, New York: Macmillan.

Wolniewicz, Bogusław (1985). *Ontologia Sytuacji [The Ontology of Situation]*, Warszawa: PWN.

Wysocka, Olga (2009). *Populism in Poland: In/visible Exclusion*, [in:] Lauren Freeman (ed.), *Junior Visiting Fellows' Conferences: In/visibility: Perspectives on Inclusion and Exclusion*, *Vol. XXVI,* Vienna: IWM. [Published on the Web].

Xenophon (1914). *Cyropaedia*, trans. W. Miller, Harvard: Harvard University Press.

Zakaria, Fareed (2003). *The Future of Freedom: Illiberal Democracy at Home and Abroad*, New York: W. W. Norton.

Zaretsky, Eli (2004). *Secrets of the Soul: A Social and Cultural History of Psychoanalysis*, New York: Knopf.

Žižek, Slavoj (1991). *Looking Awry: An Introduction to Jacques Lacan Through Popular Culture*, Cambridge: The MIT Press.

Žižek, Slavoj (1993). *Tarrying with the Negative: Kant, Hegel, and the Critique of Ideology (Post-Contemporary Interventions)*, Durham: Duke University Press.

Žižek, Slavoj (1998). *The Plague of Fantasies,* London: Verso.

Žižek, Slavoj (2000). *The Ticklish Subject. The Absent Center of Political Ontology,* London: Verso.

Žižek, Slavoj (2002). *I do not Order my Dreams,* [in:] Mladen Dolar, Slavoj Žižek, *Opera's Second Death,* New York: Routledge.

Žižek, Slavoj (2006). *Against the Populist Temptation*, "Critical Inquiry", Spring 32, pp. 551-574.

Žižek, Slavoj (2006). *How to Read Lacan*, London: Granta.

Zuckert, Catherine, H., Zuckert, Michael (2006). *The Truth about Leo Strauss*, Chicago: University of Chicago Press.

Index

Studies in Social Sciences, Philosophy and History of Ideas

Edited by Andrzej Rychard

Vol. 1 Józef Niżnik: Twentieth Century Wars in European Memory. 2013.

Vol. 2 Szymon Wróbel: Deferring the Self. 2013.

www.peterlang.de